Bodies of Law

Bodies of Law

Alan Hyde

PRINCETON UNIVERSITY PRESS

PRINCETON, NEW JERSEY

Library of Congress Cataloging-in-Publication Data

Hyde, Alan, 1951–
Bodies of law / Alan Hyde.
p. cm.
Includes bibliographical references and index.
ISBN 0-691-01229-6 (CL : alk. paper). — ISBN 0-691-01228-8 (PB : alk. paper)
1. Body, Human—Law and legislation.   2. Law—Philosophy.   3. Critical legal
studies.   I. Title.
K564.H8H93   1997   340'.1—dc21   96-50187   CIP

1 3 5 7 9 10 8 6 4 2

1 3 5 7 9 10 8 6 4 2
(Pbk.)

CONTENTS

PART THREE: *Abjection*

PREFACE

THIS BOOK tries to do three things. It would be remarkable if all three were accomplished to the same degree.

First, this book collects, classifies, and analyzes the way American lawyers talk about the body: the range of metaphors, similes, and other verbal constructions that cumulatively form a discourse of the body. When, and for what purpose, is the body said to be property that we own, or a machine that labors, or a privacy interest that is balanced? When does vivid language create a body that is metaphorically on display, visualized, and when is the body hidden from view? When and how are bodies figured as sites of difference (gendered, racial, or other), and when are our bodies the thing that makes us all like one another? When is the body represented as an individual isolated from others, and when is it understood in its relations with others? When is the body the object of mental or moral control by something or someone else, and when is the body the agent that controls our minds and morals?

These themes are developed through the close reading of a set of leading legal decisions, some of them well known to lawyers, some more obscure. I will be subjecting these iconic decisions to an eclectic mix of close readings that draws on leading lights of critical theory who are still not well known, and rarely applied, within law schools: Foucault, Kristeva, Butler, and others. The second aim of this book, then, is to advance the project of applying recent critical theory to legal analysis, to open up a dialogue between a legal academy that is often dissatisfied with the unreflective and repetitive quality of its internal discourse, and a world of critical theory, the allure of which is often diminished by its obscurity, pomposity, and disregard of standards of logic and argumentation that lawyers rightfully expect. I became interested in the construction of the body because of that subject's inherent interest and importance, but as work on this book developed it became clear that this was an excellent topic on which to help advance a dialogue between critical theory and law, for both were full of prolific, contesting discourses of the body that, if juxtaposed, might be mutually enriching. Oral presentation of some of this work has reinforced my belief that some scholars of literature or critical theory enjoy learning of legal texts on which they may strut their stuff, and at least some lawyers enjoy expanding their own reading skills and learning new kinds of questions with which to interrogate the texts they deal with daily.

It has seemed to me that this dialogue would best be advanced by keeping my readings of cases methodologically extremely light, and that is what I have done. For example, more than once in the pages that follow, I read a legal precedent in a manner that is deconstructive. This book, however, says nothing about deconstruction "as such," if that is not an oxymoron. It makes no attempt to summarize Derrida or any other deconstructionist, or define deconstructionism, or speculate on whether deconstruction is still a coming thing or has long since passed its prime, or whether, given what we now know about Paul de Man's youthful politics, we can . . . Legal scholars are extremely adept at generating this kind of chitchat, which so often represents an avoidance of theory, and its transformation into a display of the scholar's reading, a bid for professional advancement. Moreover, as I mentioned, I have been most eclectic in my own reading techniques, trying to select strategies that in each case expose the particular gaps or unreflective dead spots (the fashionable technical term is *aporiae*) of the relevant legal text. The book draws on Freudian readings, Foucault, Kristeva, and different schools of feminist and queer reading. It would burden the book unduly to provide extensive methodological discussions of each school and lead us too far away from the task of encouraging self-reflection and analysis of the stories we tell ourselves about the body and the kinds of bodies we construct.

The proof of the pudding is the reading and analysis of law's construction of the body. If the readings strike readers as interesting or illuminating, I believe it will be because of the readings themselves, not the luster of their academic influences. If the case readings seem foolish or unhelpful, fifty footnotes to famous French authors will not save them.

For similar reasons, the chapters that follow do not purport to be comprehensive introductions to the law of criminal searches, abortion, employment discrimination, the evaluation of injury for purposes of contract or tort damages, and the like. There is a worthy tradition in legal scholarship that aspires to such comprehension, so that each article must summarize existing scholarship on the topic, review all applicable cases, summarize the current state of the law, and propose sensible reforms. There is a kind of beauty in this sort of scholarship, and, simply because I have tried to do something different here, I in no way seek its replacement. Obviously this book could never have been written if I had to take the reader through the entire history of discrimination in order to analyze a particular case chosen because it constructs the body as an object of display in an interesting way. Consistent, however, with my principles announced in the previous few paragraphs, I will not defend this methodological choice, simply announce it, and hope that the reader may agree that in this fragmented age of legal scholarship, there may well be room for work that cuts across doctrinal areas to deal with a kind of abstraction, the body, that haunts them all.

Third, this book aspires to be a major jurisprudential statement from the Critical Legal Studies networks. I will be emphasizing that multiple competing constructions of the body are available to legal and other speakers; that these *are* constructions, neither natural nor limited by biology; and that speakers retain a (suppressed) freedom to select among constructions for instrumental purposes. These are familiar themes from critical legal studies, and this book could not have been written without the work of others who have explored them. This book carries the critical legal studies project of denaturalization to its core. Many people who are quite sophisticated about the social construction of various legal doctrines and social arrangements that are often presented as natural or inevitable resist this interpretation of their own bodies. If I can show that the body, too, is a discursive creation, the antinecessitarian project of critical legal studies will have been carried to its ultimate destination.

The rap on critical legal studies of course is that it is *only* critical, that no affirmative vision emerges from all this talk about social construction, and that this failure has led to the movement's current stasis. I will be attempting to develop precisely an affirmative jurisprudence of embodied personhood out of the critical reading of cases. Specifically, I seek to develop ways of talking and thinking about legal subjects that seem truer and closer to people's ethical aspirations, in which the subjects of legal analysis are people, not bodies or things or interests; in which bodies are understood quite self-consciously as discursive devices that represent other people to ourselves and that we select most self-consciously; and in which we represent others as people, as embodied, as metaphysically present to us, not estranged from us. My goal is not to abolish any particular discourse of the body. All are probably functional for some purpose, though as we dig out these purposes we may reject one or more. Rather, my goal is the opposite: to proliferate *so many* discursive constructions of the body that none may ever seem "natural" again—especially not a body's gender or race.

This reconstructive politics of legal bodies is surely less well developed than the critique of existing discourse. I have had a hard time finding the words in which to express it—does not one's own criticism knock out the legs on which one stands?—and some readers have urged me to drop it. In the end, I felt it important to take the few first steps toward a jurisprudence of human presence, conscious that these are a few steps, on a trail largely unmarked, toward an elusive goal.

My chief regret has been my inability to follow up the challenge that John Gillis posed in February 1993, when I presented a preliminary version of this study to the Rutgers Center for Historical Analysis: where are the physical bodies among all these discursive bodies? What do we know about the body position and appearance of litigants: when they stood, when they sat, when they hung their heads, when they looked judges in the eyes? What do we know about the appearance, posture, deportment of bodies as subjects and objects of legal regulation? Obviously these are difficult matters to research and would require at least an early decision to ground the study in a particular place and period. I have tried to use such historical research as I could find on physical bodies, from studies of courtroom architecture to techniques of criminal punishment. (Of course, these spectating bodies and punished bodies also fit this book on the discursive construction of bodies, because all bodies are constructed in discourse.) Still, the exclusive focus on discourse was more forced on me by materials than it was a choice of my own, and it would be nice to return some day to the issue of body appearance and practices.

Presentations of this project were made to several academic audiences, and I would like particularly to thank those whose suggestions helped shape the final work: Rutgers University School of Law Faculty Symposium (Norman Cantor, John Leubsdorf, Eric Neisser, James Gray Pope, Dorothy Roberts, George Thomas); University of Miami School of Law Reading Group (Gary Minda, Jonathan Simon, Steven Winter, all of whom did their best to stamp out any sentimental humanism); Rutgers Center for Historical Analysis (Anne-Catherine Aubert-Smith, Rachel Bowlby, Tim Burke, Belinda Davis, Victoria De Grazia, Richard Dellamora, Alan Douglas, John Gillis, David Glover, Jennifer Jones, Jackson Lears, Jim Livingston, Erica Rappoport, Niamh Reilly, Sonia Rudikoff, Scott Sandage, and Mick Taussig); University of Toronto Faculty Workshop (Alan Brudner, Brian Langille); Yale Law School Faculty Workshop (Bruce Ackerman, Akhil Amar, Ralph Sharp Brown, Robert Burt, Guido Calabresi, Robert Ferguson, Paul Kahn, Carol Rose, Peter Schuck, Vicki Schultz, Reva Siegel); Yale Department of Comparative Literature (Matt Greenfield, Steve Monte); Columbia Law School Faculty Lunch (Gerald Lynch, Kent Greenawalt). Stephen Munzer made detailed comments on the manuscript far beyond any obligations. Lucie White made telling comments on the manuscript at an early stage. David Laidlaw at Rutgers, Rachel Geman at Columbia, and Michael Likoskey, Rebecca Martin, and Sascha Rand at Cardozo provided outstanding research assistance. The students in my seminar on the Legal History of the Body, Yale Law School, fall 1993, helped shape this book too, and I draw expressly on a number of their outstanding research efforts. Ellen Gesmer, Toby Hyde, and Laura Hyde could not have been more understanding of the absences that this book and other aspects of my career have inflicted on them. Naturally all this assistance has not produced a perfect book, or one free of error. One can, however, be quite certain that all the puns and parapraxes on body parts have by now been identified and remain in the book intentionally.

Finally, I would like to thank five individuals, none a close friend and two of whom I have never met, who influenced this project, mainly through the support and inspiration their books gave me at crucial points of decision.

When Elaine Scarry's *The Body in Pain* appeared in 1985, I was wrestling in class with the stilted efforts of courts to define a "privacy interest" in urine collected for purposes of drug testing, as well as with my teaching of the first analogy taught to many American law students, in which an injured body is analogized to a defective machine. It was Scarry's book that first made me see that these were, perhaps, the same problem; that there were books to be written just about the discursive construction of the body; and that there were metaphysical and ethical implications to our discourse of the body. I doubt I would have embarked on this study without it.

Patricia Williams's *Alchemy of Race and Rights* taught me that law professors don't have to write like law professors, that the autobiographical essay could provoke more thought than the law review article, particularly on the subject of the words we use, the kinds of people and relationships we construct in legal discourse, which often leads us to thoughts of which we are ashamed when someone (Williams) points them out. Williams's book was a powerful influence, and at various stages in the gestation of my book I fooled around with autobiographical essays in the Patricia Williams mode, melodramatic essays titled "My Body" and the like. Let me tell you, those things are harder to write than they look. In the end, as the book came to focus so heavily on legal discourse, I found the autobiography unhelpful. I wonder, though, if my book retains any of the signs of the struggle I had over whether and how to make it personal.

Judith Butler's *Gender Trouble*. Gosh did I hate this one when Duncan Kennedy included excerpts from it in the reading at Critical Legal Studies summer camp in 1990! It seemed everything that so many people dislike about recent critical theory: obscure, ponderous, name-dropping, insular. I'm glad I stayed with it, though, because Butler's self-consciously "extreme position"—that *everything* about the body, specifically including its sexual differentiation, is a repeated "performativity"—came to influence my own analysis, in which no knowledge of our or of others' bodies is available unmediated by discourse, and the discursive constructions all perform acts of power and domination. In some moods, and to some audiences, I describe my book as an application to legal texts of Judith Butler's readings, through a microstudy of the political texts that literally construct our "experience" of our bodies.

Thomas Laqueur's *Making Sex* does for medical thought what I had begun to attempt for legal thought: traces the history of the discursive constructions of the body; destroys any possibility that the succeeding constructions respond simply to biological knowledge; and analyzes the schemes of political domination encapsuled in dominant medical discourse of the body. Under Laqueur's influence, I aspired at one time to do a similar history of legal thought. I abandoned this organization because I found legal thought, unsurprisingly, to be more contested and multivocal than Laqueur found medical thought. Legal discursive constructions of the body didn't always seem to have nice periodization; they tend to hang around for a long time after their purpose seems to have been served, and they always contest, generally quite visibly, with competing conceptions. Some legal bodies do have histories, of course: we can date fairly accurately both the origin and demise of the machine body and the sentimental body in pain. In the end, though, it seemed there was enough to do just to catalog and analyze contemporary legal discursive constructions of the body, but for scholars who wish to trace the histories of our contemporary constructions, Laqueur will be an inspiring model.

Finally, Mary Joe Frug tirelessly pressed the claims of the body, pleasure, sexuality, joy on all the scholars whom she influenced in her tragically short-ened life. When you were with Mary Joe, law couldn't help but be about pleasure and joy, and the shabby evasions of that fact that law made up be-came just the object of our shared laughter. I am certain I would not have written about the body without her encouragement. This book is dedicated to her memory.

Bodies of Law

INTRODUCTION

It is noteworthy that in all languages the greater part of the expressions relating to inanimate things are formed by metaphor from the human body and its parts and from the human senses and passions. Thus, head for top or beginning; the brow and shoulders of a hill; the eyes of needles and of potatoes; mouth for any opening; the lip of a cup or pitcher; the teeth of a rake, a saw, a comb. . . . Heaven or the sea smiles; the wind whistles; the waves murmur; a body groans under great weight. The farmers of Latium used to say the fields were thirsty, bore fruit, were swollen with grain; and our rustics speak of plants making love, vines going mad, resinous trees weeping. Innumerable other examples could be collected from all languages. All of which is a consequence of our axiom that man in his ignorance makes himself the rule of the universe, for in the examples cited he has made of himself an entire world. So that, as rational metaphysics teaches that man becomes all things by understanding them *(homo intelligendo fit omnia),* this imaginative metaphysics shows that man becomes all things by *not* understanding them *(homo non intelligendo fit omnia);* and perhaps the latter proposition is truer than the former, for when man understands he extends his mind and takes in the things, but when he does not understand he makes the things out of himself and becomes them by transforming himself into them.[1]

[T]he effects of oppression on the body—giving it its form, its gestures, its movement, its motricity, and even its muscles—have their origin in the abstract domain of concepts, through the words that formalize them.[2]

If you want to make it as a radical critic these days, slip the word "body" into your book title.[3]

BODIES ARE, among other things, the ways we represent other people to ourselves. Bodies are, at least in part, the linguistic, discursive devices for representing that aspect of other people, indeed of ourselves, which is not opaque

---

[1] Giambattista Vico, *The New Science of Giambattista Vico* §405 (Thomas Goddard Bergin and Max Harold Fisch trans.) (Ithaca: Cornell U. Pr., 1948) [1744].

[2] Monique Wittig, *The Straight Mind and Other Essays* xv (Boston: Beacon, 1992).

[3] Terry Eagleton, "International Books of the Year," *Times Literary Supplement,* December 3, 1993, at 10.

and inaccessible to us. We may or may not know other people. We believe we can see, touch, measure, sense, evaluate their bodies. In doing this, we often fail to appreciate our own agency in constructing those very bodies that we claim to see, bodies that, we claim, represent others. Out of our ignorance, as Vico says, we make things out of ourselves, and among the things we make up are the discursive bodies of others. We construct these bodies that are distanced from us, unlike us, threatening to us, far from us, and treat our own constructions as if they were the people they purportedly represent.

Everyone does this. Law, perhaps, does it particularly well.

The three principal theses of this book are the following: First, as employed in contemporary American law, *body* means an inconsistent and incoherent assortment of representations and visualizations, deployed to solve political problems internal to legal discourse. Second, there is no attractive alternative to this practice of representation. In particular, there is no "real" or "material" body that is available as a standard for political or legal theory, even when the precise question to be answered involves defining the boundaries of, or intrusion into, or use of, that body. We have literally no way of grasping cognitively the most intimate aspects of our bodies except through words and images of legal, that is, political discourse, developed to serve political purposes. Third, legal thinkers should recognize and confront the constructed nature of their representations of the body, and not, as they often do, inappropriately naturalize those constructions. Such inappropriate naturalizations of what are really discursive artifacts include the localizing in the body of such apparently natural or objective factors as race, sex, and disease. My goal is not to replace any particular way of talking about bodies, but, instead, to multiply the competing constructions that are available to anyone, the better to force confrontation with their provisional and artificial quality.

LAW'S COLD METAPHORS

Something is wrong with law's language of the body. In a case involving a woman named Shirley Rodriques, a United States court of appeals recently affirmed the issuance of "search warrants for appellant's apartment and vagina." Most people find this language odd, if not offensive. Whether or not a search of Shirley Rodriques's vagina ought to be permitted, it does not seem to capture our feelings about our bodies, or her body, to treat either as parallel to her apartment.[4]

Quite literally the first analogy taught to many American law students concerns the proper measure of damages in an action in which a surgeon promised to a boy, George Hawkins, with scars from an earlier burn "a hundred per cent perfect hand." The operation resulted in a hand less attractive and func-

---

[4] Rodriques v. Furtado, 950 F.2d 805 (1st Cir. 1991).

tional than it had been in the preoperative state. In the court's opinion, we read, "The present case is closely analogous to one in which a machine is built for a certain purpose and warranted to do certain work."[5] Closely analogous?

Law's language of the body is typically just this cold, this clinical, and this self-consciously metaphorical. We shall see that these opening examples are typical of many constructions of the body as property (like Shirley Rodriques's vagina) or a machine (like George Hawkins's hand). The highest development of this line of thought is the commodified body of contemporary consumer culture, in which bodily alteration, display, and suffering are imagined as contracts.

When I began to think about legal constructions of the body some years ago, my goal was to replace these cold metaphors with a new discourse of the body. In this alternative world, everyone would have a "right to bodily integrity" that would replace what we now call the "right to privacy" and would provide more protection for individuals than that beleaguered right. For example, the right to body integrity would not permit many of the restrictions on the availability of abortion that states may now impose and would also reverse the Supreme Court's decision allowing states to criminalize homosexual relations.[6]

While I still favor these legal changes, I no longer think that a new right to bodily integrity is the way to get there. For one thing, law actually recognizes such a right, sometimes by name and sometimes by deed; for example, the Supreme Court's most recent abortion decision actually invokes a right to body integrity.[7] Other bodies of law construct firm, private, integrated bodies with near-total autonomy from the demands of state or others. For example, as we shall see, people are not obligated to share blood or bone marrow with others, even siblings, no matter how much those others need the body product and how little the potential donor would be inconvenienced.[8] In other words, it's not obvious that we need a new right of bodily integrity.

The problem, rather, on which I discovered no legal literature of interest, is describing just which bodies law currently constructs and when and how it comes to construct different bodies for different purposes. A new right to body

---

[5] Hawkins v. McGee, 146 Atl. 641, 643 (N.H. 1929).

[6] Roe v. Wade, 410 U.S. 113 (1973); Planned Parenthood of Southeastern Pennsylvania v. Casey, 505 U.S. 833 (1992); Bowers v. Hardwick, 478 U.S. 186 (1986). Some attempts to sketch such a right to the body include Drucilla Cornell, *The Imaginary Domain: Abortion, Pornography, and Sexual Harassment* 31–55 (New York: Routledge, 1995); Patricia J. Williams, *The Rooster's Egg* 230–43 (Cambridge: Harv. U. Pr., 1995); Christyne L. Neff, "Woman, Womb, and Bodily Integrity," 3 *Yale J. L. & Feminism* 327 (1991); Kendall Thomas, "Beyond the Privacy Principle," 92 *Colum. L. Rev.* 1431, 1459–60 (1992).

[7] Planned Parenthood, 505 U.S. at 849.

[8] Curran v. Bosze, 41 Ill.2d 473, 153 Ill.Dec. 213, 566 NE.2d 1319 (1990) (refusing to order mother of three-year-old twins to test their bone marrow for compatibility for transplant to their older half-sibling, who later died of leukemia).

integrity would accomplish little if it merely took its place in the cavalcade of legal bodies—including those that exist *only* as constituted by their relations with others, bodies defined by their very accessibility to the gaze, by "intrusion." Perhaps what we need is not a new right, but a bringing into consciousness of the multiple constructions already immanent in law, including alternatives to the body as property or privacy right or machine, alternatives that always treat people as embodied, that do not shy away from pain, sex, or other embodied experiences, that replace the metaphors of property, machine, or privacy right with a language of bodily presence or embrace. Any lawyer who, for some instrumental purposes, wishes to construct an alternative discourse of the body, immanent in legal materials, will find alternatives here from which to choose.

The Inevitability of Constructed Representations

Such conflicting, competing constructions of the body as we all carry with us are unlikely to stem from direct knowledge of the body. We surely have knowledge of others' bodies only through the mediation of discourse. The very ease with which we construct the body as machine, as property, as consumer commodity, as bearer of privacy rights or of narratives, as inviolable, as sacred, as object of desire, as threat to society, demonstrates that there is no knowledge of the body apart from our discursive constructions of it. My thesis is that the multiple, competing constructions of the body in American law show the impossibility of knowledge of the body unmediated by discourse. And those constructions, as we shall see, are never innocent.

Seeing the world as socially constructed is a sort of academic fad, and readers may well be thinking that they have heard all this before. However, even readers quite sophisticated in understanding social construction often resist this interpretation of the body, particularly of their own body.

Let me give an example. During the 1993 mayoral campaign in New York, President Clinton gave a speech on behalf of his preferred candidate, Mayor David Dinkins, a man of African-American ancestry. The President bemoaned the fact that "too many of us are still too unwilling to vote for people who are different than we are. . . . It is not as simple as overt racism. It's this inability to take that sort of leap of faith, to believe that people who look different than we are really are more like us than some people who look just like us but don't share our values or our interests or our conduct."[9]

Even readers who have thought a great deal about social construction normally hear remarks like the President's in the following way. (I am speaking precisely for myself here). "Looking different from me" is a natural category. Some people in the world "look like me," and others "look different from me."

---

[9] "For the Record," *Washington Post*, September 29, 1993, p. A22.

That is simply a fact about the world. Moreover, everyone knows who "looks different" and who doesn't. Surely every voter in New York knew whether or not he or she "looked different from" Mayor Dinkins. So when I first heard the President's remarks, I interpreted them as assuming a fact about the world (people look different from each other) and urging that we develop a particular attitude about this fact (our voting should not be affected by the fact that people look different from us).

With effort, however, we may reinterpret the President's speech, not as an observation about the world coupled with a moral exhortation, but as a construction of the very reality it purports to find. While the President's remarks were certainly antiracist of a sort—no one would understand "look different than" as anything but a reference to race—his remarks, by identifying race with bodily appearance, naturalize catachrestically what should be understood as a social construction. There is nothing natural about "looking different from." Bodies differ in appearance in innumerable ways, along innumerable dimensions. The cultures of different times and places saw differences in ways that seem incomprehensible to us now. Even those of us who are well aware of these banalities do not often employ them when we hear remarks like the President's. It takes effort to see the social construction behind our "observation" of bodies, behind our perception of difference and sameness, desire and repulsion, which so often seems natural or foundational even to people sophisticated in interpretation.

THE MATERIALITY OF THE BODY

To say, as I do, that we know the body only through its discursive representation is not, I think, to deny the materiality of the body. At least, I do not wish to deny the materiality of the body, though in my attention to its discursive constructions I have been influenced by recent feminist scholarship that does indeed deny it.[10] I tend however, to be a philosophic pragmatist about all questions of metaphysics. While this is in fact my personal stance, this book seeks to recover and analyze the discourse of American legal culture, which, I also believe, is firmly pragmatist in its metaphysics. So I will not be spending much time on ontological questions in this book. If people, say health professionals, find it a helpful and useful account of what they do to describe a material body that actually exists apart from our discursive representations of it, as a pragmatist I can't really argue against them; the body is material for them. For myself, then, as a philosophic pragmatist, I don't doubt that there are physical bodies that exist in the world, independent of our representations of them, bodies that are therefore "real," as a philosophical realist like John

[10] Judith Butler, *Bodies That Matter: On the Discursive Limits of "Sex"* (New York: Routledge, 1993); Elizabeth Grosz, *Volatile Bodies: Toward a Corporeal Feminism* (Bloomington: Ind. U. Pr., 1994).

Searle would use the term.[11] I am not Bishop Berkeley, and no latter-day Dr. Johnson need refute this book "thus" by kicking some small child. (I do think, however, with Judith Butler, that one may always usefully confront the constructed quality of claims to materiality.) In short, this book is written to speak *both* to those (like John Searle) who insist that bodies are real *and* those (like the postmodernists who will end up quoted more frequently) who are prone to say things like "The body exists only in our discursive representations of it."

As a pragmatist, though, I don't find this metaphysical question about the ontology of the body all that interesting, because, as I shall show with respect to the legal texts we will examine, the body, whatever its ultimate reality, is unavailable to us as a standard of political analysis except as mediated through discursive constructions that, just our luck, represent, often in conflicting ways, the boundaries, nature, and features of the body. Even when the very issue is the boundary of the body, or the invasion of the body, or the use of the body, its ontology is not available, or at least, not observable in legal texts. In the legal texts that follow, there is simply nothing that may be described as reflecting the speaker's direct, unmediated knowledge of his or her own body.

Approaching the body through metaphor or representation is inevitable, and my goal is not to get us to stop metaphorizing the body, to recognize only the "real" physical body, or to stop using the body to think through or represent various political ideas. None of these is possible, as I shall show. As Mary Douglas writes, "[M]ost symbolic behavior must work through the human body. . . . the human body is common to us all. Only our social experience varies. The symbols based on the human body are used to express different social experiences."[12] The body is a kind of master symbol, the foundation of all symbolizing or representational activity of any kind, so it would be quite impossible to have any sort of politics or human interaction without body constructions. In any case, my goal throughout is rarely the suppression of any particular discursive construction of the body. It is rather the proliferation of competing discursive constructions and the acquisition of a particular psychological attitude toward our constructions, under which they come to be experienced as made, not natural.

The Politics of Representation: Bodies as Sameness, Bodies as Difference

Constructions of the body enact or perform specific regimes of political relations. Different political domination is involved when the body is property owned than when the body is a legible narrative. The body expressed domination graphically in 1305 when the lord was told to take the man found to be his

---

[11] John R. Searle, *The Construction of Social Reality* (New York: Free Pr., 1995).

[12] Mary Douglas, *Natural Symbols: Explorations in Cosmology* vii (New York: Pantheon, 1970).

villein "by his forelock."[13] In any verbal reference to the body, however, the body is discursively constructed to stand in particular relations with other people and with society.

The most basic choice that inheres in any use of the word *body* is the implicit separation of the body from something else, what Derrida would call a "dangerous supplement," like mind or spirit or soul. Another way of demonstrating the limited practical effect of the materiality of the body is to note that, in the entire section above on the materiality of the body, the word *body* might everywhere be replaced by the word *person*. Choosing to describe the existence of people in space as a "body" is always an implicit choice for an ontological construction, neither natural nor inevitable, that *dematerializes* "something else" as it *materializes* the body. "The body was born in Plato's cave"[14] and thus always represents the material at best ambiguously, since the body is material only in a world that has already constructed a great deal else as nonmaterial.

Another choice that legal discourse must make, to which I have already alluded, is when to configure the body in relationship to others: to be seen, empathized with, touched, held, chastised, or killed; and when the body is represented as isolated, the home of a person existing separate from others.

This book advances a genealogical thesis about the ugly legal constructions of the body with which this introduction began. It appears that the body did not exist as a subject of legal analysis until the early nineteenth century. In the early years of that century, a distinctively modern body takes shape in legal and popular culture, a body that represents an individuated, human spirit that is the person inside it, a person that controls that body but is not identical to it. This nineteenth-century body is legible to others, is the object of the empathy or sympathy of a viewer, feels pain, but also bears legible signs that may call for its expulsion from society. In the twentieth century, this body continues to be constructed in legal discourse, but coexists with other bodies that are represented in abstraction from their relations with others: "dehumanized" constructions of the body that are distanced, anonymous, rejected, or unavailable to us. These modern legal discursive bodies include property bodies awarded legal damages, container bodies with tax deductions, bodies as "interests" weighed against search warrants. They are distinguished from nineteenth-century sympathetic bodies precisely by being "cold" and "inhumane" in a way rarely true of bodies in, say, popular art or literature.

One thing that unites political commentators of the Right and the Left is their desire for the body. I mean the pun. All infants, and nearly all adults, hope to escape their individual loneliness through physical contact with the

---

[13] CP 40/154, m.62d, discussed in unpublished work by Paul Brand.

[14] Jean-Luc Nancy, "Corpus," in *Thinking Bodies* 19 (Juliet Flower MacCannell and Laura Zakarin eds.) (Stanford: Stan. U. Pr., 1994).

body of another. This desire unites us as humans and may be characteristically undervalued in an intellectual culture that tends rather to celebrate difference. Basic bodily experiences are a common, and still moving, metaphor for shared, human experiences, not less moving when we realize that they represent but one of many possible competing discursive constructions of the body:

> Hath not a Jew eyes? Hath not a Jew hands, organs, dimensions, senses, affections, passions; fed with the same food, hurt with the same weapons, subject to the same diseases, healed by the same means, warmed and cooled by the same winter and summer as a Christian is? If you prick us do we not bleed? If you tickle us do we not laugh? If you poison us do we not die?[15]

The English theater director Peter Brook has recently reinvoked just this bodily imagining of human likeness:

> A universal truth is that every single being as yet discovered on this planet, unlike people from Mars, has the same anatomical and physiological structure. This universal reference of the human body is also the emotional, ideological, philosophical and spiritual reference—in other words, when a truth, a dramatic truth, genuinely touches on what can be understood and felt within the human body, in its most complete sense, it is universal.[16]

Of course, this is not a complete account of the way in which the body represents human solidarity. For one thing, the body may as easily be the site for distinction and division as for unity. Hath not a Jew a circumcised penis? Hath not a Jew a large nose?[17] If, as we shall see in chapter 13, these classic constructions of the Jewish body have lost considerable resonance in contemporary culture, the same may not be said of such common constructions of difference as race and sex. Indeed, Emile Durkheim generalized in apparent contradiction to Peter Brook:

> [T]he notion of person is the product of two sorts of factors. One of these is essentially impersonal: it is the spiritual principle serving as the soul of the group. In fact, it is this which constitutes the very substance of individual souls. Now this is not the possession of any one in particular: it is a part of the collective patrimony; in it and through it, all consciousness communicate [sic]. But on the other hand, in order to have separate personalities, it is necessary that another factor intervene to break up and differentiate this principle: in other words, an individualizing factor is necessary. It is the body that fulfills this function.[18]

---

[15] William Shakespeare, *The Merchant of Venice,* Act 3, Scene 1 (1600).

[16] Peter Brook, Universal Shakespeare, broadcast, Radio 3, November 14, 1994, as quoted in N.B., *Times Literary Supplement,* November 18, 1994, at 14.

[17] See chap. 13, infra, and Sander Gilman, *The Jew's Body* (New York: Routledge, 1991).

[18] Emile Durkheim, *The Elementary Forms of the Religious Life* 305 (Joseph Ward Swain trans.) (New York: Free Pr., 1965) [1915].

How can the body be both the thing that represents our essential likeness to and solidarity with others and, simultaneously, represents our individual (as opposed to collective) personalities? Is it, rather, as the Greek medical treatises attributed to Hippocrates claimed, that Scythians and "Asiatics" resemble each other physically, while Europeans vary in size and appearance; in other words, that *our* bodies individuate, while *their* bodies solidify?[19]

Moreover, as we have known since Nietzsche and Freud, our erotic desire for the body of another must frequently be displaced when we live with others. This book is full of such displacements, one of which is the desire to claim the body as a foundation of one's political philosophy. One tradition follows Locke and defends the institution of private property from the foundational thesis that we own our own bodies. Marx purported to discover communism from economic laws self-consciously founded in the bodily needs of humans. Today we hear that we can start from the integrity of our bodies and thus develop understandings of the right to contracept, or abort, or engage in sexual activity.

The body as property, the body as human need, the body as integrity—all are social constructions that create the very foundation they invoke. None rests on bodily experience, or at least, nothing in our experiences of our bodies leads necessarily either to Lockean property or communism or abortion rights. The bodily arguments for either represent social constructions of the body, and not any person's experience. In other words, *body autonomy* is an oxymoron. Bodies may indeed be experienced as autonomous, but, where this is so, this is because of their social, discursive construction as autonomous. Body autonomy is really social, public, and conventional.

It follows that the body is not the best but the worst standpoint for defining legal subjects, particularly subjects autonomous against public intrusion (the aim of those who would replace the right to privacy with a right to body integrity or autonomy). When we see a culture self-consciously defining bodies, it is already in trouble. We define bodies in the first place only when we are conflicted, as a society and often within ourselves. When body boundaries become problematic and need definition, when we worry about whether blood or urine "is" the body, when we try to define the body's availability to state authority, to be searched or medicated, we do not draw on any strong social consensus about the nature and boundaries of the body, though it often pleases us to talk as if we do. We draw instead on the multiple conflicting constructions of the body available to any mature speaker and pretend that we have resolved our social and internal conflicts by deploying one or another metaphor, for example by describing the body as "inviolable" rather than merely "private."

[19] Hippocrates (pseudo-), "Airs, Waters, Places," in 1 *Hippocrates* xxiii (W. H. S. Jones trans.) (Loeb Classical Library, London: Heineman, 1923).

I cannot agree with the assertion that "bodies are important because the only experiences which cannot be co-opted by political systems are the inevitably personal bodily experiences of individuals."[20] Bodily experiences are not inevitably personal—inevitably social is more like it—and they most assuredly can be co-opted by and into larger systems of social order and control.[21]

FEMINISM AND BODILY PRESENCE

While this book reflects an eclectic mix of influences to be introduced in turn, including Freud, Foucault, and Kristeva, the feminist influence on this project has already become apparent in the discussion above of the materiality of the body. I will be appropriating a particular feminist critique of metaphor and a particular feminist discourse of bodily presence. Both are, I think, frequently misunderstood, so let me explain what I am doing.

Feminist scholars have done much to make the body a subject of analysis, and it is no doubt true that "neither Foucault nor any other poststructuralist thinker discovered or invented the idea . . . that the 'definition and shaping' of the body is 'the focal point for struggles over the shape of power.' *That* was discovered by feminism, and long before it entered into its marriage with poststructuralist thought."[22] Feminists have also identified much that is characteristically male about law's metaphors of the body, metaphors which, as we have "glimpsed" already, are often (though not always) metaphors of distance or absence. "By giving up their bodies, men gain power—the power to theorize, to represent themselves, to exchange women, to reproduce themselves and mark their offspring with their name."[23]

Jacqueline Rose, writing in a Lacanian framework, identifies three characteristically male aspects of metaphor that apply well to such legal discursive constructions of the body as property or machine or "liberty interest." First, metaphors work by substitution and refer to the substitution of the prohibition of the father for the absence of the mother. Second, metaphors refer to pater-

[20] Dorinda Outram, *The Body and the French Revolution: Sex, Class, and Political Culture* 5 (New Haven: Yale U. Pr., 1989).

[21] See generally Michel Foucault, *History of Sexuality* (Robert Hurley trans.) (New York: Pantheon, 1978); Norbert Elias, *The History of Manners* (*The Civilizing Process:* vol. 1) (Edmund Jephcott trans.) (New York: Pantheon, 1978) [1939]; *Zone 3, 4, and 5: Fragments for a History of the Human Body, Parts 1–3* (Michel Feher ed.) (New York: Zone, 1989); Thomas Laqueur, *Making Sex: Body and Gender from the Greeks to Freud* (Cambridge: Harv. U. Pr., 1990).

[22] Susan Bordo, *Unbearable Weight: Feminism, Western Culture, and the Body* 17 (Berkeley: U. Cal. Pr.) (1993). Bordo mentions Mary Wollstonecraft and a number of important texts of 1970s feminism. For my part, I have been particularly influenced by the works of Judith Butler, Jane Gallop, Luce Irigaray, and Monique Wittig, cited throughout this book.

[23] Jane Gallop, *The Daughter's Seduction: Feminism and Psychoanalysis* 67 (Ithaca: Cornell U. Pr.) (1982).

nity itself which can never be known directly, only inferred. Third, under a regime of metaphor, the father may stand for a place and a function that is not reducible to the presence or absence of the real father as such.[24] Legal metaphors of the body as machine or property or privacy interest have, moreover, a particularly male content. For only a woman can really produce a human body. Men, however, can produce machines and property and interests, so if bodies are these things, then men can construct them as well as (if not even better than) women.[25]

Feminists have not only criticized male metaphors for the body but have gone a long way toward an alternative discourse of the body, in which the physical body is placed, discursively speaking, in the reader's face. Consider these observations of Adrienne Rich:

> Perhaps we need a moratorium on saying "the body." For it's also possible to abstract "the" body. When I write "the body," I see nothing in particular. To write "my body" plunges me into lived experience, particularity: I see scars, disfigurements, discolorations, damages, losses, as well as what pleases me. Bones well nourished from the placenta; the teeth of a middle class person seen by the dentist twice a year from childhood. White skin, marked and scarred by three pregnancies, an elected sterilization, progressive arthritis, four joint operations, calcium deposits, no rapes, no abortions, long hours at a typewriter—my own, not in a typing pool—and so forth. To say "the body" lifts me away from what has given me a primary perspective. To say "my body" reduces the temptation to grandiose assertions.[26]

Or the following poem by Audre Lord:

> it does not pay to cherish symbols
> when the substance
> lies so close at hand
> waiting to be held
> your hand
> falls off the apple bark
> like casual fire
> along my back[27]

---

[24] Jacqueline Rose, "Introduction," to *Feminine Sexuality: Jacques Lacan and the École Freudienne* 38–39 (Juliet Mitchell and Jacqueline Rose eds.) (New York: Norton, 1982).

[25] Mark Seltzer, *Bodies and Machines* 32 (New York: Routledge, 1992).

[26] Adrienne Rich, "Notes toward a Politics of Location," in *Blood, Bread, and Poetry: Selected Prose 1979–1985* 215 (New York: Norton, 1986). There is a sense in which all of Rich's descriptions of her body are metaphors too, mostly metaphors of loss or absence. Perhaps the real dynamic in this passage is not "metaphor vs. no-metaphor" but rather metaphors of distance/alienation vs. metaphors of possession/presence, or even estranged body vs. nice body.

[27] "Walking Our Boundaries," in Audre Lord, *The Black Unicorn* 38 (New York: Norton, 1978). "The repetition of 'hand,' the pun on it, contrasts the sensuality of touching with the

These discourses of the embodied subject represent a powerful alternative to the legal discourse we have already begun to explore. It is important, I think, to see these *as* alternative discourses, and not, for example, as the privileged female voice of bodily experience, opposed to the male voice of metaphor. Some feminist writing makes something like this epistemological claim, but I prefer to link myself with that strain of feminist writing which is skeptical of any claimed epistemological privilege for bodily experiences and hostile to the notion that bodily experiences are in any sense prior to social conventions of gender and sexuality.

> In a strong sense the body is a concept, and so is hardly intelligible unless it is read in relation to whatever else supports it and surrounds it. Indeed the queer neutrality of the phrase "the body" in its strenuous colorlessness suggests that something is up. We could speculate that some of the persistent draw of this "the body" lies in the tacit promise to ground the sexual, to make intimacy more readily decipherable, less evanescent. But then this enticement is undercut by the fact that the very location of "the sexual" in the body is itself historically mutable. And "the body" is never above—or below—history. . . . [T]he sexed body is not something reliably constant, which can afford a good underpinning for the complications of the thousand discourses on "woman." How and when even the body will be understood and lived as gendered, or indeed as a body at all, is not fully predictable.[28]

"The body posited as prior to the sign, is always *posited* or *signified* as *prior*. This signification produces as an *effect* of its own procedure the very body that it nevertheless and simultaneously claims to discover as that which *precedes* its own action."[29]

Adrienne Rich, in "that most cited of citations about the body," shows how racial and gender categories are inscribed on the body even before birth:

> This body. White, female; or female, white. The first obvious, lifelong facts. But I was born in the white section of a hospital which separated Black and white babies in its nursery, just as it separated Black and white bodies in its morgue. I was defined as white before I was defined as female. The politics of location.

---

abstractness of 'symbols.'" Helena Michie, *The Flesh Made Word: Female Figures and Women's Bodies* 147 (New York: Oxford U. Pr., 1987).

[28] Denise Riley, *Am I That Name?: Feminism and the Category of "Women" in History* 104–6 (Minneapolis: U. Minn. Pr., 1988).

[29] Butler, *Bodies That Matter* 30. Butler continues: "If the body signified as prior to signification is an effect of signification, then the mimetic or representational status of language, which claims that signs follow bodies as their necessary mirrors, is not mimetic at all. On the contrary, it is productive, constitutive, one might even argue *performative,* inasmuch as this signifying act delimits and contours the body that it then claims to find prior to any and all signification." For a more general critique of the epistemological status of "experience," see Joan W. Scott, "The Evidence of Experience," 17 *Critical Inquiry* 773 (1991).

Even to begin with my body I have to say that from the outset that body had more than one identity. When I was carried out of the hospital into the world, I was viewed and treated as female, but also viewed and treated as white.[30]

Law's discourse, like other social discourse, constructs bodies as male or female, and consequences follow these constructions. This fact must be approached cautiously. Scholars of art or literature who have studied the body often assume that all bodies necessarily have genders, that the first thing the gaze notices about the painted, sculpted, or seen body is its sex.[31] Legal bodies may be different. Often the body constructed in legal discourse may have no gender at all.

At other times, however, law constructs precisely a gendered body, and that gender matters.[32] As we have seen, the pregnant body is constructed as "private" in abortion cases; the body with bone marrow needed by a sibling is "inviolable"; and these constructions matter and are surely not free of gender.

The same court of appeals that constructed the searchable vagina of Shirley Rodriques had occasion, a few months later, to construct the penis of Norman Harrington, a police officer accused of sexual abuse of children. The district attorney sought to make Harrington's employment conditional on a penile plethysmograph that would register his arousal on being shown sexually explicit slides involving adults and children. Without mentioning Shirley Rodriques's case, the court of appeals permitted Harrington to sue the town for damages (though the plethysmograph was never actually administered).[33] The cases will be discussed more fully in chapters 9 and 10. They are certainly distinguishable on numerous grounds; the decision to permit search of Rodriques's vagina in no way compels the uncovering of the narrative of Harrington's penis. All the same, it is impossible to read the cases and not be struck by the difference that gender makes. Law's construction of the penis is, we shall see, quite different from its construction of the vagina.

Let us turn now to reading some legal texts about the body. These are strange myths, and I hope the reader comes to see that strangeness. We all can

[30] Rich, "Politics of Location," 215. The description as "most cited" is from Elspeth Probyn, "Queer Belongings: The Politics of Departure," in *Sexy Bodies: The Strange Carnalities of Feminism* 5 (Elizabeth Grosz and Elspeth Probyn eds.) (London: Routledge, 1995).

[31] See also Sigmund Freud, "Femininity," in *New Introductory Lectures on Psychoanalysis* 113 (James Strachey trans.) (New York: Norton, 1965) [1933]: "When you meet a human being, the first distinction you make is 'male or female?' and you are accustomed to make the distinction with unhesitating certainty."

[32] See generally Mary Joe Frug, *Postmodern Legal Feminism* 128–45 (New York: Routledge, 1992); Zillah R. Eisenstein, *The Female Body and the Law* (Berkeley: U. Cal. Pr., 1988).

[33] Harrington v. Almy, 977 F.2d 37 (1st Cir. 1992). At the subsequent trial, the jury awarded Harrington $950,000 compensatory damages and $10,000 punitive damages. Harrington v. Cole, D.Me, 89-CV-207, June 17, 1993. The city settled the case by paying the police officer more than $900,000. 8 Individual Employment Rights (BNA) (no. 27) at 1 (December 21, 1993).

see the strangeness of, say, Kwakiutl tales in which human bodies turn into birds.[34] How strange it is to read legal stories in which people become machines, property, privacy, individuality, "interests." Stranger still when we have difficulty imagining our own bodies, apart from their metamorphoses into these legal metaphors.

[34] Susan Postal, "Body Image and Identity: A Comparison of Kwakiutl and Hopi," 67 *Am. Anthropologist* 455 (1965).

PART ONE

Regulation

Chapter 1

THE BODY AS MACHINE: *HAWKINS v. McGEE*

QUITE LITERALLY the first legal analogy taught to many American law students imagines the body as a machine, owned by its owner or buyer (someone or something other than the "body"), and used by that owner in order to make money. This parade of fantastic inferences, which law students annually swallow without significant protest, shows up in the celebrated case of *Hawkins v. McGee*.[1] I shall argue that the case's role in the first semester of law school is to introduce students to discursive bodies that are distant from, and unlike, us.

The case introduces law students, on their first day of law school, to two common legal constructions of the body: the body as a machine; and the "perfect body." As we shall see, it is likely that the machine construction had already largely had its day by 1929, the date of the *Hawkins* opinion, while the image of the perfect body was just entering legal discourse at the time, to flower in later generations. So on the first day of law school, law students implicitly learn: (1) that the body is constructed in legal discourse; (2) that the same body may be constructed in multiple ways in the same writing; (3) that bodies are machines; and (4) that lawyers are people who can see that bodies are machines, which fact helps distinguish them from ordinary people, who lack this insight. This is rather a lot to learn on the first day of law school and may help contribute significantly to the intellectual and psychological pressure that many law students experience.

I want to take a little time to explain the legal issues in the case and the possible functions in legal analysis of the court's analogy of George Hawkins's hand to a machine. Readers who are not lawyers, and some who are, may find this section tedious, so let me explain what I am doing. Any author who seeks to elaborate an extralegal structure for understanding legal discourse is often, and fairly, met with the objection that these odd terms can only be understood from a perspective internal to legal thought, for which they are functional, and not from an external perspective, from which they may be made, unfairly and inaccurately, to appear ridiculous. Ahead of us lie a num-

---

[1] 146 Atl. 641 (N.H. 1929). Lon Fuller popularized the case by putting it in the opening spot of his casebook, *Contracts* (1947). It continues to be the first case in such popular casebooks as John P. Dawson, William Burnett Harvey, and Stanley D. Henderson, *Contracts* (6th ed. 1993); Thomas D. Crandall and Douglas J. Whaley, *Contracts* (1987); and Robert W. Hamilton, Alan Scott Rau, and Russell J. Weintraub, *Contracts* (2d ed. 1992). The case has passed into popular culture; see John Jay Osborne Jr., *The Paper Chase* 6–9 (Boston: Houghton Mifflin, 1971), and the movie based on it. Its human drama excites continuing interest from law students; see Jorie Roberts, "Hawkins Case: A Hair-Raising Experience," 66 *Harv. L. Rec.* 1 (March 17, 1978).

ber of such examples, of legal authors using quite far-fetched discursive constructions of the body, for purposes that within their assigned intellectual and
professional tasks are quite mundane.

Hawkins, I will argue, is not such an example. George Hawkins's hand is
constructed as a machine for no evident internal legal purpose whatever. It
establishes no valid legal analogy. If it is the basis for a jury instruction, its
symbolic meaning is almost completely indeterminate. If I am right, *Hawkins*
illustrates several of my basic contentions: that legal speakers construct in
discourse a human body; that they have freedom to construct multiple competing bodies, none of which corresponds to any person's bodily experience, all
of which represent social conventions for understanding bodily experience;
and that, in the face of this freedom, legal speakers characteristically construct
bodies that are cold, distanced, mechanical, inhuman.

George Hawkins's precise age does not appear from the opinion, though he
is described as a "boy." Nine years before the events of the case, George's
right hand came into contact with an electric wire and was severely burned,
leaving George with a scar on the palm. McGee, a physician, attempted to
graft skin from George's chest onto his palm. There was testimony that Dr.
McGee had repeatedly solicited Hawkins's father for permission to attempt
such a skin graft, and that, while George and his father were attempting to
decide whether to go ahead, Dr. McGee said that he would "guarantee to make
the hand a hundred per cent perfect hand."

The operation was not a success. Although the court's opinion contains no
physical description of the postoperative hand, it was apparently less attractive
and functional than it had been before. George sued Dr. McGee on the theory
that the "hundred per cent perfect hand" statement created an enforceable
contract or warranty on which Dr. McGee failed to deliver. Hawkins did not
attempt to show that Dr. McGee was negligent. A jury awarded Hawkins a
verdict in an amount unspecified in the court's opinion but too large for the
trial court, which ordered that the award be set aside unless Hawkins agreed to
reduce it to five hundred dollars. Both sides appealed to the Supreme Court of
New Hampshire, George seeking the jury's verdict reinstated, and Dr. McGee
seeking to have the whole case dismissed.

The Supreme Court of New Hampshire dealt first with Dr. McGee's contention that no case should ever have been sent to the jury since the alleged
"perfect hand" statement (which Dr. McGee denied making) was, even if
made, legally insufficient to constitute a contract. Contract theory at the time
of the case, and now, supports Dr. McGee on the abstract proposition that
there is a role for courts in such matters; that a jury is not free to find absolutely any words or deeds to constitute an enforceable contract; and that a trial
or appellate court may decide that particular words or deeds would not be
understood by any reasonable hearer as a contractual commitment. A court
may make such a finding even if, or rather, just because, the individual plain-

tiff in the contract case sincerely *did* hear the words as a contractual commitment. In the language of the law, the individual plaintiff's is merely a "subjective" understanding, while contract requires an "objective" agreement in the sense that hypothetical reasonable observers would agree that agreement had been reached. It is also accepted that the finding of "objective" agreement is for the judge and not the jury, although there is no generally accepted theory of why the judge, and not the jury, is in the better position to determine how reasonable objective observers would size up a given course of communications.

The *Hawkins* court held that Dr. McGee could be sued in contract. This is an unusual holding. The court did not cite any precedent supporting the idea that physicians' promises to patients might be enforceable contracts, and very few cases have followed *Hawkins* in the past sixty-plus years in finding such contracts. The *Hawkins* court's justification of its decision helped ensure that its holding would be regarded as unusual, linked to the facts before it. The court emphasized the fact mentioned above, that Dr. McGee had solicited the operation, as tending to reinforce the reasonable hearer's belief that Dr. McGee stood by his guarantee or warranty. If this fact is indeed material to the holding, the holding will be narrow, for few surgical operations are preceded by aggressive solicitation by the physician. The court also noted expressly that much communication by doctors to patients would represent expressions of opinion, or predictions, or reassurances, on which no contractual liability would be based, since reasonable hearers do not understand such communication as creating a contract. The court's example was a statement made by Dr. McGee predicting a three- or four-day hospital stay. It would seem to follow that most communication from physicians to patients would fall into this larger, noncontractual category.

The machine metaphor shows up in the second half of the opinion, dealing with the equally novel question of the correct measure of damages for the cause of action that the court just created seconds earlier. By employing the machine metaphor, the court can treat the question of damages as an easy one:

> The present case is closely analogous to one in which a machine is built for a certain purpose and warranted to do certain work. In such cases, the usual rule of damages for breach of warranty in the sale of chattels is applied, and it is held that the measure of damages is the difference between the value of the machine, if it had corresponded with the warranty[,] and its actual value, together with such incidental losses as the parties knew, or ought to have known, would probably result from failure to comply with its terms.[2]

Since the trial court had permitted Hawkins to recover for "pain and suffering," the jury's verdict must be reversed, and the damages portion of the case

[2] 146 Atl. at 643.

retried, in order to award Hawkins only his expected gain in "value" from the operation.

Why should we analogize the operation on Hawkins's hand to the construction of a machine? The court's answer is inadequate.

The court's manifest purpose in introducing this far-fetched analogy is to explain its theory of damages: Hawkins recovers (1) his anticipated gain from the operation, that is, the value of the hand as promised less its present value, (2) but no damages for pain and suffering. The machine metaphor contributes little to either half of this formulation. It contributes nothing to the first half, the award of expectation damages, since the court treats these as the normal damages in contract, as they had in fact become. Today law students are taught that there are competing theories of damages in contract cases, not all of which seek to protect the plaintiff's expectations, but the article that first made this point for English-speaking readers had not yet been published at the time of the *Hawkins* opinion.[3] If expectation damages are normal contract damages, they apply in Hawkins's case irrespective of whether or not one accepts the machine analogy.

Nor does the machine analogy really exclude pain and suffering damages. It is true that contract plaintiffs are not normally awarded damages for the mental distress sustained on delivery of a defective machine. However, as we shall see, the theoretical basis of damages for pain and suffering, where these damages are awarded, is most unclear and, in the view of some scholars, rests *precisely* on conceptualizing the damaged body as damaged property.[4]

Under the court's damages holding in *Hawkins,* the jury must still evaluate Hawkins's "expected gain in value" from the operation. It is this figure that is wholly indeterminate. Perhaps the court introduces the machine metaphor in order to limit this figure. If Hawkins's case is "closely analogous to one in which a machine is built for a certain purpose and warranted to do certain work," then perhaps it might follow that the "value of the machine, if it had corresponded with the warranty" is the hand's economic value as a money-maker for Hawkins and not, for example, its affective value to Hawkins. We cannot be certain that the court was not concerned with this problem. A generation earlier, it would have been clear that Hawkins's hand could only be evaluated for its ability to earn money for Hawkins, but already by 1929 there

---

[3] Lon Fuller and William Perdue, "The Reliance Interest in Contract Damages," 46 *Yale L. J.* 52 (1936). As a result of this article, other measures of damages are now seen to be possible; see Sullivan v. O'Connor, 296 NE.2d 183 (Mass. 1973) (reliance damages, seeking to restore status quo ante contract, are appropriate for breach of physician's promise to obtain specific result) (dictum).

[4] E.g., A. I. Ogus, "Damages for Lost Amenities: For a Foot, a Feeling, or a Function?," 35 *Mod. L. Rev.* 1, 2–10 (1972) I will take up the construction of the injured body as the property of its owner again in chapter 3.

were glimmerings of emotional and sentimental values in damage awards, particularly when children were injured.[5]

If the court introduces the machine metaphor to limit a damage award, the metaphor becomes functional. Presumably if the case is retried, the defendant can get a jury instruction based on the machine metaphor, something like: "Gentlemen [it would have been] of the jury, in determining the value to George Hawkins of a perfect hand, you should regard that hand as if it were a machine that George Hawkins bought." If the metaphor is used in this jury instruction, it is functional, but also clearly a bad analogy; indeed it is functional just because it is a bad analogy. A machine ordered from the Sears catalog is priced to reflect a competitive market in which buyers will demand machines on the basis of their marginal contribution to productivity, and manufacturers will produce them if they can make a profit on the marginal sale. Obviously Hawkins cannot order a hand from Sears or anyone else, and we have no assurance that the price he agreed to pay Dr. McGee reflected only, or primarily, the enhanced economic value of a perfect hand.

In any case, if the court's purpose in introducing the machine metaphor is to provide an economic analogy to limit the jury's award of damages, it does not follow through on this intention. The jury still has discretion to determine the "value of the hand, if perfect"; it is not expressly limited to its economic value and is not told that the price of the operation equals the anticipated value of the hand. Moreover, the court permits the jury to award "incidental damages," without defining these or limiting them to economic losses.

Perhaps all this is wrong, and the machine metaphor is a proplaintiff metaphor, and not prodefendant. Perhaps the *Hawkins* court is not haunted by the specter of a runaway jury award, but rather by the specter of a jury that fails even to see an injury here. Perhaps in an isolated farming community in northern New Hampshire, scarred hands are common, as common as other body scars, missing digits and limbs, the myriad injuries that farming inflicts on the body. Perhaps the court fears that the jury, unless properly guided, might not regard George Hawkins's scarred hand as a legal injury at all. Ah, but if the hand is not a hand but a machine, a machine that failed to perform as warranted, any farmer should be able to see the legal and economic injury, if a scarred hand is not just a scarred hand.[6] Perhaps in the consumer society of today, it is easier to get any jury to imagine that people have a sort of right to a perfect body, but if the New Hampshire jury did not start from this point, both Dr. McGee's promise, and the machine metaphor, might be necessary to get the jury to see that George Hawkins, at least, had a right to a perfect hand.

---

[5] Viviana A. Zelizer, *Pricing the Priceless Child: The Changing Social Value of Children* (New York: Basic, 1985).

[6] Gillian Stern made this point to me.

Some support for this proplaintiff interpretation comes from our best-known observer of rural New Hampshire life in the period roughly contemporaneous with the *Hawkins* case. Robert Frost's poem "Out, Out—" concerns a boy, like George Hawkins working in a sawmill, whose hand meets the saw. By the time the doctor arrives, "the hand was gone already."

> The doctor put him in the dark of ether.
> He lay and puffed his lips out with his breath.
> And then—the watcher at his pulse took fright.
> No one believed. They listened at his heart.
> Little—less—nothing!—and that ended it.
> No more to build on there. And they, since they
> Were not the one dead, turned to their affairs.[7]

If the New Hampshire jury that heard George Hawkins's suit against Dr. McGee was like the "they" of Frost's poem, who "turned to their affairs" "since they were not the one dead," perhaps a George Hawkins who was merely disfigured would have had less claim on their attention than a George Hawkins who was the victim of a breach of warranty.

How to choose between these interpretations? We cannot be sure we know what the machine metaphor meant in the mind of the judge who wrote it or in the minds of the likely readers of the opinion in New Hampshire in 1929. The metaphor was the Supreme Court's own creation; it does not appear in the briefs of either side (which are silent on the entire question of how to measure damages). Even if a lawyer for one side or the other had first introduced the metaphor, for all we know he might have misunderstood others' likely understanding of it.

I have nothing but respect for the legal interpreter who insists as a matter of chaste self-discipline on the interpretation of legal texts solely on the basis of internal canons of interpretation. However, such an interpreter must be silent about a great deal, including, it seems to me, the discursive construction of the body in legal analysis. We know that George Hawkins's body was constructed as a machine, but we cannot say what legal argument was advanced by this construction; whether any argument was excluded by it; or precisely what the construction meant to its likely hearers.

 In the next two chapters, I seek to put the machine metaphor into the context of the legal and literary discourse of its day. The basic points to be argued are that the analogy of the body to a machine was well established by 1929 in literature and law, but that its political spin was indeterminate. As a literary and medical construction, it often emphasized the deadening effects of industrial production.[8] This construction figured in legal advocacy as well, notably

---

[7] Robert Frost, "Out, Out—," in *Mountain Interval* 65–66 (New York: Henry Holt, 1916).
[8] See generally Mark Seltzer, *Bodies and Machines* (New York: Routledge, 1992). In truth, the

in the legal campaign for statutory restrictions on work hours. By 1929, however, this progressive version of the machine metaphor was a fairly dead metaphor that had ceased to generate new ideas when heard.

At the same time, the metaphor fit well in 1929 and fits well today with a
version of the body as the property of its owner, or a commodity that is bought
or sold. This complex of metaphors continues to be a functioning part of
American law and may underlie such diverse practices as compensation for
bodily injury, the interpretation of employment contracts calling for bodily
display or alteration by employees, the tax treatment of blood donation. Any
evaluation of the body in terms of money displays what we will be calling a
"commodified" construction of the body. On the other hand, this metaphor has
always coexisted with decided legal discomfort with the idea that the body is
property, or a commodity, and there are cases that seem to reject that proposition, when put starkly. The post-*Hawkins* history of the machine metaphor
merges into a larger tension between a legal discursive construction of the
body that emphasizes its remoteness or coldness (property, commodity) and
one that constructs a "nice," humanistic body in which we imagine our selves
at home.

The *Hawkins* case is thus a creature of its time by employing the machine
metaphor (disappearing by 1929), but doing so in the service of the body as
commodity (which had a bright future). The notion that George Hawkins's
arrangement for an operation on his hand was "closely analogous" to the
purchase of a machine was, perhaps, cold and legalistic. The internal evidence
from the opinion sustaining this interpretation is mainly silence. The opinion
is silent about physical description of Hawkins's hand, details of his life, his
feelings about his body, indeed, any detail about the "person" George
Hawkins other than the fact that his doctor promised him a perfect hand. I said
above that this coldness is not necessarily functional for analysis of the legal
issues presented by the case, and I think we can see it as chronically legal.
Legal thought absorbed, without much difficulty, the invitation of Adam
Smith to imagine economic life as the workings of an invisible hand.[9]
Hawkins v. McGee makes this metaphor embarrassingly literal. Insofar as it
assumes economic meaning, George Hawkins's *is* the invisible hand; it is
made "visible" in the opinion only through the machine metaphor.

In later chapters, especially chapters 6 through 11, I will explore a complex
of discursive bodies in which the body is figured as the object of desire, often,
though not necessarily, erotic desire. I don't want to spell out that conception

---

association of "machines" with conformity, mediocrity, and absence of mental or spiritual content
has hardly changed since Thomas Carlyle's essay "Signs of the Times," in Carlyle: *Selected
Works, Reminiscences and Letters* (Julian Symons ed.) (Cambridge: Harv. U. Pr., 1970) [1829],
discussed in chap. 2.

[9] P. Atiyah, *The Rise and Fall of Freedom of Contract* (Oxford: Clarendon, 1979) traces the
reception of Smith's ideas.

here, but experience teaching this case to students leads me to believe that any reader in our culture can, at this point, imagine a counteropinion that would seek to arouse identification, pity, sympathy, or desire for George Hawkins's body. Such an opinion would include, at a minimum, physical description of Hawkins and personal details about his life. As we shall see, most invocations of twentieth-century nonerotic, nonvisualized, isolated, machine or property bodies manage all the same to invoke in spectral form the earlier sentimental body in pain.

By imagining this counteropinion, we may readily see that the actual opinion is careful to efface any erotic aspects of the body of George Hawkins. Its very abstention from physical description creates a legal voice from which desire is absent, so the reader is prevented any emotional engagement with George Hawkins as a person. (It is probably necessary to point out again that the eroticized body of desire is itself a social construction, and my contrast here is not "legal/natural" but between two social constructions, each available to speakers in our culture).

Instead, Hawkins's hand is a machine that is bought, constructed, warranted, but not performing. This hand is thus inscribed into the normal regulatory mechanisms of consumer capitalism, mechanisms that include lawsuits and expectation damages.

George Hawkins's hand is constructed as a machine, then, for no particular purpose internal to the opinion, but rather as a typical example of a legal culture oriented away from erotic desire and toward economic self-understandings. While this orientation is still found in law, the machine metaphor is rarely invoked any more to support it. When an economic understanding of the body is generally accepted, it is not supported by the machine metaphor; when we are ambivalent about such an economic understanding, we no longer employ that metaphor to help us out of our difficulties.

For a contemporary example of unproblematic economic construction of the body, consider the evaluation of disability for purposes of workers' compensation statutes. The case of Karen Jaske is as typical as one could find:

> Plaintiff, Karen E. Jaske, is a thirty-seven year old woman who has a high school education, but no other vocational skills. She is currently employed as a sales person by an insurance company. From 1978 until 1984 plaintiff was employed as a production worker by defendant, Murray Ohio Manufacturing Company, Inc. In 1983, plaintiff discovered that she had developed bilateral carpal tunnel syndrome as a result of her employment with defendant. Surgery was performed on plaintiff's wrists, and plaintiff returned to work. Additional surgery was necessary in 1985 on plaintiff's right wrist because plaintiff developed recurrent carpal tunnel syndrome. Since this surgery, plaintiff has had difficulty using her hands. Such activities as writing, typing, and driving for an extended period of time cause pain in plaintiff's hands. In addition, the pain in plaintiff's hands

makes it difficult for plaintiff to dress herself, fix her own hair, and pick up a skillet.[10]

The issue in the case was the extent of Karen Jaske's disability for purposes of workers' compensation. As a description of her disability, the opinion shows some humanization in the sixty years since *Hawkins*. We are given a laconic recitation of activities in which Karen Jaske engages, which is more than we had for George Hawkins, even though this might have been relevant in determining the value of a perfect hand. This advance for humanism, if such it be, is small. The activities are barely described and of course horribly sexist. Male claimants normally discuss their inability to engage in athletic pursuits, not their difficulties in fixing their hair or picking up a skillet.[11]

The difficulty in determining the extent of Karen Jaske's disability as the court saw it was however not the sexism of its standards but the disagreement among its experts: three experts testified respectively that Karen Jaske was 5, 10, and 62 percent permanently partially disabled. The chancellor had found that she was 20 percent permanently partially disabled, relying heavily on the fact that Karen Jaske was making more money as an insurance salesperson than she ever had as a factory operative. The Supreme Court of Tennessee specifically approved this finding and this method. Disability is not a purely medical concept. The "trial judge may properly consider several non-medical factors," including "the fact of employment after an injury, the earning power of the injured workman, and his earnings."[12]

This is just the same thing as saying that, for purposes of the workers' compensation laws, Karen Jaske's body is, at least in part, a machine that works for her, and is disabled largely insofar as it fails to make money for her. (Of course, she was found to be 20 percent disabled even though she was making more money, so her body is only in part a machine to make money, and has other, affective value to her). However, the *Jaske* court does not employ this machine metaphor, or any other. This is what I mean by saying that when we have agreed on an economic concept of the body, the machine metaphor itself need not explicitly be invoked and indeed would arguably jar, not support, the decision: wouldn't the court's laconic certainty be put into question if it explicitly held that Karen Jaske's "case is closely analogous to one in which a machine is built for a certain purpose and warranted to do certain work"?

Later chapters will take up such problems as the theory of compensation for body injury or ownership of body organs. On these issues, law seems ambivalent about an economic concept of the body yet still does not employ the

---

[10] Jaske v. Murray Ohio Mfg. Co., Inc., 750 SW.2d 150, 151 (Tenn. 1988).

[11] Ellen Smith Pryor, "Flawed Promises: A Critical Evaluation of the American Medical Association's *Guides to the Evaluation of Permanent Impairment*," 103 *Harv. L. Rev.* 964 (1990).

[12] Jaske, 750 SW.2d at 151.

machine metaphor. So this is what I mean by saying that *Hawkins* seems an old-fashioned, dying metaphor in 1929 that the *Hawkins* opinion does little to sustain—not that the machine/property/commodity construction of the body has died, but that its support through an articulate machine metaphor has.

The machine metaphor performs another function in *Hawkins* that characterizes all constructions of the body in law: it mediates between the "public" and "private" aspects of George Hawkins's body. The body often symbolizes in law the private, that which is treated as foundational for the individual self, particularly when the body is characterized as a "privacy interest." However, the body is also importantly public: our constructions of the body are social and conventional; the boundaries of the body, the sense of injury, the sense of harm, are quite significantly social, constructed, and conventional. Wittgenstein notes that the way we talk about pain presupposes a social "stage" "set" so that the word *pain* makes sense.[13] It is but a short step to the conclusion that the play performed on this stage actually changes the nature of the experience: the language of pain is *not* simply a set of reports on internal states, but largely constructs the experience undergone. We shall see that all discursive constructions of the body necessarily mediate between the public and private aspects of the body, all the more so when they self-consciously code the body as one or the other.

Because the injured hand is a machine that George Hawkins ordered, it is private to him; he "owned" it; and the injury to his hand, or the failure to deliver the "perfect" hand he was promised, calls for compensation to him. But because the hand is public, we can analogize it to other objects in our experience, we can evaluate it, we can put a dollar figure on it—and we do so "objectively," by reference to "public" or social valuations of a "perfect hand," and not to "subjective" or emotional valuations internal to George Hawkins—or to us. A marvelous metaphor, property, that is always and everywhere public and private!

Before taking up the larger history of the machine/property/commodity complex of metaphors, I want to ask one last question about the *Hawkins* case. For if we cannot determine just why the court analogized George Hawkins's hand to a machine, can we at least say why this analogy is literally the first one taught to American law students? As I said above, the case has not been influential in American law; it has rarely been cited, and few students will ever encounter a physician's contract to procure a particular result at any point in their professional careers.

There are conventional reasons for starting the class in contracts with *Hawkins v. McGee* that I do not reject or minimize. Among others, it helps introduce students to the overlap of contract and tort and how each may lie on

---

[13] Ludwig Wittgenstein, *Philosophical Investigations* §257 (G. E. M. Anscombe trans.) (New York: Macmillan, 3d ed., 1958).

the same set of facts, as well as to the basic theory of expectation damages, a contract concept not part of tort law.

Still, there are definitely elements of a degradation ritual here.[14] Attendant with their entry into higher, professional class, students undergo ritual passage and ritual degradation, and, as Mary Douglas writes, "The structure of living organisms is better able to reflect complex social forms than door posts and lintels."[15] Students must swallow (body metaphor), without whimper or protest, the idea that thinking like a lawyer about damaged hands *means* analogizing them to defective machines. If you can believe that, we promise them, you can be a lawyer. Most students can believe this, of course; few students really drop out of law school over *Hawkins v. McGee*. Being bright and adaptable, they promptly do go to work believing that hands are machines, as we know they will. What we mean is: if you can believe that, you are complicit with us, you are in fact one of us. You cannot criticize us, for you are as degraded as we are.

Of course this isn't what the machine metaphor necessarily means, although I believe that for many or most law students it is what it does mean. A competing strain in postmodernist discourse stresses the possibilities for the liberation of the spirit in developing a self-concept as a machine. If one is a machine, one is free of some of the stultifying humanism of bodies that have been constructed only as situated in webs of conventional or religious rules. Walter Benjamin remarks of works of art: "[M]echanical reproduction emancipates the work of art from its parasitical dependence on ritual. . . . Instead of being based on ritual, it begins to be based on another practice—politics."[16] Perhaps the body, like Benjamin's work of art, might similarly be understood as mechanically reproduced, freed from ritual, and liberated through politics, and this may be the spirit behind Andy Warhol's often-repeated claim that he wanted to be a machine and certainly lies behind Donna Haraway's work.[17] This postmodern sense of possibility underlies the jokey machinelike formulation "BUGS: Body Unit Grounded in a Self."[18]

---

[14] Erving Goffman, *Asylums: Essays on the Social Situation of Mental Patients and Other Inmates* 14–48 (Garden City, N.Y.: Anchor, 1961); Harold Garfinkel, "Conditions of Successful Degradation Ceremonies," 61 *Am. J. Soc.* 420 (1956).

[15] Mary Douglas, *Purity and Danger: An Analysis of the Concepts of Pollution and Taboo* 114 (London: Routledge, 1966).

[16] Walter Benjamin, "The Work of Art in the Age of Mechanical Reproduction," in *Illuminations* 224 (Hannah Arendt ed., Harry Zohn trans.) (New York: Schocken, 1969) [1936].

[17] Gene R. Swenson, "What Is Pop Art? Interview with Andy Warhol," 62 *ArtNews* (No. 7) p. 24 (November 1963), as quoted in Patrick S. Smith, *Andy Warhol: Art and Films* 110 (Ann Arbor, Mich.: UMI Research Pr., 1986); Donna Haraway, *Simian, Cyborg, and Women: The Reinvention of Nature* (New York: Routledge, 1990). The champion, if obscure, advocates of people becoming machines are Gilles Deleuze and Félix Guattari, *Anti-Oedipus* (Robert Hurley, Mark Seem, and Helen R. Lane trans.) (Minneapolis: U. Minn. Pr., 1983) [1972].

[18] In use at the Group for the Study of Virtual Systems, University of California at Santa Cruz.

Benjamin, however, did not draw this conclusion, either about art or about bodies. At the time of these remarks, it was fascism that had most fully realized the transformation of the mechanically reproduced work of art, as Benjamin argued: the cinema and other mass propaganda of fascism could aestheticize even war. There is nothing of liberation in Benjamin's use of the machine metaphor in his notes for his project on the Paris Arcades: "Comparison of human beings with a control panel on which are thousands of electric light bulbs; first these die out, then others light themselves anew."[19] Benjamin criticized Hitler's 1936 Olympics as "reactionary" because of the measurement of athletic performance in "seconds and centimeters"; "the old form of struggle disappears," to be replaced by a modern form typified by "measuring the human being against an apparatus."[20]

The law students whom I encounter on the first day of law school are more like the humanist Walter Benjamin than the postmodernist Andy Warhol and Donna Haraway; few find any liberatory potential in that paragraph in *Hawkins*. Stephen Munzer suggests another possible meaning of the machine metaphor: physical therapists, trainers, and athletes might imagine their bodies as machines, the better to understand and master them. This is true, no doubt, but the *Hawkins* court does not seem to advance the metaphor as any such advance in understanding, nor do my students seem to experience it that way. My students, when their attention is drawn to the paragraph, seem to respond more as if it is a degradation ritual.

For many years, when I have taught contracts, I have tried to break this cycle by making the students conscious of the weirdness of the machine metaphor. I refer to some selected, recent, well-publicized injury, usually of a well-known sports figure. I ask the students to imagine a lunch table conversation in which people are commiserating with the victim, speculating about the impact of the injury on the victim and on his team, whatever people have actually been saying about the injury in question. I then ask them to imagine a law student saying what the *Hawkins* court said: "You have to think about this as if Bo Jackson's hip were a machine, and now his machine is damaged." Wouldn't people feel that a psychopath was sitting at the table with them?[21]

See Allucquière Roseanne Stone, "Virtual Systems," in *Zone 6: Incorporations* 613 (Jonathan Crary and Sanford Kwitner eds.) (New York: Zone, 1992).

[19] As quoted in Susan Buck-Morss, *The Dialectics of Seeing: Walter Benjamin and the Arcades Project* 309 (Cambridge: MIT Pr., 1989).

[20] Id. 326 (quoting the notes to the artwork essay).

[21] Cf. Bruno Bettelheim, *The Empty Fortress: Infantile Autism and the Birth of the Self* 233–339 (New York: Free Pr., 1967) (on Joey the mechanical boy, a severely autistic boy who described himself as a machine run by remote control); Victor Tausk, "On the Origin of the 'Influencing Machine' in Schizophrenia," 2 *Psychoanalytic Quarterly* 519–56 (1933) [1919], reprinted in Crary and Kwitner, *Zone 6* 542 (descriptions by schizophrenic patients of machines allegedly inducing their illness, attributed by Tausk to patients' rejection of normal narcissistic libido toward their own bodies, and projection of those bodies). Psychotherapists tell me that schizophrenics today rarely present these particular symptoms, for reasons that are not clear.

I pulled this stunt in my contracts class for many years before I understood its structure. When I ask the students to imagine lunch table conversation about Bo Jackson's hip, I am not sending them into their own experience of their own bodies (however problematic the idea of "experience" of your body).[22] The contrast works equally well for students who have had hip injuries and students who have not. Rather, I was playing on what has become a central contrast of this book: the contrast between the "nice" sentimental body and the estranged legal body, that is, between two competing discursive constructions. (The "nice" body is itself a regulatory device, but I will postpone until chapters 6–11 the kind of discipline made possible when the body is represented as the sentimental object of sympathy or desire, including, in my view, certain concepts of privacy and types of search, criminal punishment, appearance regulation, and regulation of bodily display).

Because each of my students can call up the image of the "nice" sentimental body, the felt, sensed, empathized-with body, they can readily grasp the function of the machine analogy as used in *Hawkins* or elsewhere in legal analysis. The very purpose of the analogy may be to estrange the reader or hearer, specifically, the juror who hears the jury instruction based on it, from those feelings of human empathy and commiseration that dominate "normal," "lunch table" conversations about someone else's injury and thus come to seem "natural." I raised above the possibility that this is not how the analogy worked in 1929, when it may rather have created such empathy when it was lacking. However, a contemporary audience almost surely will value a perfect body more highly than a perfect machine.

The human body represents an acute instance of the tension between empathy and principle that pervades legal analysis generally. Pretty much the entire history of sociological and philosophical thinking about law could be written as the story of successive attempts to model it as a system of rules and principles divorced from human empathy and identification, followed by the amazing repeated discovery that law is shot full of human empathy and identification. (Citations seem to me both superfluous and invidious.) When conceived as principle, law often mimetically represents mind, brain, or spirit, understood precisely as dominating the body. It is in moments like these that the strategy of embodying all legal subjects discussed in the introduction, a relentless onslaught of body language, references, and descriptions, has a certain destabilizing promise.

However, as cases like *Hawkins* show, this is very much less than the whole story, for law sometimes is represented as "human," sympathetic, emotional; and, as we shall see, the precise way these bodies are constructed in law is at least as interesting as the more conventional construction in which body stands opposed to law as flesh to spirit. Any matter involving injury to the body that goes to trial, whether a tort or contract suit, will open up a space for

[22] Cf. Joan W. Scott, "The Evidence of Experience," 17 *Critical Inquiry* 773 (1991).

a lawyer whose virtually sole obligation will be to create empathy and identification with the victim through the rhetorical worlds of testimony and sum-
mation.[23] In a case such as *Hawkins v. McGee,* in which the jury must place a
value on the "hand as promised" and the "hand in its current condition," such
empathy is literally the only tool the jury can employ to fix a measure of
damages. There are other sorts of legal proceedings in which a jury may be
asked to place a value on something lost, based on their own experience in a
market economy, but in *Hawkins* it is surely equally dreamlike to ask the jury
to put a dollar figure on Hawkins's "pain and suffering" (as the trial judge
erroneously did) or the "value of a perfect hand" (the legally correct measure
of damages). Either formula invites a figure to be drawn from an enormous
range of possibilities, none more compelling than another.

Human empathy is, as I say, literally the only tool the jury brings to its task
in the damages phase of personal injury litigation. But this creates a risk: the
jury may be so carried away by identification with the victim as to render
awards that would inhibit what the system deems valuable economic activity.
It is reversible error to permit the jury to base damage awards on, for example,
what they would have to be paid to go through the plaintiff's experience.[24]

For a contemporary audience, the machine metaphor becomes central to the
court's opinion, more central than the sterile damage formulas ("expected
gain," "value of a perfect hand") that could not conceivably achieve the goal
of limiting discretion. The work of the machine metaphor is, if not to break
empathy with the victim, then to channel and limit it, in a way that the court's
preferred damage formula, "value of the hand as promised," alone and unac-
companied by the machine metaphor, cannot. We must see the body as a
machine so that we are not tempted to see it as "human."

This is what torturers described by Elaine Scarry do. "The nomenclature for
torture is typically drawn from three spheres of civilization. First, . . . the
prolonged, acute distress of the body is in its contortions claimed to be mimetic of a particular invention or technological feat: the person's pain will be
called 'the telephone' in Brazil, 'the plane ride' in Vietnam, 'the motorola' in
Greece, and 'the San Juanica Bridge' in the Philippines." This produces a
"circle of negation: there is no human being in excruciating pain; that's only a

---

[23] For a brilliant analysis of rhetorical strategies in products liability trials, see Elaine Scarry,
The Body in Pain: The Making and Unmaking of the World 297–307 (New York: Oxford U. Pr.,
1985), discussed in chap. 4.

[24] See, e.g., Stanley v. Ellegood, 382 SW.2d 572 (Ky. 1964) ("You will treat him like you
would want yourselves to be treated"; jury should have been admonished to disregard); Klotz v.
Sears and Roebuck, 267 F.2d 53 (7th Cir.), cert. denied 361 U.S. 877 (1959) (urging that jury "do
unto others as you would have them to unto you"; asking defendant's counsel how much his eye
worth; and framing tort as if defendant had purchased plaintiff's eye, all appealed to jury's sympathy rather than its reason). Compare Walters v. Hitchcock, 697 P.2d 847, 849 (Ks. 1985) ("The
comment commencing 'Who would sell . . .' is, we believe, a fair argument relative to claimed
damages and is not a 'golden rule' argument").

telephone; there is no telephone; that is merely a means of destroying a human being who is not a human being, who is only a telephone, who is not a telephone but merely a means of destroying a telephone."[25] It is what lawyers must be trained to do.

There must be no mistake about the contemporary audience for *Hawkins v. McGee*. As I said above, few lawyers or jurors will ever be exposed to its language. The case exists today as a degradation ritual for law students accompanying their entrance into a new and higher professional state. It is their tendency toward humanism that is the target in teaching *Hawkins*. Their very ability to construct alternative legal bodies must be cut loose to drift in the silences of *Hawkins,* so utterly free of descriptions of the body, representations of pain, shame, or embarrassment, metaphors of closeness or bodily presence.

[25] Scarry, *The Body in Pain* 44.

Chapter 2

THE FATIGUED BODY: ON THE PROGRESSIVE
HISTORY OF THE BODY AS MACHINE

BODIES WERE MACHINES in American law principally from 1908 to 1929, as the symbolic objects of efficient management and regulation. The analogy does not appear to have been used in American law until the early years of the twentieth century, as part of the legal campaign over legislated limits to the working day. By the time the legal body was first constructed as a machine, the machine body was an extremely complex metaphor that was in active use in medical thought and in literature to convey at least three different ideas.

First, the body is a machine because it is *like other bodies*. Because bodies are machines or mechanical, medical therapies that work for one patient should work for another. Because a body is a machine, it is possible to have accident insurance, or labor legislation.

Second, the body is a machine because of the *deadening effects of industrial production*. These machine bodies experience fatigue, wear out, require maintenance.

Third, the body is a machine when it is *perfect*. Bodies that are perfectly strong, perfectly formed, improved through effort, are all analogized to machines in the years before the machine body became a legal metaphor.

The brief history of the legal metaphor plays alternately on all three of these meanings. For example, as we have seen in *Hawkins v. McGee,* meanings one and three are punned on. George Hawkins's hand is a machine insofar as damages may be awarded for its defective delivery (machine like other machines, interchangeable). However, the hand is also a machine insofar as George and Dr. McGee can contemplate its perfection. The complexity of the metaphor may help explain its disappearance from law after the *Hawkins* case of 1929.

CLOCKWORK MACHINES IN PHILOSOPHY AND LITERATURE

The analogy of the body to a machine has origins in antiquity.[1] Centuries before the legal body was a machine, philosophers compared the body to a

---

[1] See generally Leslie M. Thompson, "People as Machines and the Body as Property," 27 *Midwest Q.* 163 (1986), tracing the metaphor from antiquity through de la Mettrie, *L'Homme machine* (1748) and then through the industrial revolution to dehumanization and mass killing. The tone is alarmist and the hope is that somehow we can get away from the metaphor.

machine, with distinct meaning for medical thought and practice, culminating in the obsession with human fatigue through which the machine metaphor entered law. As Anson Rabinbach tells the tale,[2] it begins with Descartes's description of the body as a machine. "Je suppose que le Corps n'est autre chose qu'une statue ou machine de Terre" [I assume their body to be but a statue, an earthen machine][3] Leibniz, Descartes's opponent on so many matters, joined him in this imagery. "Thus each organic body of a living thing is a kind of divine machine, or natural automaton, which infinitely surpasses all artificial automata. . . . [T]he machines of nature, that is to say living bodies, are still machines in the least of their parts ad infinitum."[4]

The machine body, in all its manifestations in this and the preceding chapter, fits well with a Cartesian dualism in which the body on the one hand and mind or spirit on the other inhabit two different worlds, neither reducible to the other. A machine body is normally a body from which the mind or spirit has been removed, as it were. The machine body can function as the synecdoche for a larger ontology in which mind and body are necessarily disjoined, or, less ambitiously, as a critical metaphor in which some set of social arrangements is criticized for, *contra naturem,* wrongfully seeking to separate mind from body.

Under Descartes's influence, eighteenth-century Europe, particularly France, was obsessed with the machine metaphor, which helped bring about useful work in medicine and science. "Whoever examines the bodily organism with attention will certainly not fail to discern pincers in the jaws and teeth; a container in the stomach; watermains in the veins, the arteries and the other ducts; a piston in the heart; sieves or filters in the bowels; in the lungs, bellows; in the muscles, the force of the lever; in the corner of the eye, a pulley, and so on . . . . It remains unquestionable that all these phenomena must be seen in the forces of the wedge, of equilibrium, of the lever, of the spring, and of all the other principles of mechanics."[5] The machines here are, naturally, eighteenth-century "clockwork" machines in which an exogenous source of power is applied, and thereafter the machine itself performs movements that are predictable, regular, and efficient. In the metaphor, the exogenous power

---

[2] Anson Rabinbach, *The Human Motor: Energy, Fatigue, and the Origins of Modernity* (Berkeley: Univ. Cal. Pr., 1990).

[3] René Descartes, *Treatise of Man* 2–4 (Thomas Steele Hall trans.) (Cambridge: Harv. U. Pr., 1972). See also René Descartes, *Discourse on Method,* Fifth Part, at 41 (Laurence J. Lafleur trans.) (Indianapolis: Bobbs-Merrill, 1960) [1637].

[4] "Monadology" Par. 64 (1714), in Leibniz, *Philosophical Writings* 15 (Mary Morris trans.) (London: Dent, 1934). See also the passage in Leibniz's "Remarks on Bayle's Dictionary," in which human bodies are compared with watches and alarm clocks, wound and set by God, id. 133.

[5] Giorgio Baglivi, *De Praxi Medica* 78 (Venice 1727), as quoted in Sergio Moravia, "From *Homme Machine* to *Homme Sensible:* Changing Eighteenth-Century Models of Man's Image," 39 *J. Hist. Ideas* 45, 48 (1978).

source represents the Cartesian mind or spirit that stays outside the body but animates and directs it; the machine represents the mindless body. This simplified model apparently accounted for remarkable progress in medical thought.

It similarly influenced the human psychology found in eighteenth-century literature. "This sort of woman is absolutely nothing but a machine for giving pleasure. You will say that we have only to turn her into one of these and our plans are suited. Well and good! But don't forget that everyone is soon familiar with the springs and motors of these machines; and that, to make use of this one without danger it will be necessary to do so with all speed, to stop in good time, then to destroy it."[6] This machine metaphor speaks the language of science, reason, and progress but does so in order to parody them. Because the body is a machine, it can be made by a man as easily as by a woman. Because the body is a machine, it can be the more easily controlled, predicted, known—and destroyed.

It is not clear that either the eighteenth-century medical or literary body-machine had much influence on legal thought.[7] In our surviving legal texts of the era society may be a machine, the Constitution may even be a machine, but the body does not seem to be a machine.[8]

DYNAMIC MACHINES IN PHILOSOPHY, LITERATURE, AND MEDICAL THOUGHT

In European and American medical thought of the late eighteenth and early nineteenth centuries, "mechanists" temporarily lost ground to medical "vitalists," who argued that principles other than the mechanical were necessary to explain human illness. Specifically, the "body was seen, metaphorically, as a system of dynamic interactions with its environment. Health or disease resulted from a cumulative interaction between constitutional endowment and environmental circumstance."[9] It was natural for each healthy body to be in "balance," but just what was that balance depended greatly on specific features of each body, including its ethnic background, social class, and occupa-

[6] Pierre-Ambroise-François Choderlos de Laclos, *Les Liaisons dangereuses,* letter 106, at 254 (P. W. K. Stone trans.) (Harmondsworth: Penguin, 1961) [1782].

[7] See Stephen Rice, forthcoming dissertation (Yale, American Studies), on body machine in eighteenth-century America. Daniel A. Cohen, *Pillars of Salt, Monuments of Grace: New England Crime Literature and the Origins of American Popular Culture, 1674–1860* (New York: Oxford U. Pr., 1993) demonstrates both a national obsession with crime fiction and reporting following the American Revolution and (at 219–30) at least one jury's lack of interest in a "medical" defense of somnambulism.

[8] Cf. Michael G. Kammen, *A Machine That Would Go of Itself: The Constitution in American Culture* (New York: Knopf, 1986).

[9] Charles E. Rosenberg, *Explaining Epidemics and Other Studies in the History of Medicine* 12 (Cambridge: Camb. U. Pr., 1992).

tional type. Naming a disease was not considered a trustworthy guide to treatment, since good treatment for a Frenchman might not be appropriate for an American.[10]

We may take Thomas Carlyle's great essay of 1829, "Signs of the Times," as an interestingly nonobvious philosophic analog to this nonmechanized medical body. "Were we required to characterise this age of ours by any single epithet, we should be tempted to call it, not an Heroical, Devotional, Philosophical, or Moral Age, but above all others, the Mechanical Age. It is the Age of Machinery, in every outward and inward sense of that word; the age which, with its whole undivided might, forwards, teaches and practises the great art of adapting means to ends. Nothing is now done directly, or by hand; all is by rule and calculated contrivance." The body is not a machine in this lament; rather, it stands opposed to Machine, as "hand" stands against "rule" in the last sentence. "On every hand, the living artisan is driven from his workshop, to make room for a speedier, inanimate one. The shuttle drops from the fingers of the weaver, and falls into iron fingers that ply it faster."[11] The weaver and the machine both have fingers, but no one doubts that these are different in kind.

The same confident distinction between the human and the mechanical lies behind even such as sentence as "Men are grown mechanical in head and in heart, as well as in hand. They have lost faith in individual endeavour, and in natural force, of any kind. Not for internal perfection, but for external combinations and arrangements, for institutions, constitutions,—for Mechanism of one sort or other, do they hope and struggle."[12] In this conventional contrast, the antidote to the "mechanical" is "the imperishable dignity of man." "If Mechanism, like some glass bell, encircles and imprisons us; if the soul looks forth on a fair heavenly country which it cannot reach, and pines, and in its scanty atmosphere is ready to perish,—yet the bell is but of glass; 'one bold stroke to break the bell in pieces, and thou art delivered!' " "[A]ll but foolish men know, that the only solid, though a far slower reformation, is what each begins and perfects on *himself*."[13]

Carlyle's contrast between the mechanical and the human is conventional and comes easily to us today, as we saw in the discussion in the last chapter of our "natural" responses to bodily injury, and as we shall see most clearly when we take up the sale and donation of organs (chap. 3), and the history of criminal punishment (chap. 11). It influences Captain Ahab's justification of the cash bonus he offers his sailors in the quest for Moby Dick: "In times of

[10] John Harley Warner, *The Therapeutic Perspective: Medical Practice, Knowledge, and Identity in America, 1820–1885* 62–90 (Cambridge: Harv. U. Pr., 1986).

[11] Carlyle: *Selected Works, Reminiscences, and Letters* 22 (Julian Symons ed.) (Cambridge: Harv. U. Pr., 1970).

[12] Id. 25.

[13] Id. 41–44.

strong emotion mankind disdain all base considerations; but such times are evanescent. The permanent constitutional condition of the *manufactured* man, thought Ahab, is sordidness."[14] The sentimental human body that feels pain, that is opposed to the mechanical, that rises above base and sordid considerations, that must be envisioned as intact and perfect, is one of the finest creations of legal discourse, and will be repeatedly invoked in legal texts throughout this book. Its power is in no way diminished by the fact that it seems to be a creation of the final decades of the eighteenth century and is imaged as a kind of mimesis of philosophic liberalism and individualism similarly becoming established at that time.

Such is the power of this sentimental body that it may be harder for a contemporary reader to capture a way in which the human *is* mechanical, not to bemoan but to illuminate. Just this feature of eighteenth-century medical thought reappeared in the nineteenth century's rejection of the therapeutics of the "natural."

In the 1860s through 1880s a "therapeutic revolution" took place, the most radical departure of which was the demand that therapies be proven in laboratory experimentation, not merely in physicians' observations. Therapy became redefined as restoring the body to the "normal," not the "natural." Illness was not a specific body out of harmony with its environment for reasons possibly idiosyncratic to it, but rather a malfunctioning part, which normally should be treated in the same way that the part would be treated if it malfunctioned in other bodies.[15]

This focus on specific, functioning parts helped revive the machine metaphors of early-eighteenth-century medicine; indeed causation is hard to pin down when so many contemporaneous conceptions linked hands. "Breakdown of a part" is of course already a machine metaphor and linked with it in medical thought, where machine imagery always shapes a set of assumptions about disease, including focus on isolated bodily processes and mechanisms and a Cartesian separation of the "body" from the something else that is mind or spirit or agency.[16] For example, if the woman's body is a machine with different parts, women's reproductive organs could become "the active agents in reproduction; women were merely the passive instruments of nature's purposes, their agency appearing only as they *interfered* with the purposes nature intended for their bodies."[17] The medical idea of the healthy body as essentially alike to others in their healthiness doubtless helps reinforce such other late-nineteenth-century conceptions as statistical persons, acting in actuarially

[14] Herman Melville, *Moby-Dick; or, The Whale,* chap. 46, "Surmises" (1851).

[15] Warner, *The Therapeutic Perspective* 235–64.

[16] Mark Johnson, *The Body in the Mind: The Bodily Basis of Meaning, Imagination, and Reason* 127–37 (Chicago: U. Chi. Pr., 1987).

[17] Reva Siegel, "Reasoning from the Body: A Historical Perspective on Abortion Regulation and Questions of Equal Protection," 44 *Stan. L. Rev.* 261, 291–92 (1992) (emphasis original).

predictable ways and easily replaceable by others, insurance against disease and accident, and a Taylorist workforce performing deskilled tasks which any replacement worker might perform as well.[18]

However, the nineteenth-century concept of machine differed from Descartes's. The body was now not a set of simple moving parts put into motion by an exogenous motor. Rather, the body was a motor itself, a motor subject to decline, entropy, and work fatigue.[19] Physiologists and hygienists like Etienne-Jules Marey and Angelo Mosso "discovered" fatigue (in the precise sense of loss of energy due to overwork) in the 1870s, ushering in a flood of medical literature on the problem, in which the strain of modernity was blamed for the apparent dissipation of bodily strength and energy.[20]

The association of the body with a machine, in order to symbolize the fatigue of industrialization, became a common figure in popular literature as well. During the middle third of the nineteenth century we may trace the move from Carlyle to Marey and Mosso, that is, from mechanical analogies as metaphors for degradation, to mechanical analogies as sources of personal power.[21]

As the mill owner in Rebecca Harding Davis's *Life in the Iron Mills* says, " 'If I had the making of men, these men who do the lowest part of the world's work should be machines,—nothing more,—hands. It would be kindness. God help them: What are taste, reason, to creatures who must live such lives as that?' He pointed to Deborah, sleeping on the ash-heap."[22] Elsewhere Davis rings some beautiful changes on the machine metaphor, as the bodies of the workers become a clock:

> Not many even of the inhabitants of a manufacturing town know the vast machinery of system by which the bodies of workmen are governed, that goes on un-

---

[18] Mark Seltzer, *Bodies and Machines* 47–66 (New York: Routledge, 1992); Jonathan Simon, "For the Government of Its Servants: Law and Disciplinary Power in the Work Place, 1870–1906," 13 *Stud. L, Politics, & Soc.* 105, 131–32 (1993); Jonathan Simon, "The Ideological Effects of Actuarial Practices," 22 *L. & Soc. Rev.* 71 (1988). On accident insurance, I have benefited from an unpublished student paper by Gunnar O'Neill, whose tragic early death is an acute loss. Gunnar O'Neill, "Speculations on Accident Insurance: Risking Security" (1990).

[19] "With the invention of the steam and internal combustion engines, however, the analogy of the human or animal machine began to take on a modern countenance. As the philosopher Michel Serres has noted, the eighteenth-century machine was a product of the Newtonian universe with its multiplicity of forces, disparate sources of motion, and reversible mechanism. By contrast, the nineteenth-century machine, modeled on the thermodynamic engine, was a 'motor,' the servant of a powerful nature conceived as a reservoirs of motivating power." Rabinbach, *The Human Motor* 52, quoting Michel Serres, *Hermes: Literature, Science, Philosophy* 71 (Baltimore: Johns Hopkins U. Pr.,1982).

[20] Rabinbach, *The Human Motor.*

[21] See generally Daniel T. Rodgers, *The Work Ethic in Industrial America, 1850–1920* 65–90 (Chicago: U. Chi. Pr., 1978) ("mechanicalized" man).

[22] Rebecca Harding Davis, *Life in the Iron Mills; or, The Korl Woman* 34 (Old Westbury, N.Y.: Feminist Pr., 1972) [1861].

ceasingly from year to year. The hands of each mill are divided into watches that relieve each other as regularly as the sentinels of an army. By night and day the work goes on, the unsleeping engines groan and shriek, the fiery pools of metal boil and surge. Only for a day in the week, in half-courtesy to public censure, the fires are partially veiled; but as soon as the clock strikes midnight, the great furnaces break forth with renewed fury, the clamor begins with fresh, breathless vigor, the engines sob and shriek like "gods in pain."[23]

The furnaces and engines are alive; they display "fury" and "vigor," "sob and shriek." The people, however, are "hands" and "watches" of the clock that governs their schedules.[24]

Jack London employed machine metaphors alternatively as metaphors of degradation and of human power. His short story "The Apostate: A Child Labor Parallel," illustrates the degradation version; it is not so different from Thomas Carlyle or Rebecca Harding Davis in its identification of the machine with degradation; liberation lies in freedom from the mechanical.[25]

The child Johnny was the perfect worker. He knew that. He had been told so, often. It was a commonplace, and besides it didn't seem to mean anything to him any more. From the perfect worker he had evolved into the perfect machine. When his work went wrong, it was with him as with the machine, due to faulty material. It would have been as possible for a perfect nail-die to cut imperfect nails as for him to make a mistake. And small wonder. There had never been a time when he had not been in intimate relationship with machines. Machinery had almost been bred into him, and at any rate he had been brought up on it.

In the story, factory labor turns not only Johnny and his coworkers but their overseer into a machine: "It seemed to him as useless to oppose the overseer as to defy the will of a machine. Machines were made to go in certain ways and to perform certain tasks. It was the same with the overseer."[26] At the end of the story Johnny leaves home and the factory to ride the rails, but he "did not walk like a man. He did not look like a man. He was a travesty of the human. It was a twisted and stunted and nameless piece of life that shambled like a sickly ape, arms loose-hanging, stoop-shouldered, narrow-chested, grotesque and terrible."[27] Throughout, machine is opposed to human.

London's novel *The Sea-Wolf* identifies bodies with machines quite differently, as a metaphor for power. When the narrator, a doctor, first sees Captain Wolf Larsen "stripped . . . the sight of his body quite took my breath

[23] Id. 19.

[24] Seltzer, *Bodies and Machines*.

[25] Jack London, *Novels and Stories* 797, 801 (New York: Library of America, 1982) [1906; with the subtitle "A Child Labor Parable"].

[26] Id. 801.

[27] Id. 815–16.

away. . . . Wolf Larsen was the man-type, the masculine, and almost a god in his perfectness. . . ."

> "God made you well," I said.
>
> "Did he?" he answered. "I have often thought so myself, and wondered why."
>
> "Purpose—" I began.
>
> "Utility," he interrupted. "This body was made for use. These muscles were made to grip, and tear, and destroy living things that get between me and life. . . . Feet with which to clutch the ground, legs to stand on and to help withstand, while with arms and hands, teeth and nails, I struggle to kill and to be not killed. Purpose? Utility is the better word."
>
> I did not argue. I had seen the mechanism of the primitive fighting beast, and I was as strongly impressed as if I had seen the engines of a great battleship or Atlantic liner.

Earlier, the narrator watches Larsen's "biceps move *like a living thing* under its white sheath." Isn't the biceps really a living thing? Stephen Munzer reminds me that the English word "muscle" comes from the Latin *musculus,* meaning "little mouse," so buried in the idea of a muscle is the idea that it is like an independent living thing. But the idea may also be that for a battleship like Larsen, it is indeed surprising that any of it is like a living thing.[28]

So by 1904 the machine body was an extremely complex intellectual creation that compressed several ideas in some tension with each other. Bodies were machines when they were powerful, like Wolf Larsen. The mechanical aspects of the body are the rawest and most brutal, not exactly natural, for they reflect careful physical cultivation, but nevertheless in some opposition to civilization. Bodies were also machines when they were fatigued. This machine, like the powerful body-machine, was sometimes also a dynamic, motorized nineteenth-century machine, but one that had been abused and neglected. Both these machines stand opposed to "nature": factory work has turned Johnny into a machine (exhausted); Wolf Larsen's regime has turned him into a machine (power, perfection); both are estranged in their machinehood from a natural or human state.

Finally, the critical machine metaphor, as a critical mimesis of industrial civilization, contains elements of the older, Cartesian machine body from which mind has been removed, but now employed as critical social theory, not ontology. If Deborah's body is a machine in Rebecca Harding Davis's novel (or Johnny's in Jack London's story), it is precisely in the sense that her mind has been disconnected from her body and her work, but this is not an ontologic truth but an economic and political crime, and restitution requires that her mind and body be reconnected, as no one doubts possible. American lawyers

[28] Jack London, *The Sea-Wolf,* chap. 15, in id. 593–94 [1904].

adopted just this complex construction of the body as part of the struggle over legislated limits on the working day.

THE MACHINE BODY IN THE STRUGGLE TO LIMIT THE WORKING DAY

The struggle of working people for shorter days predates this machine imagery and was originally justified without it. "The reduction of working hours constituted the prime demand in the class conflicts that spawned America's first industrial strike, its first citywide trade union councils, its first labor party, its first general strikes, its first organization uniting skilled and unskilled workers, its first strike by females, and its first attempts at regional and national labor organization."[29] "Some of the most dramatic and significant events in the history of labor, such as the strikes of 1886, the Haymarket riots, and the steel strike of 1919 . . . were part of this century-long struggle for shorter hours."[30]

Through most of the nineteenth century, shorter days were claimed as a sort of natural right. For example, the New England Workingmen's Association resolutions, adopted in their first meeting in October 1844, stated, "[T]he time now devoted to manual labor is unreasonable and unjust. [It] amounts to the denial of the invaluable right every man should possess to an opportunity for recreation and social enjoyment."[31] An eight-hour day, it was said by its proponents, would permit workers to be more active and effective democratic citizens and prevent the worker from becoming a slave. In the 1860s and 1870s "[F]ew of the workers favoring shorter hours suggested that such reduction would 'spread the work' or would reduce industrial accidents . . . two of the favorite arguments of the early twentieth century."[32] But by an odd twist of judicial reasoning, the machine metaphor, and not natural right or democratic citizenship, became an essential part of the constitutionality of American statutory limits on the working day.

The story is familiar. Statutory restrictions on working hours were challenged in state and federal court, frequently successfully, as deprivations of the liberty of contract between employers and workers.[33] A statute limited to

[29] David R. Roediger and Philip S. Foner, *Our Own Time: A History of American Labor and the Working Day* vii (London: Verso, 1989).

[30] Benjamin Kline Hunnicutt, *Work without End: Abandoning Shorter Hours for the Right to Work* 1 (Philadelphia: Temple U. Pr., 1988).

[31] Quoted in Charles E. Persons, "The Early History of Factory Legislation in Massachusetts," in 2 *Labor Laws and Their Enforcement* 31 (Susan M. Kingsbury ed.) (New York: Longman's, Green, 1911).

[32] David Montgomery, *Beyond Equality: Labor and the Radical Republicans, 1862–1872* 237 (New York: Knopf, 1967).

[33] William E. Forbath, *Law and the Shaping of the American Labor Movement* 37–58 (Cambridge: Harv. U. Pr., 1991).

miners was upheld in the United States Supreme Court,[34] but then came *Lochner v. New York,* striking down hours limitations.[35] Labor law reformers did not abandon the fight but did change their tactics. The next Supreme Court confrontation with hours legislation was *Muller v. Oregon,* in which Louis Brandeis, representing Oregon, filed his famous "Brandeis brief," summarizing some of the (mostly European) scholarship on work and fatigue. As the statute in *Muller* was limited to women workers, the brief often discussed supposed special needs of women workers, but for the most part summarized, without reference to sex, the European medical literature on worker fatigue. This was an attempt to maneuver between the two Supreme Court precedents. The earlier miners' case, *Holden v. Hardy,* in light of *Lochner,* now appeared to be a case of workers with "special needs." In *Lochner* itself, the Supreme Court noted that bakers were not a special class.[36] This invited the kind of argument made in *Muller.*

Brandeis's brief adopts the machine metaphor of the European medical scholarship on almost every page of the brief:

> Machinery imposes on man a crushing task. Feeble appendage of a mighty force, a tiny engine bound to an engine of immense power, the workman must bow to its attractions, give way to the rapidity of its movements, follow it in its incessant pace—in a word, he must turn, twist, and toil just as much as the untiring machinery pleases.[37]

The body is a source of power or working capital.[38] However, it may "break down."[39] "[T]he flesh and blood of the operatives have only so much work in them, and it was all got out in ten hours, and no more could be got out in twelve; and what was got extra in the first month was taken right out of the life of the operatives."[40] To maximize efficiency, hours had to be cut back.[41]

The Supreme Court did uphold the statute limiting working hours in *Muller.*[42] Later generations concluded that this was because the statute was limited to women, but this was not the conclusion that was drawn at the time, either by labor reformers or the Supreme Court itself.

Reformers concluded instead that advocacy must stop talking of rights and keep talking of science. After *Muller,* a leading reformer wrote: "The whole

---

[34] Holden v. Hardy, 169 U.S. 366 (1898).

[35] 198 U.S. 45 (1905).

[36] Lochner, 198 U.S. at 56–57.

[37] Brief at 25. The brief is reprinted in 14 *Landmark Briefs and Arguments of the Supreme Court of the United States: Constitutional Law* (Philip B. Kurland and Gerhard Casper eds.) (Arlington, Va.: University Publications of America, 1975).

[38] Brief at 54, 63, 73.

[39] At 20, 22.

[40] At 67–68 (quoting Massachusetts Bureau of Statistics of Labor, 1881).

[41] At 49, 50, 67, 73.

[42] 208 U.S. 412 (1908).

procedure in defense of labor laws has thus been revolutionized. Instead of abstract discussions of abstract freedom, the procedure is, to-day, to ascertain the exact facts, to show what the existing working hours are, what other nations and states have done about it, and what the medical profession says on the subject. The final deciding factor is not 'freedom' but health."[43]

These words were vindicated when the Supreme Court returned to, and upheld, gender-neutral hours regulation in *Bunting v. Oregon*.[44] The statute was supported by the mother of all Brandeis briefs, almost a thousand pages of excerpts from scientific and social science studies and foreign legislation.[45] Much of this is the very scholarship discussed by Anson Rabinbach; for example, the brief quotes Angelo Mosso extensively:

> [T]he law of exhaustion sets an insuperable barrier to the greed of gain. . . .

> [Factory] machines are not made to lessen human fatigue, as poets were wont to dream. The velocity of the flying wheels, the whirling of the hammers, and the furious speed at which everything moves, these things tell us that time is an important factor in the progress of industry, and that here in the factory the activity of the workers must conquer the forces of nature. The hiss of the steam, the rattling of the pulleys, the shaking of the joints, the snorting of these gigantic automata, all warn us that they are inexorable in their motion, that man is condemned to follow them without a moment's rest, because every minute wasted consumes time that is worth money, seeing that it renders useless the coal and the movements of these colossi.

> Marx, in his celebrated work (*Le Capital,* Karl Marx, p. 161), devotes a chapter to machinery, and arrives at the following conclusions: that all our inventions have not diminished human fatigue, but simply the price of commodities; that machinery has rendered worse the condition of the worker, because by rendering strength of no avail it has entailed the employment of women and children; instead of shortening the working-day it has prolonged it, instead of reducing fatigue it has rendered it more dangerous and injurious; that to the accumulation of riches corresponds an increase in poverty; that owing to machinery society is

[43] Florence Kelley, *Modern Industry in Relation to the Family, Health, Education, Morality* 72 (New York: Longman's, Green, 1914). See also Felix Frankfurter, "Hours of Labor and Realism in Constitutional Law," 29 *Harv. L. Rev.* 353 (1916) (drawing similar conclusion). Labor abandoned much of its understanding of its claim to "abstract freedom" at the turn of the century, assisted in this process by judicial indifference or hostility to labor's philosophy of freedom. See generally Forbath, *Law and Shaping;* 128–41 James Gray Pope, "Labor's Constitution of Freedom," 106 Yale L. J. 941 (1997).

[44] 243 U.S. 426 (1917). The opinion does not mention *Lochner.*

[45] Brandeis apparently participated in the early preparation of the brief but was named to the Supreme Court during the proceedings. The brief as filed carried the names of his associates, Felix Frankfurter and Josephine Goldmark. I used the version in the New York University Law Library, reprinted by the National Consumers' League under the title "The Case for the Shorter Work Day."

receding further and further from its ideal; that the reality has not corresponded to our hopes.

. . . The powerful automaton of mechanics wants nothing but intelligence and a nervous system; this want a child or a woman can supply and guide the blind giants by the hand.[46]

It is remarkable to imagine a time when Karl Marx might be quoted in a brief to the United States Supreme Court; did Brandeis, Frankfurter, and Goldmark expect anyone to read this?

Mosso shows (particularly in the last paragraph quoted) how the machine had become a person (with a hand, lacking intelligence). The image of the worker as a machine is also prominent elsewhere in the Frankfurter and Goldmark brief.

The Locomotive and the Human Motor. Accidents to the locomotive correspond to the germ diseases, which are really accidents, and in time will doubtless all be prevented. In the wear and tear of the valves, boiler tubes, cylinders, bearings and other vital parts of the locomotive we have organic diseases—the diseases of degeneration, for the life of the locomotive, like that of man, is determined by the strain which is put upon its hardest worked parts. . . . But we treat this machine of metal better than we do the human machine.[47]

When the Supreme Court upheld Oregon's ten-hours law, Kelley's and Frankfurter's point had been established (despite the fact that the Court's opinion cites none of the material from the brief). Workers could win nothing by arguing their rights, their "abstract freedom." They could win shorter days if their bodies became the passive subjects of the medical gaze, became machines that would now be cared for almost as well as a locomotive engine.

Muller and *Bunting* also show the triumph of the therapeutic revolution in medical thought, for the employers did not seek to revive an older medical literature under which the illness of a particular baker or worker would have stemmed from the lack of balance between his individual racial or ethnic constitution and his environment. Had anyone still believed in this version of disease, it would have provided powerful medical support for the "substantive due process" vision of liberty of contract, for the power to make individualized contracts on working hours, that would trump uniform legislation, would have been the only way to bring about individual health.

---

[46] Angelo Mosso, *Fatigue* 168–74 (Margaret Drummond and W. B. Drummond trans.) (New York: Putnam, 1904), as quoted in Brief in *Bunting* at 214–15.

[47] Brief at 29–30 ("Protecting the Human Machine. Condensed from an Address before the Board of Trade of Washington, D.C., Delivered by President E. E. Rittenhouse, of the Life Extension Institute"). Frankfurter later recanted the analogy of the worker's body to a machine. "The coming of the machine age tended to despoil human personality. It turned men and women into hands." AFL v. American Sash and Door Co., 335 U.S. 538, 542–43 (1949) (Frankfurter, J., concurring).

Hawkins v. McGee came just twelve years after *Bunting* and thus comes at the tail end of a generation of deploying the body-machine metaphor to convert "freedom" to "science." The ambiguity and complexity of the machine metaphor in *Hawkins* thus reproduces a systemic complexity in law, medicine, and popular discourse. A hand can be a machine because it is very powerful; because it has been separated from mind or spirit or agency; because it has been dehumanized or degraded by industrial capitalism; or because it is fungible with other hands and thus amenable to modern medical therapies that abstract from individual peculiarities and treat diseases, not individuals.

Since 1929, law rarely discursively constructs the body, or even the hand, as a machine. For example, there are a number of cases involving assaults with bare fists in which prosecutors seek to charge defendants with assaults with "deadly weapons"; the courts normally do not permit hands to be classed as weapons.[48]

There are several reasons why the machine metaphor died. Probably the main factor is a general loss of interest in the kind of machine represented by locomotive engines. Just as the eighteenth-century clockwork gave way to the nineteenth-century dynamic engine, twentieth-century machine imagery is much more likely to emphasize information networks, systems, computers. While these metaphors have indeed influenced people's constructions of their bodies, they do not yet seem to have exerted much influence on law.[49] Perhaps the machine metaphor simply came to seem trite, or to call unnecessary attention to itself; I suggested this in the last chapter when I raised the possibility that a contemporary legal text that adopts the metaphor, in everything but name, would compromise rather than reinforce its persuasiveness by calling the body a machine.[50] The machine metaphor always meant too many different things, in particular, standing in simultaneously for Cartesian dualism, the body's raw power, the fungibility of persons, and a social critique of industrialism. Finally, the machine body always fit poorly with the other great construction of the body in *Hawkins v. McGee:* the sentimental, intact, perfect human body that feels pain. It is that body that has the more cultural resonance today, although as we shall see it is still only one of many competing bodies of law.

This brief legal and cultural history of the machine body, however, is in-

[48] See, e.g., Dixon v. State, 603 So.2d 570 (Fla.App. 1992). Contra, State v. Zangrilli, 440 A.2d 710 (R.I. 1982). See generally Parts of the Human Body as Dangerous Weapons, 8 ALR4th 1268.

[49] Emily Martin, *Flexible Bodies: Tracking Immunity in American Culture—from the Days of Polio to the Age of AIDS* 113–92 (Boston: Beacon, 1994) explores the imagery of "flexible systems" as applied to corporations, government, work organization, and immunity, disease, and the body. David F. Channell, *The Vital Machine: A Study of Technology and Organic Life* (New York: Oxford U. Pr., 1991) explores the continuing romance of technological metaphors for the body, in which a "bionic" worldview replaces an earlier "mechanical" one.

[50] Jaske v. Murray Ohio Mfg. Co. Inc., 750 SW2d 150 (Tenn. 1988), discussed in chap. 1.

structive, for it shows that the bodies constructed in legal discourse have a history. In some cases, we can date the creation of a legal body and note its demise. Our legal bodies are not only not true or natural, are not only discursive creations, but are often created quite self-consciously and terminated in the same way.

The fact that life goes on without the machine metaphor creates a tantalizing possibility that I will raise here but defer to the conclusion: that law might do without the body altogether. In this alternative view, there would be no bodies. There would only be persons. Or rather, the bodies of law could only be experienced as inevitably artificial, the sentimental body no less than the machine body. As Gabriel Marcel pointed out, if the body is a tool, there must be a second, more primordial body that uses it, ad infinitum.[51] Perhaps the point is of broader application, and law may come to see that all bodies are really people, were always already just people, just our own representations to ourselves of the people with whom we could not otherwise commune.

We have many bodies of law to scrutinize before we reach that point, however. For if the machine body is now largely dead, many of its intellectual functions—fungibility, estrangement, desentimentalization—have been taken over by the discursive construction of the body as property or a commodity. When, how, and why are the subjects of the next chapter.

---

[51] Gabriel Marcel, *Metaphysical Journal* 246 (Bernard Wall trans.) (Chicago: Henry Regnery, 1952). See discussion in Drew Leader, *The Absent Body* 179 n. 70 (Chicago: U. Chi. Pr., 1990).

Chapter 3

THE BODY AS PROPERTY

Thus, the man, identified [by Stirner] with the "unique," having first given thoughts corporeality, i.e., having transformed them into specters, now destroys this corporeality again by taking them back into his own body, which he thus makes into a body of specters. The fact that he arrives at his own corporeality only through the negation of the specters, shows the nature of this constructed corporeality of the man, which he has first to "announce" to himself, in order to believe in it. But what he "announces to himself" he does not even "announce" correctly.[1]

On Embodied Concepts

The chief function of law in advanced societies is to provide a totalizing vocabulary, under which people will become incapable of articulating any modalities of human interaction except as the relations between buyers and sellers in markets, and between bearers of abstract rights. Legal discourse powerfully and relentlessly translates all other and earlier ways of describing human relations into its preferred formulations. Thus love becomes marriage, which is conceptualized as a *contract;* intrafamily relations become described as the clash of parental and children's *rights,* and so on. Even a particular doctrine or decision that may uphold, say, children's as against parents' rights, thus reinforces the entire Orwellian structure, which oppresses at the level of words and concepts, until all forms of human interaction become literally unthinkable—except as variations on market relations or the relations among abstract rights holders. The discourse of commodification normalizes the personal, the subjective, the abnormal—George Hawkins's hand—and reinscribes them into the normal regulatory apparatuses of consumer, market society.

So, at least, runs the most original left-wing contribution to twentieth-century legal thought.[2] If valid, it apparently suggests a powerful if excessively simple thesis about the construction of the body in such a legal regime. The body's needs, its desires, its passions, all must be tamed in society, so the

---

[1] Karl Marx, *The German Ideology,* in 5 Karl Marx and Friedrich Engels, *Collected Works* 125–26 (New York: International Publishers, 1976) [1845–46], as quoted in Jacques Derrida, *Specters of Marx: The State of the Debt, the Work of Mourning, and the New International* 128 (Peggy Kamuf trans.) (New York: Routledge, 1994).

[2] Evgeni Pashukanis, *Law and Marxism: A General Theory* (Barbara Einhorn trans.) (London: Pluto Pr., 1989); Karl Renner, *The Institutions of Private Law and Their Social Functions* (Agnes Schwarzschild trans.) (London: Routledge and Kegan Paul, 1949).

body would appear a particularly urgent target for the effacement-and-replacement mechanism of legal thought. One might predict therefore that law would construct only bodies that related to each other as market commodities, or the transient locations of abstract rights, so that one would be unable to articulate pain except as a sort of property damage, unable to articulate desire except as a subspecies of consumer preference, unable to experience the joy of movement except as a consumer activity called sports, unable to articulate love except as a sort of contract.

These constructions of the body are no parody, although as we shall see they are not the whole story either. They are no parody, as we have already seen in the discussion of George Hawkins's case, in which disfigurement became precisely a sort of breach of warranty. While that machine metaphor is no longer a living one—or perhaps our concepts of machines merely altered—the basic underlying property construction is quite vigorous in American law.

What is equally interesting, however, is that this construction of the body as property has not totally effaced noncommodified constructions of the body. Anyone is equally capable both of conceptualizing one's body as property, and of recoiling in horror at the very conception. I will occasionally be using the term *sacred body* to refer generally to any Carlyle-like construction of the body as a sort of refuge outside the boundaries of market and political society. As I will be using the term, it need not necessarily connote religious thought or the body of Jesus. A sacred body in this sense, that is, a master symbol of what is *not* a subject of contract or barter, is, as we shall see in this chapter, as vital a part of American law as is the body as property. Study of law's discursive construction of the body confirms a postmodern rather than a Marxist account. The point of the story will be, not only the dead reifications we habitually deploy to figure our own bodies, but also the range and variety of our constructions of our bodies, and our freedom and power to construct bodies in ever-changing and even contradictory ways.

We might conceptualize this coexistence, of the body as commodity and the body as sacred refuge from market society, as reflecting merely an incomplete colonization, of the aboriginal world of affection and sentiment, by the discourse of market and politics. Terry Eagleton has recently argued, by contrast, that the competing sacred discursive construction of the body, like the work of art in the discourse of aesthetics, is not at odds with market society, but a sort of necessary supplement to it. A world discursively constructed entirely on the basis of market economics and political rights lacks a vocabulary of cohesion or unity; it runs the risk that nothing links individuals at all. "This is one reason why the 'aesthetic' realm of sentiments, affections and spontaneous bodily habits comes to assume the significance it does. Custom, piety, intuition and opinion must now cohere an otherwise abstract, atomized social order."[3]

In any case, the discursive body that is either a commodity or an abstract

---

[3] Terry Eagleton, *The Ideology of the Aesthetic* 23 (Oxford: Basil Blackwell, 1990).

right coexists with a sacred discursive body and could discursively colonize society only if it acquired some bodily meaning, in the way citizens explain their own bodies to themselves. There is a close link between the rise of modern market democracy, and the dense rules and practices of manners, civility, body control, and deportment that separate the modern and medieval world as surely as attitudes toward interest rates and market expectations. Controlling one's bodily deportment, odors, and emissions, in the interest of harmonious living with other, provides a crucial cognitive map for what would otherwise be the abstract, if not even mystified, concept of self-government.[4] Such a self-controlled citizen may imagine himself as "autonomous and self-determining," a subject who "acknowledges no merely extrinsic law but instead, in some mysterious fashion, gives the law to itself. In doing so, the law becomes the form which shapes into harmonious unity the turbulent content of the subject's appetites and inclinations. The compulsion of autocratic power is replaced by the more gratifying compulsion of the subject's self-identity."[5]

Citizens must be able to imagine their bodies as property or a zone of rights for the political and economic order to be able to function: for one thing, they must be able to sell their labor power every day without going mad or rebelling. This imagining of the property or rights body must itself take place in a physical, not merely ideational, way, so that the citizen must stand, lift, or lower eyes, approach or remain distant from others, control odors and emissions, in a way that performs or mimes the political theory of liberal market society. At the same time, these ideas and body gestures are not a complete repertoire of either political ideas or body gestures and carry with them a spectral older body of sentiment and pain. These remarks raise two themes that will be important throughout this study: first, the mutually self-constitutive quality of bodily experience and abstract concept; second, the way in which apparently contradictory discursive constructions of the body may be seen as alternative aspects of the same rhetorical project: the discursive production of the autonomous subject, the "nice body with a self at home in it."[6]

---

[4] See Norbert Elias, *The History of Manners* (*The Civilizing Process:* vol. 1) (Edmund Jephcott trans.) (New York: Pantheon, 1978) [1939]; Georges Vigarello, "The Upward Training of the Body from the Age of Chivalry to Courtly Civility," in *Zone 4: Fragments for a History of the Human Body, Part 2,* 149 (Michel Feher ed.) (New York: Zone, 1989); for America, Richard L. Bushman, *The Refinement of America: Bodies, Houses, Cities* (New York: Knopf, 1992); John F. Kasson, *Rudeness and Civility: Manners in Nineteenth-Century Urban America* (New York: Hill and Wang, 1990); Aihwa Ong, "Making the Biopolitical Subject: Cambodian Immigrants, Refugee Medicine, and Cultural Citizenship in California" 40 Soc. Sci Med. 1243 (1995).

[5] Eagleton, *Ideology of the Aesthetic* 23.

[6] Rachel Bowlby used this phrase, to my undying gratitude, in commenting on a presentation of an earlier version of this book at the Rutgers Center for Historical Analysis, February 2, 1993.

First Theme: Bodily Experience and Legal Thought as Mutually Self-Constitutive

Throughout this study, I will be linking, as Eagleton just did, abstract legal concepts, with common, sometimes universal, bodily experiences, as those experiences are represented discursively. For example, I will explore at length in chapters 12–15 the idea that the universal, infantile, preverbal experience of expelling body wastes, what Julia Kristeva calls "abjection," provides a kind of mental script for the recurring legal pattern in which a fictive group identity is constructed and kept pure by the expulsion of the polluting Other. I have suggested in this chapter and will explore further in the next the idea that the experience of bodily self-control characteristic of modern notions of civility and politeness—these not universal bodily experiences, but body practices with a distinct history—provide a similar kind of mental script for the abstract political concepts of freedom and autonomy under law.

Very few of the body experiences that enact political ideas are like abjecting waste, that is, biological in the sense of being universal and unavoidable. Most of the body experiences that seem important in political and legal theory are of the type explored in this chapter, the acquisition of particular postures, deportment, manners, athletic behavior, and the like, where not only the discourse but the body practices themselves vary sharply among cultures. But whether the body practice is biologically necessary (like urination) or "merely" culturally prescribed (like upright deportment), what matters most for our purposes is its discursive construction. Here I am following recent work on popular *and medical* representations of the body that stress the evolution of particular imagery and representation in response to exogenous social variables, even when purely medical knowledge has not changed. Thomas Laqueur has traced the succession of theories of sexual differentiation, which respond more to social factors than to medical knowledge, indeed constitute and structure that medical knowledge.[7] Emily Martin has explored the biases and assumptions in the way medical textbooks and physicians discuss women's reproductive systems and, more recently, immune systems—when bodily processes are figured as mechanical, intelligent, self-regulating, and so on.[8]

It is much easier to show the influence of political theory on body "experience" than it is to show the contrary. The body is knowable only through the discursive mediation of our metaphors and visualizations, and these in turn have political content. Political and economic systems and their accompanying discourse become embodied, so that people experience their own bodies in

[7] Thomas Laqueur, *Making Sex: Body and Gender from the Greeks to Freud* (Cambridge: Harv. U. Pr.) (1990).

[8] Emily Martin, *The Woman in the Body: A Cultural Analysis of Reproduction* (Boston: Beacon, 1987); Emily Martin, *Flexible Bodies: Tracking Immunity in American Culture from the Days of Polio to the Age of AIDS* (Boston: Beacon, 1994).

a way that fits with the dominant social discourse: as "theirs," or as mechanical, or private, or pure or impure. I suspect that it is unlikely or impossible for any abstract concept of legal or political theory truly to become part of a culture unless it can be linked with such a bodily experience. As George Orwell wrote, "no feeling of like or dislike is quite so fundamental as a *physical* feeling."[9] It is liberalism, not nature, that makes us "experience" our bodies as independent and self-controlled; and it is unlikely that liberalism could have endured had it not been able to structure bodies in accord with its political requirements.

This morning my daughter asked me what were the proper internal temperatures for our refrigerator and freezer, and I realized that I had only the vaguest idea, although I have undoubtedly read the correct figures dozens of times in articles about food safety and the like. "I don't know," I told her. "I just know what the inside of the refrigerator feels like when it's at the right temperature."

This is the kind of body experience that seems to me central in the establishment and maintenance of political and economic systems. This kind of body experience is *not* "natural"; a less primal or natural experience would be hard to imagine. My body's experience of "the inside of a refrigerator functioning at the proper temperature" is the product of technological advances in home refrigeration; the wealthy society in which I live has made these miracles part of every home. (Some might want to add: heedless, for generations, of the profligate use of resources, the damage to the ozone layer). Thick layers of the discursive construction of "home refrigeration" mediate between my body's experience of a cold blast (should I put on a coat?) and my understanding (the refrigerator is working properly). But because I have the experience of that cold blast from the refrigerator, I can get along without the useful knowledge of the temperature at which it is supposed to operate. And because I have the experience of controlling my body's posture, appearance, odors, and emissions, I could similarly get along, should I choose, without much liberal theory, which so often represents political freedom as bodily control ("My freedom to swing my arm ends at your nose" and so forth). Richard Sennett has recently reminded us how much of the self-conscious creation of Athenian democracy revolved around the architects' or planners' issues about the body: spaces to speak, to sit, to stand, to hear.[10] These problems are effaced when the dominant theories of democracy, such as John Rawls's or Jürgen Habermas's, model it as the deliberations of disembodied voices.

[9] George Orwell, *The Road to Wigan Pier* 160 (New York: Harcourt, Brace, 1958) [1937]. We will have more to say about this observation in chapter 15.

[10] Richard Sennett, *Flesh and Stone: The Body and the City in Western Civilization* 52–67 (New York: Norton, 1994).

The discourse is thus as powerful as anatomy even as to body processes, such as feeling cold, that are both inevitable and salient to us. (Many crucial body processes, such as blood circulation, or the immune system studied by Emily Martin, are not salient to us and are known to us cognitively *only* through the mediation of the dominant discourse, such as pumps and machinery for blood, military defense for immune systems). Expelling bodily wastes is indeed a universal body experience. Waste expulsion is available to anyone, I should say, as a bodily script for acts of political exclusion and purification. However, only a thick layer of mediating discourse will tell us how many of us will draw on these infantile experiences in adult political acts of cultural definition through expulsion.

By contrast, the bodily self-control typical of bourgeois orders is not even a universal experience, indeed is an experience only because partly constituted by an accompanying political discourse of individual autonomy. Political thought is a kind of bodily "experience," was always already a bodily experience, just as bodily experience itself is lived political thought.

This chapter takes up the discourse of property ownership, the bodily experiences sometimes drawn on to construct legal bodies that are alienable property, though not drawn on in every instance when they might be relevant. My focus, here as throughout this book, is on the discursive constructions, their origins, usage, and history, and not on the issues of cognitive theory that might sort out—if we had such an accepted theory, which it appears to me we do not—precisely how body and mind work together in the creation of discourse.

Second Theme: Constructing the Autonomous Subject

Many of the dizzying dances law makes around the body are thus in the service of a larger mission, law's construction of an autonomous legal self, a self that must be both property and never-property, free and ordered, autonomous and socialized, and so on. A fuller picture of how law constructs bodies, in the service of this larger mission of constructing the self, must await, not only our early expeditions into machine and property constructions, but also chapters 4 and 7–11, on the construction of the private self. As I have suggested in my discussion of *Hawkins v. McGee* and again in this chapter, it is common for legal discussions of the body to invoke, explicitly or implicitly, a contrast between a sentimental body in pain with which another empathizes or desires, and a modern dehumanized machine or property body. In the end I want to subvert this way of thinking about the body, but we have still to explore how law obsessively reestablishes this supposed contrast.

In the end, I hope these accumulated contrasting bodies will assist my own subversive intervention: the construction of the postmodern body, in which individuals experience their command of the multiple discursive constructions

of their body as a kind of power, a liberation from any single dominant discourse of the body, including the dominant legal discourse of the autonomous
self. We still have much work, however, in understanding the constructions of
the body internal to dominant legal rhetoric, before we can turn these self-
contradictions on themselves.

Constructing the Body as Property: The Philosophic Structure of the Claim

Do we own our bodies as property under American law? The question is
surprisingly difficult to answer.

The analogy of the body to property is familiar from antiquity and shows up
for different purposes in many different discourses. The very derivation of the
word *property,* which derives from the Latin *proprius* (one's own) and is akin
to the French *propre* (close or near, one's own, proper, clean), just starts the
complex associations.[11] The central pun involved in every invocation of
"property" is inherent in its name: *property,* however defined, always mimetically represents both a supposed private, individual, isolated self (*propre,*
one's own), and, at the same time, the proper, as defined publicly or socially
through the social conventions that give us *propriety, propre* (clean).

When law needs to decide whether the body is property, the issue is usually
one of deciding the just limits of the domination of one person by another. The
complex metaphor of the property body may be deployed either in the service
of domination or the service of limiting domination.

The body may be property in order to explain or justify human domination,
in either or both of two somewhat different ways. In the first, a human may be
dominated because, after all, its body is just property. Aristotle derives a justification for the government of some over others from the domination of the
slave by the master.[12] Leibniz justifies domination over animals by analogizing them to machines: "If we are compelled to view the animal as being more
than a machine, we would have to become Pythagorians and renounce our
domination of animals."[13] If people are property, or machines, they may be
dominated too.

A countertradition, however, constitutes the body as property to emphasize
autonomy. John Locke moves from the claim that "every man has a property

---

[11] George A. Miller and Philip N. Johnson-Laird, *Language and Perception* 563 (Cambridge:
Belknap Pr. of Harvard U. Pr., 1976).

[12] Aristotle, *Politics,* par. 2.

[13] "Letter to Conring," March 19, 1678, as quoted in Georges Canguilhem, "Machine and
Organism," in *Zone 6: Incorporations* 52 (Jonathan Crary and Sanford Kwitner eds.) (New York:
Zone, 1992). See generally Gary L. Francione, *Animals, Property, and the Law* (Philadelphia:
Temple U. Pr., 1995).

in his own person"[14] to a general theory of the institution of private property. Locke was, after all, a physician and may have meant this quite literally. "Locke took his first step toward political influence by working on the body of Anthony Ashley Cooper," later earl of Shaftesbury and prime minister. Locke cured Ashley of tapeworm, and it was Ashley who then urged Locke "to turn from the body to the body politic."[15]

It has also been claimed that Locke's entire move from body ownership to private property rests on nothing but an unsophisticated pun on the possessive adjective ("my body"), what Claude Bruaire has aptly called "le monstre juridique de la possession: j'ai un corps," contrasting it with "je suis un corps."[16] Contrary to Locke, usage of the possessive adjective in English does not always imply the legal status of possession (A's cold, A's golf game, the labors of Hercules), though it may always represent a kind of pun on that legal relationship.[17] Other languages employ different possessive adjectives that distinguish between the inalienable and alienable. "In Fijian 'uluqu' means 'my head' in the sense of the inalienable object attached to my neck, whereas suffixing the possessive morpheme, 'kequ ulu,' means 'my head' in the sense of the alienable object that, say, I own and am about to eat. The ambiguity of the English possessive in these examples is worth remarking since it has sometimes been taken as an index of inalienable or inherent possession."[18]

The possessive adjective may represent fragmentation and alienation as easily as it represents some kind of inalienable essence. When Odysseus addresses his heart ("Be patient, my heart! . . . Soon his heart obeyed him and staunchly endured. But he himself still rolled to and fro"), the image, contra Locke, is internal division and estrangement. "The individual as subject is still unreconciled to himself, still unsure. His affective forces (his mettle and his heart) still react independently to him."[19] Patricia Williams has recently pointed out that claims of self-possession may suppose *either* a fragmented relationship in which a "person as transactor" owns a "body as commodity," *or* an "inalienable corporeal integrity."[20]

So there is nothing inevitable about Locke's association of the owned, body

[14] "An Essay Concerning the True Original Extent and End of Civil Government" (Second Treatise), par. 27, in John Locke, *Two Treatises of Government* 287 (Peter Laslett ed.) (Cambridge: Camb. U. Pr., 1960) [1690].

[15] Wayne Glausser, "Locke and Blake as Physicians: Delivering the Eighteenth-Century Body," in *Reading the Social Body* 223–24 (Catherine B. Burroughs and Jeffery David Ehrenreich eds.) (Iowa City: U. Ia. Pr., 1993).

[16] Claude Bruaire, *Philosophie du corps* 232 (Paris: Editions du Seuil, 1968).

[17] J. P. Day, "Locke on Property," 16 *Phil. Q.* 207, 212–15 (1966).

[18] Miller and Johnson-Laird, *Language and Perception* 562.

[19] Theodor W. Adorno and Max Horkheimer, *Dialectic of Enlightenment* 47 n. 5 (John Cumming trans.) (London: Verso, 1972) [1944].

[20] Patricia J. Williams, *The Rooster's Egg* 230 (Cambridge: Harv. U. Pr., 1995).

as property, with any claim of autonomy and freedom in the self that owns that body. If that metaphor works, it is at a complicated discursive level. However, people who think Locke's views very influential in shaping the law of property would not be exaggerating to find just this metaphor of the body as property underlying a great deal of modern law, including the entire law of property, derived by analogy from subjects' relations to their bodies.

This construction makes for a complex map of human domination. For the Locke property-as-autonomy-and-freedom claim *is* a claim to dominate others. Any system of property is necessarily a map of the domination of some who lack, by others who have.[21] The freedom and autonomy that property gives its owners is precisely the freedom that comes from the power to be heedless of others. A property claim is, analytically, always the claim to power that consists of the power of ignoring others, and as such tracks what Eve Kosofsky Sedgwick calls the "privilege of unknowing."[22]

A claim that the body is property in any particular context thus reproduces an extremely complex three-part structure, a complexity magnified by the fact that, if Locke is right, a claim that the body is property underlies analogically *any* property claim at all. First, if my body is property, this may naturalize others' domination of it (Aristotle). For example, as we shall see in chapters 5 and 6, my employer will be able to impose and enforce demands for particular display or even alteration of my body, because, after all, if my body is my property, then my alienation of it to others is just a contract. Second, if my body is property, this may reinforce my freedom and autonomy, and not just in the freedom to make contracts, but equally in the freedom not to. My body may be property to emphasize my power not to submit to others' demands on it. Third, however, the second claim, the freedom and autonomy claim, is

---

[21] Morris Raphael Cohen, "Property and Sovereignty," 13 *Corn. L. Q.* 8 (1927), reprinted *Law and the Social Order: Essays in Legal Philosophy* 41 (New Brunswick, N.J.: Transaction, 1982); Robert Hale, "Coercion and Distribution in a Supposedly Non-Coercive State," 38 *Pol. Sci. Q.* 470 (1923). A powerful illustration is Amartya Sen, *Poverty and Famines: An Essay on Entitlement and Deprivation* (Oxford: Clarendon, 1981), showing how starvation in a famine is rarely a function of the absence of food, but rather the absence of property rights to the food. See also Martin Ravallion, *Markets and Famines* (Oxford: Clarendon, 1987); Jean Drèze and Amartya Sen, *Hunger and Public Action* (Oxford: Clarendon, 1989).

[22] Cf. Eve Kosofsky Sedgwick, "Privilege of Unknowing: Diderot's *The Nun*," in *Tendencies* 23 (Durham: Duke U. Pr., 1993): "Knowledge is not itself power, although it is the magnetic field of power. Ignorance and opacity collude or compete with it in mobilizing the flows of energy, desire, goods, meanings, persons. If M. Mitterand knows English but Mr. Reagan lacks French, it is the urbane M. Mitterand who must negotiate in an acquired tongue, the ignorant Mr. Reagan who may dilate in his native one. . . . [I]t is the interlocutor who has or pretends to have the *less* broadly knowledgeable understanding of interpretive practice who will define the terms of the exchange. . . . Such ignorance effects can be harnessed, licensed, and regulated on a mass scale for striking enforcements—perhaps especially around sexuality, in modern Western culture the most meaning-intensive of human activities."

always and necessarily a claim of domination, an assertion of my privilege not to share, not to respond to others. Later in this chapter, we will see a court denying a claim of property in the body precisely because, as the court saw it, this would empower claimants to frustrate beneficent medical research.

As this implies, a final element of the complex structure, one always available in any contest for meaning, is to construct a body that is not property. It is true that for many technical legal purposes, body parts and products may be bought, sold, transferred. Yet the construction of the body as property is not complete, and we shall see judges recoiling in horror from this construction, judges whose attachment generally to a regime of markets and rights could not be questioned. I think this ambivalence, or dialectic if you like, reproduces precisely the tension that Eagleton has identified: a fear that a discourse in which the body was *always* unproblematically property would be incapable of constructing human subjects, without whom neither market, nor any other, society could function. The body that cannot be property (which I shall sometimes call the *sacred body*) thus marks the boundaries of an aesthetic realm that defines the boundaries of, and supplements, market society.

Some Legal Examples

BLOOD: A CLEAR CASE OF PROPERTY RIGHTS IN THE BODY

The clearest case is blood, which we surely do own. Blood has more clearly become a legal commodity in the past thirty years, during which period it has become much less likely actually to be an object of sale, and during which time controversy has raged in the courts and legal literature over whether markets should exist in transplantable organs. So let us first examine the rhetorical process through which blood has been, rather unproblematically, constructed as a commodity that is ownable and salable. As I have just implied, this process of discursive commodification does not occur automatically for all body parts and products and does not occur merely because efficiency gains may be had. We shall also see that discursive commodification does not necessarily require either a persuasive distinction or a bright line between the commodified and uncommodified.

The practices of transfusing blood and even paying for donations grew up, despite what law-and-economics types might prefer to believe, against a decided lack of clarity about the relevant property rights.[23] In the 1950s, courts held that a blood transfusion by a hospital was not a sale for purposes of warranty laws.[24] In the 1960s, blood was held to be a commodity for purposes

---

[23] See generally Andrew Kimbrell, *The Human Body Shop: The Engineering and Marketing of Life* 6–23 (San Francisco: Harper, 1993).

[24] E.g., Perlmutter v. Beth David Hospital, 308 N.Y. 100, 123 NE.2d 792 (1954).

of the antitrust laws, trade in which may not be restrained.[25] At that time, perhaps 80 percent of the blood transfused in the United States was obtained by paying donors.[26]

A series of cases under the tax laws have clarified the commodity status of blood, sale of which is taxable income to the seller.[27] Particularly interesting to students of law's discourse of the body is *Green v. Commissioner,* which neatly displays law's ambivalence in treating the body as a machine.[28] Margaret Green, who lived with her three teenage children, supported herself through repeated sale of her rare, type AB-negative blood. In 1976 she made ninety-five trips to the blood laboratory some twenty miles from her home to "donate" blood. She reported and paid taxes on this income. The issue in the Tax Court was the deductibility of expenses she had claimed as business expenses.

The Tax Court held that her blood was a "tangible product" that she sold "in the ordinary course of business." "The rarity of petitioner's blood made the processing and packaging of her blood plasma a profitable undertaking, just as it is profitable for other entrepreneurs to purchase hen's eggs, bee's honey, cow's milk, or sheep's wool for processing and distribution. Although we recognize the traditional sanctity of the human body, we can find no reason to legally distinguish the sale of these raw products of nature from the sale of petitioner's blood plasma."[29]

Since Green was "in the trade or business of selling blood plasma," some, but not all, of her expenses were "ordinary and necessary" to the carrying on of her business. The court permitted deduction of expenditures for special high-protein foods and diet supplements, and also for travel to the laboratory. While "commuting expenses are clearly personal expenses and not deductible," these were different. "Unique to this situation, petitioner was the container in which her product was transported to market. Had she been able to extract the plasma at home and transport it to the lab without her being present, such shipping expenses would have been deductible as selling expenses."[30]

On the other hand, Green could not deduct her health insurance premiums

[25] Community Blood Bank of the Kansas City Area, Inc., 70 F.T.C. 728 (1966), reversed on other grounds 405 F.2d 1011 (8th Cir. 1969).

[26] Douglas MacN. Surgenor, The Nation's Blood Resource: A Summary Report (NIH Pub. No. 85-2028, 1985).

[27] See generally Douglas Kahn, *Federal Income Tax* 77–79 (Mineola, N.Y.: Foundation Pr., 1992), discussing United States v. Garber, 607 F.2d 92 (5th Cir. 1979) (taxability of sale of blood a novel issue; remanding for further proceedings on whether taxpayer who failed to report profits from sale of her blood acted willfully); Green v. Commissioner, 74 T.C. 1229 (1980) (payment received from sale of blood is gross income); Lary v. United States, 787 F.2d 1538 (11th Cir. 1986) (denying charitable deduction for blood donation).

[28] 74 T.C. 1229 (1980).

[29] 74 Id. 1234.

[30] 74 Id. 1238.

as business insurance. "Although petitioner attempts to justify the deduction by comparing her body to some insured manufacturing machinery, the instant set of facts prevents such a comparison; her body is not a replaceable, or easily repairable, machine maintained solely for the production of blood plasma."[31]

Thus, the court held that her body was a "container" for "shipping" the product the business sells but not a "machine" for its manufacture. It's not entirely clear what line is being drawn here. The distinctions have more to do with the integrity of the Internal Revenue Code, maintenance of which is after all an institutional function of the Tax Court, than with the development of any philosophically coherent concept of the body in law, something about which the Tax Court as an institution could not, presumably, care less. Specifically, Green's claimed deduction for her health insurance raised a long-standing and vexatious issue under the tax laws, namely distinguishing the things taxpayers do to preserve their income-earning capacity, which are deductible business expenses, from the things they do to stay alive, which aren't. For example, taxpayers may depreciate business property but not their own bodies, even if the taxpayer is a skilled craft worker whose body is in fact deteriorating. It is likely that the *Green* court would have let Green deduct some of her insurance payments if there were some workable way of dividing the "business" portion from the "personal" portion, the precise line the court draws as to her food and vitamins.

Finally, Green was not allowed a depletion deduction for the loss of her blood's ability to regenerate. That deduction was intended "to promote exploration and development of geological mineral resources. . . . Bodies and skills of taxpayers are not among the 'natural deposits' contemplated by Congress in these depletion provisions."[32] This seems unsatisfactory. Blood is, among other things, a mineral resource, and the court has just told us that Green's plasma is a "raw product of nature." Perhaps people with valuable blood are just as deserving of subsidies to encourage them to "explore and develop" that product as are owners of (other) mineral resources.[33] Surely it is not difficult to imagine the nation's blood supply as a "natural resource," and in other official publications the government does just that.[34]

For all I know, the *Green* case is a competent, even brilliant, exposition of difficult issues in tax law. For students of the legal discursive construction of

[31] 74 Id.

[32] 74 Id.

[33] Compare Anthony Kronman, "Mistake, Disclosure, Information, and the Law of Contracts," 7 *J. Leg. Stud.* 1 (1978) (property rights, there in information, as incentives to induce investment in scarce information, such as location of mineral resources).

[34] See, e.g., Department of Health, Education, and Welfare, Food and Drug Administration, "Current Good Manufacturing Practice for Blood and Blood Components," 39 Fed.Reg. 18614 (May 28, 1974) ("Human blood is a priceless natural resource"); Surgenor, *The Nation's Blood Supply.*

the body, however, it is unquestionably a hoot. Green's body is a container, but not a machine; her blood is a "raw product of nature," but not a "natural deposit"; her body in its "sanctity" produces a product sold "in the ordinary course of business." How could we think or talk this way if we had unmediated access to bodily experience, a sort of bedrock experience that would check the proliferating metaphors in *Green,* that would tell us whether we "really" are containers, machines, sacred, raw, natural?

Whatever the extent and limits of body experience as an epistemological category, particularly that unattainable phantom, "body experience unmediated by discourse," the production and circulation of our blood is a good example of a function that we cannot control, understand, or even really experience apart from the mediating imagery provided by medical accounts, accounts in which the heart is inevitably a sort of pump, the cells a sort of factory. The fact that we cannot directly experience our own blood while it remains inside our body has made blood a particularly lively site for the generation of competing fantastic discourses.[35] The more fundamental lesson of the *Green* case is that we are not, in the end, the passive consumers of these machine metaphors. We are amazingly free to construct directly competing discursive bodies, only lines apart, in the same legal text.

Why blood? Can we speculate about why blood, of all body parts or products, is the clearest example of a commodity? I want these remarks to be quite tentative, since I regard our discursive practices regarding property and commodification to be quite radically unstable, as I shall be demonstrating throughout our discussion of the commodification of the body and sexual activity as well. Blood was not always so clearly a commodity, and for all we know, corneas and kidneys may someday be commodities as unproblematically as blood is today.

Perhaps the body experience is fundamental to the establishment of the property right. Once people routinely have the experience of donating blood, of watching blood being extracted from the body, assuming a new shape and form, then donated to others, then it is easier for them to construct property out of the body experience. Marxists believe that all capital is congealed labor, of course, but this idea, however compelling to some of us, is not self-evident to most people. However, like George Hawkins's invisible hand, made visible

---

[35] See Laqueur, *Making Sex* 142–48 (sexual aspects of Harvey's theories); Françoise Héritier-Augé, "Semen and Blood: Some Ancient Theories Concerning Their Genesis and Relationship," in *Zone 5: Fragments for a History of the Human Body, Part 3,* at 159 (Michel Feher ed.) (New York: Zone, 1989); Piero Camporesi, *Il sugo della vita: Simbolismo e magia del sangue* (Milan: Saggiatore, 1984); Richard Toellner, "Logical and Psychological Aspects of the Discovery of the Circulation of the Blood, in *On Scientific Discovery: The Erice Lectures* 239 (M. D. Grmek ed.) (Dordrecht: Reidel, 1981). Popular explanations of heart disease are the last bastion of a mechanical explanation of the body (heart a pump that gets clogged), although even here there are signs of a reconceptualization in which heart disease will be understood in the newer vocabularies of complex, flexible immune systems. Martin, *Flexible Bodies* 192.

only through its discursive construction as a defective machine, blood, pumped from the body and then assuming a new shape, is a particularly vivid enactment of the extraction of surplus value and its transformation into capital. This seems plausible, although it has the problem common to all our arguments from bodily experience, namely that the experience has meaning only as mediated through discourse, and this simply raises the question of why, if the discursive construction of a bodily product as property may be made to work with blood, such construction is not universal for all body parts and products. Perhaps the simple answer is that many more people, including judges, have had the experience of donating blood and have thus been forced to represent this experience discursively to themselves.

Perhaps the important factors are economic: legal discursive creation of a property right follows, not precedes, the establishment of well-functioning markets in the questionable item. Or perhaps blood came first because of medical factors unique to blood: it is easily replaceable by the body, little pain or risk is involved in its donation, and so forth. Sperm shares these characteristics and is similarly said to be the property of its donor.[36]

The example of blood teaches by letting us eliminate some plausible theories of the discursive construction of the body as property. Efficiency, as the term is used by law-and-economics moralists, is neither necessary nor sufficient for legal recognition of a property right. It is not sufficient, since, as we shall discuss momentarily, markets like the market for blood do not exist for other bodily products.

Nor was efficiency necessary to the construction of blood as property. This is the great irony of this legal development. While cases like *Green* begin to establish a firm legal foundation for paid blood donation, the social importance of that institution has declined dramatically over the last quarter-century. Paid donors, who accounted for 80 percent of blood transfused in the United States in 1966, account for less than 1 percent today.[37] Apparently concern about infection, particularly hepatitis, has led the United States to follow the practice of the many other countries that have long relied on systems of voluntary donation.[38]

[36] Hecht v. Superior Court, 20 Cal.Rptr.2d 275 (D.Ct.App. 1993) (frozen sperm stored at sperm bank property of donor and part of his estate).

[37] Douglas MacN. Surgenor et al., "Collection and Transfusion of Blood in the United States 1982–1988," 322 *N. Eng. J. Med.* 1646 (June 7, 1990); Surgenor, *The Nation's Blood Supply.*

[38] See generally Richard M. Titmuss, *The Gift Relationship: From Human Blood to Social Policy* (New York: Pantheon, 1971). Perhaps some participants in this change in U.S. policy were also quietly motivated by Professor Titmuss's moving appeal that we recognize people's need to engage in altruistic relations. I know I was moved by that appeal when I first read his book. The United States's move toward voluntary blood donation has not been an unqualified success either as a way of guaranteeing adequate supplies for transfusion or as a way of spreading experiences of altruism. The number of annual donors has been either static or dipping slightly in recent years. Lawrence K. Altman, "U.S. Blood Supply Hits Lowest Level since World War II," *New York Times,* February 1, 1994, p. A1.

What is the alternative in *Green?* A body that is "sacred" and "private," that is *never* a machine or commodity? What then? Would Green and her children be denied the income she realizes from selling her plasma? Would she be denied the ability to deduct any of her business expenses? Would we indulge our humanist fantasies that we are truly embracing the sacred body of Margaret Green if we denied her her livelihood? So we stagger from case to case, now insisting the body is a machine, now denying that it ever could be. Law supposes that we might, collectively, enter into a relationship with Margaret Green (the person) solely through the medium of her body, but then constructs that body in self-contradictory ways.

These constructions of the body are also instrumental, designed to solve particular technical legal problems and not otherwise generalizable, even within law. For example, the city officials of Hanover, New Hampshire, have long attempted to deal with a perceived problem of drinking by teenagers by arresting, for "internal possession" of alcohol, teenagers who possess alcohol only inside their digestive systems.[39] The city has changed its procedures following complaint by the local chapter of the American Civil Liberties Union. Whether or not such criminal charges would ultimately have held up in court would have had nothing whatever to do with the fact that Margaret Green's body is the container of her blood.

COMPENSATION FOR BODY INJURY: CONSTRUCTING THE BODY AS PROPERTY

So if blood is property, the overall significance of this doctrine is not so clear. Other ways in which bodies are property in American law are even less clear, more self-consciously chosen as a figure of speech for a particular effect. For example, I believe that the very practice of awarding monetary compensation for physical injury hypothesizes the body as property "had" and "lost," and the same is true for awarding damages for "pain and suffering," although I recognize that alternative explanations are possible.[40]

The really interesting question here is how it ever became natural to think that a reasonable social response to the damaged body is the payment of monetary compensation. Other responses are possible: public expiation, punishment, apology, ritual healing, and the like. Our culture happens to prefer monetary "compensation," which is every bit as mythical as ritual expiation. Its mythical qualities are evident in the refrain, like *Hawkins v. McGee* also

---

[39] "N.H. Town Can't Stomach Drinking Law; Hanover Abolishes Rule on 'Internal Possession,'" *Boston Globe,* April 18, 1995, p. 17.

[40] A. I. Ogus, "Damages for Lost Amenities: For a Foot, a Feeling, or a Function?" 35 *Mod. L. Rev.* 1, 2–10 (1972) rationalizes English approaches to the award of nonpecuniary tort damages by analogy to "the law of property. The plaintiff's life, his faculties, his capacity for enjoying life are all 'valuable' personal assets, akin to his house, his shares or his china vase. To deprive him of one or more of these assets is to deprive him of something to which he has a 'proprietary right.'" Ogus nevertheless recognizes competing approaches.

taught early to first-year law students, that tort damages "are called compensatory" even though "[t]he sensations caused by harm to the body or pain or humiliation are not in any way analogous to a pecuniary loss."[41]

Behind of the entire practice of monetary compensation for bodily injury must lie a hazy notion of the body as "property" "lost" to its owner. The law recognizes the market, exchange value of intact, attractive bodies, in a variety of contexts discussed in chapter 5, such as the sale of labor power, or particular bodily displays or alterations. Since this is so, awarding damages for loss of an intact or attractive body is not even "nonpecuniary," although it may reflect the difficulty of imagining the particular kind of transaction for which the damages substitute. Bodies in pain and suffering are less employable, attract less desirable sexual and life partners, may have diminished social opportunities. Virtually none of these is quantifiable, yet perhaps awarding damages for pain and suffering makes some effort at compensation for the loss of a chattel: the intact, pain-free body.[42]

Since I do support monetary compensation for tort victims, this account is not, then, a humanist cri de coeur against the dehumanizing allegedly involved in body commodification.[43] In a classical Marxist analysis, the commodification of anything was ineluctably associated with alienation and domination. However, postmodernists have broadened our perspectives here. The commodification of something may shift power and advantage in unpredictable ways.[44] The liberation and autonomy purchased through consumer purchases

[41] Restatement, Second, Torts, Sec. 903, Comment a (1979). Richard Abel made this point to me. See also Cornelius J. Peck, "Compensation for Pain: A Reappraisal in Light of New Medical Evidence," 72 *Mich. L. Rev.* 1355, 1371 n. 79 (1974).

[42] Damages for pain and suffering are somewhat undertheorized, given that, where awarded, they comprise more than two-thirds of damages recovered. W. Kip Viscusi, "Pain and Suffering in Product Liability Cases: Systematic Compensation or Capricious Awards?" 8 *Int. Rev. L. & Econ.* 203, 208 (1988). Supporting the claim that these damages "compensate" for loss are David W. Leebron, "Final Moments: Damages for Pain and Suffering Prior to Death," 64 *NYU L. Rev.* 256 (1989); Randall R. Bovbjerg, Frank A. Sloan, and James F. Blumstein, "Valuing Life and Limb in Tort: Scheduling 'Pain and Suffering,'" 83 *Nw. U. L. Rev.* 908 (1989). The older suggestion in Louis L. Jaffe, "Damages for Personal Injury: The Impact of Insurance," 18 *L. and Contemp. Prob.* 219, 222 (1953) that such damages may be "consolation" to the victim does not explain the award of such damages to persons who had no consciousness of the pain or did not survive it. Margaret Jane Radin, *Contested Commodities* 184–205 (Cambridge: Harv. U. Pr., 1996), defends a "noncommodified conception" in which the award shows the victim that her rights are taken seriously but does not treat her pain as commensurable with any one else's. I find it hard to square this account with actual legal practice, in which, of all the ways law might show victims they are taken seriously, law restricts itself to monetary damages, varying "systematically with a variety of injury types." Viscusi, "Pain and Suffering" 213.

[43] For an anthology of cris de coeur on behalf of a sort of sacred body, see the collection *Politics and the Human Body: Assault on Dignity* (Jean Bethke Elshtain and J. Timothy Cloyd eds.) (Nashville: Vanderbilt U. Pr., 1995) (eugenics, genome project, organs for sale, surrogacy, torture, slavery).

[44] My thinking here has been influenced by Kobena Mercer, "Black Hair/Style Politics," 3

is always fragile and partial, supplied by enterprise and manipulated by advertising, but I'm not arguing that there is no liberation at all. Domination would come discursively if our experience of our bodies as commodities really drove out all the alternatives, so that we were incapable of constructing any other sort of body for ourselves than the commodity (or rights-holder). This sort of danger is worth worrying about but, as this whole book tries to show, is beyond law's power, no matter how hard it tries sometimes to establish just this discursive hegemony. A celebration precisely of the postmodern freedom to construct the body might well take a kind of partial Andy Warhol–Donna Haraway–Gilles Deleuze pleasure in the language of commodification (as a proof of the underlying freedom) in a way that a different version of liberation (Kantian, Marxist) might not.

RECOILING IN HORROR: LEGAL REFUSALS TO TREAT THE BODY AS PROPERTY IN THE SALE AND DONATION OF BODILY ORGANS

The law of sales and donation of bodily organs is also at best ambiguous support for the idea that the body is property.[45] A federal statute prohibits the acquisition or transfer of organs for transplantation if valuable consideration has been paid.[46] Similarly, a Uniform Anatomical Gift Act in effect in most American jurisdictions prohibits the purchase or sale of body parts if the removal of the part is to occur after death.[47] Analogous statutes in most countries discourage or forbid payment for transplantable organs.[48] The meaning of such of prohibition is certainly ambiguous; absent the statute, would it have been obviously the case that one's liver and kidney were one's property, subject to sale or donation? In a funny way, the statutory prohibition may be read to reinforce a construction of the body as property, albeit property that is subject, as what property is not, to regulation.

There has been considerable academic criticism of these statutes, mainly from a law-and-economics perspective, asserting that markets for the sale of

---

New Formations 33 (1987), reprinted in *Welcome to the Jungle: New Positions in Black Cultural Studies* 111 (New York: Routledge, 1994), who shows how marginalized groups have asserted control over commodified artifacts, in creative, empowering ways.

[45] A popular account of the legal framework surrounding the practice of transplanting and other uses of body parts from living or deceased donors was published under that very title: Russell Scott, *The Body as Property* (New York: Viking, 1981). A more technical legal introduction to some of these issues is David W. Meyers, *The Human Body and the Law* (Stanford: Stan. U. Pr., 2d ed., 1990).

[46] National Organ Transplant Act, 42 U.S.C. §274e.

[47] Uniform Anatomical Gift Act §10.

[48] World Health Organization, Human Organ Transplantation: A Report on Developments under the Auspices of WHO (1987–1991), 42 *International Digest of Health Legislation* 389 (1991); S. S. Fluss, Legal Aspects of Transplantation: Emerging Trends in International Action and National Legislation, 24 *Transplantation Proceedings* 2121 (No. 5, Oct. 1992); S. S. Fluss, "Preventing Commercial Transactions in Human Organs and Tissues: An International Overview of Regulatory and Administrative Measures," in *Organ Replacement Therapy: Ethics, Justice, and Commerce* (W. Land and J. B. Dossetor eds.) (Berlin: Springer-Verlag, 1991).

human organs will have the beneficent distributional consequences these writers ordinarily attribute to markets.[49] These proposals are often opposed by invoking a concept that it violates the sacredness of the human body to treat it as a commodity, a concept that both its proponents and opponents often find vague and unspecific.[50]

Participants in this debate often attribute importance precisely to the discursive construction of acquiring organs for transplantation, assuming a kind of pragmatic attitude consistent with the legal practice we have been observing, under which people are free to draw on a range of competing discursive constructions of the body, deploying particular constructions strategically, for particular objectives. For example, a recent internal report to the board of directors of United Network for Organ Sharing, a nonprofit organization that coordinates the nation's transplant supply under federal contract, reported a nationwide telephone poll in which 48 percent of those interviewed favored some form of donor compensation. The report recommended no action, however, until such incentives "are widely accepted as different from the purchasing of organs." Change the name of the rose, apparently, and the smell changes too. As the Network's spokesman told the *New York Times,* paying donors "can lead basically to Pandora's box," a characteristic construction of

---

[49] See, e.g., Lori B. Andrews, "My Body, My Property," 16 *Hastings Ctr. Rpt.* 28 (October 1986); James F. Blumstein, "Federal Organ Transplantation Policy: A Time for Reassessment?" 22 *UC Davis L. Rev.* 451 (1989); Lloyd R. Cohen, "Increasing the Supply of Transplant Organs: The Virtues of a Futures Market," 58 *Geo. Wash. L. Rev.* 1 (1989); Henry Hansmann, "The Economics and Ethics of Markets for Human Organs," 14 *J. Health Politics, Policy, & L.* 57 (1989); Roy Hardiman (student author), "Toward the Right of Commerciality: Recognizing Property Rights in the Commercial Value of Human Tissue," 34 *UCLA L. Rev.* 207 (1986); Richard Schwindt and A. R. Vining, "Proposal for a Future Delivery Market for Transplant Organs," 11 *J. Health Politics, Policy, & L.* 483 (1986); but see Paul P. Lee, "The Organ Supply Dilemma: Acute Responses to a Chronic Shortage," 20 *Colum. J. L. and Soc. Prob.* 363, 398–99 (1986) (criticizing proposals: "The cost of buying or otherwise paying for organs that are currently provided free is one drawback. Others are the backlash effect on voluntary giving, the 'inequity' of using an income test to determine recipients and the need to regulate such a market"); R. A. Sells, "The Case against Buying Organs and a Futures Market in Transplants," 24 *Transplantation Proceedings* 2198 (1992). See also Erik S. Jaffe (student author), "She's Got Bette Davis['s] Eyes": Assessing the Nonconsensual Removal of Cadaver Organs under the Takings and Due Process Clauses," 90 *Colum. L. Rev.* 528 (1990) (deriving theory of cadaveric organs as property so as to be able to argue that statutes "presuming" consent to organ donation are unconstitutional "takings" of property).

It is interesting that few of the advocates of markets for organs have written much else about health policy or expressed any concern about other shortages in the delivery of medical services, such as workers without health insurance. Much of the advocacy of markets for organs seems designed rather to advance arguments for markets generally, and specifically to challenge, quite aggressively, the alleged sentimental humanism of people who support some sort of regulation of markets. I am, however, willing to accept this challenge in attempting to construct, as one among many competing bodies, just this humanistic body.

[50] Kimbrell, *The Human Body Shop.* See discussion in Hansmann, "Economics and Ethics" 74–78.

the female body as not only a tangible commodity, a "container" like Margaret Green, but a container of evil out of control. "The body becomes a commodity."[51]

It is this resistance to the commodified body that I would like to explore, through the vehicle of a recent state court decision deploying that concept in a somewhat unlikely political context. As usual, my interest is in the different constructions of bodies in legal analysis, here, a body that is not the property of the person inside it and not an article of commerce; how, through what language, such bodies are figured in legal discourse, and what the examination of those texts tells us about the history and philosophy, the mental universe in short, that are associated with the particular body being discursively constructed.

I will not summarize the philosophic arguments for or against body non-commodification here nor add new arguments.[52] This stance gains support from one recent legal philosophic analysis of the process of commodification, which in the end is less a philosophy of commodification than a practical guide to coping with our collective lack of such a philosophy. Margaret Jane Radin identifies intermediate positions between "universal commodification" and "universal noncommodification," such as "market inalienable" property that may be given away but not sold. Radin argues that there should be neither universal commodification nor universal noncommodification, but that the question of whether to commodify in disputed areas, such as sexual services or reproductive services, should be approached case by case, in order to promote "human flourishing." In making these determinations, law should be attentive to all the consequences of its decisions, including in particular the possibility that once we discursively construct a commodity we may be unable to refrain from doing so in situations we would prefer to leave noncommodified.[53] This modest and sensible position would seem to include just

---

[51] Peter S. Young, "Moving to Compensate Families in Human-Organ Market; Legal Scholars and Doctors Lead Way," *New York Times,* July 8, 1994, p. B7. The headline is most misleading and reflects a minor public relations success by the proponents of markets for organs. No "move" to compensate families is revealed in the article, and buried in paragraph twenty-nine comes the information that "the House approved renewal of the National Organ Transplant Act without allowing for donor compensation; a similar version of the bill is awaiting action in the Senate." From one perspective, nothing in the law, then, is changing, and the legal scholars and doctors who got themselves quoted in the *Times* are just self-promoting. However, from the perspective of this book on the discursive construction of the body, the appearance in a headline in the *New York Times* of the solecism "human-organ market" is a sort of small victory for the proponents of this way of talking.

[52] A good philosophical discussion from a Kantian perspective is Stephen R. Munzer, "An Uneasy Case against Property Rights in Body Parts," in *Property Rights* 259 (Ellen Frankel Paul, Fred D. Miller Jr., and Jeffrey Paul eds.) (Cambridge: Camb. U. Pr., 1994), and Stephen R. Munzer, "Kant and Property Rights in Body Parts," 6 *Canadian J. L. & Jurisprudence* 319 (no. 2, July 1993).

[53] Radin, *Contested Commodities* 51–114. An interesting critique of Radin from a Lacanian perspective that shares many points with this book is Jeanne Lorraine Schroeder, "Virgin Terri-

about everyone who ever walked the earth, with the possible exceptions of Mao Tse-tung on the one hand and a few professors at the University of Chicago on the other, and their respective overenthusiastic disciples. As we shall see, at least some courts adopt just Radin's position.

Nor do I claim any expertise in health policy or any original contribution to the consequentialist debate in the journals on whether there ought to be markets for organs. I assume that treating organs as commodities would indeed increase the supplies available for transplantation, but I express no opinion on whether this would come about primarily through benign incentives for voluntary transfers or, instead, through the murder and dismemberment of the powerless, though my instincts run to the latter rather than the former.[54] In general, I assume that ways could be found to encourage greater voluntary donation out of a sense of altruism and reinforced community, and that any proposal to pay people for what they ought to do is merely a tribute to our ignorance of the institutional framework for a caring society. At the moment, though, I am pursuing the more descriptive task of understanding why people in our legal system, who have at hand access to vocabularies of the body-as-property/commodity (blood, for example) and the sacred noncommodified body, choose one or the other in particular contexts.

MOORE V. REGENTS OF THE UNIVERSITY OF CALIFORNIA: WHY WE DON'T OWN OUR SPLEENS

The much-publicized recent case of *Moore v. Regents of the University of California* saw the court split five to two precisely on the question of whether plaintiff's spleen, removed in a surgical operation, was his "property."[55] At least according to plaintiff's version of the story, the doctors who recommended removal of his spleen to arrest the spread of his leukemia knew, but did not tell him, that the spleen had research and commercial value since it

---

tory: Margaret Radin's Imagery of Personal Property as the Inviolate Feminine Body," 79 *Minn. L. Rev.* 55 (1994), but I cannot pursue these points here.

[54] Kimbrell, *The Human Body Shop* 29–35, is a work of journalism, not scholarship, but some of the horror stories of organ sales in the less-developed countries are quite chilling.

[55] Moore v. Regents of the University of California, 793 P.2d 479 (Cal. 1990), cert. denied, 499 U.S. 936 (1991). The case has been much commented on its journey through the California courts and has already entered popular culture as a symbol of alienation. "There was a sense of being used for a purpose that was beyond my control, like the Seattle man whose freakish, highly immune blood cells were taken from him, cultured and patented without his consent." Susan Daitch, *The Colorist* 40 (New York: Vintage Contemporaries, 1990). Among the best of the extensive law review commentary are Michelle Bourianoff Bray (student author), "Personalizing Personality: Toward a Property Right in Human Bodies," 69 *Tex. L. Rev.* 209 (1990); Jeffrey A. Potts (student author), *"Moore v. Regents of the University of California:* Expanded Disclosure, Limited Property Rights," 86 *Nw. U. L. Rev.* 453 (1992). A marvelous treatment of the case as one over control of information, in which the fact that it's about a body part is of no distinctive interest, is James Boyle, *Shamans, Software, and Spleens: Law and the Construction of the Information Society* 21–24, 97–107 (Cambridge: Harv. U. Pr., 1996).

could be used to manufacture valuable cells. (The metaphor of possession is unavoidable: his spleen, his leukemia.) The spleen was removed, the medical staff established a cell line from Moore's T-lymphocytes, patented the cell line and became quite wealthy through commercial exploitation of the patent. The California Supreme Court, disagreeing with both the trial and intermediate appeals court, upheld plaintiff's cause of action for breach of fiduciary duty. The court did not, however, sustain Moore's cause of action for conversion.[56]

In most conversations about the ethics of payment for useful organs, and certainly in the legal and health policy literature cited above, participants line up predictably along political lines. Political conservatives favor the establishment of markets for organs, in which voluntary sales will take place, promoting, they say, the freedom of individuals and the efficient production and distribution of transplantable organs. Political liberals oppose markets in body organs, often in the name of preserving a place in society for altruism or other noncommodified vocabularies of interaction.

One of the amusing paradoxes of the *Moore* case is that the lineup of justices of the California Supreme Court was exactly the opposite of the "normal" lineup. The political liberals on the court favored payment to Moore for his spleen, while the conservative majority denied his action for conversion. In understanding the discursive constructions of John Moore's body that were intellectually available to the court, and why they did what they did, this is a puzzle to be explained.

Conversion is the tort of dominion or control over a thing so as to interfere with the rights of another (usually, the owner) to control it, and thus to call for compensation to that owner.[57] Moore's conversion theory thus forced the court to consider whether his spleen and its cells were Moore's property.

I mentioned above that this is a question left open by the American statutes on organ sales, since they are narrowly drawn and do not state whether body parts are property in a more general way. In fact, neither the prohibition of

---

[56] The court was unanimous in upholding the cause of action for breach of fiduciary duty. There were two dissents from the failure to recognize a cause of action for conversion, 793 P.2d at 498 ("concurring and dissenting" opinion of Broussard, J.); 793 P.2d at 506 ("dissenting" opinion of Mosk, J.).

[57] Restatement, 2d, Torts (1965), §222A: What Constitutes Conversion

(1) Conversion is an intentional exercise of dominion or control over a chattel which so seriously interferes with the right of another to control it that the actor may justly be required to pay the other the full value of the chattel.

(2) In determining the seriousness of the interference and the justice of requiring the actor to pay the full value, the following factors are important:
    (a) the extent and duration of the actor's exercise of domination or control:
    (b) the actor's intent to assert a right in fact inconsistent with the other's right of control;
    (c) the actor's good faith;
    (d) the extent and duration of the resulting interference with the other's right of control;
    (e) the harm done to the chattel;
    (f) the inconvenience and expense caused to the other.

sales in the National Organ Transplant Act nor that of the Uniform Anatomical Gift Act applied to Moore's case, the former because Moore's spleen was
not sought "for transplantation," and the latter because the spleen was removed while Moore was still living. Since neither statute prohibited payment
for Moore's spleen, the court had to decide this more basic question of
whether Moore's spleen was his property. Under legal principles basic to
common-law systems like America's, this is a question to be decided by
judges—in America, normally state court judges—applying general principles and precedents developed by other courts defining "property."

The court's analysis recreated the inglorious past of the legal body-as-
property: as in medieval rape law or the law of chattel slavery, Moore's cells
were property, but they weren't his. For surely they were the property of the
medical researchers after they were removed from Moore's body.[58] The court
did not replicate the situation said to obtain in French law, in which there can
be no property rights in the body at all, so that if I sever my finger, intending to
keep it, and you take it, you have not committed any crime.[59] In America, by
contrast, the cells clearly belonged to the researchers who removed them,
since they patented the cell line itself—a property interest created by the
United States government. Another researcher who stole the spleen or cells
from their laboratory could presumably have been sued for conversion. Yet if
the spleen was the property of the medical researchers, how did they acquire
it? California, like other states, provides for anatomical gifts, but Moore made
no such gift.[60]

The court decided Moore's spleen was not his property without any explicit
reference to any theory of property. Nor did the court see, feel, embrace, even
mimetically, the body of John Moore, invisible in the opinion, any more than
the New Hampshire court could face the hand of George Hawkins or the Tax
Court the body of Margaret Green.

Rather, the court decided that Moore's spleen was not his property by eval-
uating the competing needs of patients and medical researchers. Currently, the
court says, cells removed from patients' bodies are kept, copied freely, supplied to other researchers. Moore's argument would "impose a tort duty on
scientists to investigate the consensual pedigree of each human cell sample
used in research. . . .[which] implicates policy concerns far removed from the
traditional, two-party ownership disputes in which the law of conversion
arose."[61] The court, then, has a theory of property, despite its absence of

[58] 793 P.2d at 510 (Mosk, J., dissenting).

[59] Jean-Pierre Baud, *L'Affaire de la main volée: Une histoire juridique du corps* (Paris: Editions du Seuil, 1993).

[60] Uniform Anatomical Gift Act, adopted in California as Health and Safety Code §7150 Et
Seq.; 793 P.2d at 501–2 (Broussard, J., concurring and dissenting). As noted, this statute applies
only to gifts that take place after the donor's death. Nevertheless, Justice Broussard read the
statute as stating a more general policy of "donor control."

[61] 793 P.2d at 487 (footnote omitted). These observations are literally the court's first response

theoretical citation: property is that which is defined by a court as property, doing so in order to promote some sort of utilitarian greatest good for the greatest number, under which John Moore may appropriately be asked to sacrifice if society is thereby improved. It is possible that Professor Radin might criticize this utilitarianism and might argue that a different conception of personhood here would better advance "human flourishing." But it is hard to see how she could criticize the court's case-by-case consequentialism.

The adoption of such a nominalist theory of property by the so-called conservative wing of what is now a "conservative" (Republican-appointed) court shows the indeterminate political spin of all our legal metaphors for the body. The idea that a property right grants a sort of sovereignty to the owner to ignore others is usually associated with the radical wing of American legal realism (Morris Cohen, Robert Hale) or those in the critical legal studies movement who have revived the idea.[62] Here we have a conservative court deploying precisely that argument in order to deny a claim of property. John Moore's spleen can't be his property, because this would privilege him to disable medical research.

The "liberal" dissenters also resorted to political poaching as they developed their argument that John Moore's spleen was his property. They invoked the property metaphor in one of its common conservative guises, as a metaphor for individual autonomy and control in the face of alien forces.

[E]very individual has a legally protectable property interest in his own body and its products. First, our society acknowledges a profound ethical imperative to respect the human body as the physical and temporal expression of the unique human persona.[63] One manifestation of that respect is our prohibition against direct abuse of the body by torture or other forms of cruel or unusual punishment. Another is our prohibition against indirect abuse of the body by its economic exploitation for the sole benefit of another person. The most abhorrent form of

---

to Moore's argument on conversion, after restating the argument and noting that "No court, however, has ever in a reported decision imposed conversion liability for the use of human cells in medical research." 793 P.2d at 487 (footnote omitted).

[62] Cohen, "Property and Sovereignty," 41; Hale, "Coercion and Distribution," 470; Joseph William Singer, "The Legal Rights Debate in Analytical Jurisprudence from Bentham to Hohfeld," 1982 *Wis. L. Rev.* 975; Duncan Kennedy, *Sexy Dressing Etc.* 83–125 (Cambridge: Harv. U. Pr., 1993).

[63] 793 P.2d at 515. Does Justice Mosk really mean "persona"? What Hobbes called "the *disguise,* or *outward appearance* of a man, counterfeited on the Stage; and sometimes more particularly that part of it which disguiseth the Face, as a Mask or Visard"? Thomas Hobbes, *Leviathan* 133–34 (New York: Dutton, London: Dent Everyman, 1950) [1651]. My desk dictionary defines *persona* as "1.[pl.] the characters of a drama, novel, etc. 2. *psychol.* the outer personality or facade presented to others by an individual." *Webster's New World Dictionary of the American Language* 1062 (2d college ed.) (New York: Simon and Schuster, 1984). Read this way, Justice Mosk's opinion becomes radically postmodern. Probably he just used the wrong word and meant to write "personality."

such exploitation, of course, was the institution of slavery. Lesser forms, such as indentured servitude or even debtor's prison, have also disappeared. Yet their specter haunts the laboratories and boardrooms of today's biotechnological research-industrial complex.[64]

One might share Justice Mosk's commitment to the abolition of exploitation and abuse and nevertheless question the relevance of recognizing "property" in the body to that crusade. The slavery example is telling, since surely the essence of slavery is that the body *is* property, just not the property of the person inside it. Perhaps if legal discourse were completely incapable of constructing the body as property, slavery would have had a harder time institutionalizing itself legally. Furthermore, in none of the successful campaigns for the dignity of the body mentioned by Justice Mosk, that is, to abolish slavery, indentured servitude, debtor's prison, and torture, was the body discursively constructed as property. Rather, the operative body, as we shall see in chapter 11, was constructed as the object of discipline through intimacy and love.[65]

This just points out the deeper problem with Justice Mosk's invocation of property, the complex three-part argument we said above is part of any claim of property. If John Moore's spleen is his property, it necessarily follows that Moore has a certain freedom to make or not to make contracts for its alienation; that he will become subject to the domination of others who purchase or rent his property in the market; and that he will have the freedom to dominate others that comes from the privilege of not heeding them. In the *Moore* case, the majority largely rested on the last of these claims, while a separate concurrence seemed to hover around the second. (Of course property can be disaggregated as a concept, for which the standard metaphor is a bundle of sticks, but I think that at least these three features necessarily follow from any construction of property).[66]

Behind Justice Mosk's invocation of property to stand in for freedom from torture and slavery lies a sort of absolute right of dominion of the owner over his property, which is not a trope often found in the judicial opinions of contemporary political liberals. Contemporary liberals often prefer to imagine property as a social construction in the service of social needs and subject to various social restrictions. Calling the body property would, however, provide comparatively little autonomy if that concept carried with it such concepts as land use planning, zoning, easements, or condemnation for public use. In fairness, Justice Mosk's dissent, which did try to operate from a broad philo-

---

[64] 793 P.2d at 515 (Mosk, J., dissenting).

[65] Richard H. Brodhead, "Sparing the Rod: Discipline and Fiction in Antebellum America," in *Cultures of Letters: Scenes of Reading and Writing in Nineteenth-Century America* 18 (Chicago: U. Chi. Pr., 1993); Elizabeth B. Clark, "'The Sacred Rights of the Weak': Pain, Sympathy, and the Culture of Individual Rights in Antebellum America," 82 *J. Am. Hist.* 463 (1995).

[66] For others, see Jeanne L. Schroeder, "Chix Nix Bundle-o-Stix: A Feminist Critique of the Disaggregation of Property," 93 *Mich. L. Rev.* 239 (1994).

sophic definition of property, also recognized that property is often subject to legal regulation of one kind or another, but he made this point only to establish that Moore might still own his spleen even if statutes limited how it might be disposed of after his death, not to raise the larger question of whether constructing the body as property is genuinely in the service of autonomy and freedom.[67]

On the other hand, the "conservative" majority assumed the responsibility to define property. They treated the question of property rights in the body as entirely open, though did not discuss any of the bodies of law we have discussed so far to show property conceptions of the body: not *Hawkins v. McGee,* or compensation for injury generally, or even the regulation of blood, which is quite clearly both property and a commodity. The majority then stated that it was reluctant to recognize property where the consequences of recognizing property would be to impede medical research. The "policy consideration" weighing against calling Moore's spleen his property "is that we not threaten with disabling civil liability innocent parties who are engaged in socially useful activities, such as researchers who have no reason to believe that their use of a particular cell sample is, or may be, against a donor's wishes."[68] "[T]he theory of liability that Moore urges us to endorse threatens to destroy the economic incentive to conduct important medical research."[69]

This approach could not be applied generally to other recognized property rights. While the court does not generalize its approach into a principle, one might say that they will not recognize any property right where the consequence of such recognition would be to impede the free flow of cooperation, information, and knowledge. However, few legally recognized property rights can pass that test. The literature on the economic analysis of property rights oscillates dizzily between the claim that recognition of a property right in information will lower transaction costs (by creating markets for information that will get information to most valued uses) or raise transaction costs (as parties overinvest in duplicative research, screening of potential contract partners).[70] The same contradictory results may be generated in asking whether recognizing property rights in diseased organs would or would not be efficient. Conservative legal scholars assume that permitting or requiring researchers to purchase spleens would increase the supply and efficiently guide spleens to their highest and best use. Conservative judges in California come down on the side of not paralyzing research.

Some of the philosophic considerations absent from the majority opinion found their way into Justice Arabian's extraordinary separate concurrence,

[67] 793 P.2d at 509–10 (Mosk, J., dissenting).

[68] 793 P.2d at 493.

[69] 793 P.2d at 495.

[70] Kim Lane Scheppele, *Legal Secrets: Equality and Efficiency in the Common Law* 165–66 (Chicago: U. Chi. Pr., 1988).

which turned the dissenters' property metaphor back on them, by invoking the sentimental sacred body that is its usual spectral supplement:

> Plaintiff has asked us to recognize and enforce a right to sell one's own body tissue *for profit*. He entreats us to regard the human vessel—the single most venerated and protected subject in any civilized society—as equal with the basest commercial commodity. He urges us to commingle the sacred with the profane. He asks much. . . . Does it uplift or degrade the "unique human persona" to treat human tissue as a fungible article of commerce?

This is cloddish and awkward, Carlyle repeated as farce, but its very awkwardness helps break through the surface of legal analysis and threatens to destabilize the opinion. It would even be possible to see this opinion as standing alone against the rest of the court, by grouping the majority *and* dissents as advocates of a modern, isolated, nonvisualized body that is somebody's property, while seeing Justice Arabian as an advocate from a wholly different tradition of the sacred, noncommodified body. This turns out not to be true, however. First, as I have argued throughout, the modern dehumanized body always already carries with it the spectral sentimental body, so Arabian merely makes explicit what was there all along. Second, as a technical legal matter, Arabian does not follow through with his invocation of the sacred body, which might, if he took it seriously, prohibit ownership of Moore's cell line by the defendant researchers, or indeed, the practice of wage labor. So Arabian does not stand alone but instead lines up with the majority, and the opinion sputters off into the usual clichés about judicial inaction ("not, in my view, ours to decide . . . [The] mark of wisdom for us as expositors of the law is the recognition that we cannot cure every ill. . . . Clearly the Legislature . . . is the proper deliberative forum. . . . Courts cannot and should not seek to fashion a remedy for every 'heartache and the thousand natural shocks that flesh is heir to.'").[71]

The *Moore* case well illustrates the impoverished nature of our legal discourse about the body, the indeterminacy of at least one key discursive construction, the body as property, and our foolishness in thinking that the deployment of these indeterminate constructions constitutes thinking about a problem. Moore's spleen is and is not property; calling it property makes Moore autonomous and degrades him; calling it property stakes out his autonomy from others yet does so only through a metaphor that judges can bestow on things or not, as they see fit, guided by their notion of the greatest social good.

I repeat that I find the whole question of markets for organs to be a difficult one, in which I do not feel myself expert and certainly feel internally divided, in the guts, as it were. However, while I may not be sure what is the right way

---

[71] 793 P.2d at 497 (Arabian, J., concurring).

to think about organ donations, I am quite sure that *Moore* is the wrong way. Legal discourse provides, ready-made, discursive constructions of the body, handy in any situation: machines, property, sacred and noncommodified. We can always pluck the construction we like and insert it into the context in which we find ourselves, secure that by doing so we in no way constrain our ability to react flexibly to the next context. I don't think there's any alternative to this flexibility. We are just this free, existentially, and may come to gain power from the fact that there is no essence to our bodies, and we are free to construct them anew. I also don't think, however, that we should treat deploying any particular body construction as if it were thinking about a problem. Margaret Radin's admonition to case-by-case consequentialism in the service of human flourishing does not add anything to our repertoire of moral reasoning *if* any problematic use of the body can be restated as the choice of two discursive constructions, commodified and noncommodified, and we may select the one that discursively figures the body to line up with our ethical aspirations, knowing that we are free to select another tomorrow.

SHOULD BODIES BE DISCURSIVELY CONSTRUCTED AS PROPERTY?

We are not done by any means with excavation of the discursive construction of the body as a commodity. We have yet to take up the field of employer-employee relations, in which employer demands for body display or alteration are often discursively constructed as contracts; or the difficult question of the valuation of lost sexual relations, in damages known as loss of consortium. However, we have seen enough to begin to raise some questions whether the discourse in which bodies are constituted property is functional for legal analysis or consistent with our best ethical aspirations.

I will argue momentarily that we would be better off abandoning any attachment to all the legal constructions that figure the body as somebody's property, or commodity, or machine, so that, if we employed them at all, we could do so only knowing that other people in the conversation would automatically be thinking about their opposite. On this view, arguing that "my body is my property" would always be an invitation of the form "don't think about an elephant." We would know that anyone who urged us to see our bodies as property, or commodities, or machines, would expect us to be thinking, "Well, yes, only as one of competing discursive constructions of the body, which I control, so the issue is really how I want to live, not who owns what."

The argument will be on philosophic grounds—that calling the body property, to the extent it drives out and eats up competing discursive constructions (body metaphors), is not consistent with our ethical aspirations but instead just reproduces anxieties and ambivalences that should be confronted directly. However, as before, a philosophic critique of legal discourse should carefully consider whether a particular discursive construction is functional within legal analysis, however comic or illogical it may appear from an outsider's perspective. Just as it was hard to make such as case for the machine metaphor, there is not much of an internal legal case to be made for constructing the body as property. We will still be forced to construct bodies discursively, for we still have no way of catching hold of that chimera, the "real" body unmediated by discourse. I hope, however, to present more appealing discursive figuring of the body than the trite and fairly comic constructions that dominate lawyer talk.

American legal realism has left us a staple argument that the ordinary legal problems that daily life throws our way—should the doctors who removed John Moore's spleen share any of their profits; should Margaret Green be allowed the tax deductions she claims; to what damages is George Hawkins entitled—are not normally made easier to solve by referring them to a large abstraction like property. This is because the large abstractions will be malleable if not meaningless; because the move to abstraction will distance us from the facts of particular cases that in fact are influencing the outcome, so that the move to abstraction estranges us from our own judging process; because it is impossible to generate consistent results from such an abstraction as property, so that exceptions and refinements will inevitably creep in that soon allow any result to be reached in any case.

The few cases we have examined so far in which the body is constructed as property seem to confirm this analysis. How can it be that we own our blood, not our spleen, and can barely answer the question of whether we own our bodies under American law? Moreover, we cannot answer the question whether we own our bodies, not because there are gray areas, but because we lack firm grasp on the most basic definitional questions, such as what it means to own property.

Certainly the courts do not employ any general concept called *ownership* or *property*. Cases like *Green* or *Moore* or pain-and-suffering cases are bereft of general definitions or theories of property. The courts are legal realists too, or, rather, the abstractions they deploy to decide specific cases are no longer "ownership" or "property" but "medical research" and "business expense." As a result, the bodies constructed in particular cases have little or no resonance beyond the boundaries of that particular case, which is why the ownership question comes out differently for blood and organs, and why the bodies figuratively constructed in these cases are so elusive and rarely link up with each other. (This point will become particularly important in later chapters as we examine cases that define bodily privacy or bodily boundaries, cases that, as we shall see, do not and cannot invoke visualizations of the body found in other areas of the law). This is just another way of noting that in neither Margaret Green's case nor John Moore's can a judge consult anything called one's sense of "one's own body"; the judge is therefore compelled to construct a new body each time.

Body Property as Foucauldian Regulation

I find it easier to see property or commodity constructions of the body as a kind of Foucauldian regulatory process, rather than as any contribution to solving the concededly difficult legal issues presented. Bodies are figured as machines, property, commodities, not to resolve ethical-legal issues about which we are divided as a society or within ourselves. Rather, bodies are so figured in order to inscribe them into the normal regulatory apparatus of consumer and market society, a world of contracts and compensation, domination mystified as economic exchange. I am generalizing my explanation of "pain and suffering" damages, then, to apply to all constructions of the body as property.

For the success of this project of regulation through discursive construction, it is unimportant whether John Moore owns his spleen in the end. What is important is that everyone be able to imagine a world in which our relation to our bodies is one of ownership and sale. This is the common ground between the majority and dissent, and the way in which Justice Arabian's cloddish concurrence, in the few sentences when it breaks free of cliché, is momentarily fresher and more radical than the sterile dispute between majority and dissenters—only momentarily, for we will soon explore the regulatory aspects of Justice Arabian's construction of the sacred body.

Michel Foucault, in his famous lecture at the Collège de France on January 14, 1976, generalized from his studies of insane asylums and prisons by associating them with a "new mechanism of power" arising in the seventeenth and eighteenth centuries, incompatible with earlier "relations of sovereignty," and abiding to the present. "This new mechanism of power is more dependent upon bodies and what they do than upon the Earth and its products. It is a mechanism of power which permits time and labour, rather than wealth and commodities, to be extracted from bodies. It is a type of power which is constantly exercised by means of surveillance rather than in a discontinuous manner by means of a system of levies or obligations distributed over time."

The legal codes and other aspects of state power, holdovers from the earlier era of sovereignty, survive largely "to conceal [the] actual procedures" of the disciplinary society, "the element of domination inherent in its techniques, and to guarantee to everyone, by virtue of the sovereignty of the State, the exercise of his proper sovereign rights. . . . Modern society, then, from the nineteenth century up to our own day, has been characterised on the one hand, by a legislation, a discourse, an organisation based on public right, whose principle of articulation is the social body and the delegative status of each citizen; and, on the other hand, by a closely linked grid of disciplinary coercions whose purpose is in fact to assure the cohesion of this same social body." These disciplinary coercions have their own discourse, not a discourse of right, but of "normalisation." Social conflicts often represent just this conflict between disciplinary normalization and judicial sovereignty; we lack a mediating discourse between the two and have difficulty criticizing either except in the language of the other.[72]

Once one realizes that, particularly in the United States, legal personnel are as likely to be employed to develop the discourse of "disciplinary normalization" as of "sovereignty," this passage from Foucault offers a more illuminating explanation of the discursive construction of the body as property than any explanation internal to legal thought.[73] After all, by definition only marginal subpopulations are disciplined through such blunt and obvious coercions as the prison and mental hospital. Most people who have not been defined as marginal—the "general population" we will encounter particularly when we construct diseased bodies—are subject to social regulation and coercion largely through two great disciplines of power, the discipline of sexuality and gender, about which Foucault wrote so much, and the discipline of the market and economic activity, about which he did not.

I will have more to say about the construction of the legal body in order to facilitate the discipline of gender and sexuality. While there is an eroticized component to the discursive construction of the bodies of George Hawkins, Margaret Green, and John Moore, primarily in the way the very absence of their bodies suggests the eroticized repression of a more visualized discourse, I want to concentrate here on the discursive construction of bodies so as to enable them to function in market society.

Most adults in our society survive, and are expected to survive, by selling their labor power, renting, if you like, their brains and bodies for specified times at specified rents. While we all understand what Justice Arabian is saying in his concurrence in *Moore v. Regents* ("Plaintiff has asked us to recognize and enforce a right to sell one's own body tissue *for profit*. He entreats us to regard the human vessel—the single most venerated and protected subject in any civilized society—as equal with the basest commercial commodity"), we also understand that any adult in our society who consistently took the principled position that he would not sell the labor of his body "for profit," that he would not equate the "venerated and protected" "human vessel" with "the basest commercial commodity,"[74] that he would not submit his "body by

---

[72] Lecture: 14 January 1976, in Michel Foucault, *Power/Knowledge: Selected Interviews and Other Writings 1972–1977* (Colin Gordon ed.) (New York: Pantheon, 1980).

[73] Other professionals besides legal professionals may play their role in the normalizing discursive construction of the body. Compare the medical texts analyzed by Emily Martin that treat the body "as a small business that is either winning or losing," so that menstruation and menopause are *losses* that *weaken* the body. Martin, *Woman in the Body* 35. See also Susan Sontag's analysis of the economic imagery in the popular representation of tuberculosis and cancer. Susan Sontag, *Illness as Metaphor and AIDS and its Metaphors* 62–63 (New York: Anchor, 1990) [1978].

[74] 793 P.2d at 497 (Arabian, J., concurring).

its economic exploitation for the sole benefit of another person,"[75] would either have to be a very wealthy individual or would not survive long.

We don't normally think of work as sale of the body, preferring formulations like sale of labor or worktime or labor power. Marxists prefer the formulation "labor power," but, as Carole Pateman has argued, this really just carries forward the domination that Marxists like to criticize: "The answer to the question of how property in the person can be contracted out is that no such procedure is possible. Labor power, capacities or services, cannot be separated from the person of the worker like pieces of property. . . . The worker and his labor, not his labor power, are the subject of contract. . . . he sells command over the use of his body and himself."[76]

Labor markets, the disciplinary coercion that touches more adults than any other, excepting again the system of gender and sexuality, must generate, as Foucault says, their "normalizing" discourse, a discourse in which domination, compulsion, coercion come out as the language of contract of employment. There is indeed, as Foucault says, a constant tension between the discourse of sovereign subjects holding rights, and the economic discourse of normal market life. Much of the tension and difficulty in American law comes from the fact that, moreso than in most societies, American legal personnel are called on to advance both of these competing discourses, often on the same occasion and in the same text.

I don't want to argue that market society requires that Margaret Green's blood be a commodity, or John Moore's spleen his property. That would be reductionist and surely wrong. Market society may require, however, that adults at least be able to comprehend the claim that blood is a commodity, a spleen, property. Moreover, I do think it is helpful to see the tortured rhetoric of those cases driven partly by factors internal to legal culture, but also by larger social disciplinary requirements.

Society will cohere and function as best it can, goods and services will be produced, whether or not John Moore's doctors may be sued for conversion. However, in the larger social project of the construction of the self, people must be able to imagine themselves both as sacred individuals, and as sellers of labor power, always and at the same time. For, as I said, if people construct selves for themselves so fine that they cannot submit to economic exploitation, the economic system will not survive. Yet, as Terry Eagleton observed, if people are *only* the passive subjects of authoritarian orders, they may not be able to comprehend elementary solidarity.

So legal discourse must produce images both of individual autonomy and of social cohesion. In particular, it must construct bodies appropriate to each discursive order. We find in law the body constructed as property and com-

---

[75] 793 P.2d at 515 (Mosk, J., dissenting).
[76] Carole Pateman, *The Sexual Contract* 150–51 (Stanford: Stan. U. Pr., 1988).

modity, normalizing exploitation and coercion into contract and market. And we find the autonomous, sacred body, seat of the sacred and unique individual, giving the law to itself and withstanding state intrusion. While we will come back to more bodies constructed to facilitate regulation, I would like to glimpse some of the competing discursive constructions of the autonomous body in American law. The body as property has a role to play here, too, but competes with other bodies discursively constructed as autonomous.

Chapter 4

CONSTRUCTING THE AUTONOMOUS LEGAL BODY:
PRIVACY, PROPERTY, INVIOLABILITY

Of course, one cannot think without metaphors. But that does not mean
there aren't some metaphors we might well abstain from or try to retire.[1]

IF GEORGE HAWKINS owns his hand, a machine, and Margaret Green owns the
container in which her blood is transported to market, does Jane Roe own her
body for purposes of determining whether the Texas can forbid her from obtaining an abortion? Does the answer to this question matter? If the answer is,
no, it does not matter, because Jane Roe's right of privacy guarantees her at
least some possibility of abortion, then how and why is this private body
constructed in legal discourse? The common thread among George
Hawkins's, Margaret Green's, and John Moore's cases is the juxtaposition of a
commodified body, property of its owner, with a vaguer notion of the sentimental, private body. Jane Roe, as everyone knows but as we shall examine
carefully, has a private body but may or may not have a property body. Does it
matter how law figures Jane Roe's body? If not, did it matter how law figured
the others?

In the last chapter I invited the reader to begin the process of imagining a
legal discourse in which bodies could not be constructed as property, or rather,
could only be constructed as property through a self-conscious process in
which the speaker constructing the body as property was necessarily aware of
alternative constructions (and aware that hearers were also aware of those
alternative constructions), and self-consciously deployed a particular construction only as a device for representing another person. My interest is not in
suppressing any particular metaphor, but in encouraging an explosion of competing metaphors, in which property metaphors would not be able to drive out
the competition. I also pointed out, however, some specific defects of the
property construction, specifically, its ability to facilitate domination as well
as autonomy; the kind of autonomy it constructs, that is, the privilege to ignore others; and the aporiae opened up when property constructions of the
body coexist, as inevitably they will, with noncommodified conceptions in
which the body is constructed as a refuge, a private hermitage from the economic and political life of civil society.

---

[1] Susan Sontag, "AIDS and Its Metaphors," in *Illness as Metaphor and AIDS and Its Metaphors* 93 (New York: Doubleday Anchor, 1990).

None of this is necessarily a knockout argument for doing away with the property construction. I confess that my biggest concern about doing so would be the potential blow to human freedom, dignity, and autonomy. All readers of this book will want to find room in their legal discourse for some vocabulary with which to articulate some conception of the autonomy of the body, its power to withstand the demands of others. This is so even though the core example of such autonomy will vary with the reader, each imagining resistance to some different proposed use of or intrusion into the body. For some, perhaps, the core violation of autonomy would be slavery, for others, perhaps, compelled pregnancy to term, or police search, or economic regulation, or compulsory heterosexuality. Indeed, the first journal advocating what we would now term gay rights was published in German from 1899 to 1933 under the title *Der Eigene,* which might be translated "The Self-Owner," and the movement around that journal termed itself *die Gemeinschaft der Eigenen,* or community of self-owners.[2]

I take as the starting point for this chapter this assumption that any reader will have some such core examples of body freedom and autonomy, though these will differ among readers. For the moment I want to respect, rather than deconstruct, our individual visions of autonomy, secure that everyone has one, and that some notion of freedom or autonomy would play a part in almost everyone's ethical aspirations. This is so even when we can be sophisticated about the constructed if not mystified quality of our experiences of individual autonomy. As Susan Bordo puts it nicely, paraphrasing Foucault: "[T]he heady experience of feeling powerful or 'in control,' far from being a necessarily accurate reflection of one's social position, is always suspect as itself the product of power relations whose shape may be very different."[3] For the moment, however, let us try to imagine a core case of autonomy. I wish then to contrast three discursive constructions of the body current in American law, all ostensibly employed in order to construct an autonomous body capable of resisting intrusion. These constructions differ greatly in their structure and effect. I invite readers to explore the deeper structure of these discursive bodies and test each against their individual core examples of the kind of body autonomy that is normally desirable.

The three bodies are the body constructed as the property of its owner (the person or self "inside" that body), as analyzed in chapter 3; the body constructed as a privacy interest; and the body constructed as inviolable in the sense of being unavailable for redistribution. I will have much more to say

---

[2] *Homosexuality and Male Bonding in Pre-Nazi Germany: The Youth Movement, the Gay Movement, and Male Bonding before Hitler's Rise. Original Transcripts from "Der Eigene," the First Gay Journal in the World* (Harry Oosterhuis and Hubert Kennedy eds.) (New York: Haworth, 1991).

[3] Susan Bordo, *Unbearable Weight: Feminism, Western Culture, and the Body* 27 (Berkeley: U. Cal. Pr., 1993).

about "private" bodies in this book (chaps. 6–11); some more to say about bodies as property (chap. 5); and some, though far less, about inviolable bodies. Having invited the reader to do without one of these constructions, however, it seemed only fair to begin to raise the question of the competing discursive constructions of the body that law employs *in the service of the same end,* that is, the body autonomous and able to withstand the demands and intrusions of others. Soon enough, we will contrast the discursive practices that construct bodies that are hardly autonomous at all: bodies subject to military drafts, compulsory inoculations, forced medications, imposed invisibility, or exclusion from society on account of their odors or other offense.

Two Alternative Autonomous Bodies: "Natural Constitution" and "Animal Economy"

The Body as Privacy Interest

As everyone knows, the bodies of pregnant American women are constituted as "privacy interests" for purposes of analyzing restrictions on abortion. Imagining one's body as a privacy interest isn't necessarily any less weird than imagining it to be a machine. While the abortion decision, *Roe v. Wade,* is surely one of the more controversial Supreme Court decisions of modern times, the body constructed, as we shall see, is, like women's bodies in our culture generally, significantly available to others.[4]

Much of the rest of this book glosses Roe's construction of the body as a privacy interest or zone. The "private body" is a *right,* conceptualized as *space, weighed* against other interests and therefore not absolute; it is, therefore, public and social. Women lose their bodies, which are metaphorically assumed by states, law, or judges.

Rights are often visualized with spatial metaphors; in *Roe v. Wade,* typically, they are "areas or zones." So already the contrast with the body as property is blurred, because the body as privacy right is always already a kind of area or zone, that is, a piece of property.

Why are rights visualized as spaces? The basic reason, from which the others flow, is that rights are not absolute. They exist on an infinite and perhaps darkling plain, along with innumerable other rights and interests. Because they are conceptualized spatially, they have boundaries and enclose areas. "This right of privacy . . . is *broad enough* to *encompass* a woman's decision whether to terminate her pregnancy." Some rights are broad enough

---

[4] On the difference between male and female bodies in their comparative availability to and accessibility by others, see Colette Guillaumin, "The Constructed Body," in *Reading the Social Body* 55–57 (Catherine B. Burroughs and Jeffrey David Ehrenreich eds.) (Iowa City: U. Ia. Pr., 1993).

to enclose lots of area, like enormous cattle ranches or real-estate developments, and some are as narrow as the strip of sidewalk on which the homeless person lies.

Most importantly, perhaps, these big and little spatial rights may be invaded or intruded upon by others or by the regulatory state itself. "[S]ome state regulation in *areas* protected by that right is appropriate." "Our cases recognize 'the right of the *individual,* married or single, to be free from unwarranted governmental *intrusion* into matters so fundamentally affecting a person as the decision whether to bear or beget a child.' *Eisenstadt v. Baird, supra,* 405 U.S., at 453 ([first] emphasis in original). Our precedents 'have respected the private realm of family life which the state *cannot enter.*' *Prince v. Massachusetts,* 321 U.S. 158, 166 (1944)."[5]

Sometimes rights have mass instead of area. They are characteristically "balanced" or "weighed" against asserted state interests in their diminution.[6]

Indeed, this has been the fate of the right to abortion recognized in *Roe v. Wade.* Most recently, the Supreme Court has permitted states to require counseling on alternatives to abortion, waiting periods, and parental consent for minors (so long as a court may authorize the abortion over parental objections).[7] For present purposes I am neither praising nor criticizing these limitations on *Roe v. Wade,* merely pointing out that the discursive possibility of some such limitations was created precisely by the construction of the pregnant body as a right with mass weighed against other masses, or space with boundaries and invasions. "On the other side of the equation is the interest of the State in the protection of potential life." The mathematical metaphor grates, for an equation is just what it's not, since contested constitutional cases don't end in ties. At the end of the day there will be no equal sign, but rather a greater-than or less-than sign.

"Only where state regulation imposes an undue burden on a woman's ability to make this decision does the power of the State reach into the *heart* of the liberty protected by the Due Process Clause."[8] In this passage, the spatial metaphor joins hands (as it were) with a body metaphor, so that the state, like a vampire, "reach[es] into" liberty, but only sometimes touches the "heart." The state has hands to reach (like the factory in Rebecca Harding Davis), and the liberty protected by the Due Process Clause has a heart, but the pregnant woman involved in the case has, discursively, no body at all.

Rights are thus discursively constructed as projections of the human body,

5 Planned Parenthood of Southeastern Pennsylvania v. Casey, 505 U.S. 833, 851 (1992) (all emphasis supplied except the word "individual").

6 See generally T. Alexander Aleinikoff, "Constitutional Law in the Age of Balancing," 96 *Yale L. J.* 943 (1987).

7 Planned Parenthood, 505 U.S. 833.

8 Id. 874.

like the chairs and other artifacts discussed by Elaine Scarry: they have space, boundaries, borders, weight, and hearts—all the features of physical bodies, and—most importantly—thereby may efface physical bodies.[9] For example, a state law requiring notification of husbands before abortion, though struck down by the Supreme Court in the most recent abortion case, is not conceptualized as an appropriation by the State of Pennsylvania of the *bodies* of Pennsylvania women, or even an "intrusion" by Pennsylvania into those bodies, let alone an appropriation of "women." Rather, the unconstitutional law is an intrusion into a "zone" of liberty or "bodily integrity." Zones of liberty, as we saw in the last passage, have hearts; it is almost a matter of indifference whether women do:

> It is an inescapable biological fact that state regulation with respect to the child a woman is carrying will have a far greater impact on the mother's liberty than on the father's. The effect of state regulation on a woman's protected liberty is doubly deserving of scrutiny in such a case, as the State has touched not only upon the private sphere of the family but upon the very bodily integrity of the pregnant woman.[10]

This is about as embodied as subjects ever become in constitutional law, so I suppose I should praise this passage. But would it have killed them to say "touched . . . upon the body" as opposed to "touched . . . upon the bodily integrity"? How can it be that the state, an abstract entity, can "touch," something that normally only a body can do, while women's bodies are not "touched," but only their "bodily integrity"? The discourse of rights constructs a state that, like the ironworks in Rebecca Harding Davis's story discussed in chapter 2, takes on human attributes while denying humanity to genuine people.

The Supreme Court's most recent abortion case contains a dazzling oscillation between the body of the pregnant woman constructed as a private realm and that body constructed as a metaphor for society. When that body is "private," the imagery is intensely sexual. As we have seen, the woman's body becomes a right that is figured as a realm or zone that law or the state, coded perhaps as male, aggressive, and thrusting, seeks to "enter" or "intru[de]" and possess, a sort of female body.[11]

Women lose their bodies, which become rights or zones. At the same time, law acquires a metaphorical body. "The inescapable fact is that adjudication of substantive due process claims may call upon the Court in interpreting the

[9] Elaine Scarry, *The Body in Pain: The Making and Unmaking of the World* 278–328 (New York: Oxford U. Pr., 1985).

[10] Planned Parenthood, 505 U.S. at 896.

[11] Id. at 851. "[A]t a later point in fetal development the State's interest in life has sufficient *force* so that the right of the woman to terminate the pregnancy can be restricted." Id.

Constitution to exercise that same capacity which by tradition courts always have exercised: reasoned judgment. Its *boundaries* are not susceptible of expression as a simple rule. That does not mean we are free to invalidate state policy choices with which we disagree; yet neither does it permit us to *shrink* from the duties of our office." The "boundaries" of the woman's body, the rule, and reasoned judgment all come into focus. Lesser men than the Court might "shrink" at the task, but not this Court, which remains erect as it defines all those "boundaries."[12] The Court's drawing the boundaries, of the woman and the law, is legitimate precisely because the judges of the Court are themselves embodied, not machines. "See also *Rochin v. California, supra,* 342 U.S., at 171–172 (Frankfurter, J., writing for the Court) ('To believe that this judicial exercise of judgment could be avoided by freezing "due process of law" at some fixed stage of time or thought is to suggest that the most important aspect of constitutional adjudication is a function for inanimate machines and not for judges')."[13]

Thus the discursive private body, at least in our first glimpse of it, is every bit as complex as the discursive property body, combining multiple and somewhat self-deconstructing images. The private body is constructed as a refuge from social demands, but of course the construction itself is a social and public act. Moreover, the refuge is not really the body, but the body as constitutional right, a kind of discursive body, what Henry Fielding in the eighteenth century called the "Natural Constitution," and that body is as often a metaphor for society, for law, and for judicial wisdom and intellectual labor, as it is for the exclusion of these potential intruders.[14]

This self-deconstruction, this private body that simultaneously represents the public and private, follows from any claim of a constitutional right in the body. The doctrine of "privacy" reinforces this internal self-deconstruction of the doctrine, not its fortitude as a bastion of individual resistance to others. As we have seen, abortion rights are sometimes characterized as privacy rights,

[12] Id. 849 (emphasis supplied).

[13] Id. 850. As we saw in chapter 2, in his earlier career as an advocate for labor legislation in the Supreme Court Felix Frankfurter had helped efface any difference between machines and humans by justifying labor legislation in the name of a "science" of fatigue. As a judge, however, Frankfurter could more easily recapture the distinction between men and machines, in their capacity to reason. Perhaps the distinction was between elite men, who reasoned, and working-class people, who remained machines.

[14] Henry Fielding, *An Enquiry into the causes of the late increase of Robbers and Related Writings* 65 (Malvin R. Zirker ed.) (Oxford: Clarendon, 1988) [1751]. The title essay is a sort of anthology of comparisons between the "body" and the "body politic": both are diseased, both need physicians, both must be understood to include habits and humors, both contain bad habits that cannot be eradicated but must be palliated, and so on. Fielding uses the term "Natural Constitution" to refer to "the several Members of the Body, the animal Oeconomy, with the Humours and Habit."

and there has been much criticism of this particular formulation from both the Right[15] and the Left.[16] I do not however think the word privacy adds anything to the structure described above, in which rights, modeled on bodies, stand in for bodies. The possibility of "balancing" and "compelling interests" exists in normal American rights discourse, as we shall see in later chapters, whether the individual right is denominated one of liberty, privacy, or property. For example, some legal scholars have called for a "right to bodily autonomy" to replace the "privacy" right of *Roe v. Wade*.[17] While this may or may not be preferable, it would not, under American constitutional law, exclude limitations on that right, of a kind already recognized. Indeed the Court, in its most recent abortion opinion, posits just such a right to "bodily integrity"[18] and, elsewhere, "physical autonomy."[19]

These commonplaces may best be appreciated by contrasting the competing discourse of the body that we have been analyzing: the body as property. It is sometimes suggested that abortion rights, rather than reflecting a privacy interest that may be vague or of uncertain constitutional location, might rest rather on a woman's ownership of her body.[20] For example, during the vice-presidential debates in the 1992 presidential election, Admiral James B. Stockdale, candidate on Ross Perot's independent ticket, supported abortion rights by saying: "I believe that a woman owns her body and what she does with it is her own business, period."[21] Is this an accurate statement about American law? We saw in chapter 3 that it is far from clear that her body is her property: her blood is, her spleen isn't, and her kidneys are up for grabs.

What would abortion regulation look like if we asked whether a woman's body is her property? It is hard to see that it would look any different than it does now. John Moore's spleen is not his property, not because it wasn't "his" (in some sense involving the correct use of English possessive adjectives), but

[15] Robert H. Bork, *The Tempting of America: The Political Seduction of the Law* (New York: Free Pr., 1990).

[16] Rosalind Pollack Petchesky, "Reproductive Freedom: Beyond a Woman's Right to Choose," 5 *Signs* 661 (1980).

[17] See, e.g., Drucilla Cornell, *The Imaginary Domain: Abortion, Pornography, and Sexual Harassment* (New York: Routledge, 1995); Christyne L. Neff, "Woman, Womb, and Bodily Integrity," 3 *Yale J. L. & Feminism* 327 (1991).

[18] Planned Parenthood, 505 U.S. at 849. ("It is settled now, as it was when the Court heard arguments in *Roe v. Wade,* that the Constitution places limits on a State's right to interfere with a person's most basic decisions about family and parenthood, as well as *bodily integrity*"(citations omitted).

[19] Id.

[20] See, e.g., Susan E. Looper-Friedman, "Keep Your Laws Off My Body": Abortion Regulation and the Takings Clause, 29 *N. Eng. L. Rev.* 253 (1995). A recent invocation to women to conceptualize their bodies as "inviolable," under analogy to a castle or sanctuary, is Linda C. McClain, "Inviolability and Privacy: The Castle, the Sanctuary, and the Body," 7 *Yale J. L. & Humanities* 195 (1995).

[21] Transcript of the Vice Presidential Debate (Part II), *Washington Post,* Oct. 14, 1992, p. A17.

because it hasn't clearly been recognized as property until now and, all things considered, the court thought things would be better if the spleen weren't property.

Specifically, the grammar of a property claim is that it grants autonomy to the holder by privileging him or her to ignore the needs of others. Thus John Moore was not permitted the kind of property that would have permitted him to "threaten with disabling civil liability innocent parties who are engaged in socially useful activities."[22] It would not be a particularly challenging drafting exercise to write an opinion similarly denying a pregnant woman property in her body wherever this carried with it a threat to "innocent parties," and no reason to think this category, if developed in constitutional law, would turn out to be anything but what the Court is now pleased to call "the State's profound interest in potential life."[23]

Moreover, calling Jane Roe's body property would provide comparatively little autonomy if that concept carried with it such concepts as land-use planning, zoning, easements, or condemnation for public use. We might imagine that a state law that required a woman, who wanted to abort, to carry instead a child to term, could be figured discursively as a "taking" of her body, her property. But so what, if the state could still take that body, required only to pay her some kind of fair market value of the property taken, or perhaps none at all if the "taking" were not for a "public use."[24]

This glimpse at two significant legal decisions on abortion is obviously not a comprehensive introduction to the law of abortions but has been done to make two points about law's discursive construction of the body.

First, we have already seen how easily legal analysis proceeds by constructing two conflicting bodies, the property/commodity/machine body and the sacred private body, and then plucking one or another construction. Readers may have developed a haunting sense that these were two sides of the same coin, as indeed they are, for many purposes. Both efface the physical body and refigure it as an abstraction. Each is profoundly complex, both a symbol of autonomy and a very map of domination, and thus either can be made to symbolize any of a great range of regulation of (say) abortion. Each normalizes the body in an act of Foucauldian regulation, inscribing it in the normal regulatory mechanisms of society. It is for this reason that the novelist and London magistrate Henry Fielding, in the passage referred to above, may in the same thought construct the body, in each case as a self-conscious metaphor, as both the "animal economy" and the "natural constitution":

22 Moore v. Regents, 793 P.2d 479, 493 (Cal. 1990).

23 Planned Parenthood, 505 U.S. at 878.

24 Those interested in an introduction to the difficult corner of American constitutional law dealing with taking of private property for public use might start with Jed Rubenfeld, "Usings," 102 *Yale L. J.* 1077 (1993).

the several members of the body, the animal economy, with the humors and habit, compose that which is called the natural constitution.[25]

Perhaps the only difference between the property and privacy formulations is that property inscribes the body into normal economic or market life and thus represents (I believe) what Foucault calls "disciplinary" power, while privacy inscribes the body into juridical personhood as a site or bearer of abstract political rights, what Foucault calls "sovereignty." Our occasional indecision between these two discursive formations: Is Margaret Green a container or sacred? Is John Moore's spleen property or sacred? Do abortion rights stem from a right to privacy or property in the body?—may now be identified as a symptom of what Foucault correctly described as our inability to criticize the realm of economic regulation except in the language of abstract political right, our inability to criticize political right except in the abstract language of economics and markets.[26]

Second, we have seen that some people who oppose figuring bodies as property or commodities do so because they fear that this discursive construction will eat up others and deny space for experiences of altruism or dignity or other human nonmarket interaction that they would like to spare. Some who are drawn to this argument may fear, however, that abandoning property conceptions of the body may hurt the weak by removing an important discursive support for conceptions of individual autonomy that they think are worth saving. The language of abortion rights shows that bodily property is but one figure of speech used to construct discursively autonomy from the use of others. Law has other languages of bodily autonomy. If law refuses to commodify bodies or make them property, we cannot be certain of all the discursive ramifications. There is no reason to think, however, that abortion rights as we know them would necessarily be affected.

The Body as Inviolability

The strongest concept of body autonomy known to American law constitutes the body neither as privacy right nor as property, at least, not in so many words. Body parts are not available for distribution to others, no matter how needy those others are, how little the donor needs the part. Income and property may be taxed, but body parts may not. Nor has anyone else a claim on our body parts.

Consider the recent case of *Curran v. Bosze*.[27] The father of a boy dying of leukemia asked the mother of three-year-old twins whom he had fathered,

---

[25] Fielding, *Enquiry.*

[26] Michel Foucault, *Power/Knowledge: Selected Interviews and Other Writings, 1972–1977* 107–8 (New York: Pantheon, 1980).

[27] 41 Ill.2d 473, 153 Ill.Dec. 213, 566 NE.2d 1319 (1990).

half-siblings to the boy, to consent to test the twins for bone marrow compatibility and, if the tests were encouraging, to donate some of their bone marrow to their half-brother. Without a transplant, the older boy would die. All other relatives of the boy had been tested and found incompatible. Bone marrow donation is dangerous only because of the risks involved in general anesthesia. While the prognosis for a successful transplant from half-siblings was not good (estimates for success at trial ranged from five to twenty percent), it was the only possibility that offered any hope of saving the older boy's life.

All legal analyses of the case start from the unquestioned idea that, had the twins been adults, they would have been entirely free to refuse to donate bone marrow to their half brother.[28] The principle that body products need not be shared with others is so fundamental that it is not even discussed in the opinion. Indeed, if your adult sibling or half-sibling simply refuses to share bone marrow with you, there is normally simply no point in suing.

The litigated issue in *Bosze* was rather, the twins being minors, whether their mother's refusal to permit the bone marrow testing should be final, or whether the court should substitute its judgment.[29] The court held that it could substitute its judgment only in the best interests of the children, that is, the three-year-old twins. The mother's refusal was not a threat to those children's interests. As the court saw it, the only advantage a bone marrow donor gains is psychological, benefits that occur only "when there is an existing relationship between a healthy child and his or her ill sister or brother" and not "personal, individual altruism in an abstract theoretical sense."[30] The mother's refusal to permit testing was therefore final; the older boy died of leukemia.

This strong result did not once constitute the twins' bodies as property, owned either by themselves or their mother. The trope of the body as property does not appear once in the opinion. Rather, the court reached its strong rule,

[28] See, e.g., McFall v. Shimp, Pa. County Ct., Allegheny County, No. 78-17711, July 16, 1978, summarized in Russell Scott, *The Body as Property* 127–36 (New York: Viking, 1981), refusing to order an unwilling bone marrow donation. A case sometimes cited as a contrary holding is not. Strunk v. Strunk, 445 SW.2d 145, 35 ALR3d 683 (Ky.App. 1969) was for practical purposes a case of voluntary consent to donation, approved by an equity court. The donor was severely retarded, but his parents, his court-appointed guardian, and the donor himself, as nearly as anyone could tell, all favored the donation.

[29] For discussion of these issues in the historic context of children's rights, see Rachel M. Dufault (student author), "Bone Marrow Donations by Children: Rethinking the Legal Framework in Light of Curran v. Bosze," 24 *Conn. L. Rev.* 211 (1991).

[30] 566 NE.2d at 1343. Compare Richard Titmuss, *The Gift Relationship: From Human Blood to Social Policy* 195–246 (New York: Pantheon, 1971), on the psychic, social, and economic benefits of altruism toward strangers. See also the study comparing voluntary organ donors with a control group of nondonors, and finding the donors higher in self-esteem and lower in depressive effect. Roberta G. Simmons, "Long-Term Reactions of Renal Recipients and Donors," in *Psychonephrology 2: Psychological Problems in Kidney Failure and Their Treatment* 275 (Norman B. Levy ed.) (New York: Plenum, 1983).

of autonomy from forced distribution, by constituting their bodies as "the foundation of self-determination and inviolability of the person."[31]

This is such a strong category of property, albeit a property without the name, that it is no wonder that people seeking a firm ethical foundation for the institution of private property, such as Robert Nozick, have returned to John Locke's argument that all property stems by analogy from our ownership of our bodies. If *Curran v. Bosze* did not exist, Robert Nozick would surely have had to invent it, for bone marrow need not be shared with others even if they will die without it, I have plenty more, and I may share it with only minimal discomfort, and no monetary cost, to me.

It is hard to say much about the discursive construction of this "inviolable" body of James and Allison Curran, however, since, remarkably, the inviolable body is constructed largely in silence, as an "of course," taken-for-granted feature of bodies. The court spends no time on whether the body is property, or on deriving privacy interests, or on the sacred body. There is no discussion of any possible limitations on this construction. There is no equivalent to *Roe v. Wade,* which rejected as "unpersuasive" any claim of "an unlimited right to do with one's body as one pleases," since "a State may properly assert important interests in safeguarding health, in maintaining medical standards, and in protecting potential life."[32] This is a thought which might well have disrupted the "inviolability" cadences of the *Curran* decision had it been dropped therein. But what was "unpersuasive" in *Roe v. Wade* was apparently self-evident in *Curran v. Bosze.*

Indeed, juxtaposing *Roe v. Wade* and *Curran v. Bosze* immediately raises the question of the relationship between the inviolable body of James and Allison Curran, and the private body of a woman carrying a viable fetus, who may be denied access to abortion and required to carry the fetus to term.[33] Both lines of cases conceptualize the person refusing to share the body ("her"

---

[31] 566 NE.2d at 1326 (quoting In re Estate of Longeway, 133 Ill.2d 33, 49, 139 Ill.Dec. 780, 549 NE.2d 292 (1989).

[32] Roe v. Wade, 410 U.S. 113, 154 (1973).

[33] Judith Jarvis Thomson, "A Defense of Abortion," 1 *Phil. & Pub. Aff.* 47 (1971). Susan Bordo, "Are Mothers Persons? Reproductive Rights and the Politics of Subject-ivity," in *Unbearable Weight* 71–97, makes a similar argument covering not only access to abortion but the line of cases involving forced cesarean deliveries over the objection of the pregnant woman, such as In re A.C., 573 A.2d 1235 (D.C. 1990) and Jefferson v. Griffin Spalding County Hospital Authority, 274 SE.2d 457 (Ga. 1981). The extensive law review literature includes Joel Jay Finer, "Toward Guidelines for Compelling Cesarean Surgery: Of Rights, Responsibility, and Decisional Authority," 76 *Minn. L. Rev.* 239 (1991) (supporting court-compelled cesarean surgery where necessary for mother's health or where she lacks decisional maturity); Goldberg, "Medical Choices during Pregnancy: Whose Decision Is It Anyway?" 41 *Rut. L. Rev.* 591 (1989); Neff, "Woman, Womb,"; Lawrence J. Nelson, Brian P. Buggy, and Carol Weil, "Forced Medical Treatment of Pregnant Women: Compelling Each to Live as Seems Good to the Rest," 37 *Hast. L. J.* 703 (1986); Nancy Rhoden, "The Judge in the Delivery Room: The Emergence of Court-Ordered Caesarians," 74 *Cal. L. Rev.* 1951 (1986).

body) as asserting a liberty or privacy or "inviolability" "interest" which is balanced against "interests" in others to life. The pregnant woman must share her body; the potential bone marrow donor need not. What is the difference between them?

Is it the claim or interest asserted by the prospective "user" of or "intruder" into the body? In the bone marrow cases, the person asserting (unsuccessfully) the right to the bone marrow of another is a legal person asserting his own interest in life; in the abortion cases, the viable fetus's "interests" in life are not asserted by the fetus, which is not a legal person, but by the state, pursuing its claimed interest in fetal life. If this distinction affects the result, it should give women greater power to refuse pregnancy than Allison and James Curran have generally to refuse bone marrow to Jean-Pierre Bosze, who would ultimately die without it, since how can the claims to life of a viable fetus, asserted derivatively through the state, be greater than the claim to life of the late Jean-Pierre Bosze? (The report in *Curran v. Bosze* does not reveal any briefs filed amicus curiae by any of the self-styled "right-to-life" organizations).

Is this difference rather in the nature of the use of the body being imposed? Is testing for bone marrow compatibility more intrusive than requiring an unwilling mother to carry a fetus to term? The *Curran* court stated: "The primary risk to a bone marrow donor is the risk associated with undergoing general anesthesia. The risk of a life-threatening complication occurring from undergoing general anesthesia is 1 in 10,000. [The anesthesiologist called as an expert by Nancy Curran, the defendant resisting bone marrow testing, had actually testified that the risk of death "would be in the range of one to ten thousand to one in one hundred thousand, and that risk admittedly is very low"; the court, as lawyers so often do, selected the expert with which it agreed and only one end of his range of estimates]. As noted by the circuit court, the risks associated with general anesthesia include, but are not limited to, 'brain damage as a result of oxygen deprivation, stroke, cardiac arrest and death.'"[34] The risks from pregnancy are comparable. The anesthesiologist called by Nancy Curran testified that anesthesia "has transient risks, including nausea and vomiting, headaches, sore throat and drowsiness."[35] This does not distinguish pregnancy, to put it mildly. Opposition to autonomy and power for women seems the only possible explanation for the different results.

In fact, there is a sense in which the abortion cases and *Curran* are consistent at an ideological level. Both construct an image of the good mother who protects her children. That is why a pregnant woman may not abort a viable fetus, and why no court can substitute its judgment for Nancy Curran's when she refuses to let her twins be tested for bone marrow compatibility. The unwillingly pregnant woman is legally responsible for a fetus that is "hers"

---

[34] 566 NE.2d at 1344.
[35] 566 NE.2d at 1337.

(possessive adjective). But neither Nancy Curran, nor James nor Allison Curran, is in any way responsible for Jean-Pierre Bosze.

This intuition may be tested by imagining the following hypothetical variant of *Curran v. Bosze*. Suppose, as in the actual case, that the potential donor is a minor child whose mother is her custodial parent and who has always lived apart from the potential recipient. Suppose, however, that the recipient is the biological offspring of that mother, adult and living apart. Are we so sure that the court would defer to this mother's refusal to permit testing that might save the life of "her own" child? Or do we think the court might "substitute its judgment"? My students who pressed this hypothetical on me are convinced this second mother would lose; I think it possible but lack firm intuition. If my students are right, the agenda of constructing and enforcing "being a good mother" outweighs any body constructions, or privacy or autonomy concerns, in these cases.

Of course it does not follow that advocates for abortion rights should at once attempt to establish access to abortion by constructing the body of a pregnant woman as "inviolable" in the sense of *Curran v. Bosze*. Many feminists dislike conceptualizing abortion as either the pregnant woman's "privacy" or "bodily autonomy," finding these isolating, privatizing, and untrue to the actual emotional resonance of the decision to abort, which for most women is said to be relational and the application of an ethic of care.[36] Many legal scholars have advanced alternative defenses of abortion rights recently that do not rest on the "privacy" rights of the mother.[37] I do not quarrel with this analysis but wish to point out the public or social dimension to *any* construction of the body employed to establish the right to an abortion, whether privacy, property, inviolability, or relational. The figurative language may be "privatizing," but it is also inevitably social, for in each case social institutions construct the body that society seems to require. One could as well defend

[36] Petchesky, "Reproductive Freedom," 661; Carol Gilligan, *In a Different Voice* (Cambridge: Harv. U. Pr., 1983); Robin West, "Jurisprudence and Gender," 55 *U. Chi. L. Rev.* 1, 30–36 (1988); Robert D. Goldstein, *Mother-Love and Abortion: A Legal Interpretation* (Berkeley: U. Cal. Pr., 1988).

[37] For defenses of the right to abortion that do not invoke the woman's body as property or "privacy," see Petchesky, "Reproductive Freedom" 661 (1980); Catharine A. MacKinnon, *Toward a Feminist Theory of the State* 184–94 (Cambridge.: Harvard U. Pr., 1989) (defense of abortion rights as necessary to redress male domination of women); Guido Calabresi, *Ideals, Beliefs, Attitudes, and the Law: Private Law Perspectives on a Public Law Problem* 99–114 (Syracuse: Syr. U. Pr., 1985) (abortion rights as implementing value of equality); Ronald Dworkin, *Life's Dominion: An Argument about Abortion, Euthanasia, and Individual Freedom* 160–66 (New York: Knopf, 1993) (abortion rights as free exercise of religion); Cass Sunstein, *The Partial Constitution* (Cambridge: Harv. U. Pr., 1993) (equality); Reva Siegel, "Reasoning from the Body: A Historical Perspective on Abortion Regulation and Questions of Equal Protection," 44 *Stan. L. Rev.* 261 (1992) (equal protection).

abortion rights as a way of facilitating women's participation in the public sphere.[38]

WHY CONSTRUCTING THE BODY OR BODY PARTS AS PROPERTY IS NOT A GOOD WAY TO THINK ABOUT QUESTIONS OF AUTONOMY FROM THE DEMANDS OF OTHERS

From John Locke to *die Gemeinschaft der Eigenen* to some contemporary advocates of access to abortion stretches a curious tradition of arguing for the freedom of the individual to resist certain social or private regulation because of the supposed fact that that individual owns his or her body. I can bring us no freedom from the continuing need to argue about the fairness, justice, and wisdom of various demands by others on individuals, various resistances by individuals to those demands. These arguments are the raw stuff of law and political theory, and no verbal formulation will give us respite from them.

I do believe I have shown that the conception of the body as property contributes nothing at all to these arguments. Let me sum up the major points I have been making over the last two chapters.

First, the autonomy that individuals gain from owning their bodies can be achieved only when authoritative legal institutions recognize such property, so freedom from social demands is illusory, and we are simply arguing about which social demands, and who decides. This is only partly the Nietzschean point about every morality being the product of language. It is also a particular point about legal and political institutions, which deploy various competing discourses to construct bodies that are either open to others or closed to others, and are not required as institutions or individuals to reconcile these discordant constructions. Moreover, these problematic cases of body definition may at times be shaped by social needs and concerns, which seem to have real weight in the decisions, and hardly at all by strong conceptions of the psychological or ethical needs of individuals, about which we are strongly divided and which do not figure in the opinions except as makeweight slogans.

Second, and purely pragmatically, property is simply not that magic a word in American courts. The strongest bodily autonomy known to law, freedom from compulsory donation of bone marrow (or blood or other body parts) does not employ the term at all.

Third, the philosophers do not employ property in a way that makes it likely that it would become a magic word in American courts. For an example of the unhelpfulness of the property metaphor, consider the debate mentioned above among philosophers of distributive justice over what sorts of property might be available for public distribution. Nozick argued that people, even political

---

[38] Cf. Kristin Luker, *Abortion and the Politics of Motherhood* (Berkeley: U. Cal. Pr., 1984).

egalitarians who believe in redistribution from the rich to the poor, do not intuitively regard their eyes and bone marrow as available for redistribution. Nozick argued that both money and eyes are property and challenged redistributionists to defend their distinction. This challenge turned out not to be particularly difficult to defeat. Some defended, or did not deny, self-ownership but denied the analogy to other property.[39] Presumably others might accept the analogy and would permit socialization of scarce body parts.[40]

What has happened here? Constituting the body as property turns out to be irrelevant to solving the distributional problem. The distributional problem is difficult, but the property argument simply layers confusion on top of it. Even if we could decide whether the body is property, and then whether or not it is the "same kind" of property as money, we have not solved the problem of distributive justice.

Fourth, since law could and does construct only some parts of the body as property, it would and does not follow from a general concept of property in the body that women would control their reproduction. Catharine MacKinnon has with characteristic brilliance made just this criticism of any attempt to base reproductive rights on a slogan such as "control of the body" or "laws off my body."

> Even before *Roe v. Wade,* arguments for abortion under the rubric of feminism have rested upon the right to control one's own body, gender neutral. This argument has been appealing for the same reasons it is inadequate: socially, women's bodies have not been theirs; women have not controlled their meanings and destinies. Feminists have tried to assert that control without risking pursuit of the idea that something more than women's bodies might be at stake, something closer to a net of relations in which women are gendered and unequal.[41]

Fifth, a really firm basis for dividing public from private is simply too much to ask from a poor figure of speech. Just how far we as a culture want to go with the body-as-property is often a difficult problem that the figure itself cannot answer. If I am right in this book, however, discursive figurations of the human body are characteristically extremely fragile and self-

[39] Stephen Munzer, *A Theory of Property* 44–58 (Cambridge: Camb. U. Pr., 1991) (some, but not all, body rights are property rights); Margaret Jane Radin, *Contested Commodities* 102–53 (Cambridge: Harv. U. Pr., 1996) (developing theory of "incomplete commodification" to explain prostitution and "market-inalienability" to explain restrictions on sale of babies or surrogate mothering, while generally accepting sale of property), id. 97 (sale of human organs as potential example of incomplete commodification); G. A. Cohen, *Self-ownership, Freedom, and Equality* (Cambridge: Camb. U. Pr., 1995) (rejecting self-ownership *and* lotteries for eyes; "our resistance to a lottery for natural eyes shows not belief in self-ownership but hostility to severe interference in someone's life"); Sara Ann Ketchum, "The Moral Status of the Bodies of Persons," 10 *Soc. Theory & Prac.* 25 (1984).

[40] No articles have been located actually advocating this.

[41] MacKinnon, *Toward a Feminist Theory* 189.

deconstructing, since they mediate a contradiction: the extent to which we experience our bodies as private, and the extent to which we experience them as social. Since this really is a contradiction, the figure we select to grasp the body is never more than a truce line drawn in the sand. To ask it to function in a different legal context is to ask a line in the sand to be a castle. The breakdown of our discourse is not the weakness of the figure of speech but our genuine social confusion about the legitimate claims of the individual and the collective.

All of these deficiencies—abstraction, self-contradiction, malleability, empowering social regulators—are shared by property constructions with other discursive constructions of the body. Property constructions, as we have seen, have several distinctive and undesirable features.

The biggest weakness of the discourse of property as a defense of human autonomy is the history of making the body the property of someone other than the person inside it. Figures of speech can't determine their own usage, of course, but there must be some relationship between law's continuing readiness to treat the body as the property of its owner and law's former readiness to take the next step and treat that property as capable of ownership by another. For centuries at common law, human beings were bought and sold as slaves. Body commodification or property is not a metaphor but a performative: the slave's body really was a commodity and treated as such at law.[42] The commodification rationalizes, naturalizes, disguises what in other discourse might be analyzed as domination. While human slavery is no longer a feature of common law, it is interesting that such fundamental aspects of common law as property and contract that permitted human slavery have never been rethought for that reason—why doesn't every teacher of contracts and property in America recognize this appalling moral rot at the center of the very subjects normally required of first-year law students and presented as bastions of human freedom?[43] Moreover, continuities between the law of slavery and contemporary law are not hard to find.[44]

Finally, as I have discussed at length, the discursive construction of property directs our attention from the subjective to the objective, the personal to

[42] Dorothy Roberts made me see this.

[43] A number of classic teaching cases in contracts concern property in slaves, e.g., Boone v. Eyre, 1 H&P 273, 126 Eng.Rep. 160(a) (King's Bench 1777) (Mansfield, C.J.) (independent covenants), discussed in, e.g., E. Allan Farnsworth and William F. Young, *Cases and Materials on Contracts* 708 (5th ed.) (Westbury, N.Y.: Foundation, 1995). For an insightful analysis of the lessons taught by these cases and the phenomenology of participating in such class discussions, from the point of view of an African-American scholar, see Kimberlé Williams Crenshaw, "Foreword: Toward a Race-Conscious Pedagogy in Legal Education," 11 *Natl. Black L. J.* 1, 1–6 (1988–89).

[44] On continuities between the attitudes of a system of slave law and contemporary law, not limited to the machine metaphor, see Patricia J. Williams, *The Alchemy of Race and Rights* 154–65, 216–30 (Cambridge: Harvard U. Pr., 1990).

the abstract, the emotional to the cold, and thereby inscribes the bearer into the normal regulatory apparatus of a consumer society, naturalizing domination as contract or business. It is these contemporary manifestations of the commodified body that I wish to address next, examining employer domination of the bodies of employees.

Chapter 5

REPRODUCTIVE CAPACITY: UNSALABLE,
COMMODIFIED, COMPENSABLE

CAN PEOPLE legally sell their capacity to reproduce? In the famous *Baby M* case, the court, in refusing to enforce a contract in which a "surrogate" mother agreed to become impregnated and then give up the child, described the contract disparagingly as "the purchase of a woman's procreative capacity."[1] There is, however, no general barrier in American law to the sale of one's reproductive capacity. Employers may require that employees sterilize themselves before work that exposes them to dangerous toxins, and there does not appear to be any doctrine of labor or civil rights law that prevents such contracts. This absence is a telling demonstration of how the commodified body may efface completely the autonomous body, supposedly able to resist the intrusions of others.

Reproductive capacity, interestingly, is also constructed in a third way, besides being unsalable *(Baby M)* and a commodity (employment contracts to sterilize). If an accident destroys a married person's capacity to engage in sexual relations, the spouse may be compensated for loss of "consortium." It would be possible to see the doctrine of consortium as another example of body commodification (as we argued in chapter 3 was true of damages for pain and suffering). We shall see, however, that the discourse of consortium is quite different from the discourse of machine bodies and property bodies. In a real alternative to the bodies of law we have discussed so far, we shall meet the *narrated* body: the highly visualized object of empathy. In many ways, the body of the victim in a consortium case will be a prototype for the body of law that should be constructed much more frequently.

STERILIZATION OF EMPLOYEES: REPRODUCTIVE CAPACITY AS A COMMODITY

The assumption that absolutely everything is for sale, all the time, including one's reproductive capacity, underlies a remarkable recent victory in the Supreme Court for women's rights and sexual equality. The Johnson Controls Company, a manufacturer of batteries, adopted a "fetal protection policy" that excluded "women who are pregnant or who are capable of bearing children" from jobs involving exposure to lead. The policy defined "women . . . capable of bearing children" as "[a]ll women except those whose inability to bear

[1] In re Baby M, 537 A.2d 1227, 1248 (N.J. 1988).

children is medically documented." Some women chose to become sterilized in order to avoid losing their jobs; others accepted transfers to other positions at lower pay. The Supreme Court held that the company's policy violated Title VII of the Civil Rights Act of 1964, which prohibits sex discrimination in employment.[2]

The case raises many important issues of discrimination law that I shall not deal with.[3] Nor does the case belong here because of the discursive construction of the bodies of the affected women, who are largely absent from the opinion. Three individual plaintiffs are mentioned by name and characterized briefly, but then not heard from again in the course of the opinion:

> Among the individual plaintiffs were petitioners Mary Craig, who had chosen to be sterilized in order to avoid losing her job, Elsie Nason, a 50-year-old divorcee, who had suffered a loss in compensation when she was transferred out of a job where she was exposed to lead, and Donald Penney, who had been denied a request for a leave of absence for the purpose of lowering his lead level because he intended to become a father.[4]

There is no further representation of these people, their bodies, hopes, fears, desires, experiences. As used here, they function, like many "individual" plaintiffs in class litigation, on the model of individuals seen using products in television commercials, with whom they share an economical, laconic, stereotyped characterization. For legal purposes, they display or represent "individual" injuries thought necessary for litigation, but without genuine individual idiosyncrasies that would only distract from the legal issues. The techniques of establishing character familiar from television advertising thus commend themselves to counsel and courts.

Instead, I raise *Johnson Controls* to show how all our talk of the integrity of the body, its resistance to intrusion, and the privacy of decisions on reproduction, may vanish if sterilization is treated as a kind of contract, fertility as a kind of commodity. For *Johnson Controls* assumes throughout that, apart from the discrimination, there is nothing remarkable—no one remarks on it—about an employer purchasing its employees' reproductive capacity.

The *Johnson Controls* opinion does not have much detail about just how the company induced sterilization or how it paid for it. In a similar case a few years ago, involving American Cyanamide, the plant director of industrial relations met with small groups of female employees to explain the company's decision not to let any women between the ages of sixteen and fifty work in

---

[2] International Union, United Automobile Workers v. Johnson Controls, Inc., 499 U.S. 187 (1991).

[3] Law review commentary includes Mary Becker, "Reproductive Hazards after Johnson Controls," 31 *Hous. L. Rev.* 43 (1994); Samuel Issacharoff and Elyse Rosenblum, "Women and the Workplace: Accommodating the Demands of Pregnancy," 94 *Colum. L. Rev.* 2154 (1994).

[4] 499 U.S. at 192.

the pigments plant unless they sterilized themselves. "A company doctor and nurse accompanied [the director] to these meetings and addressed the women. They explained to the women that such 'buttonhole surgery' was simple and that it could be obtained locally in several places. The women were also told that the company's medical insurance would pay for the procedure, and that sick leave would be provided to those undergoing the surgery. [The director of industrial relations] told the women that once the fetus protection policy was fully implemented the plant would have only about seven jobs for fertile women in the entire facility."[5] It is hardly necessary to point out how "buttonhole surgery" constructs a legal body as a sort of domestic sewing chore.

Johnson Controls holds that subjecting only female employees to these contracts violates the Civil Rights Act. But what if an employer announced that *all* employees, of any sex, would have to sterilize themselves before working in a battery factory? I can think of no doctrine of employment law, civil rights law, or contract law that would prevent an employer from imposing such a requirement. An employee who promises to become sterilized under such a sex-neutral policy and then breaches that promise could be fired. (The employer would be unable to get an injunction ordering the employee to become sterilized or damages for breach of the promise, but this reflects the sense that the employer is not damaged if another, sterile, employee can be found to do the work. A legal concept of body integrity would not be part of the case).

An employee, fired for refusing to sterilize him- or herself, can bring no suit to recover the lost job. Employees can normally be fired for no reason at all. There is no public policy favoring fertility or preventing an employer from a sex-neutral job requirement of sterility. Since there is no discrimination, the civil rights laws have not been violated.

We also know that employers' sterilization policies present no issues under the Occupational Safety and Health Act. Or at least that is what the Occupational Safety and Health Review Commission held in the case mentioned before, in which five women employed at an American Cyanamide plant had sterilized themselves in order to keep their jobs. The commission held that the women were sterilized because of an employer "policy," and employer policies were not "hazards" covered by the Occupational Safety and Health Act. (It was not "economically feasible" for American Cyanamide to reduce the levels of lead in the air, and there would have been some risk to fetuses at any technologically feasible level of ambient lead.) A reviewing court of appeals backed up the commission.[6] In short, in the sterilization cases, reproductive capacity is a pure commodity, bought by employers, sold by employees, and extinguished.

[5] Oil, Chemical, and Atomic Workers Int. U. v. American Cyanamid Co., 741 F.2d 444 (D.C. Cir. 1984).

[6] Oil, Chemical, and Atomic Workers, 741 F.2d 444 (Bork, J.).

CONSORTIUM: NARRATED BODIES

When an accident destroys the sexual capacity of a married person, the tort-feasor may have to pay the spouse damages for "loss of consortium." That action originated in a husband's action for loss of his wife's economically valuable household services, and it would be possible to see its continued development as another example of the commodification of reproductive capacity, in line with the sterilization cases and contrary to the dictum in *Baby M*. Examination of the most famous modern consortium case, however, reveals quite a different construction of the body.

The bodies of Richard and Mary Anne Rodriguez are as well known as any in the consortium cases. Their case was the one in which California first let wives sue for loss of consortium; the opinion is rather ostentatiously overwritten, perhaps to make it into the casebooks.

On May 24, 1969, Richard and Mary Anne Rodriguez were married. Both were gainfully employed. In their leisure time they participated in a variety of social and recreational activities. They were saving for the time when they could buy their own home. They wanted children, and planned to raise a large family.

Only 16 months after their marriage, however, their young lives were shattered by a grave accident. While at work, Richard was struck on the head by a falling pipe weighing over 600 pounds. The blow caused severe spinal cord damage which has left him totally paralyzed in both legs, totally paralyzed in his body below the midpoint of the chest, and partially paralyzed in one of his arms.

The effects of Richard's accident on Mary Anne's life have likewise been disastrous. It has transformed her husband from an active partner into a lifelong invalid, confined to home and bedridden for a great deal of the time. Because he needs assistance in virtually every activity of daily living, Mary Anne gave up her job and undertook his care on a 24-hour basis. Each night she must wake in order to turn him from side to side, so as to minimize the occurrence of bedsores. Every morning and evening she must help him wash, dress and undress, and get into and out of his wheelchair. She must help him into and out of the car when a visit to the doctor's office or hospital is required. Because he has lost all bladder and bowel control, she must assist him in the difficult and time-consuming processes of performing those bodily functions by artificial inducement. Many of these activities require her to lift or support his body weight, thus placing a repeated physical strain on her.

Nor is the psychological strain any less. Mary Anne's social and recreational life, evidently, has been severely restricted. She is a constant witness to her husband's pain, mental anguish, and frustration. Because he has lost all capacity for sexual intercourse, that aspect of married life is wholly denied to her: as she explains in her declaration, "To be deeply in love with each other and have no way of physically expressing this love is most difficult physically and mentally." For the same reason she is forever denied the opportunity to have children by him—she is, for all practical purposes, sterilized: again she explains, "I have lost what I consider is the fulfillment of my existence because my husband can't make me pregnant so as to bear children and have a family." The consequences to her are predictable: "These physical and emotional frustrations with no outlet have made me nervous, tense, depressed and have caused me to have trouble sleeping, eating and concentrating." In short, Mary Anne says, "Richard's life has been ruined by this accident. As his partner, my life has been ruined too."

At the time of the accident Richard was 22 years old and Mary Anne was 20. The injuries, apparently, are permanent.[7]

I hope it will not seem callous in the face of this tragedy to examine the discursive construction of the bodies of Richard and Mary Anne Rodriguez, particularly in comparison with the differently constructed bodies of such victims of disaster as Jane Roe or Mary Craig.

In the discourse of consortium, as of much contemporary personal injury litigation, the dominant literary trope is narrative, typically chronological, with an emphasis on before and after the accident. Figurative language of any sort is self-consciously at a minimum. Richard Rodriguez's body is not a machine, or property, or commodity; it is not private, or sacred, or "the physical and temporal expression of the unique human persona."[8] Anyone satiated with the parade of figures of speech presented up to this point, might be forgiven thinking that the discursive construction of Richard Rodriguez' body is somehow more direct, natural, nonmetaphorical than the constructions up to this point. Anyone convinced by the deconstructive readings of the figures of speech in preceding chapters might have supposed that plain narrative like this is what we have been leading up to as the desired legal discourse.

This would be quite wrong, however. The "plain speech" of the plaintiff's personal injury lawyer provides the discourse in which Richard Rodriguez's body is constructed, and it is selected, self-consciously, for a kind of effect. It is neither more or less "natural" than machine bodies or privacy bodies.

Narrated bodies, as we shall call them, are indeed more salient, less distant, to the hearer. We find them when empathy is sought with the plight or condition of the person inside the body, so professionally they are more basic to the repertoire of the personal injury lawyer than the civil liberties or public interest lawyer. This is not meant to compliment the latter group. It is worth considering what abortion rights might look like if civil rights and liberties lawyers had employed similar narrations to construct the body of Jane Roe, or Norma McCorvey, as we now know her to have been.[9] Indeed, I have considerable sympathy for the argument made long ago that the disgraceful failures

---

[7] Rodriguez v. Bethlehem Steel Corp., 525 P.2d 669, 670–71 (Cal. 1974).

[8] Moore v. Regents of the University of California, 793 P.2d 479, 497 (Mosk, J., dissenting). Justice Mosk was also the author of the court's opinion in *Rodriguez v. Bethlehem Steel Corp.*

[9] Norma McCorvey, *I Am Roe: My Life, Roe v. Wade, and Freedom of Choice* (New York: Harper Collins, 1994).

of the American Civil Liberties Union to challenge the two most serious assaults on civil liberties during the lifetime of that organization, the wartime internment of Japanese-Americans and the anticommunist repression of the 1950s, are attributable to that organization's devotion to principle, in a way that excludes such human values as loyalty and friendship.[10]

Elaine Scarry observes that personal injury litigation "will be organized around the skeletal structure of a discrete action, the path of an accident, a sequence of occurrences that (for the plaintiff) carried the whole world from being normal to being abnormal." In the course of a trial, the story "will be told ten, or forty, or two hundred times, sometimes in its forty-five second entirety, and other times in one of its ten-second or five-second subunits."[11] But

the most crucial difference between the "unifying plot action" of a play and the "unifying plot action" of the trial [is that] the action of the first is complete and cannot be altered; its audience must passively bear it. The action of the trial is incomplete and can be mimetically altered; its audience, the jury, is empowered to in some sense reverse it, and it is *only* because this possibility exists that the story is being retold. That is, the audience of *Oedipus Rex* or *Hamlet* can only mentally reverse it: they will be engaged in the counterfactual wish, let Oedipus not move down that road, let him not marry the Queen, let Polonius this time not be behind the curtain, let Hamlet at least not act moronic to Ophelia. But the trial audience, the jury, is there to "make-real" what the audience of a play can ordinarily only "make-up." . . . That "the making real of the counterfactual" is centrally at issue in the legal contest and differentiates the defense and plaintiff positions becomes most overt in the closing arguments. The lawyer for the defense will often in such a case attempt to persuade the jury that they are powerless in this regard by saying some version of the following statement: "A terrible accident has happened; we all wish it weren't so; but there is nothing anyone can do that will change the fact that it happened." The lawyer for the plaintiff, in contrast, will often take great care to remind the jury that they indeed have at this moment a very special power ("I try to give jurors a feeling of royalty," explains one of New York City's leading plaintiff lawyers), that some of the remaining body damage can be reversed and undone by medical care, that the problems of being out of work can be reversed or diminished by being paid for, that even the objectlessness of acute suffering can in some sense be mimetically reversed by a more bountiful object world, that, in effect, the first two hundred recitations of the

[10] Jonathan D. Caspar, *Lawyers before the Warren Court: Civil Liberties and Civil Rights, 1957–66* (Urbana: U. Ill. Pr., 1972) contrasted the lawyers who actually represented accused communists, who did so largely out of personal loyalty to old colleagues and friends, and thus helped vindicate civil liberties, when the organized civil liberties bar convinced itself that devotion to principle meant siding with the government.

[11] Elaine Scarry, *The Body in Pain: The Making and Unmaking of the World* 297 (New York: Oxford U. Pr., 1985).

story they have heard can be displaced by a two-hundred-and-first recitation in which the story of the failure of artifice can be displaced by a story about the medically and psychologically curative strategies of artifice.[12]

While the bodies of Richard and Mary Anne Rodriguez are constructed discursively by an appellate court, not a jury, the narrative is identical, and the function too. A significant issue in the Supreme Court of California was whether that court had the power to reverse tradition and permit wives to sue for loss of consortium (one justice dissented on just this point),[13] so Justice Mosk's narrative "making real the counterfactual" had the same empowering effect on his colleagues, empowering them to mimetically reverse reality, as the narrative normally does for jurors.

But of course Oedipus must take that road, Polonius must be behind the curtain, and the six-hundred-pound pipe must fall on Richard Rodriguez's head and destroy his mobility and Mary Anne's dreams. Here is the awful aporia in *Rodriguez,* that having employed the discourse of narration, storytelling to empower the hearer into "making real the counterfactual," the court can do no such thing.

What it can do is let Mary Anne sue for money damages, a substitute counterfactual. " 'Money . . . cannot truly compensate a wife for the destruction of her marriage, but it is the only known means to compensate for the loss suffered and to symbolize society's recognition that a culpable wrong—even if unintentional—has been done.' That the law cannot do enough, in short, is an unacceptable excuse for not doing anything at all."[14]

The narrated body of Richard Rodriguez is a powerful alternative to the body figured as property, commodity, or interest. While Richard Rodriguez's reproductive capacity, like Mary Craig's, is turned into dollars, the discursive process is quite different.

A COMMODIFIED VERSION OF THE BODY OF RICHARD RODRIGUEZ

The thrust of much legal discourse for at least a generation has been to make it impossible to distinguish between a contract for labor and a contract for sterilization. The conventional way of contrasting Mary Craig's body with Richard Rodriguez's is not to contrast commodity bodies from narrated bodies, but rather property rules from liability rules.

Legal academics, in the twenty years since Guido Calabresi's germinal article, have developed a particularly chilling discourse that distinguishes rather between the way in which Richard Rodriguez's reproductive capacity and

[12] Id. 298–99.

[13] Rodriguez, 525 P.2d at 687 (McComb, J., dissenting).

[14] Rodriguez, 525 P.2d at 682. The internal quotation is from Millington v. Southeastern Elevator Co., 239 NE.2d 897, 902 (N.Y. 1968).

Mary Craig's may be said to be commodified.[15] (It is also profoundly ideological in the classic sense, a discursive construction of a practice that disguises
its nature from participants. I am not, of course, saying that participants would
otherwise have access to anything that might be termed the "true" or "unmediated" bodies of Mary Craig or Richard Rodriguez. Rather, the legal academic
discourse is ideological in the sense of estranging practitioners from what
might otherwise be their overriding ethical impulses, or more ordinary, meaning simply not distinctively legal, discursive practice).

In Calabresi's terminology, Mary Craig's reproductive capacity is hers under a *property rule* that enables her to sell it to the Johnson Controls Company
in exchange for a better job. Richard Rodriguez's is his under a *liability rule*
that lets Bethlehem Steel take it from him, so long as they pay him for it
afterward, in amounts specified by legal institutions. (A third possibility is that
reproductive capacity might be *inalienable,* as in the famous *Baby M* case).

While Calabresi's analysis of why one or another rule is selected by law in
particular contexts is typically subtle and nuanced, unusually alert to many
moral factors, it is fair to say that the bulk of that article deals with the problem of transaction costs: property rules are said to be efficient when property
holders can easily negotiate optimal transfers; liability rules are efficient when
free-rider and other collective action problems prevent efficient transfers. This
may explain the different rules here.

It is true that both Mary Craig and Richard Rodriguez were deprived of
their reproductive capacity by the action of their employer, and that transaction costs in individual employment contracts are not usually high, since the
employer imposes what it wants and employees either accept it or quit. (It is
also true that these are both somewhat unusual transfers, inasmuch as, after
the transfer, the employee no longer has reproductive capacity, but the employer doesn't exactly have it either. Still, it doesn't seem far-fetched to me to
describe Johnson Controls as "buying" Mary Craig's capacity to reproduce).

As Mary Craig's example shows, employers can get employees to sell their
reproductive capacity for comparatively small sums of money, with low transaction costs. Was such an "efficient transfer" possible in Richard Rodriguez's
case? The problem there was that Bethlehem Steel didn't particularly want his
mobility and reproductive capacity; they just took them from him in an accident. Perhaps the cognitive barriers that would have prevented either
Rodriguez or Bethlehem from appreciating the likelihood and severity of such
an accident before it happened stand in for transaction costs and explain why
Rodriguez's reproductive capacity is protected only by a liability rule.

This way of talking well illustrates law's cold metaphors for the body:
machine, property, privacy. The cases in this chapter show, however, that

---

[15] Guido Calabresi and A. Douglas Melamed, "Property Rules, Liability Rules, and Inalien-
ability: One View of the Cathedral," 85 *Harv. L. Rev.* 1089 (1972).

these cold metaphors have brought us none of the benefits that their defenders might assert. They do not abstract from individual characteristics to bring us rules of equality, of treating like cases alike: they construct bodies as sites of meticulous individuation. They do not reduce passion or will in adjudication or enforce reason: they are the very vehicles of passion. They do not bring about predictability or other rule-of-law values: they inscribe into law the very oscillation described by Foucault: we can criticize disciplinary regulation of the body only through construction of a juridical subject, bearing rights, independent of others, rights conceptualized as rights against intrusion, or sharing, or to independence. And we can criticize this judicial subject only through construction of an economic body, imbricated in commodity exchange, whose freedom lies, like Margaret Green's, in the freedom to alienate for money all bodily products, functions, and labors.

Can we break through this circle? Can we conceptualize people as people in relations? Can we create a bodily discourse of pleasure, of sexuality? Can we develop a constitutional jurisprudence of how we want to live with each other, so that rights could be secured for subjects by imagining them as other than isolated? What about a better vocabulary of domination, particularly gender domination?

I will make some tentative starts at such a jurisprudence in the final chapter. For now, let us leave the regulated body, alternating between sacred and commodified. Let us continue to explore the legal discursive figuration of sexuality, through various contexts in which the body is figured as the object of another's desire.

PART TWO

Desire

Chapter 6

SANDWICH MAN; OR, THE ECONOMIC AND POLITICAL HISTORY OF BODILY DISPLAY

ON DESIRE

To every construction of the body as a commodity or property, there exists some moment at which everyone recoils in horror. Everyone has a point of insistence on a relationship to the body of another that is noncommodified and nonutilitarian, the meaning of which would be destroyed were participants to attempt to experience it as an economic exchange. I shall be using the term *desire* as a nontechnical term to cover all relations in which someone wants to see, be close to, understand, possess the body of another but that are not characteristically experienced as relations of economic exchange. For example, someone who resisted the idea that the body of Richard Rodriguez in the last chapter was property or a commodity might claim instead that his was a *desired* body in the sense in which I am using the term.

I want the term *desire* to be as broad as possible, mainly because, as we shall see, law invariably refigures desire into some other sort of relationship and thus lacks its own theory or discursive construction of desire. In particular, I want to include as *desire* all the erotic object attractions that Freudians normally mean by the term, but also various infantile or mimetic attractions to others that might be, but need not, classified as erotic. For example, under the psychoanalytic theories of Jacques Lacan, the infant literally acquires an identity and symbolic competence in a "mirror stage" in which the infant enjoys gazing at the images of other people (typically, the mother) or itself in a mirror. Only through this gaze could the infant translate the disorder of sense experience, which could never give it a unified sense of its own body, into a sense, which is necessarily a symbolic construction, an act of interpretation, that it has a single body in which it lives.[1] So it is not surprising that people like to look at other people; they have their identities to maintain in doing so.

---

[1] Jacques Lacan, "The Mirror Stage as Formative of the Function of the I as Revealed in Psychoanalytic Experience," in *Ecrits: A Selection* 1 (Alan Sheridan trans.) (New York: Norton, 1977) [1949]. A most helpful introduction to the writing of this essay is Martin Jay, *Downcast Eyes: The Denigration of Vision in Twentieth-Century French Thought* 338–53 (Berkeley: U. Cal. Pr., 1993). Obviously it is a matter of complete indifference to me whether the mirror stage is really a stage, or a lifetime process, or, if a stage, whether Lacan has the timing right, and so on. I confess to having laughed out loud at the Podsnappian savaging of Lacan on these points in Raymond Tallis, *Not Saussure: A Critique of Post-Saussurian Literary Theory* 131–63 (New York: St. Martin's, 2d ed., 1995).

The idea that identity formation is partly interpretive and normally involves visual inspection seems plausible enough to me, although I don't think people actually fall apart if they don't pass a mirror for a week or so, or that blind people never acquire personal identities. The word *desire* may add distracting and unnecessary erotic allusions to the possibly simple fact that people like looking at other people, but there doesn't seem to me to be a better term, and it is the very term that Deleuze and Guattari have used in their expressly non-Freudian account of "desire," which I also intend to include, if not exactly comprehend, in my usage.[2]

Although *desire* is a Freudian term, I do not use it to ally myself with any particular school of psychotherapy. The Freudian term is commonly used by intellectuals to order our thought, rather like Bentham's *utility* or Marshall's *equilibrium,* and that is how I use it here. It is a matter of complete indifference to me whether or not desire or utility or equilibrium ever "existed," or whether Freud, Bentham, or Marshall was a good person or desirable role model, or whether any ever did anything interesting or practical with his concepts. It seems likely that Freud was a complete failure as a psychotherapist, and while that is important to psychotherapists, for my purposes it is just about as interesting a question as whether Marshall ever made any money from his concept of economic equilibrium.

The chief *desired* bodies of law are bodies that are visually displayed or searched. As we shall see, the task of legal discourse is to displace the erotic desire to know the displayed body.

THE BODY AS TEXT

In his exploration of the nineteenth-century Parisian arcades, Walter Benjamin gravitated to a singular figure who seemed to encapsulate the spectacle of commodification: the sandwichman. The sandwich (board) man stood for the animation of the inanimate; this figure roamed the streets of Paris bearing advertisements of commodity exchange values mounted on the front and back of his body. As an animated text, the sandwichman was an allegory of the body reified by the logic of capitalism.[3]

Walter Benjamin has given us much of our imagery of the birth of consumer society, in the arcades of nineteenth-century Paris, and of the characteristically modern body that was constructed at that time and that, as we shall see

[2] Gilles Deleuze and Félix Guattari, *Anti-Oedipus* (Robert Hurley, Mark Seem, and Helen R. Lane trans.) (Minneapolis: U. Minn. Pr., 1983) [1972].

[3] Allen Feldman, *Formations of Violence: The Narrative of the Body and Political Terror in Northern Ireland* 7 (Chicago: U. Chi. Pr., 1991), citing Susan Buck-Morss, *The Dialectics of Seeing: Walter Benjamin and the Arcades Project* 306 (Cambridge: MIT Pr., 1989).

throughout part 2, figures in much contemporary legal discourse, even in un-
expected places and times: the displayed body, the "legible body" with its
"paths of . . . expropriability,"[4] the body that is scrutinized with an aim toward its possession, where possession encompasses erotic enjoyment, domination, and other creation of meaning. This chapter deals with the political
economy of the visual display of the body, as seen in contemporary legal cases
in which motels, airlines, and other employers require employees to display
their bodies in particular ways.

The legal puzzle is that law sometimes requires unwilling employees to
display their bodies in particular ways (because their employer requires it) and
sometimes suppresses particular body displays (that violate something called
morality). Having seen the body constructed as commodity in part 1, one might
hypothesize that law facilitates display of the commodified body, but not the
body as a means of individual self-expression. This is not a bad starting point
but as we shall see is an oversimplification: there are limits on the body displays that employers may require, and there are circumstances in which gratu-
itous display of the body is permissible where commercial display of the same
body would not be. So an inquiry into the cultural meaning of body display
must supplement our repertoire of commodified bodies from part 1.

Body Display in Consumer Culture

"What modern consumer culture produces, then, is not so much a way of
being as a way of seeing."[5] For Benjamin, that way of seeing is the dreamlike
state in which urban pedestrians observe displayed objects, anticipating possessing them. "Marx had used the term 'phantasmagoria' to refer to the decep-
tive appearances of commodities as 'fetishes' in the marketplace. . . . But for
Benjamin . . . the key to the new urban phantasmagoria was not so much the
commodity-in-the-market as the commodity-on-display, where exchange
value no less than use value lost practical meaning, and purely representational value came to the fore. Everything desirable, from sex to social status,
could be transformed into commodities."[6]

Consumer society, like market society, liberalism, and group identity, is
grasped by its participants through particular embodied experiences. Benjamin said the arcades sent a "dreaming collective" "into its own innards,"
heightening their sensation of their bodies. Like the other embodied correlates
of political ideas we have studied, what was ultimately most significant about

[4] Eve Kosofsky Sedgwick, *Tendencies* 198 (Durham: Duke U. Pr., 1993).

[5] Jean-Christophe Agnew, "The Consuming Vision of Henry James," in *The Culture of Consumption: Critical Essays in American History, 1880–1980* 73 (Richard Wightman Fox and T. J.
Jackson Lears eds.) (New York: Pantheon, 1983).

[6] Buck-Morss, *The Dialectics of Seeing* 81–82. This reconstruction of Benjamin's lost book
on the Paris arcades is probably the best introduction to Benjamin in English.

these sensations was their discursive representation, what Benjamin called the "hallucinations or dream images that translate and explain" the body's sensations.[7]

The body, of course, makes an excellent commodity-on-display, as Benjamin's example of the sandwich man shows. Desire for the body of another has a long history, after all, with quite a head start on the nineteenth century. However, several aspects of looking at the body on display are indeed new in the mid–nineteenth century and, I would suggest, are associated with the discursive construction of consumer goods: the body becomes semiotic; images of the body are mass produced; the legible body becomes female, often pornographic.

The external appearance of the body suddenly becomes semiotic to the internal "character" (or, as we would say, "personality").[8] Shakespeare omitted physical description of most of his characters. It was the Victorians, with their obsession with prosopography (description of characters' external appearance) and physiognomy (moralized description), who remedied this omission.[9] The nineteenth century loved its catalogs of visual facial types, each in mimetic recreation of distinctive characters, its Daumier caricatures and *cris de Paris* imagery, its skull measurements and phrenology.[10] (Contemporary American lawyers continue to love at least the Daumier caricatures.) Victorian law allied with Victorian criminology in which criminal tendencies were said to lie in the body and be legible on its surface, to Sherlock Holmes, at least, if not to Watson. "Once it could be shown how criminals were in part biological

---

[7] Id. 272.

[8] On the change from character to personality, see Christopher Lasch, *The Culture of Narcissism: American Life in an Age of Diminishing Expectation* (New York: Norton, 1978); Richard Sennett, *The Fall of Public Man* (New York: Knopf, 1977).

[9] Mary Cowden Clarke, *The Girlhood of Shakespeare's Heroines* (London: Bicker and Son, 1864), discussed in Helena Michie, *The Flesh Made Word: Female Figures and Women's Bodies* 84 (New York: Oxford U. Pr., 1987). W. S. Gilbert lampooned this insistence on the body's revelation of character in his ballad "The Bishop and the Busman," in which a Jewish bus-director converts to Christianity, at which time his body is instantly transformed, losing all "Jewish" traits. See Ina Rae Hark, "Writ of Habeas Corpus: Bodies as Commodities in the *Bab Ballads*," 26 *Victorian Poetry* 319, 325 (1988).

[10] An outstanding history of visual knowledge in art and medicine is Barbara Maria Stafford, *Body Criticism: Imaging the Unseen in Enlightenment Art and Medicine* (Cambridge: MIT Pr., 1991); pp. 91–129 deal with the reception of Johann Caspar Lavater, *Physiognomische Fragmente* (1775) and later excursions into phrenology, cranial criticism, etc. See also Judith Wechsler, *A Human Comedy: Physiognomy and Caricature in Nineteenth-Century France* (Chicago: U. Chi. Pr., 1982); Christopher Rivers, *Face Value: Physiognomical Thought and the Legible Body in Marivaux, Lavater, Balzac, Gautier, and Zola* (Madison: U. Wis. Pr., 1994); *Victorian Literature and the Victorian Visual Imagination* (Carol T. Christ and John O. Jordan eds.) (Berkeley: U. Cal. Pr., 1996); as well as Joanne Finkelstein, *The Fashioned Self* (Cambridge: Polity, 1991), a critique of the fallacy that much can be learned about the personality from inspection of the external body.

anomalies, it proved a relatively simple matter to medicalize other kinds of deviance as well."[11] All this helps establish a way of looking at the exterior of others' bodies as commodities on display.

Technologies for the mass production of images: first lithography and photography, later film and television—increasingly educate large numbers of people as to the "perfect body." Left behind would be a pre–consumer society observation like Denis Diderot's: "On the entire surface of the earth, there is not a single man perfectly constituted, perfectly sound. The human species is only a mass of individuals more or less deformed, more or less ill."[12] Now Diderot was not a typical member of the eighteenth century (or of anything else), but in this he spoke for his time, a time before mass-produced images of the perfect body. In the next century, however, beginning in Paris, lithographs and photographs daily brought the disproof of Diderot's statement into every home. There is a kind of aesthetic link between eighteenth-century etching and the dissected body as an anatomical engraving,[13] as there was later between photography and a kind of glossy body; film and a kind of heavy attractiveness in close-up, the excitement of massed bodies in distance.

But the most surprising aspect of the perfect body, displayed through technologies of mass reproduction, is this: that body is female. Benjamin missed this point, but it is central in important work on nineteenth-century French lithography, not yet published, by the art historian Abigail Solomon-Godeau.[14] As lithographic images proliferated in nineteenth-century France, they were typically of women, often nude, often pornographic. All this time the male nude, which in the eighteenth century often served as a symbol of beauty, perfection, Greece, Rome, as virile or ephebe, essentially disappeared from art, not to be revived until a twentieth-century homosexual revival (to be discussed in chapter 7). Théophile Gautier: "The ideal of beauty for the moderns is inclined towards woman and it is rare that a painter of today would seek it in the expression of the most perfect virile type. Among the Greeks, the ideal had no sex, and man could represent the ideal as well

---

[11] Robert A. Nye, *Crime, Madness, and Politics in Modern France: The Medical Concept of National Decline* 99 (Princeton: Prin. U. Pr., 1984).

[12] Denis Diderot, *Eléments de physiologie,* 9 *Oeuvres complètes de Diderot* 272 (Paris: Garnier, 1875) [1778] ("il n'y a pas sur toute la surface de la terre un seul homme parfaitement constitué, parfaitement sain. L'espèce humaine n'est donc qu'un amas d'individus plus ou moins contrefaits, plus ou moins malades").

[13] Stafford, *Body Criticism* 53–69.

[14] Abigail Solomon-Godeau, *The Other Side of Venus,* adapted from her doctoral dissertation (City University of New York) and presented to the Rutgers Center for Historical Analysis, fall 1992. A portion appears in *The Sex of Things: Gender and Consumption in Historical Perspective* 113 (Victoria de Grazia ed.) (Berkeley: U. Cal. Pr., 1996). She explores similar themes for a somewhat later period in her "Reconsidering Erotic Photography: Notes for a Project of Historical Salvage," in *Photography at the Dock: Essays on Photographic History, Institutions, and Practices* (Minneapolis: U. Minn. Pr., 1991).

as woman. Apollo is not less beautiful than Venus; Paris could compete with Helen."[15]

Solomon-Godeau: "In theater, in opera, and above all, in the ballet, masculinity was reconfigured as femininity became the gender elected to exclusively represent the erotic, the beautiful, and indeed, corporeality itself." Representations of women's bodies link high art and low, salon and avant-garde, elite and popular culture, "commodity culture and the image world of consumable femininities."[16] "[A]n overemphasis on the stylistic and qualitative distinctions between avant-garde and official painting of the later nineteenth century obscures their shared agency in the modern construction of femininity." While women are of course present in rococo art, "the notion that a painting of a woman, nude or clothed, divorced from any narrative context whatsoever, *could* be a subject for an ambitious, important, or public painting, was utterly uncountenanced in classical art theory."

Yet a generation or two later, all had changed. "The explicitly heterosexual erotics of art production as they became mythologized (e.g. the artist and his model, the female nude as genre, the mythos of bohemian sexuality) are in fact nineteenth century formations, fully coalesced by 1848. . . as women were banished from the public sphere, images and discourses of femininity proliferated enormously. It is as though the real absence of women as actors in the bourgeois civil sphere was filled by compensatory fantasies—or constellations of fantasies—about femininity."[17]

Solomon-Godeau's is a detailed analysis of images of women in lithographs, often pornographic, of midcentury France. Lithography, which officially debuted as an industrial product in the Salon of 1817, brought print images into ordinary French homes by the early 1830s.

What is remarkable, as Solomon-Godeau establishes with care, is how many of the poses and motifs of contemporary erotica and pornography were well established by this early date. Body parts are displayed, of course, but accompanied by "the solicitous and coquettish gaze of the girl. . . . This solicitous look is a staple feature of the legal erotic, and to state the obvious, it  retains its currency to this day. . . . To the extent that the viewer both recognizes and assents to this visual solicitation he is himself constructed as masculine. While here too there are prototypes for this mode of address going back as far as the Renaissance [e.g., Lucas Cranach] these newer—modern—gazes are addressed to a potential purchaser and emerge from artifacts that make no aesthetic or intellectual claims."

[15] Théophile Gautier, "Guide de l'amateur au Musée du Louvre," in 8 *Oeuvres complètes* 14 (Geneva: Slatkine Reprints, 1978) [1882], as quoted and translated in Solomon-Godeau, *Other Side of Venus* 182.

[16] Id. 218.

[17] Id. 184–90.

The book the girl is interrupted reading, "the swathe of curtain, silk-covered sofa, embroidered foot cushion and carved table declare the print's setting as the bourgeois home," and this adds significance to the lithographs. "Compliant, chic, titillating, these icons of femininity are significant not only because they are the first true mass produced commodities designed to purvey 'the feminine.' They are also important because they offer to the purchaser more than the fantasy of possession of the woman (or women) but the fantasy of possession of the world it depicts—mondaine, but private, and above all, profoundly 'feminine.' In its feminization and eroticization of the private interior, such iconography repeats the social separation of the spheres and the fantasized confinement of (desirable) femininity to hearth or harem. In this it presages the mechanisms of modern advertising in which desire is provoked not merely or only for the commodity, but for the ambiance or 'lifestyle' of which the commodity is a metonym."[18]

A typical rococo gallant scene is erotic in its way but nearly disappears in lithography and photography. In the dying rococo imagery, "What is represented is a world in which the erotic is still inseparable from a courtly notion of *sociabilité,* where eroticism is not yet fully privatized." The males courting, escorting, and accompanying the rococo woman disappear as "lithographic production gradually narrows the focus to boudoir or sitting room and concentrates increasingly on the feminine alone."[19]

It is impossible not to wonder whether a consumer society *requires* the specularization of women, "the idea that what is involved in the construction of modern femininity has to do with a condition of pure specularity, a condition hypothesized by Luce Irigaray and famously described by Laura Mulvey as 'to-be-looked-at-ness.' "[20] Perhaps it is mere historical coincidence that the technologies of mass production and marketing that typify consumer society (lithography and photography) simultaneously facilitated the proliferation of images of women. Perhaps, had lithography been perfected in the eighteenth century, lithographs of classical male nudes would have been popular.

We cannot be sure, but there seems to me to be a link here that is stronger

---

[18] Id. 213–15.

[19] Id. 216–17.

[20] Id. 223. For Luce Irigaray, see particularly *Speculum of the Other Woman* 133–213 (Gillian C. Gill trans.) (Ithaca: Cornell U. Pr. 1985) [1974]. The Laura Mulvey quote is from her essay "Visual Pleasure and Narrative Cinema," in *Visual and Other Pleasures* 19 (Bloomington: Indiana U. Pr. , 1989).

Women purchased and displayed these nineteenth-century French lithographs to a surprising degree, as Professor Solomon-Godeau commented in her oral presentation at the Rutgers Center for Historical Analysis, perhaps like buying today's magazines like *Vogue:* respectable women displayed photographs of models and actresses along with family photographs and *cartes de visite.* Perhaps this just goes to show that, when analyzing "the sexual economy of looking," masculine and feminine "are understood to be subject *positions,* not biological givens." Solomon-Godeau, "Reconsidering Erotic Photography," 220.

than temporal coincidence. Rather, technologies of the mechanical production of images, a consumer society built on new "modes of seeing," and male economic agency all reinforce each other through the dream image of the woman-to-be-possessed. (The new modes of seeing that are typical of Benjamin's consumer society include the stimulation and even creation of desire, the channeling of desire into seeing, and the examination of images with an eye toward their possession, a possession that takes place only in the realm of "representational value," while the commodity or service actually purchased is some sort of metonymic substitution, a giant bait-and-switch).[21]

I would like to explore these themes with a group of contemporary American cases in which the actual bodies of living women become specularized as part of consumer culture, examining the legal discourse that permits Howard Johnson's and American Airlines to order the display of women's bodies with particular representational values. Of course others might want to explore these themes, of the specularization and commodification of women, with reference to contemporary legal battles over the definition and regulation of graphic pornography. I will not be exploring those themes here, only partly because this book is limited to constructions of the body that exist in official legal culture and does not pursue proposed regulations, of whatever merit, that are so far established mainly in the academy. I shall let Abigail Solomon-Godeau explain further: "To identify the problem of women's oppression or violence against women with the pornographic modes we can recognize 'on sight' is to greatly oversimplify the matter. On the contrary, it may well be that the most insidious and instrumental form of domination, subjugation, and objectification are produced by mainstream images of women rather than by juridically criminal or obscene ones. . . . The pressing need, it seems to me, is not to locate and censor a 'worse offender' class of images, but rather to better understand—in order to effectively combat—the complex network of relations that meshes power, patriarchy, and representations."[22]

I share this perspective, as should be evident. Much of this book analyzes the body fetishism, commodification, and display well established in normal legal culture, in the hopes of what would at best be a gradual transformation of that culture. Some readers will think I am being coy by not weighing in on contemporary antipornographic efforts like the proposed statute of Andrea Dworkin and Catharine MacKinnon.[23] Let me just state simply and not de-

---

[21] Lauren Berlant, "National Brands/National Body: Imitation of Life," in *Comparative American Identities: Race, Sex, and Nationality in the Modern Text* 110–35 (Hortense J. Spillers ed.) (New York: Routledge, 1991) powerfully explores these and other themes in discussing the "trademarking" of the body of "Aunt Delilah," the Aunt Jemima character in Fanny Hurst's *Imitation of Life* and the movies based on it.

[22] Solomon-Godeau, "Reconsidering Erotic Photography," 237.

[23] Catharine MacKinnon, *Only Words* (Cambridge: Harv. U. Pr., 1993); Andrea Dworkin, "Against the Male Flood: Censorship, Pornography, and Equality," 8 *Harv. Women's L. J.* 1, 25–26 (1985).

velop here what I believe to be implicit in this entire book. I am not a liber-
tarian, I believe in culture, and have no philosophic objection to people working together to develop discursive practices that are acceptable to all that
might well involve constraints on sexual display. In any culture, restrictions
on discursive practice are inevitable, and the choice in ours is typically
whether they will be developed democratically or imposed by capitalism. I am
most interested in a discourse of the body that is relational, empathetic, not
estranging and fetishistic, though institutionalizing this would require larger
social transformations that cannot be imposed by municipal ordinance. On the
other hand, in our observable legal culture, with its courts, lawyers, judges,
legal techniques, and, in particular, the discursive constructions, regulation,
and abjection of the body that are the subject of this book, the antipornographic statute that would not do more harm than good has yet to come to
my attention. All such statutes would be most likely to harm the expressive
discourses that challenge discursive hegemony—outlaw sexualities, Bakhti-
nian parody—without which the kind of social transformation in which I am
interested becomes even less thinkable.[24] The characteristic product of the
legal profession demonstrates a desire to overcome the domination of women
far less frequently than it displays fear and hatred of the body and its submission to the regulatory apparatus of capital. The following legal materials reinforce my point.

Legal Construction of Female Bodies on Commercial Display: Man's Own Private Disneyland

Let us examine a recent legal case involving a dispute between an employer
and a female employee over the use of her body as a consumer artifact and
analyze the construction of the legal body of Sondra Tamimi as an object of
specularization.

> Sondra Tamimi was employed as a desk clerk at a Howard Johnson's Motor
> Lodge in Montgomery, Alabama on two separate occasions. She was first em-
> ployed there in June, 1981, working there for only a short time before quitting
> because of difficulty in arranging transportation to her job. She was hired by
> Howard Johnson a second time in October, 1981. On both occasions, she was
> hired by the manager of the motor lodge, Albert Gallof. Gallof's testimony indi-
> cates that on both occasions when he hired Tamimi she was wearing no makeup

---

[24] See generally Drucilla Cornell, *The Imaginary Domain: Abortion, Pornography, and Sexual Harassment* 95–163 (New York: Routledge, 1995); Carlin Meyer, "Sex, Sin, and Women's
Liberation: Against Porn-Suppression," 72 *Tex. L. Rev.* 1097 (1994); Jeffrey G. Sherman, "Love
Speech: The Social Utility of Pornography," 47 *Stan. L. Rev.* 661 (1995). On the political message
of at least some historical pornography, though not the examples that most outrage contemporary
reformers, see Robert Darnton, *The Forbidden Bestsellers of Pre-Revolutionary France* (New
York: Norton, 1995); *The Invention of Pornography: Obscenity and the Origins of Modernity,
1500–1800* (Lynn Hunt ed.) (New York: Zone, 1993).

and had a fair complexion. At the inception of her employment each time, Tamimi was informed that she would be required to report to work in a standard Howard Johnson uniform for women; however, on neither occasion did Gallof inform her that she had to wear makeup and lipstick while she was working behind the front desk. . . .

At a meeting of the office staff of the motor lodge on June 17, 1982, Gallof announced that he was installing a new dress code effective immediately. This dress code was not based upon an order from corporate headquarters but sprang solely from the mind of Gallof. The new dress code required, among other things, that all women wear makeup and lipstick. Tamimi was the only woman then employed at the motor lodge who did not already wear makeup, and since she had already told Gallof on several occasions that she would not wear it, it seems that the new makeup requirement was directed specifically at her. . . .

Gallof claims that he instituted this new dress code because Tamimi had been coming to work looking pale, with her face broken out, and occasionally with unbrushed hair. Tamimi claims that she had no problems with her complexion related to her pregnancy. The beginning of this period when Gallof claims that he began to notice that Tamimi looked pale and that her face was breaking out apparently coincides with Tamimi's having become pregnant. Tamimi learned that she was pregnant and so informed Gallof in mid-June. Prior to that time, he had never complained about her appearance or complexion.

Tamimi was fired eleven days later for failure to meet this new dress code.

Several recent articles review comprehensively the law of employer regulation of employee appearance. This permits us to review quickly the state of the law and take up momentarily the discursive construction of the body of Sondra Tamimi that facilitates a regime of employer regulation of appearance.

The district court, affirmed by the court of appeals, found that Sondra Tamimi's firing was sex discrimination, but its reasoning was instructive. The court found that it did not need to decide "whether an employer under certain circumstances may require its female employees to wear makeup."[25] Had it reached this issue, it could have found only that employer dress and grooming codes are normally upheld by courts against charges that they constitute sex discrimination.[26] The district court in Sondra Tamimi's case specifically noted

[25] Tamimi v. Howard Johnson Co., Inc., 807 F.2d 1550, 1554 (11th Cir. 1987).

[26] Karl E. Klare, "Power/Dressing: Regulation of Employee Appearance," 26 *N. Eng. L. Rev.* 1395, 1412–25 (1992), a detailed review of the law on all aspects of employee appearance and a strong plea for the autonomy of employees' appearance. In normally upholding dress codes, courts continue to treat employment discrimination legislation as aimed at "differences," not "domination," as Catharine MacKinnon has criticized in a different context. Catharine MacKinnon, *Sexual Harassment of Working Women: A Case of Sex Discrimination* (New Haven: Yale U. Pr., 1979). That is, they search for whether men and women are treated differently. They do not consider themselves authorized to root out institutions that particularly hold back women although applying nominally to men as well.

that mandatory makeup rules might well constitute the kinds of "bona fide occupational qualifications" that are recognized exceptions to the statute prohibiting discrimination against women.[27] How does wearing makeup constitute a "bona fide occupational qualification" for a motel desk clerk? Makeup does not assist her in checking customers in or out; it assists the customers in checking her out. Makeup reinforces Walter Benjamin's dream state, in which the customer fantasizes possession of the body-commodity, but that body is never actually exchanged, has only representational value, is a metonym for the motel room that is actually engaged.

Howard Johnson had "not demonstrated that requiring that female employees wear makeup is necessary to maintain the defendant's public image," in which case such a rule would (says the court) have been a bona fide occupational qualification.[28] Would Howard Johnson have to demonstrate the semiotics of that "public image"? Would that "image" have to have some necessity or demonstrated economic significance for Howard Johnson's business? Or could a court just take judicial notice of the frequent pornographic motif, mentioned by Abigail Solomon-Godeau, in which the image of an isolated woman mimetically represents the luxury of a domestic interior?[29]

The discrimination laws do give employees some significant protection against employer appearance requirements, as Karl Klare notes in a recent article. Tamimi's discharge, for example, was illegal because the makeup rule had been developed to apply only to her (she was the only female employee not already wearing makeup) and only when she became pregnant. Firing an employee because she is pregnant violates the Civil Rights Act. Gallof denied vehemently that he had any objection to pregnant employees, claimed to have employed others and to have been concerned only about the issue of facial appearance, but the court did not believe him. Secondly, the employer may not impose a uniform requirement on female employees while leaving male employees to wear any customary business attire. The court in that case noted that the grooming code was premised on the offensive stereotype "that women cannot be expected to exercise good judgment in choosing business apparel, whereas men can."[30]

---

[27] Civil Rights Act of 1964, §703(e), 42 U.S.C. §2000e-2(e).

[28] Tamimi, 807 F.2d at 1554.

[29] In the employer sterilization case mentioned in the last chapter, decided subsequent to Sondra Tamimi's case, the battery manufacturer argued that sterility was a "bona fide occupational qualification" for battery plant workers. The Supreme Court rejected this argument and gave a narrow reading to "bona fide occupational qualification." "By modifying 'qualification' with 'occupational,' Congress narrowed the term to qualifications that affect an employee's ability to do the job." International Union, United Automobile Workers v. Johnson Controls, Inc., 499 U.S. 187, 201 (1991). This is easier to apply to battery workers than to motel desk clerks; what is "the job" that motel desk clerks "do," and does requiring makeup affect their ability to do it?

[30] Carroll v. Talman Fed. Sav. and Loan Ass'n, 604 F.2d 1028 (7th Cir. 1979), cert. denied, 445 U.S. 929 (1980); followed in Department of Civil Rights v. Edward W. Sparrow Hosp. Ass'n, 377

However, as long as there are some regulations that apply to each sex, the specific content of the regulations may reflect "generally accepted community standards of dress and appearance," and, as Klare notes, this "opens the door to the imposition of onerous and discriminatory 'attractiveness' standards upon women."[31] In the most famous case, a television anchorwoman lost her job because of negative management and viewer reactions to her hair and appearance.[32] Employers may not generally exclude men or women as a group from jobs (such as flight attendant) because of "customer preference,"[33] but apparently customer preference (as revealed through surveys) may control employee appearance, even when the effect is to reinforce traditional stereotypes. (The station had employed viewer surveys to determine reactions to its male and female newscasters, but only female newscasters had ever been subject to viewer questions about their looks).

Whether an employer can really require all female employees to wear makeup—the question reserved in Sondra Tamimi's case—thus is difficult to answer. Is this discriminating against women, because there is no equivalent requirement for men? Do the men have to wear makeup too? What *would* an equivalent for men be? (Karl Klare suggests, facetiously, use of aftershave cologne or toupees to cover balding).[34] Or is it the other way around: men can be fired if they *do* wear makeup, as another court has held?[35]

Naomi Wolf has pointed out the cruel double-bind of cases like *Tamimi:* the woman may be discharged for refusing to wear revealing or conventionally attractive attire; yet her wearing of such attire will be introduced into evidence against her should she be sexually harassed.[36] A woman worker may be or-

---

NW.2d 755 (Mich. 1989); O'Donnell v. Burlington Coat Factory, 656 F.Supp. 263 (S.D.Ohio 1987).

[31] Klare, "Power/Dressing," 1417.

[32] Craft v. Metromedia, Inc., 766 F.2d 1205 (8th Cir. 1985), cert. denied, 475 U.S. 1058 (1986).

[33] Diaz v. Pan American World Airways, 442 F.2d 385 (5th Cir. 1971), cert. denied 404 U.S. 950 (1971).

[34] Klare, "Power/Dressing," 1419 n. 99.

[35] Williamson v. A. G. Edwards and Sons, Inc., 876 F.2d 56 (8th Cir. 1989). Williamson was dismissed for "disruptive and inappropriate" conduct, namely, that he had continually discussed "the details of his homosexual lifestyle" and had worn makeup to work. Williamson's claim of discrimination was dismissed, as the court had to construct a series of references for comparison. Other employees discussed their sex lives, but theirs were heterosexual. White homosexual men (Williamson was African-American) were not discharged, but they wore only earrings, no makeup. See Mary Eaton, "Homosexual Unmodified: Speculations on Law's Discourse, Race, and the Construction of Sexual Identity," in *Legal Inversions: Lesbians, Gay Men, and the Politics of Law* 54–56 (Didi Herman and Carl Stychin eds.) (Philadelphia: Temple U. Pr., 1995).

[36] Naomi Wolf, *The Beauty Myth: How Images of Beauty Are Used against Women* 38–39 (New York: William Morrow, 1991); Meritor Savings Bank v. Vinson, 477 U.S. 57, 68–69 (1986) (defendant in sexual harassment case may introduce evidence of allegedly provocative dress of plaintiff).

dered *both* to appear conventionally feminine *and* to "cover herself from neck to toe" in order to avoid harassment.[37] Wolf cites a complaint alleging that "a dress code of short skirts was set by an employer who allegedly sexually harassed his female employees because they complied with it."[38]

Sexual-harassment law creates one limit to employers' general privilege to market fantasies through the specularization of women. The managers of an office building in Manhattan, showing a deep appreciation of the teachings of Walter Benjamin and Abigail Solomon-Godeau, employed "lobby attendants" to advise building visitors, receive elevator complaints and the like. Male attendants had all given way to female attendants, who were dressed in ever-changing, fanciful costumes that seem largely to have been drawn from porno-graphic films (riding apparel; cowgirl outfits; tennis skirts). Things went too far in 1976 when the women were required to wear revealing bicentennial ponchos, flags gathered on the side but open to reveal their thighs and but-tocks. Margaret Hasselman wore the outfit for two days and was constantly sexually importuned. She refused to wear it again and was fired. This was found to be sex discrimination; while there were no male lobby attendants, the court found this kind of specularization would not be imposed on the male body. Interestingly, the building owner's unsuccessful defense of its practice was that the costumes enacted its First Amendment right to theatrical repre-sentation, "in the same sense as the Walt Disney creation of his Disneyland," as the lawyer put it.[39]

Despite this case, it is not difficult to find waitresses and other employees who are indeed required to wear outfits that invite sexual harassment. Nor is it clear that it matters, legally, whether these revealing dress requirements were made known to women when they took the job, or imposed on incumbent employees as part of a change ordered by management. Outside the jurisdic-tion of American antidiscrimination law is the case of the restaurant in Perth, Australia, closed by authorities because topless women were used as plates by customers who ate fruit salad and cream off the stomach of their waitress.[40]

As the excerpts from Walter Benjamin and Abigail Solomon-Godeau sug-gest, employer demands for the alteration or display of women's bodies are not a simple excrescence on an efficient system but are deeply imbricated in all the relations of a consumer society. For Sondra Tamimi's body to function as the commodity on display, as the representational mimesis of a motel room (or Margaret Hasselman's an office suite), we suggested above, it should, from Howard Johnson's perspective, be as close to "perfect" as possible, and where

[37] Bohen v. City of East Chicago, 799 F.2d 1180, 1187–88 (7th Cir. 1986).

[38] Wolf, *The Beauty Myth* 39.

[39] Equal Employment Opportunity Commission v. Sage Realty Corp., 507 F.Supp. 599, 609–10 (S.D.N.Y. 1981).

[40] Woody Igou, "Appall-O-Meter: Outback in the Stone Age," *In These Times,* September 20, 1993, p. 6.

possible, "perfected" through artifice; it should be isolated from sociability; silent; stare invitingly at the viewer; and be accompanied, not by other people, but by the accoutrements of middle-class comfort. This is a stereotyped image for Howard Johnson's to present, and it is one that law discursively constructs in its words even more effectively than Howard Johnson's was able to do in social practice.

Tamimi is nearly silent to us. She barely speaks to us in the opinion, and the basis for her antimakeup stance is left obscure. Tamimi claimed that on being told of the makeup policy, she exclaimed, "Oh, no, my mother is going to die, because this is against my religion," but Gallof and another employee at the meeting denied hearing the statement. Gallof must, however, have linked Tamimi's attitude to family pressure, because he admitted that, after having met Tamimi's sister, he asked Tamimi why her sister wore makeup and she didn't, to which Tamimi allegedly responded, "Well, I am not my sister." Tamimi denied that conversation, at least on the date that Gallof remembered it. Since the court turned the whole case from one of appearance regulation to one of pregnancy discrimination, these conflicts were never resolved and became irrelevant to the outcome. I think their continuing relevance is precisely to facilitate a silent and inviting Sondra Tamimi, about whom the reader of the opinion will learn little else. (She is married to an immigrant).

The "perfect body" is constructed in the court's observation that, were makeup "necessary to maintain [Howard Johnson's] public image," this "would have established a 'bona fide occupational qualification'" that could be imposed even if it disqualified more women than men. This is a distinctly modern understanding of body desire. While demands for body display presumably have a long history, the demand to alter appearance to conform to the perfect body, as the quotation from Denis Diderot earlier suggested, is a characteristically modern use of the body that could only have grown up in the last few centuries. There was until fairly recent times a great deal of uncertainty about the bodily basis of gender division, whether there were really two bodily sexes at all, and whether genders might change over the course of a lifetime.[41] Thus it is only recently that ideal body types have become firmly enough fixed to permit criticism of women who do not measure up to the ideal.

Because of the diffusion of images of the perfect body, particularly in television and advertising imagery, male customers, managers, and viewers now know what the perfect woman looks like. The manager of the Howard Johnson's recalled quite clearly how Sondra Tamimi appeared at her two job interviews. The man who cannot really possess a perfect woman still feels entitled to possess one in his gaze, as he checks into a motel or watches a television news show, and, if asked by the employer, he will have an opinion about how

[41] Thomas Laqueur, *Making Sex: Body and Gender from the Greeks to Freud* (Cambridge: Harv. U. Pr., 1990).

the employee's "looks" measure up. (It is interesting that someone's "looks" refers not to her own acts of looking, but her appearance and construction in the eyes of another).

Many people, but women vastly disproportionately, spend a great deal of time dissatisfied with their failure to own a perfect body in this sense, and a number of feminist writers have written on behalf of accepting one's own body, and against the increasing prevalence of eating disorders, cosmetic surgery, and other self-inflicted and culture-inflicted abuse in the name of body perfection.[42] These authors do not entirely deny the liberation we have discussed from time to time that may come from seeing oneself as a machine or commodity, freed from the sacred, ready to make oneself over afresh, a theme heavily exploited (as Susan Bordo shows) in advertising products and services for diet and fitness, but not entirely fictional either. So, once again, I am not undertaking a humanist cri de coeur against the dehumanizing involved in body commodification, but a postmodern plea for the multiplication of bodily performances. My complaint about employers putting the bodies of Sondra Tamimi and Renee Rogers (the heroine of the next section) on display is not that this adds a new body to the discourse, the displayed, legible body, but rather that it closes off the un-made-up face of Sondra Tamimi and the braided hair of Renee Rogers that those women adopted as their presentations of their selves. The employer is not just "purchasing" body alteration when it can lawfully terminate employees who refuse.

Appearance norms are thus as tough on the one who tries fruitlessly to comply with them as to the one who rebels against them, the Sondra Tamimis who refuse makeup. For most ordinary people, the control they exercise over their dress and appearance is a kind of basic control, the handiest and easiest way of making a kind of social or political statement that many people cannot make in any other way. When employers can normalize appearance, this denigrates nonmainstream looks and shuts off avenues of expression that are often very important to people.

As Karl Klare writes,

The genius of appearance law as discipline lies in indirection and decentralization. We have no government or clerical commissions that lay down directives for proper dress. We have "freedom" in America—with some exceptions (for example, public cross-dressing), people can buy (if they have money) and wear whatever clothes they want. However, employers generally have the countervailing right to set grooming standards and to punish nonconformists. That is, usually the law does not operate by forbidding deviance from centrally promulgated norms.

---

[42] Wolf, *The Beauty Myth* 39; Susan Bordo, *Unbearable Weight: Feminism, Western Culture, and the Body* (Berkeley: U. Cal. Pr., 1993). See the material in chapter 7 on the shirtfree movement.

Rather, by delegating power to employers (and other authority figures), appearance law raises the cost of nonconformity. . . .

So the system is decentralized, variegated, and flexible. Yet over the long run the system consistently generates what, to my taste anyway, are powerful forces of dress conservatism and conformity in the world of work, a regrettable narrowness of prevailing taste and sensibility. And precisely because appearance regulation is so decentralized, even obscure, this persistent conformism is experienced as "natural" rather than as a socially constructed artifact deeply influenced by law.[43]

Law facilitates this regime discursively through the normalizing force we have observed before of conceptualizing employment as a contract in which every aspect of the employee's body is available for sale or rent, and discursively constructing women's bodies that are silent, inviting, domestic, perfect, and possessable. Other discursive constructions of the body are of course available. It is worth examining how else the body of Sondra Tamimi might be discursively constructed.

It would be a simple rhetorical matter to deal with employers' appearance requirements by deploying something called a "right" in employees to control their own bodies, including a subsidiary right of control over their bodies' form and display. Karl Klare has recently advocated such a right, which I happily endorse; he has also discussed some of its weaknesses, and I shall add others. Klare mainly discusses the problem we have already observed many times: that rights of appearance autonomy could be alienated, could just be invitation to bargain away that autonomy to the demanding employer. Constructing the body discursively as a right, like property and commodity, is the language of what Foucault calls regulation and serves thereby to inscribe that body into the normal regulatory mechanisms of consumer society.

If the employer can just purchase the body, configured as a right to appearance autonomy, the right either changes nothing or raises transaction costs. Klare recognizes the need for individual bargains about appearance; many firms do have legitimate needs for uniformity, cleanliness, safety, and so on. He places a number of restrictions on these bargains: for example, employees waiving appearance autonomy would have to do so in writing and could not consent to discrimination or sexual harassment. Of course, these restrictions on alienability create litigation issues, and Klare recognizes readily that the "irony of the rights approach is that it transfers decisionmaking from one set of authority figures (employers) to another (judges, officials)."[44]

In the end, the value of the right to appearance autonomy might lie in the employee actions it would help mobilize, the subtle changes in consciousness it might evoke. It would be interesting to know more about the issue on which,

[43] Klare, "Power/Dressing," 1431–32.

[44] Klare, "Power/Dressing," 1442–51 (the quoted sentence is at 1446).

we noted above, the opinion is silent: how Sondra Tamimi expressed her desire not to wear makeup, to herself and to her boss. The court did not go into the question, partly because there were differences of recollection as to what was said, and the court chose to transform the whole case into one of pregnancy discrimination. It is interesting but quite speculative to wonder how conversations like those between Tamimi and Gallof would be altered if employees characteristically believed that they had something called a "right to appearance autonomy" or, better yet, our old friend the judicially rejected "right to do with their bodies what they pleased." Could one expect much difference in the workplace?

Immutable Bodies of Nature, Mutable Bodies of Artifice: Regulating Employees' Hairstyle

One much-criticized case attempts a theoretical framework to determine which employer demands on employee bodies constitute impermissible discrimination. Renee Rogers, an African-American woman and airport operations agent for American Airlines, who had worked for that company for eleven years, was forbidden from wearing her hair in an all-braided, cornrow style. The court dismissed her claim under the Civil Rights Act, finding no race discrimination.[45]

Renee Rogers alleged that the cornrow style has been "historically, a fashion and style adopted by Black American women, reflective of cultural, historical essence of the Black women in American society."[46] To this the court had several responses, not all of them equally cogent or even comprehensible. The court first observed that the grooming policy applied to all employees, and that all-braided hair is worn by white people, too, noting that Renee Rogers first wore her braids to work *after* the white actress Bo Derek had done so in the movie *10*. It is rather as if suggesting that discrimination on the basis of skin color was all right because after all some people of non-African ancestry had dark skin and some people of African ancestry had lighter skin. The Bo Derek point is even more obscure, as if African-Americans are not protected from discrimination on the basis of any African-American visual or cultural manifestation *after* it has been copied—as what African-American cultural institution is not?—by white people.

---

[45] Rogers v. American Airlines, 527 F.Supp. 229 (S.D.N.Y. 1981) (employer ban on braided hairstyles does not violate Title VII of the Civil Rights Act as either race or gender discrimination). For a brilliant analysis of the racial and sexual domination involved, see Paulette M. Caldwell, "A Hair Piece: Perspectives on the Intersection of Race and Gender," 1991 *Duke L. J.* 365. Professor Caldwell particularly criticizes the court's "premise that, although racism and sexism share much in common, they are nevertheless fundamentally unrelated phenomena." Id. 371. I shall not be pursuing these important themes here.

[46] 527 F.Supp. at 232 (quoting Plaintiff's Memorandum in Opposition to Motion to Dismiss).

The court's theory that is worth discussing comes next. It distinguishes between the "natural" or "immutable" aspects of the body, and the "mutable" or "artificial" aspects. The Civil Rights Act, said the court, prohibits "discrimination on the basis of immutable characteristics." Thus, addressing a hypothetical case advanced by Renee Rogers's attorney, "an employer's policy prohibiting the Afro/bush style might offend" the civil rights statutes.[47] "[A]n all-braided hairstyle is a different matter. It is not the product of natural hair growth but of artifice."[48]

This suggests possible theories, both of the protection of the civil rights laws generally and the scope of specific employer power to enforce appearance regulation: employers may not discriminate against, and the civil rights laws protect, immutable characteristics. On the other hand, employers may enforce rules against, and the civil rights laws do not protect, artificial aspects of personal presentation.

Let us deal here only with the question of employer-specific regulation of body display, although both theories end up in the same place: an inquiry into the role of nature and artifice in the acquisition of identity. I should note that, as a theory of civil rights law, the court's statement might suggest that homosexuals, who are not protected as such under federal civil rights statutes, might be protected under the Equal Protection Clause of the Constitution if, but only if, their homosexuality is a "product of nature" or "immutable." Professor Janet Halley has recently criticized just this argument, in an article with which I am happy to agree, relying on much of the recent literature about the social construction of sexuality that I am deploying throughout this book as it applies to the social construction of the body.[49]

There is obviously nothing "natural" about an Afro hairstyle that distinguishes it from the "artifice" of cornrows. Contrary to the court, if the question is which hairstyle performs *African* identity, the all-braided style is "natural" and the Afro or bush style "artificial." "[T]here was nothing particularly African about the Afro at all. Neither [Afro nor dreadlocks] had a given reference point in existing African cultures, in which hair is rarely left to grow 'natu-

---

[47] The court may have been thinking of, but did not specifically mention, two earlier decisions upholding the right to wear Afro hairstyles and finding bans on them to violate the Civil Rights Act. Jenkins v. Blue Cross Mut. Hosp. Ins., Inc., 538 F.2d 164 (7th Cir. 1976) (plaintiff alleges race discrimination in alleging supervisor told her she "could never represent Blue Cross with her Afro"); E.E.O.C. Dec. No. 71-2444, 4 Fair. Emp. Prac. Cas.(BNA) 18 (June 10, 1971). Professor Caldwell comments on these cases in "A Hair Piece" 384 n. 59. But see Equal Employment Opportunity Commission v. United Va. Bank / Seabord Nat'l, 615 F.2d 147, 155 (4th Cir. 1980) (noting ban on Afro or bush hairstyle not evidence of race discrimination: "In view of the fact that bank employees must deal with the public when on company assignment, we cannot see that comments concerning unusual hair styles indicate racial discrimination").

[48] 527 F.Supp. at 232.

[49] Janet E. Halley, "Sexual Orientation and the Politics of Biology: A Critique of the Argument from Immutability," 46 *Stan. L. Rev.* 503 (1994).

rally.' Often it is plaited or braided, using 'weaving' techniques to produce a rich variety of sometimes highly elaborate styles that are reminiscent of the patternings of African cloth and the decorative designs of African ceramics, architecture and embroidery."[50]

"[A]ll human hair is 'cultivated' . . . insofar as it merely provides the raw material for practices, procedures, and ritual techniques of cultural writing and social inscription. . . . [N]obody's hair is ever just natural but is always shaped and reshaped by social convention and symbolic intervention." What is "natural" about the Afro hairstyle of the 1960s, apart from its alternative name, was precisely its

> embrace of a "natural" aesthetic as an alternative ideological code of symbolic value. . . . Its names suggested a link between "Africa" and "nature" and this implied an oppositional stance vis-à-vis artificial techniques of any kind, as if any element of artificiality was imitative of Eurocentric, white-identified, aesthetic ideals. . . .
>
> However radical this counter-move was, its tactical inversion of categories was limited. One reason why may be that the "nature" invoked was not a neutral term but an ideologically loaded *idea* created by binary and dualistic logics within European culture itself. The "nature" brought into play to signify a desire for "liberation" and "freedom" so effectively was also a Western inheritance, sedimented with symbolic meaning and value by traditions of science, philosophy and art. . . . The counterhegemonic tactic of inversion appropriated a particularly romanticist version of nature as a means of empowering the black subject; but by remaining within a dualistic logic of binary oppositionality (to Europe and artifice) the moment of rupture was delimited by the fact that it was only ever an imaginary "Africa" that was put into play. Clearly, this analysis is not to write off the openings and effective liberations gained and made possible by inverting the order of aesthetic oppression; only to point out that the counterhegemonic project inscribed in these hairstyles is not completed or closed, and that this story of struggles over the same symbols continues.[51]

I have quoted at length from Kobena Mercer's book because his semiotic analysis of hairstyle, as an appropriation and critique of the division of "nature" from "culture," applies generally to the construction of the body in *every* manifestation we have seen (and will see) in this book, not just when it comes to employers' appearance regulation. Legal construction of a body is *always* artificial, social, and conventional, even, or perhaps especially, when the body that is constructed is *represented* as natural and immutable. Recall my comments in the introduction about the *construction* of difference involved in a

---

[50] Kobena Mercer, "Black Hair/Style Politics," in *Welcome to the Jungle: New Positions in Black Cultural Studies* 111 (New York: Routledge, 1994), orig. published in 3 *New Formations* 33, 42 (1987).

[51] Id. 105–10.

phrase like "people who look different from them" that purports merely to *represent* difference. (We will have more to say about law's construction of racial identity in chapter 13, in which the dynamic is typically the creation and maintenance of a fictive group identity by the identification and expulsion of a polluting Other.)

If only "immutable" bodies are protected under the civil rights laws, there is no protection at all, for all bodies are mutable. Hair may be cut, grown, straightened, curled, "cultivated," as the Jamaican hairdresser quoted by Kobena Mercer says. Skin may be lightened, noses reshaped through plastic surgery. Of course an employer who required African-American employees to lighten their skins, straighten their hair, and undergo surgery on their noses in order to keep their jobs would discriminate. But how can this be, if these characteristics are not "immutable"?

Does skin, nose, or hair texture symbolize, enact, perform African-American "identity" in a way that cornrows do not? Who decides what performance enacts what identity, anyway? Why can Judge Sofaer in Renee Rogers's case make this interpretation, rather than Kobena Mercer—or better yet, Renee Rogers? Must we choose between two readings of Renee Rogers's body? Is it the commodity on display, the mimetic representation of comfort for airline passengers, in which Judge Sofaer mimetically represents the gaze of the airline passenger, possessing Renee Rogers, or at least interpreting the semiotics of her dream image? Or the vehicle for the performance and enactment by Renee Rogers of her (African-American) (female) (individual) identity?

Or is it that skin lightening, hair straightening, and plastic surgery seem like especially "invasive" and "obtrusive" uses of the body? So they seem to me— but more invasive than sterilization (which I argued employers probably can legally require)? What metric of intrusion, what construction of the body, do we invoke in our images and discourse when we decide what employers may or may not impose? We have watched law trying and failing throughout this book to construct such a body withstanding intrusion (John Moore's spleen, the pregnant woman denied an abortion), and we shall encounter numerous other invasions of that body in the chapters that follow.

Indeed, the entire panoply of employer appearance regulation, the demands for employees of particular weight, fitness, appearance, demonstrates the quite fundamental mutability of all the most basic aspects of the body. The displayed, legible body mocks that discourse of the "sacred" nice body that attempts to reify this refuge from the commercial world, often because this sacred vessel is figured as natural, immutable, firm of boundary and free of pollution. Employers know better; they are able to make use of employees' body display precisely because the human body is mutable. In relatively short periods of time, exercise and diet may create bodies of extraordinary size, girth, strength, and appearance.[52] Employers have imposed even more extreme demands for body modification and presumably are free to do so if the demands fall equally across genders. The mutability of the body is the foundation of significant enterprise, such as cosmetic surgery, exercise, diet, and cosmetics.[53]

Even the sex of a particular body, conventionally treated in our culture as fixed at birth, static and immutable, may not be so immutable as all that, or immutability may reflect merely the conventional, among competing acceptable, ways of thinking about gender.[54]

This is central to such theorists emphasizing the social construction of gender and sexuality as Judith Butler, Monique Wittig, and Eve Kosofsky Sedgwick, all of whom have strongly influenced the present essay on the social construction of the body. "[G]ender attributes, however, are not expressive but performative. . . . these attributes effectively constitute the identity they are said to express or reveal."[55] Human bodies differ from each other in innumerable ways (some people look different), just as they share many features ("Hath not a Jew eyes?"); it is culture, not nature, that normally (but by no means inevitably) divides bodies into two "fundamentally" different genders.[56] "'M. saw that the person who approached was of the opposite sex.' Genders—insofar as there are two and they are defined in contradistinction to one another—may be said to be opposite; but in what sense is XX the opposite of XY?"[57] Considerable apparatuses of social control are necessary in order to maintain and preserve the division of humanity into two, and only two, genders, including suppression of intermediate alternatives.[58] And, of course, surgical operations permit the alteration of even the embodied aspects of sexuality.

Thus, attempts to figure a pure or inviolable body, pure *because* or *insofar as* it is "natural" and "immutable," are doomed to fail, are deeply out of touch

[52] For an amusing and amazing account of this form of mutability of the physical human body, see Samuel Wilson Fussell, *Muscle: Confessions of an Unlikely Bodybuilder* (New York: Poseidon, 1991).

[53] Wolf, *The Beauty Myth.*

[54] Laqueur, *Making Sex.*

[55] Judith Butler, *Gender Trouble: Feminism and the Subversion of Identity* 141 (New York: Routledge, 1990).

[56] For some deviant (ha ha) cases, see *Third Sex, Third Gender: Beyond Sexual Dimorphism in Culture and History* (Gilbert Herdt ed.) (New York: Zone, 1994). Legal implications are discussed in Mary Anne C. Case, "Disaggregating Gender from Sex and Sexual Orientation: The Effeminate Man in the Law and Feminist Jurisprudence," 105 *Yale L. J.* 1 (1995).

[57] Eve Kosofsky Sedgwick, *Epistemology of the Closet* 28 (Berkeley: U. Cal. Pr., 1990).

[58] Marjorie Garber, *Vice Versa: Bisexuality and the Eroticism of Everyday Life* (New York: Simon and Schuster, 1995); Marjorie Garber, *Vested Interests: Cross-Dressing and Cultural Anxiety* (New York: Routledge, 1992).

with the complicated circuits of will, control, and power that condemn the modern body to constant mutability as to weight, appearance, and muscle tone.

Nor is it so clear that "nature" even lines up discursively with "immutable" any longer in our larger culture. Legal opinions like *Rogers,* or the cases on gay rights that Janet Halley criticizes, may be fossilized remains of a figure of speech in which "biological" was a metonym for "immutable," a figure that the larger culture has begun to deconstruct for at least some bodily identities.

> [J]ust as it comes to seem questionable to assume that cultural constructs are peculiarly malleable ones, it is also becoming increasingly problematical to assume that grounding an identity in biology or "essential nature" is a stable way of insulating it from societal interference. If anything, the gestalt of assumptions that undergird nature/nurture debates may be in the process of direct reversal. Increasingly it is the conjecture that a particular trait is genetically or biologically based, *not* that it is "only cultural," that seems to trigger an estrus of manipulative fantasy in the technological institutions of the culture. A relative depressiveness about the efficacy of social engineering techniques, a high mania about biological control: the Cartesian bipolar psychosis that always underlay the nature/nurture debates has switched its polar assignments without surrendering a bit of its hold over the collective life.[59]

Once again, our legal bodies prove far frailer than our discourse of them supposes. A purely commodified body is always for sale, and we have no doctrine that can prevent employees from submitting to any employer demands. If the antidiscrimination laws are to be that doctrine, they are hobbled by adherence to a construction of the body as natural and immutable, a limit to human experience, when the precise problem we face is that the body is always constructed, always performs narratives of existential identity, may always be altered in form and in discourse. The question is, rather, who may alter any given body? Once again the discourse that attempts to give that power to the person "inside" the body is the discourse of the commodified body, and that body, while empowering in some ways, simultaneously advances the specularization of the body, particularly the female body, which is an essential element of visual possession and dream consumption which so many women find particularly oppressive.

---

[59] Sedgwick, *Epistemology of the Closet* 43. Sedgwick writes about so-called gay or homosexual identity, and surely she is correct to suggest that our culture would regard a hormonally based "sexual identity" as *more* mutable than a culturally based identity. I think (as she does) that the point is of broader applicability, as employment lawyers know: the fact that a human trait is *bodily* grants it no immunity from employer demands for alteration.

Chapter 7

SUPPRESSING BODILY DISPLAY: LEGAL BREASTS, SUNBATHING, DANCE, PHOTOGRAPHIC IMAGES

DESIRE FOR THE BODY is not limited to the particular dream imagery associated with marketing and discussed in the last chapter. Nude bodies or their representations excite desire for other purposes and thus present other problems in legal regulation, the obverse of the problem of the last chapter: not the specularization of the dominated, but the suppression of the display of the willing. The cases involving Sondra Tamimi and Renee Rogers, like the works of Michel Foucault and his followers, have conditioned us to imagine the body, often female, constituted as the object of the male gaze.[1]

A common competing legal response, though, is not to gaze at the body, but to make it disappear entirely.[2] An example of this response is the suppression of nude dancing or other display of the female (or male) body. The responses are only superficially opposed to each other, since they share a common discourse in which legal authority overcomes a claim of individual body autonomy. Both effect this result by constructing the regulated body, not for its utilitarian-commodity or rights-holding value, but as object of some gaze's desire.

---

[1] Michel Foucault has linked the "gaze" with particular forms of domination by professionals, here, medical professionals. Michel Foucault, *The Birth of the Clinic: An Archaeology of Medical Perception* 159–70 (A. M. Sheridan Smith trans.) (New York: Pantheon, 1973). Feminist scholars have linked "seeing" with characteristically male ways of apprehending the universe and contrasted this sort of seeing with a fuller repertoire of sensory knowledge. Evelyn Fox Keller and C. R. Grontkowski, "The Mind's Eye," in *Discovering Reality: Feminist Perspectives on Epistemology* (Sandra Harding and Merrill B. Hintikka eds.) (Dordrecht: Reidell, 1983); Viviane Forrester, "Le Regard des Femmes," in *New French Feminisms* 181–82 (Elaine Marks and Isabelle de Courtivron eds.) (New York: Schocken, 1981), as well as calling for a redefinition of seeing, not as rapacious possession of the other, but as caress, affinity, and empathy. Luce Irigaray, *An Ethics of Sexual Difference* (Carolyn Burke and Gillian Gill trans.) (Ithaca: Cornell U. Pr., 1993) [1984]. If "seeing" is the *limited* kind of knowledge one would expect from male professionals, it doesn't seem too much to ask legal professionals to see more when they turn their attention to human bodies. A demand that law "see" the body is thus useful, though a fuller range of sensory knowledge, and a redefinition of seeing, would be even better.

[2] See generally Jane Gallop, *Thinking through the Body* 3–4 (New York: Colum. U. Pr., 1988); K. M. Figlio, "Theories of Perception and the Physiology of Mind in the Late Eighteenth Century," 13 *Hist. Sci.* 177 (1975). For a general philosophic study of the ways in which bodily experience disappears from perception, see Drew Leader, *The Absent Body* (Chicago: U. Chi. Pr., 1990).

There are some mysteries here, all the same. If (some) men like to see naked women, and if men make the law, why aren't women on display whenever anyone wants them to be? Why is nudity ever suppressed? Secondly, if, as we have seen, aspects of the body sometimes considered sacred or beyond contract may nevertheless become alienable property, one might conclude that commercial nudity would be permitted wherever noncommercial nudity was—and this is not the case, legally, as we shall see.

The current legal framework under which some bodily displays are suppressed in the "public" interest is totally incoherent, since nudity is not private and suppression is not a public interest. This gap necessitates the construction of a particularly slippery body that is and is not private, is and is not public, is and is not sexual or sexually differentiated, and other similar incoherencies. Some recognition of law's active social construction of the body has begun to appear in this corner of law. To my mind, however, as I hope to show, law would be better off with a discourse of power and domination than by merely stopping at the recognition that bodies are socially constructed.

THE LEGAL FEMALE BREAST: NATURE, FETISH, DIFFERENCE

Despite the commonness of representations of the female breast in advertising, magazines not considered legally obscene, and film, it continues to be illegal in many places for women to expose their breasts.

> On a summer day in June of 1989, Ms. Biocic, an adult female, was walking on the beach on the Chincoteague National Wildlife Refuge in Accomack County, Virginia, with a male companion. "To get some extra sun," as she put it, she removed the top of her two-piece bathing suit, fully exposing her breasts. She was observed in this state of partial nudity by an officer of the federal Fish and Wildlife Service who issued her a summons charging a violation of 50 C.F.R. §27.83, which provides that
>
> > [a]ny act of indecency or disorderly conduct as defined by State or local laws is prohibited on any national wildlife refuge.
>
> A magistrate judge convicted Ms. Biocic of violating this regulation after a trial in which the facts above summarized were established without essential dispute. Specifically, the magistrate judge concluded that Ms. Biocic's conduct constituted an "act of indecency" within the meaning of §9.3 of the Accomack County Code. In relevant part, that "anti-nudity" ordinance, following a Preamble which recites that the enacting body "deems it necessary to prohibit certain conduct . . . in order to secure and promote the health, safety and general welfare of the [county's] inhabitants," makes it
>
> > unlawful for any person to knowingly, voluntarily, and intentionally appear . . . in a place open to the public or open to public view, in a state of nudity.
>
> "State of nudity" is then defined in a definitional section as

a state of undress so as to expose the human male or female genitals, pubic
area or buttocks with less than a fully opaque covering, or the showing of the
female breast with less than a fully opaque covering on any portion thereof
below the top of the nipple.

Jeanine Biocic's conviction and fine of twenty-five dollars were affirmed on
appeal.[3]

Legal discourse enacts an event like Jeanine Biocic's removing her top
through a series of binarisms, switch points that direct the train of legal proceedings to one destination or another. Jeanine Biocic's removing her top
either exposes a *body part* or *nudity,* is either *public* or *private,* is either *expression* or *conduct,* either *like men* or *distinctly female,* either *sexual* or *not.*
As her body may be constructed in legal discourse as *any* or *all* of these, even
within the same opinion, it is not surprising that her body will function as a
condensed symbol of these and other binarisms, around which liberal legalism
organizes and rationalizes the fragmentation of our individual spirits, and the
state's powers.

Body Part/Nude Body

Law discursively mimetically represents Jeanine Biocic's lack of control over
her own body in its discursive fetishistic fragmentation of that body, through
legal prose, into body parts. In the excerpt quoted above, the word "body"
appears once, but not to refer to Jeanine Biocic. Jeanine Biocic attempts to get
"some extra sun" without specifying a body part; by contrast, in the eyes of
the law, she exposes her breasts. Jeanine Biocic is discursively figured to have
"breasts," "conduct," commit an "act of indecency," be in a "state of nudity."
The discourse fragments Jeanine Biocic's body into morsels, some of which
she owns or controls, others that she does not.

In the history of art, the appearance of a body fragment, as Linda Nochlin
has recently shown with care, has no single determinate meaning. The body
fragment may represent nostalgia for a lost whole (such as a fragment of an
antique statue), or the horror of mutilation, or the flow of modern life, glimps-
ing bodies obliquely, or a fetish (that is, an object of misplaced worship in
substitution for something else), or a suggestion of sexual availability "outside" the painting, or a signboard advertising a commodity. While Nochlin
thus resists any "grandiose, all-encompassing 'theory of the fragment in relation to the concept of modernity,'"[4] it is striking that Nochlin discusses no
example in which the body represented in fragments or fragmented glimpses,
belongs to an individual with more power than those individuals represented

---

[3] United States v. Biocic, 928 F.2d 112 (4th Cir. 1991).

[4] Linda Nochlin, *The Body in Pieces: The Fragment as a Metaphor of Modernity* 56 (New
York: Thames and Hudson, 1995).

as whole: the fragmented bodies in her book belong to the long-dead, the replaced aristocrat, or women.

The court's breaking up of Jeanine Biocic's body into parts thus emphasizes the viewpoint of the gazer (with power) that homes in on particular parts of the body, in a kind of visual fetishism in which "the historically unnameable parts of the female body come to stand for the rest of it."[5] Monique Wittig among others has criticized this kind of anatomical synecdoche, this refusal to see the female body as whole (even when evoked by feminist authors like Luce Irigaray), as "an uncritical replication of a reproductive discourse that marks and carves up the female body into artificial 'parts' like 'vagina,' 'clitoris,' and 'vulva.' At a lecture at Vassar College, Wittig was asked whether she had a vagina, and she replied that she did not."[6]

So Jeanine Biocic is fragmented in law's discourse, embodied, even "possessing" a body, only virtually, in virtue of her breasts "standing in" for it. This interpretation would apply whenever law focuses discursively on a particular body part. Of course, there is an extensive corpus of writings, particularly by Freudians, on the symbolic aspects particularly of the human breast. I am not certain how illuminating all this is with respect to the legal breast, which clearly exists as a member of a broader category of hidden body parts; the opinion in Jeanine Biocic's case would be have been even less sympathetic to her had she exposed her genitals or buttocks or her male companion's genitals. (Interestingly, as Iris Marion Young writes, "[T]here is an amazing absence of writing about women's experiences of breasts"; her essay, from which I will be quoting, is a valuable first step).[7]

Readers interested in exploring further the Freudian version of the relationship between the symbolic breast and body fragmentation might recall that, for Freud and all Freudians, the breast is the original object of desire, from which desire is later transferred to the genital region in normal sexual development, though the process is said to be different for boys and girls.[8] As Peter

---

[5] Helena Michie, *The Flesh Made Word: Female Figures and Women's Bodies* 141 (New York: Oxford U. Pr., 1987) ("[I]n Victorian literature and culture various parts of the body came to be fetishized sexually and representationally, as nameable, accessible parts of the body came to stand for the unnameable whole/hole. Twentieth-century sexual culture, the sexual 'revolution,' has produced an inversion of Victorian representational tropes, where the historically unnameable parts of the female body come to stand for the rest of it." On fetishism, see generally Emily Apter, *Feminizing the Fetish: Psychoanalysis and Narrative Obsession in Turn-of-the-Century France* (Ithaca: Cornell U. Pr., 1991).

[6] Judith Butler, *Gender Trouble: Feminism and the Subversion of Identity* 157 n. 54 (New York: Routledge, 1990).

[7] Iris Marion Young, "Breasted Experience: The Look and the Feeling," in *Throwing Like a Girl and Other Essays in Feminist Philosophy and Social Theory* 205 (Bloomington: Ind. U. Pr, 1990).

[8] Sigmund Freud, "Three Essays on the Theory of Sexuality" [1905], 7 *Standard Edition of the Complete Psychological Works of Sigmund Freud* 222 (James Strachey ed.) (London: Hogarth, 1953).

Brooks has recently reminded us, following Freud and Melanie Klein, the breast is an original object of the desire to *know* as well as to eat or possess sexually.[9] In Jacques Lacan's account, the stage of desire for the breast is a stage at which the infant lacks a unified sense of its own body, experiencing only *le corps morcelé* (the fragmented body), so desire for the breast is of a piece with body fragmentation. All this precedes, for Lacan, the celebrated mirror stage, at which the child simultaneously acquires (through the image of the Other) a sense of its integrated body; rejects the mother; and acquires linguistic and symbolic competence; all of which inscribes the child into a world of phallic authority.[10] For Judith Butler, as for other feminists writing in a Freudian tradition, the association of the phallus with symbolic ordering reflects a sexist society; other body parts might well play this integrating role, and the very need of the Lacanian script to be reiterated in performance opens possibilities for alternative resignifications.[11] This might suggest that what is being repressed in a case like *United States v. Biocic* is precisely an infantile desire for the breast, as the lost, foregone object of desire, and that the court's visual fetishism reenacts the prohibited state. This might also suggest why male and female breasts are treated differently in public nudity statutes, in a way that genitals are not.

Jeanine Biocic has no body, only a fetishized collection of body parts. Who has a body? The legislative arm/organ/body of Accomack County has a body, for it is the "enacting body" of which the court speaks, the "enacting body" that "deems it necessary to prohibit certain conduct." Jeanine Biocic may remove her top, but she cannot be the "enacting body," since she is deprived of hers. Law, legislatures, appropriate the body.

It is, incidentally, absolutely remarkable how often this pun will reappear (see particularly chap. 14). A remarkably high percentage of legal cases involving use, invasion, or other definition of the body employ the *word* "body" repeatedly to refer, never to the body being regulated, always to the governmental authority.

Public/Private

This fundamental contradiction, on which a large critical literature exists,[12] requires constant policing. The body, as we have observed, often mimetically represents a *private* world of domesticity, autonomy, and freedom, as well as a

[9] Peter Brooks, *Body Work: Objects of Desire in Modern Narrative* 7 (Cambridge: Harv. U. Pr., 1993).

[10] Jacques Lacan, "The Mirror Stage as Formative of the Function of the I as Revealed in Psychoanalytic Experience, in E*crits: A Selection* 1, 4 (Alan Sheridan trans.) (New York: Norton, 1977) [1949].

[11] Judith Butler, "The Lesbian Phallus," in *Bodies That Matter: On the Discursive Limits of "Sex"* 89 (New York: Routledge, 1993).

[12] Symposium, 130 *U. Pa. L. Rev.* No. 6 (June 1982); Robert Hale, "Coercion and Distribution in a Supposedly Non-Coercive State," 38 *Pol. Sci. Q.* 470 (1923).

public world of politics, the social order. It thus often symbolically polices the line between public and private. In Jeanine Biocic's case, Accomack County has a body, but she does not.

A second issue, in which legal discourse must construct a "public" that is binarily opposite to "private" in a way that effaces intermediate or third terms, is a feature of all cases, like Jeanine Biocic's, that construct something called "public nudity." The most oppressive government never forbids all nudity, after all, yet the statutes require a construction of "public" binarily opposi- tional to "private" in a way that is inevitably artificial.

In Jeanine Biocic's case, the statute is violated only by one who appears in the statutory "state of nudity" "in a place open to the public or open to public view." Was the beach at Chincoteague such a place? A concurring judge pre- sents a rather different picture than the majority. Biocic "was first careful to scan the scene in an attempt to insure no one would be offended." "She exer- cised vigilance to be out of sight of everyone but her male companion. He obviously perceived no indecency in Biocic's act, at least the record reveals no objection on his part to what she was doing."

So in what sense is her nudity in a "public place"? First, the beach was a place "where members of the public who might be potentially offended *might* venture upon her in her state of deshabille."

Second, "the valiant Fish and Wildlife service officer who skillfully eluded detection by Biocic through skulking behind sand dunes until the opportunity to swoop down like a wolf on the fold first presented itself" "may have been an essential ingredient of the crime charged."[13] The crime of "public nudity" is created by the public official; before he appears, there may have been no crime. This is true in a strict legal sense; equally true discursively. Judith Butler addresses Senator Jesse Helms's "antipornography" amendments (about which more momentarily) but is equally apt on sec. 9.3 of the Ac- comack County Code: "Is this a production of a figure that it itself outlaws from production, a vehement and public way of drawing into public attention the very figure that is supposed to be banned from public attention . . . ?"[14]

The United States Supreme Court recently had a tough time explaining what makes "public nudity" "public." Like Accomack County, the State of Indiana forbids nudity "in a public place."[15] The Supreme Court held that this statute could be applied to the totally nude dancing by Darlene Miller and

[13] Biocic, 928 F.2d at 118 n. 2 (Murnaghan, J., concurring).

[14] Judith Butler, "The Force of Fantasy: Feminism, Mapplethorpe, and Discursive Excess," 2 *Differences* 105, 117 (1990).

[15] Indiana Code § 35-45-4-1, sec. 1(a) (1988), quoted in Barnes v. Glen Theatre, Inc., 501 U.S. 560, 569 n. 2 (1991). As in the Accomack County ordinance, "nudity" had a specialized meaning: "the showing of the human male or female genitalia, public area, or buttocks with less than a fully opaque covering, the showing of the female breast with less than a fully opaque covering of any part of the nipple, or the showing of the covered male genitals in a discernibly turgid state."

Gayle Ann Marie Sutro, proposed to be shown inside the Kitty Kat Lounge in South Bend. The statute followed a long line of prohibitions of public nudity, dating at least from 1831 and thus long predating barroom dancing. It had however been held by the Indiana Supreme Court to apply as well to nudity in places of "public accommodation," despite the fact, urged by counsel for the lounge, that "[i]n such places . . . minors are excluded and there are no non-consenting viewers." If nudity in bars with restricted admission is nevertheless public and suppressible, as the Supreme Court held, then it cannot matter in Jeanine Biocic's case whether or not someone who might have been offended might have seen her.

The application of the public indecency statute to barroom dancing did have the effect of suppressing what the Court grudgingly described as "expressive conduct within the outer perimeters of the First Amendment, though we view it as only marginally so." As the Court punningly put it, quoting from an earlier decision, "the customary 'barroom' type of nude dancing may involve only the barest minimum of protected expression."[16] The Court under its precedents thus had to identify a purpose or public interest secured by the application of the public-indecency statute to such expression. (Don't miss, however, as we pass, the recurring figure in which a constitutional provision, here, the First Amendment, is figured as occupying a geographic area with "perimeters" that may be pierced or intruded upon, as noted in chapter 4 above. Here the First Amendment is personified as if it, not the dancers, had body boundaries. We will return to this figure in chapter 12 when, armed with the anthropological writings of Mary Douglas, we further analyze the trope of hyperconcern for boundaries under invasion).

This way of setting up the problem requires the body of a nude dancer in a bar to be both public and private. Her body must be public, else there has been no violation of the "public indecency" statute. That crime requires not only a nude body but a "public" gazer to constitute an offense. Since the actual exposure of the body took place on private property to which admission was controlled, the body is public only in Benjamin's sense of the commodity on display, imaginarily possessed by the eye though not physically exchanged. On the other hand, there must be a "public" interest in the suppression of that "public" display. The body of the nude dancer may not be permitted synecdochally to represent "the public interest," res publica or the public body, in the way that successful invokers of the First Amendment, political speakers and newspapers, synecdochally represent, with their bodies, an imagined political body. Here, by contrast, a "public" interest must be constructed that supports suppression of the nude dance, which thus becomes a "private" and partial interest.

So, under established principles of First Amendment law, having found that

---

[16] 501 U.S. at 565, quoting Doran v. Salem Inn, Inc., 422 U.S. 922, 932 (1975).

Indiana's statute infringed protected expression, the Court had to determine a permissible public purpose served by that infringement, a purpose itself unrelated to the suppression of free expression.[17] It turned out that the permissible public purpose served by a prohibition on public nudity was . . . prohibiting public nudity. (Don't ask about how these apply inside bars). "Public indecency statutes such as the one before us reflect moral disapproval of people appearing in the nude among strangers in public places."[18]

The dissent had a hard time understanding how the suppression of nude dancing expressed a purpose, suppression of public nudity, that was unrelated to the effect of suppressing expression. Indeed, the statute *only* prohibited publicly expressive nudity, not nudity as such, so reached exclusively expression: everything that made the dancing "public" also, definitionally, made it "expressive." Legal discourse fragments the nudity from the body, just as economic discourse fragments the labor power from the body, without in either case explaining how this fragmentation is possible.

Since the posthumous release of Justice Marshall's papers, we now know that *Barnes v. Glen Theatre* was a case in which the Court majority decided simply to uphold the Indiana statute and then flailed around for a rationale that could command five votes, and that Chief Justice Rehnquist in particular could take opposite sides of a subsidiary issue so long as one would get him to the result he sought.[19] I will not pursue an analysis of the legal issues in *Barnes,* except to note with concern the willingness of four justices, Rehnquist, O'Connor, Kennedy, and Scalia, to treat conventional "morality" as sufficient ground, indeed a putatively neutral public purpose, for suppressing protected expression; the implications of this approach for such protected expression as art, dance, and theater have yet to be explored.[20]

For a high proportion of my students these days, including most self-described conservatives as well as liberals, the most pressing task in American constitutional law is to strengthen the boundaries of a "sphere" called "privacy," immune from state regulation and interference. This sphere would in-

---

[17] I am passing over all the legal intricacies of the First Amendment, which offers several competing schemes of categorization that might have been employed by the Court. A good introduction to the legal issues and the potential modes of analysis that might have been adopted is Daniel Yves Hall (student author), "Stripping Away First Amendment Protection: Barnes v. Glen Theatre, Inc.," 57 *Mo. L. Rev.* 631 (1992).

[18] Barnes, 501 U.S. at 568. Note again the embodiment of the statute: the statute stands "before us" as if it had a body; Darlene Miller and Gayle Ann Marie Sutro, the dancers do not stand "before us," since "we" hold that their bodies may not be seen.

[19] Mark Tushnet, "Rule of Law, or Rule of Five?" *The Nation,* November 1, 1993, at 497, 498.

[20] See "State Restrictions on Nude Dancing," 105 *Harv. L. Rev.* 287, 287–97 (1991); Vincent Blasi, "Six Conservatives in Search of the First Amendment: The Revealing Case of Nude Dancing," 33 *Wm. & Mary L. Rev.* 611 (1992); Zachary T. Fardon, "*Barnes v. Glen Theatre, Inc.:* Nude Dancing and the First Amendment Question," 45 *Vand. L. Rev.* 237 (1992); Gianni P. Servodidio, "The Devaluation of Nonobscene Eroticism as a Form of Expression Protected by the First Amendment," 67 *Tul. L. Rev.* 1231 (1993).

clude a woman's right to abortion as well as a right to engage in private consensual homosexual relations; the shadow of *Bowers v. Hardwick,* in which the Supreme Court did not find such a right included in the constitutional right to privacy, falls as heavily on the current generation of law students as *Brown v. Board of Education* or *Roe v. Wade* fell on some of their predecessors. For these students, control over one's own body is the core, defining concept of this expanded right to privacy, understood precisely as an extension of control of the body. When I discuss *Barnes* with these students, the key to the case for them is often the fact that the dancing at the Glen Theater took place between consenting adults in a private place for which admission was charged, facts that argue for them in favor of placing nude dancing into their expanded notion of the private. I often accuse law students these days of being ready to revive *Lochner v. New York* (the Supreme Court's striking down of a maximum-hours law in 1904 as a violation of "liberty of contract"; see chap. 2) in a minute if it would get them a reversal of *Bowers v. Hardwick.* Lawyers who wanted to establish just this expanded "zone of privacy," which would include rights to abort, homosexual sex, and to work as a nude dancer, could avail themselves of the commodified body as a construction of autonomy discussed and criticized in chapters 3 through 5.

While I certainly support the right to an abortion in *Roe v. Wade* and the reversal of *Bowers v. Hardwick,* I prefer to see both choices as ways of including people in participation in public life, not as stakes supporting boundary fences that lock people into their bodies as a kind of refuge from public life. On this view, mentioned briefly in chapter 4, women have a right to abortion in order to be able to participate in all social roles (and invent new ones), as gay people have a right to participate honestly in society without having to suppress their identities.[21]

Readers need not join me in this or any other defense of abortion rights or gay rights, but anyone tempted to base either on a right to privacy or bodily integrity might confront the question whether the body may be made to function successfully as a private refuge from civil society, or even as the foundation for a concept of the private. Cases like *Biocic* and *Barnes* show me that it cannot. First, they display the sheer range of constructions of the body on which law draws, so that, even if law deploys a construction of the private body in *Roe v. Wade,* and could be made to do so in our hypothetical reversed *Bowers v. Hardwick,* it is still a public, social, conventional act of construction going on. Second, neither the body of Jeanine Biocic nor Darlene Miller is constructed as a site of self-definition and control, suggesting how weak is our law's commitment to any such idea and how readily law recognizes public intrusions into any supposed body autonomy. As we have seen, positing a right to bodily control for Jeanine Biocic or Darlene Miller would not neces-

---

[21] See Janet E. Halley, "The Politics of the Closet: Towards Equal Protection for Gay, Lesbian, and Bisexual Identity," 36 *UCLA L. Rev.* 915 (1989).

sarily mean that they would win their cases, as those rights would be weighed against other interests. The failure even to invoke the concept of body autonomy on their behalf shows how weakly it is established. Third, those legal bodies are easily constructed as a kind of a public threat, even where unobserved by anyone but the willing and paying. Fourth, those bodies become public precisely when law adopts the subject position of a fictive gazer, metaphysically present, making the body public, when it watches the body through the eyes of "conventional morality." This gazer would inevitably define our new, proposed "body integrity" and would define it as the passive object of its own possessing gaze. Jeanine Biocic and Darlene Miller could expose their bodies only as permitted or ordered by the gaze.

Fifth, like the body of Jeanine Biocic, the bodies of the nude dancers in *Barnes* are discursively appropriated to personify (punningly) the statute:

> It is without cavil that the public indecency statute is "narrowly tailored"; Indiana's requirement that the dancers wear at least pasties and a G-string is modest, and the bare minimum necessary to achieve the state's purpose.[22]

It is hard to think this is unintentional. I don't personally find the pun clever or amusing but regard it as a display of power in which tailoring, modesty, and bareness are discursively transferred from the body to the metaphorical body of the state.

So from my students' perspective, cases like *Biocic* and *Barnes* are failures. They fail to construct a firm, private body with the power to order its own display and enter its own contracts. What if we turned this failure around? *Biocic* and *Barnes* are public bodies, publicly constituted, publicly performed. Like the bodies discussed by Judith Butler, they are the site of an erotic love that, theatrically represented and performed reiteratively, represents society, not an exemption from it.[23] We should not look for just that body fragment that grounds an isolated world of privacy, but rather the reiterated public performances that place loving bodies in the center of public space, constructing a whole world out of them.

Expression/Conduct

The binarism between expression and conduct is surely less fundamental than that between public and private.[24] For legal purposes the body must continually mediate between public and private, and vast quantities of legal regulation make no sense unless people can be induced to feel this distinction at the level of the body experiences they construct. By contrast, the distinction between expression and conduct is internal only to certain problems under the First Amendment, where it inevitably appears somewhat artificial. Nevertheless,

---

[22] Barnes, 501 U.S. at 572.

[23] Butler, *Gender Trouble* 134–49, *Bodies That Matter* 1–16.

[24] This section draws in part on a seminar paper by Michelle J. Anderson.

like other binary fragmentation, the distinction between expression and conduct is played out on the surface of the body, which stands in both for expression and for conduct.

We have seen this fragmentation already. Nude dancing at the Kitty Kat Lounge is "expression," though a low order of expression that may be suppressed in the name of conventional morality. The nudity, however, as "distinct" from the nude dancing, is not expression. In apparent contrast, the concurring judge in Jeanine Biocic's case lamented that Ms. Biocic had not pursued a First Amendment argument that her removing her top was protected expression.[25] One judge would protect nudity as expression under the Constitution; the majority on the Supreme Court would not; yet both share a discourse of body fragmentation in which the nudity is reified into something distinct from the body, so that whatever result is reached as to this factitious "nudity" has no resonance in cases seeking to define the autonomy of the "body."

Exposure of the body as a kind of political expression is not the facetious argument of counsel or limited to contexts such as artistic representation; there is a political movement the very content of which includes body exposure as a political act. Of course, this does not require courts to construct the naked body as expression rather than conduct, and one court with an opportunity to make this choice decided, rather, to refigure what was intended as a self-consciously political display of the body, into "conduct" rather than "expression." This shows once again the oxymoron involved in the legal recognition of individual or group self-expression, for in law self-expression is identifiable as such only as mimetically represented by a body of the state.

Although the opinion of the court breathes no hint of the fact, the criminal prosecution for "exposure of a person" that reached the New York Court of Appeals in *People v. Santorelli* grew out of a planned political protest in the name of a particular group of feminists whose cause is to overturn the laws that mandate that women's breasts remain hidden.[26] The "shirtfree" movement is associated with, if not the creation of, an activist and gadfly named Nikki Craft, one of the defendants in *Santorelli*.[27] Many of its themes receive philosophic support in a careful essay by Iris Marion Young.[28]

According to this group, statutes banning the exposure of women's breasts perform several functions, none of them admirable. First, they create a spu-

[25] Biocic, 928 F.2d at 117 n. 1 (Murnaghan, J., concurring).

[26] People v. Santorelli, 600 NE.2d 232 (N.Y. 1992). See Reena N. Glazer (student author), "Women's Body Image and the Law," 43 *Duke L. J.* 113 (1993).

[27] Nikki Craft, "A Crafty Zapper," in *In Stitches: A Patchwork of Feminist Humor and Satire* 156–60 (Gloria Kaufman ed.) (Bloomington: Indiana U. Pr., 1991). See also Kathy Shorr, "An Interview with Nikki Craft," *Provincetown Magazine,* July 29, 1986, at 15; Diana E. H. Russell, "Nikki Craft: Inspiring Protest," in *Femicide: The Politics of Woman Killing* 325–45 (Jill Radford and Diana E. H. Russell eds.) (New York: Twayne, 1992).

[28] Young, "Breasted Experience."

rious inequality between men and women. Men's and women's breasts are anatomically virtually identical, apart from the ability to lactate in recently-pregnant women, and average size and fat content, neither of which is a relevant factor in statutory prohibitions (which apply to women who are flat-chested). Both men's and women's breasts have nipples with erectile capacity.[29] Nor can male and female breasts be distinguished, it is claimed, by the social fact of being stimulating sexually to members of the opposite sex; some researchers claim to have found that the chest is the male body part most sexually stimulating to women (and even if it's not the *most* stimulating, it's certainly stimulating).[30] Indeed, men were arrested and fined for being shirtless on the beach as late as 1934.[31] A simple argument for equal protection of the laws is that women should be permitted the freedom men have had for sixty years or so.[32]

The shirtfree movement makes more than this rather abstract equality claim. They argue that the taboo on the voluntary exposure of women's breasts artificially maintains a market scarcity supporting such sexually exploitative industries as pornography. "Women seemingly can only take their tops of whenever there's money to be made. We can go-go dance in strip clubs and pose for girlie magazines. But try breast-feeding in public or topless sun-bathing and you're liable for public disapproval."[33] The taboo against woman-controlled exposure supports such typically male-controlled exposure as topless doughnut shops, car washes, and the kinds of advertising appeals discussed in the last chapter.

Finally, the shirtfree movement argues that the statutes against exposure permit women's images of breasts to be dominated by the media-created image of the perfect breast. "Women's self-esteem about their own bodies plummets when they are forbidden from viewing the delightfully imperfect variations of their sisters' torsos, while dangerous cosmetic surgery surges when the only breasts seen are silicone-injected."[34] Unintentionally comic confirmation of this concern came in the reported comments of a Miami City Commissioner: "I'm not against breasts. My point is that they shouldn't be displayed on the beach in front of kids and women."[35]

[29] Jack Morin, "Male Breast: Overlooked Erogenous Zone," 20 *Medical Aspects of Human Sexuality* 85, 128 (1986).

[30] Robert Wildman et al., "Note on Males' and Females' Preferences for Opposite-Sex Body Parts, Bust Sizes, and Bust-Revealing Clothing," 38 *Psychol. Rep.* 485–86 (1976).

[31] *New York Times,* June 22, 1934, p. 3.

[32] Two members of the New York Court of Appeals would have reversed the conviction in *Santorelli* on equal-protection grounds. 600 NE.2d at 234 (Titone, J., concurring).

[33] Anna-Liza Kozma, "Breasts Emancipation May Be a Setback," *Chicago Tribune,* Sept. 20, 1992, p. 13.

[34] Michelle J. Anderson, "Shirtfree Rights and the Legal Status of Breasts" 3 (unpublished seminar paper) (May 1994).

[35] Neil Brown, "Morality in Striking Contrast," *Miami Herald,* June 12, 1983, p. B1.

The cases that came to the New York Court of Appeals as *Santorelli* grew out of a pair of public demonstrations against New York's gendered "exposure of the person" law in which women in Rochester removed their tops. While the court did reverse their convictions and narrowed the statute, reading it not to apply to noncommercial exposures that are not "lewd," the court did not recognize that the exposures were a political protest or reach any issues under the First Amendment.[36] All of which goes to show that legal rights linked to body "expression" simply empower adjudicators to construct fairly ordinary body activities as either expression or conduct. The paradox is drawn nicely by contrasting Jeanine Biocic, who wanted more sun but is treated by a concurring judge as if she might have engaged in expression, with Ramona Santorelli, who thought she was engaged in political protest but was said to have engaged in "conduct," albeit conduct uncovered (as it were) by the relevant statute.

Nudity itself is a kind of disguise. My favorite judicial construction of the unclothed body is over two hundred years old but well illustrates the power of the gaze to construct the body it chooses to see. This particular body was male. E. P. Thompson discusses a conviction and execution in 1725 under a criminal statute providing death for those who joined, "in disguise," any riot or assault on an officer. The indictment of Charles Towers alleged his entry into the bailiff's house "with a large stick, his hair clipt off, without hat, wig or shirt, only with a blue pea-jacket, which flying open showed his breast as well as his face black and besmeared with soot and grease." Towers "told a sympathetic crowd that 'he was not disguised when he rescued Mr. West, unless the dirty condition he was commonly in could be so termed.' It is a nice comment on eighteenth-century polite sensibility that cropped unpowdered hair and the absence of a wig, and a jacket flying open to reveal his bare breast, should be taken to constitute 'disguise.'"[37]

Sex Discrimination/Real Differences

We have noted before how the body figures classically both as the site par excellence of human similarity (Hath not a Jew eyes?) and difference (some people don't look like us). The protesters in *Santorelli* sought reversal of their convictions on the grounds that a statute prohibiting exposure of the female, but not male, breast constituted sex discrimination. Are female breasts "the same" or "different" from male breasts? The differences we observe in aver-

---

[36] A separate concurrence pointed out, quite accurately, that the majority's limiting the statute to lewd, commercial exposures flew in the face of the expressed desire by sponsors, and the governor, to reach public nude sunbathing. 600 NE.2d at 235 (Titone, J., concurring). See also Glazer, "Women's Body Image," 119–21.

[37] E. P. Thompson, *Whigs and Hunters: The Origin of the Black Act* 247–49 (New York: Pantheon, 1975). The statute was 9 George I c.28.

age size and shape matter, or not, only as figured in larger discursive constructions of sexual difference, in which "gender ontologies always operate within
established political contexts as normative injunctions, determining what
qualifies as intelligible sex."[38] Not only does the finding or not of difference
reproduce larger political narratives within which particular differences are
produced and given meaning, but the very search for or questioning of difference are political narratives in which some regulatory purpose motivates and
shapes the inquiry into difference. Difference between the sexes is never just
difference, is always political. This is clear enough when a judge in California
in 1975 writes:

> Nature, not the legislative body, created the distinction between that portion of a
> woman's body and that of a man's torso. Unlike the situation with respect to men,
> nudity in the case of women is commonly understood to include the uncovering
> of the breasts. Consequently, in proscribing nudity on the part of women it was
> necessary to include express reference to that area of the body.[39]

Readers who have come this far can now deconstruct this discursive creation
of the very difference that it attributes, albeit uncertainly, to Nature. Women
have a "portion" of a "body," men have a "torso," the legislature has a "body."
Woman's body is taken from her and attributed to the legislature; for a
woman, the unnameable part stands in and represents the missing body. Reference to that unnameable area is, dizzyingly, within three short sentences,
"necessary to . . . refer," "commonly understood," and given by "Nature."
Obviously if it's given by Nature, it doesn't matter whether it's commonly
understood, but it's the construction of sexual difference as "necessary" that
gives the game away. "Necessary" effaces the court's own agency in constructing the differences it claims to find; it's the oldest move in the book;
courts never do anything with claims of "necessity" except efface their own
agency.

   The concurrence in *Santorelli* attempted to flip this one around, attempted,
not without difficulty, to construct male and female breasts as "the same,"
where two decades earlier the California court had seen only difference. Judge
Titone admitted that "public sensibilities" might well be different respecting
male and female breasts, but he denied that these could support different treatment as to gender if they were "grounded in prejudice and unexamined stereotypes."[40] He repeated with apparent approval the argument of defendants that
any perception of prurient interest attached to the female breast "cannot serve

---

[38] Butler, *Gender Trouble* 148.

[39] Eckl v. Davis, 124 Cal.Rptr. 685, 696 (2d Dist. 1975). The invocation of "Nature" as a
source of authority is reminiscent of the philosophy of the French Enlightenment, until Sade
demonstrated the range of behavior consistent with "Nature" and the consequent unavailability of
"Nature" as a moral standard.

[40] 600 NE.2d at 236.

as a justification for differential treatment because it is itself a suspect cultural artifact rooted in centuries of prejudice and bias towards women."[41]

As judicial utterances go, this is quite up-to-date in its recognition of the social construction of gender. The next step down this particular road would come if the female breast "itself," not merely "perception" of it, were recognized as a "cultural artifact." It is not so long ago that feminist legal debates about "sameness" and "difference" often treated the body as the one and only unproblematic site of permissible sexual difference.[42] Cases like *Santorelli* (the concurrence, at least) help show that the body itself signifies sexual difference only under prior discursive choices that reify normal variations and institutionalize gender opposition.

Legal writers who want to construct more narratives, like Judge Titone's concurrence in *Santorelli,* that emphasize the discursive production of sexual difference, may already have begun gravitating to the work of Judith Butler, the most thoroughgoing of postmodern feminists who understand *all* attributes of gender and sexuality as performed, not "natural." " '[S]ex' not only functions as a norm, but is part of a regulatory practice that produces the bodies it governs, that is, whose regulatory force is made clear as a kind of productive power, the power to produce—demarcate, circulate, differentiate—the bodies it controls."[43] To be sure, some bodies have vaginas and some penises, but then again some bodies have freckles and some warts (and some both), some blue eyes and some brown, and only what Judge Titone might call "prejudice" produces that "cultural artifact," the sexed body.

When Butler calls sex "performed," she is self-consciously punning: sex is "performative" in her broadened version of what J. L. Austin called "performative" speech acts. For Austin, a "performative" is "authoritative speech," "statements that, in the uttering, also perform a certain action and exercise a binding power." Butler: "The centrality of the marriage ceremony in J. L. Austin's examples of performativity suggests that the heterosexualization of the social bond is the paradigmatic form for those speech acts which bring about what they name. 'I pronounce you . . .' puts into effect the relation that it names."[44] However, what Butler calls "performance" also suggests the element of theatricality and specularity in sexual identity, and the possibilities— drag, queer performance—of reversing, miming, rendering hyperbolic the enforced, normative, discursive conventions.

Greater legal consciousness of the multiplicity of gender roles and the con-

---

[41] 600 NE.2d at 235.

[42] For example, the Civil Rights Act of 1964, forbidding sex discrimination in employment, permits sex to be used as a "bona fide occupational qualification" (BFOQ). A popular way of limiting this loophole among legal feminists has been to anatomize it, that is, to treat it as covering only jobs that require a penis or vagina.

[43] Butler, *Bodies That Matter* 1.

[44] Butler, *Bodies That Matter* 224–25.

ventional and performative aspects of gender would, on balance, be a great improvement in legal analysis. That does not make Butler's postmodernism a complete theory of gender, needing no supplementation, or even an abiding truth. Like other narratives of difference, postmodernism, too, is a kind of normative injunction, drawn in power, subject to later deconstruction.

Some deconstructions of Judge Titone's Butler-like narrative of the social construction of difference are not hard to imagine. For one thing, Titone partakes of the linkage nature/immutable : cultural/mutable that, following Eve Kosofsky Sedgwick, I criticized in the last chapter. Moving "distinctions between breasts" from the first to the second column maintains the distinction, one that may be losing its hold on the public, nonjudicial, imagination. We may soon or already live in a world in which the "natural" will be figured as responsive to our will while "cultural" will seem hopelessly dead and unresponsive, in which case the warriors for changed gender roles in that world, whoever they will be and whatever they will want, will need to establish with care the "natural" (hence mutable) essence of observable sexual difference.

Another deconstruction of Titone's narrative of the social construction of sex might note that Titone's is a discourse of difference, not power. His language effaces his own agency even more effectively than the California judge twenty years earlier. But all narratives of sexual difference and sameness, including all narratives of bodily difference and sameness, enact and enforce political orders. A judge who constructs (that is, claims to find) sexual sameness when it comes to taking off one's shirt in the park may have to retreat when chests and torsos are legally constructed in scenes of domination. If female breasts are the same as male, does the unconsented fondling of the breasts of a ten-year-old girl no longer constitute sexual assault?[45] Are photographs of a fourteen-year-old girl nude from the waist up, in provocative poses, no longer child pornography?[46]

---

[45] A Wisconsin trial judge gained some notoriety a few years ago in dismissing the indictment of an adult man who fondled the breasts of a ten-year-old girl on the grounds that her undeveloped breasts were not "intimate parts." An embarrassed court of appeals reversed, treating the trial court as if it had been making an inartful finding as to the defendant's lack of intent. Their opinion is not officially reported but is available on Westlaw. State of Wisconsin v. Flores, 1984 WL 180593 (Wis.App., No. 83-1663-CR, May 9, 1984). Are little girls' breasts "the same" as boys'? Is fondling either or both "sexual contact" with a minor? If law wants to maintain a category of "sexual contact" distinct from generic assault, it might make sense to define that category with a discourse of power: adult power over children, men over women. Butler's emphasis on the social construction and performativity of gender is not the easiest starting point from which to develop a discourse of power and may disable law from doing so in a case like the Flores case.

[46] Massachusetts (among other states) maintains laws prohibiting certain nude displays of minors. Massachusetts's does not distinguish the prepubertal male breast from the female breast. An earlier version of the statute was found to be overbroad by the Massachusetts Supreme Judicial Court, not because of the inclusion of boys, but because the statute prohibited essentially all nude display, including family photographs and legitimate artistic and theatrical productions. The

A decision on the sameness or difference of male and female breasts, abstracted from considerations of domination, can only reproduce a fetishizing discourse that isolates and scrutinizes isolated body parts. A legal discourse that substitutes this figure for a more holistic discourse of integrated bodies in particular social relationships of power just operates as another form of estrangement and effacement of our bodies. This would be just as true if a judge, more intellectually au courant than Judge Titone, justified that result with references to Judith Butler. Judith Butler's denaturalizing of gender and her theories of the performance of gender are wonderful, important, and very true in many ways; they have had a large influence on me and on this book. But as they seep into law's stony discourse, they have a real potential to support a kind of fetishizing abstraction unless accompanied by the kind of attention to power, and relationships of power, that characterize an earlier genre of feminist writing, and to which Butler's postmodernism is often cheerfully heedless.

Sex/Not Sex

In Judge Titone's consideration of whether different legal treatment of female and male breasts was justified by either anatomy or culture, he made the fur-

---

case reached the United States Supreme Court, by which time Massachusetts had amended the statute to apply only to defendants with lascivious intent. The United States Supreme Court then fragmented, with three justices agreeing that the original statute, under which defendant was convicted, was overbroad; two finding that it was constitutional; and four declining to reach the overbreadth issue in light of the intervening statutory amendment. Massachusetts v. Oakes, 491 U.S. 576 (1989). On remand, the Massachusetts Supreme Judicial Court held that it, too, should not now find the statute overbroad, in light of the amendment that followed its earlier decision; rejected Oakes's facial constitutional challenge to the statute; and affirmed his conviction. Commonwealth v. Oakes, 551 NE.2d 910 (1990). The state court held that while issues involving dissemination or display of the *photographs* involved pure issues of expression, the posing of the *stepdaughter* was mixed speech and conduct and therefore proscribable.

The story is full of ironic choices for feminists. The earlier statute was completely gender-neutral as to prepubertal children: all nude displays were prohibited. This is certainly equal treatment. It was also a statute so broad as to make it difficult to convict anyone, including Oakes, the actual defendant, who had forced his stepdaughter to pose topless for pornographic photographs; she was so embarrassed that she attempted to destroy the negatives, and it was her mother who (on finding the photographs) took them to the police.

The revised statute continues to make no formal gender distinctions but limits prosecution to cases of lascivious intent. Is this now a statute that the shirtfree movement would like, because it treats boys and girls alike and focuses rather on the gazer's intent? But is the statute really gender neutral? Will this statute rather silently reinscribe gender differences? Will prosecutors and juries characteristically find displays of the prepubertal female chest lascivious and never make this determination as to boys' chests? On the other hand, is this a gender distinction that even shirtfree feminists would want to see in the law, because the display of little girls' chests is just different from little boys'? What happens to the arguments from anatomical sameness and cultural stereotypes now?

ther observation that (quoting the defendants) "the female breast is no more or less a sexual organ than is the male equivalent."[47] Whatever could this mean?

The precise legal issue being addressed in the concurrence is whether a statute treating female breasts differently from male denies equal protection of the laws. Is Judge Titone inventing some inarticulate theory under which only "sexual" organs provide a "real" legal basis for unequal treatment, while "nonsexual" organs cannot? Under this theory, elements of the reproductive process *constitute* sex. It is just this sort of essentialism that Titone's other references to "prejudice" and "cultural artifact" might be seen as deconstructing. In fact, this remark is just the sort of normative performative that Judith Butler likes to question, in which the voice of authority *starts* by looking for difference and *makes* of sex the very difference which it claims to *find*.

"Sexual organ" is not a natural category in either Ramona Santorelli's case, or the case of the ten-year-old girl under Wisconsin's "sexual contact" statute.[48] The body may be configured as sexual in narratives of reproductive process, or physical development, or, as we are working toward in this book, as one or another discursive construction, each of which performs a Foucauldian regulation, enacts and performs a certain power. Power, not nature, tells us when and whether a breast is a sexual organ.

Suppressing Male Display: Robert Mapplethorpe's Photographs

Display of the male body is also suppressed in law, for example through the criminal prosecution of the Contemporary Art Center of Cincinnati, and its director, for an exhibition of photographs by Robert Mapplethorpe. Like nude dancing, the nude photographic studies were first constituted as objects of the male gaze and then, in the eyes of the prosecutor, were to be suppressed as images.[49]

It is tempting to see this attempted suppression, like the suppression of Jeanine Biocic's breasts and Darlene Miller's nude dance, as a metonym for the larger legal discourse in which bodies are made to disappear, in which people are divested of their bodies and in which bodily attributes are appropriated and redistributed to the state. On this view there is a continuity between legal acts of repression and the legal discourse in every chapter that turns bodies into something else or seems to deny human embodiment.

[47] Santorelli, 600 NE.2d at 236 (citing a textbook on human sexuality).

[48] Flores, 1984 WL 180593.

[49] City of Cincinnati v. Contemporary Arts Center, 57 Ohio Misc.2d 9, 566 NE.2d 207 (1990) (denying motions to dismiss indictment); 57 Ohio Misc.2d 15, 566 NE.2d 214 (1990) (photographs to be evaluated for obscenity apart from larger exhibit). After a jury trial, the defendants were acquitted. For discussion of some of the legal issues, see Owen M. Fiss, "State Activism and State Censorship," 100 *Yale L. J.* 2087 (1991). A journalistic account is Steven C. Dubin, *Arresting Images: Impolitic Art and Uncivil Actions* 170–90 (1992) (New York: Routledge).

This account treats the sex, race, and sexual orientation of Mapplethorpe's models, male, often African-American, and gay, as adventitious, and the offense of the photographs the same as other instances of nudity discussed in this chapter. The discourse of the *Barnes* case facilitates this construction, in which a "public" morality, disapproving of nudity, is counterposed to the "private," partial, individual claim to display. This framework is not substantially different whether the "individual" claim to display is constructed as a claim of liberty, or privacy, or even, as Ramona Santorelli tried, of political speech. Freedom opposes morality, and Mapplethorpe's photographs are defended, as they were (successfully) before the jury, as fine art, not politics.[50] For purposes of legal strategy, both prosecutors and defense share this strategy, prosecutors because it lets them associate the suppression of photographs with such less questionable activity as the suppression of public nudity, and also lets public morality assume a discursive position, while the defense can claim the First Amendment's protection for works of artistic merit.

Neither side need establish just why some people find Mapplethorpe's photographs so threatening as to call for suppression. Questions arise concerning the ontological status of photographic representation, as well as the content of the photographs. One aspect of the moral suppression of nudity story that the Mapplethorpe prosecution adds is the suppression of a photographic representation of nudity rather than the public nudity itself, relying, as Judith Butler says, "upon a representational realism that conflates the signified of fantasy with its (impossible) referent."[51] In the Platonism of antipornography activists, the artistic representation has whatever reality it has only insofar as it signifies a "realer" world of concepts (such as women's subjugation), and influences the viewer only through the viewer's tendency toward mimesis of the representation. As Butler points out, these prohibitions eroticize the forbidden and end up perpetuating monopolies of discursive production that perpetuate the very reproductions they seek to forestall.

The bodies displayed in Mapplethorpe photographs are male; does this affect their legal construction, and, if so, how? Peter Brooks has suggested that "what was deemed offensive and censorable in Mapplethorpe's work was essentially the penis, and in particular the erect penis." Women's genitals are displayed frequently, but men's may not be; one might add that the division of the genders is challenged when the to-be-looked-at-ness that performs female subjugation to the gaze is transferred to male subjects. Still, as we have seen, law is not so ready as film and advertising perhaps to guarantee full specularization of the female body. Brooks further suggests that the display of the

---

[50] Interviews with jurors after the acquittal stressed their deference to the strong opinion of the expert witnesses that the photographs were "art." See, e.g., Jonathan Yardley, "In Cincinnati, Experts as Witnesses," *Washington Post,* October 15, 1990, p. B2.

[51] Butler, "Force of Fantasy," 105–6.

penis is suppressed insofar at the penis is "the organ of patriarchy, which in a culture where patriarchy is the basis of knowledge and power, and the gaze is phallic, must be veiled."[52] I am not certain about this. Mapplethorpe's homo-erotic models, penises and all, don't seem like "patriarchs" to me, any more than the models in Bloomingdale's Father's Day advertising look at all like "fathers"; both parody fatherhood and patriarchal authority, and, as Brooks also suggests, it is their jokiness and demystification of patriarchy, gender, and gay sex that may be their most threatening element.

Within established frameworks of First Amendment analysis, then, Mapplethorpe's photographs are unquestionably a kind of political speech, a visualized version that denatures the natural, affirms the excluded. In the overall project of this book they stand for power to construct multiple bodies, freedom to remake the traditional, the power and freedom of evolving people, fashioning their bodies in constant confrontation with others. Law must resist its urge to repress, to make the body disappear, to turn it into something metaphorical, in particular metaphors of distance, loss, and estrangement. It is more consistent, I believe, with law's ethical aspirations, to embrace human embodiedness, to appreciate, not turn away from, the body, especially the excluded, the diseased, the outlaw body. A first step here is to appreciate how we construct bodies that we can ignore or make disappear; a second, to appreciate the power and regulation involved in doing so. Nudity is not a "private" expression that counters "public" morality; it is public in its construction, definition, and exclusion, suppressed when we choose to construct one politics rather than another.

[52] Peter Brooks, *Body Work: Objects of Desire in Modern Narrative* 278–79 (Cambridge: Harv. U. Pr., 1993).

Chapter 8

THE BODY'S NARRATIVES

THE BODIES that raise "privacy" claims are all *desired* bodies in the broad, not-necessarily-erotic sense that we defined in chapter 6. They have stories to tell us, secrets that we desire to possess. In their veins and urine and organs lie tales of crimes committed, drugs ingested and smuggled, madness uncontrolled.

In deciding which bodies may be searched, and how far, law constructs a distinctive body, different from others we have seen: the body constructed as an "interest" in "privacy." The characteristic features of this body, as we shall see in greater detail, are that it is distinct from the person; that it is private, not public; that it is conceptualized as having interests in privacy with determinate weight; that it lacks individuating or personal narrated characteristics *other* than its interests. At the same time, the legal desire to know is also reified into an interest with weight, "balanced" against the weight of the body's interest in privacy, and often represented as having personality and emotions that are rhetorically denied to the person inside the body.

I am not at all certain that the balancing metaphor is a bad way to proceed. It has the effect of creating a body of law that is quite fact-specific and resists easy generalization, for the bodies constructed in this discourse of interest weighing do not retain similar weights from case to case. I am not suggesting that this is a bad thing. In the end there may be no alternative to something like this weighing process, for body uses as to which the larger culture is quite ambivalent. In any case, I will not be defending any particular construction of the body as correct here. I will instead be studying the precise discursive mechanisms used to construct bodies that lack firm boundaries or determinate weight as moved from context to context. I shall also be contrasting alternative bodies, deployed in other legal contexts, that might, if deployed in body search cases, yield different legal outcomes. This is not to advocate the deployment of any of these alternative bodies, merely to raise the contrast for the reader.

I confess to finding the legal problems in this chapter to be difficult ones. I often lack firm intuition as to how to create hierarchies of bodily privacy, or how otherwise to evaluate the claimed need of the police for searches inside what would often be considered the boundaries of the body. More damaging, perhaps, to the plan of the book, I am somewhat less certain here just what is the legal effect of the particular body constructed. The discourse of weighing interests seems internal to legal discourse and to lack the kind of larger cultural resonance of such other bodies as the property or machine or sentimental body in pain. As we shall see, bodies constructed as privacy interests are sometimes capable of withstanding police searches, and sometimes not. Particularly as to these problems, I want to be careful not to reify the particular discursive construction by attributing to it a kind of causative agency.

Before examining the construction of the body, however, let us first examine the construction of desire to know the body, with which desire the body will be, in this and the next two chapters, dialectically linked.

The Body as a Bearer of Narratives

In an important recent book, Peter Brooks has drawn our attention to the importance of literary and artistic representations that attempt to present the secret narratives of the body, for example, that common motif in which the scar, birthmark, or brand on the body reveals a secret, represents a lost identity.[1] "My subject is the nexus of desire, the body, the drive to know, and narrative: those stories we tell about the body in the effort to know and to have it, which result in making the body a site of signification—the place for the inscription of stories—and itself a signifier, a prime agent in narrative plot and meaning."[2]

For Brooks, following Freud and Melanie Klein, the infant's original object of knowledge, of the desire to know, is the mother's body. Her breast is "the original object of symbolization, and then the field of exploration for the child's developing 'epistemophilic impulse,' the urge to know."[3] A major theme in art and literature is the body as a symbol and bearer of symbols. For example, the body is a site of sexual differentiation: "The radical structuring of human nature by sexuality ensures that the body will always be a problem in meaning."[4]

Since growing up involves a great deal of repression of bodily instincts, knowing how to decode messages from the body reveals us to ourselves. (Indeed, in Jacques Lacan's account, to which we referred at the beginning of chapter 6, a knowledge or sense of one's own body as an integrated whole could *never* come from "bodily experience," inevitably fragmented, but could only follow the ocular experience of the integrated, albeit symbolic, body of an Other and then the entry of that subject into a symbolic order of language; that Lacan's account is doubtless overstated should not discourage further investigation [like Brooks's] into the relationship between visual inspection of the body and the psychological development of the gazer.)[5] Since female

---

[1] Peter Brooks, *Body Work: Objects of Desire in Modern Narrative* (Cambridge: Harv. U. Pr., 1993).

[2] Id. 5–6.

[3] Id. 7.

[4] Id. 14.

[5] Jacques Lacan, "The Mirror Stage as Formative of the Function of the I as Revealed in

bodies are draped and covered, their uncovering to the male gaze in art and literature often symbolizes mystery revealed. "What presides at the inscription and imprinting of bodies is, in the broadest sense, a set of desires: a desire that the body not be lost to meaning—that it be brought into the realm of the semiotic and the significant—and, underneath this, a desire for the body itself, an erotic longing to have or to be the body."[6]

The problems that follow in this and the next two chapters illustrate Brooks's point with legal texts. The texts involve a body that is desired by what Brooks calls an "epistemophilic impulse," a desire to know: to know its evidence, its narrative. In Brooks's Freudian account, any such desire for knowledge of the body is a kind of erotic longing, "a gaze subtended by desire," intermingling the desire to know with the desire to possess.[7]

Some readers will resist this interpretation as applied to the police searches in this chapter. Recall, however, that my analysis is not of the motivation of police officers, but rather of the discursive construction of the body. A body may be discursively constructed as open and available to others by employing the figuration of the body as the object of desire, even where this is done strategically, and is not best explained as some kind of thwarted erotic desire.

These bodies, the objects of the desire to know, are constructed as private. The private body is a kind of narrative total of all the moral choices made by the subject that owns the body, the individual protagonist of the narrative: the crimes committed, the drugs ingested. Such bodies are narrative texts to which law relates as a reader. Such bodies are, as Brooks says, often mysterious in the sense of holding secrets, but, often, available to the law's scrutiny.

GETTING THE EVIDENCE: LEGAL CONSTITUTION OF THE BOUNDARIES OF THE BODY

How does legal discourse constitute the body as a holder of legally relevant evidence? How does it, for example, evaluate the state's claim that surgery should be performed to get evidence? The body constructed here is distinct from the person; private, not public; and holding interests in privacy with factitious weight.

Bodies Distinct from Persons

The cases that follow apply the Fourth Amendment to the United States Constitution, which states: "The right of the people to be secure in their *persons, houses, papers, and effects,* against unreasonable searches and seizures, shall not be violated" (emphasis supplied). The language of the amendment is most

Psychoanalytic Experience," in E*crits: A Selection* 1 (Alan Sheridan trans.) (New York: Norton, 1977) [1949].

[6] Id. 22.

[7] Id.

interesting, not least because it plays no part in the discursive constructions of the body that follow. All the legal bodies, discursively constructed as the bearers of narrative, exist already in substitution for the "person," constructed by the Constitution, but missing from the cases. As we shall see, contemporary Fourth Amendment cases do not speak of searches of "persons," even though that is the constitutional language.

When the amendment says "person," it *means* body.[8] It is interesting to imagine the jurisprudence that might have resulted had the Constitution's figuration of the body been employed subsequently. Would the "person" being searched be identical with the legal subject, so that we could not have contemplated any kind of discontinuity between the subject and the body? Would the subject simply have *been* the "person," so that we could not have imagined the subject "owning" or "having" a person (let alone buying, selling, alienating, that "person")?[9]

Private, Not Public

The cases that follow construct, rather, a symbolic bearer of this Fourth Amendment "right of the people." That right is borne, not by the person, nor the body, but rather an "interest in privacy," which is then counterposed to, sometimes balanced against, the state's or "public's" interest in obtaining evidence. We have seen this move before, at different levels of generality. At the most general, any body figured as the location of the private or individual reenacts this construction.

All these bodies might as easily be figured as performing the public's interest in fair and humane law enforcement procedures. In First Amendment cases dealing with freedom of speech or the press, the individual speaker sometimes represents a public interest in free speech or the press. Ronald Garet has recently spotted the same body, representing the public, in the Supreme Court's opinion in *Griswold v. Connecticut,* striking down state prohibitions on contraception as violations of the right to privacy. "Once the body incorporates and publishes the meaning of constitutional liberty, the violation of the person

---

[8] Compare George Eliot, *Daniel Deronda* (Harmondsworth: Penguin, 1967) [1876], chap. 3, p. 57: "One of his advantages was a fine *person,* which perhaps was even more impressive at fifty-seven than it had been earlier in life.".

[9] For other ways in which Fourth Amendment jurisprudence has traveled from the language of the amendment, see Akhil Reed Amar, "Fourth Amendment First Principles," 107 *Harv. L. Rev.* 757 (1994). Professor Amar drew my attention to the relevance of the constitutional language to my project. Grand jury subpoenas, for example for a blood sample to be used for DNA matching, have been held to be "searches" for Fourth Amendment purposes, though the Supreme Court has not spoken to the issue. See Floralynn Einesman, "Vampires among Us—Does a Grand Jury Subpoena for Blood Violate the Fourth Amendment?" 22 *Am. J. Crim. L.* 327, 351 n. 214 (1995).

is at once revealed and denounced as a violation of the Constitution."[10] Similarly, bodies in constitutional cases might figure or mediate between public and private; the body might be the "gateway" or "doorpost" or "boundary" between these important realms. By contrast, in criminal search cases, as we shall see, the constitutional person or subject instead becomes a body, which becomes an "interest in privacy."

Interests with Weights

Instead, the body is figured as, metamorphoses into, an interest. We saw this done in chapter 4 in cases involving the right to abortion. It is a discursive formation that results in a body that is substantially open to the needs of others, as available as a mother. The body as interest is rarely figured with impermeable boundaries (as is the healthy body politic, discussed in chapter 12) or imagery of the sacred and is not inviolable (as is the body in bone marrow cases discussed in chapter 4). A body is constructed as an interest so as to occupy an object position in a plane of interests competing for space.

Nor is the body as interest the narrated body that we saw in the loss of consortium cases in chapter 5. Rather, the body as interest is largely constructed through a discourse of absence and distance; there is little use of narrative or description to attempt to render the body metaphorically present. When the court finishes by holding that the body in question was properly available to the scrutiny of law enforcement personnel, it may reinforce that holding by distancing language that keeps the body veiled from the reader of the opinion. As we shall see, the body-as-privacy interest is normally isolated from others, specularized, a fetishized collection of body parts, and Cartesian in the sense that the body is stripped from the person or spirit.

Law, at the same time, is coded as equally Cartesian in the sense that reason controls law's body. Unlike the private, specularized body, law is socially integrating, and embodied in the sense that it takes on such human attributes as watching and sentimentality. Law provides the language of social integration that could arise from bodies conceived in union and relation with others but could not, and does not, arise from bodies represented as fragmented and isolated. For this reason, law will often be represented as human while the body is represented as a thing.

I have argued generally that the body as interest is substantially available to others, but that does not mean that this discursive construction inevitably results in approving whatever search law enforcement personnel propose. Lest it appear that the deck is being stacked, let us examine the discourse in a case in which the court refuses to order surgery.

[10] Ronald R. Garet, "Gnostic Due Process," 7 *Yale J. L. & Humanities* 97, 113 (1995). Griswold v. Connecticut is 381 U.S. 479 (1965).

The body in question was Rudolph Lee Jr.'s. The state's interest in Rudolph Lee's body was principally for the bullet that was lodged an inch into Lee's chest. Lee was already the chief suspect in an armed robbery, having been apprehended near the store because of his resemblance to the storeowner's description and then picked out of a lineup. However, the storeowner had fired a gun at the robber, and Lee had a bullet in his chest. The state sought an order requiring Lee to undergo surgery so that the bullet could be recovered and matched to the storeowner's gun.

The Supreme Court unanimously held that such surgery would be an unreasonable search in violation of the Fourth Amendment.[11] What made the search "unreasonable"? The Court's precedents offered little assistance. Searches without any suspicion of guilt, ordinarily 'probable cause,'" are often unreasonable, but in Lee's case there was probable cause. "Beyond this point, it is ordinarily justifiable for the community to demand that the individual give up some part of his *interest in privacy and security* to advance the community's vital interests in law enforcement; such a search is generally 'reasonable' in the Amendment's terms" (emphasis supplied). That sentence would have been very hard to write if the Court had had to use the constitutional language: "it is ordinarily justifiable for the community to demand that the individual give up some part of his *person*."

The surgery here would have required Lee to give up "too much" of "his interest in privacy and security," that is, his body, his person. Why? To reach this conclusion, no rules could be invoked. "The reasonableness of surgical intrusions beneath the skin depends on a case-by-case approach, in which the individual's interests in privacy and security are weighed against society's interests in conducting the procedure."[12]

Now the funny thing about this "balance" in Lee's case is that "society's interests," as seen by the Court, were fairly high. The Court agreed that there was probable cause to suspect Lee, that the state had followed all proper procedural steps, that a warrant had been obtained, that Lee had had a full opportunity to litigate, and that the potential evidence inside his body was relevant and probative. The state had failed to show a "compelling need" for the bullet mainly because the case against Lee even without the bullet was so overwhelming.

The legal body that the Court constituted was powerful enough to resist an otherwise proper search. Yet it was the same legal body-as-interest that we have seen before. "A compelled surgical intrusion into an individual's body for evidence, however, implicates expectations of privacy and security of such

---

[11] Winston v. Lee, 470 U.S. 753 (1985). Justices Blackmun and Rehnquist concurred only in the judgment but did not file a separate opinion, and Chief Justice Burger concurred separately to reserve an issue then pending in another case.

[12] 470 U.S. at 760.

magnitude that the intrusion may be 'unreasonable' even if likely to produce evidence of a crime."[13] Rudolph Lee loses his "person" or "body" and its magnitude. It is replaced by a signifying "interest," and the interest alone is reified into a thing with "magnitude," just such magnitude as the Court chooses to give it. This legal flesh narrates and performs the legal word. Here, as often in Fourth Amendment law, that thing with magnitude is constructed as "expectations," as if the expectations were not themselves a judicial artifact, as if the Court were not the chief shaper of people's expectations of what the police can do to them. The Court performs its own power as it denies its own agency.

The Court flirted with and rejected a possible rule that surgery under general anesthetic was, or was normally, an unreasonable search.[14] Having rejected the only general rule that seemed possible, the Court had nothing left to explain why this search was "unreasonable." So it returned to the general anesthetic, but in purpler prose. "In this case, however, the Court of Appeals noted that the Commonwealth proposes to take control of respondent's body, to 'drug this citizen—not yet convicted of a criminal offense—with narcotics and barbiturates into a state of unconsciousness,' and then to search beneath his skin for evidence of a crime. This kind of surgery involves a virtually total divestment of respondent's ordinary control over surgical probing beneath his skin."[15] This is ripe, juicy, lawyer overstatement, presumably from the brief of someone who talks to juries a lot, but in plain fact it says no more than that the state sought general anesthetic and surgical removal of the bullet, and Lee's "ordinary control" is what the Court must determine here, not look up as if it were written down someplace else. The Court then characterized this as a "severe" "intrusion on respondent's privacy interests,"[16] which of course it was, once those "privacy interests" had been defined to include the privilege to resist surgery under general anesthetic.

The Court apparently has a hierarchy of bodily intrusions, under which surgery under general anesthetic is more intrusive, less likely to be ordered, than a urine sample or breath test, which, as we shall see momentarily, may be ordered even without individualized suspicion. However, the hierarchy that places "surgery" in a different box than "urine sample" is still constructed without any real grasping of the relevant human body. What's missing from the construction of Rudolph Lee's body in legal discourse? Rudolph Lee, for one. The surgery isn't intrusive because of its meaning to Lee, or to society; because of its historical association with "public" or "private"; because Lee's body synecdochally represents either the social order or its undermining. The

13 470 U.S. at 759.
14 470 U.S. at 758–63.
15 470 U.S. at 765.
16 470 U.S. at 766.

justices just thought that surgery went too far; there is no other store of cultural meaning they can consult in order to make that decision.

Most importantly, the legal body constructed in *Lee* has no resonance outside that single case. The legal body that can resist surgery has strong, impermeable borders, while the body that must donate a blood or urine sample has weak borders.[17] The legal body that can withstand surgery gives up nothing to another, while John Moore has given up his spleen. Nothing in the specificity of Lee's body, or Lee's case, explains why the state that could get a blood or urine sample, or draft him or imprison him or require a woman to carry a fetus to term, can't compel surgery under general anesthetic, or require a kidney or bone marrow donation. I doubt there are any clear social expectations that compelled a result one way or the other in *Schmerber* or *Lee*. If the Court had a case for either of those results, it could have convinced much of the audience that cares about these things. Since the law finds it difficult to talk about bodies, or even see them, we are left, as usual, with "balancing tests" that don't balance, and a nagging feeling that the justices have nothing to consult except their own subjective senses of the fragility of their own bodies and their reactions to a list of possible social demands on it.

Judges must consult their own sense of their own bodies; where else can they turn to learn the cultural meaning of transgressing body boundaries? It is like telling them they must decide cases according to our society's conception of honor. Yet their "senses of their own bodies" are nothing but the parade of stereotyped bodies that we have identified: narrated bodies on display; sentimental bodies in pain; threatening, suppressed bodies; property bodies; machine bodies; private bodies; inviolable bodies. Any of these might have provided the imagery for a different opinion in *Winston v. Lee*.

THEORIZING THE PUBLIC USE OF THE BODY: THE LIMITS OF PRIVACY

Winston v. Lee can be a banner nailed to the post of dignity of the body. The body was permitted, after all, to resist a search. I prefer to think of it, however, as illustrating the weak presence of bodies in the eyes of the law and the law's facility at constructing a legal body with precisely those attributes with which the law chooses to endow it. The metaphor of balancing reinforces this, for the body, or rather the "interest" in body privacy, is balanced just as if the govern-

---

[17] The Supreme Court has held that public authorities may obtain urine samples for purposes of testing for recent drug use from personnel involved in a train accident, without search warrants or individualized suspicion. Skinner v. Railway Labor Executives' Assn., 489 U.S. 602 (1989). Public employers may also obtain urine samples randomly from employees if "reasonable," and this at least includes employees directly involved in drug interdiction or who carry firearms. National Treasury Employees Union v. Von Raab, 489 U.S. 656 (1989). I will take up these cases in chapter 13; while they might also have gone here, they are, interestingly, much more concerned with the definition of "boundaries" than with the "privacy interest" of those tested, on which they are embarrassingly silent.

ment sought to search a desk and the court balanced that interest in privacy against the government's need for the information.[18] The metaphor thus strips the body (or the desk, for that matter) of the "weight" that it bears in pounds, metamorphoses the body into an interest, then reifies the interest as if it had weight to be put into a balance. This double maneuver is a kind of body disappearance, even if it should turn out that, in the mirror world of the balance, a body always weighed more than a desk. The very agency of the court in investing the body with whatever weight it possesses in the mirror world shows how law assumes power over the body.

Again, I make no claim for present purposes that the "balance" is being struck incorrectly in particular cases, merely trying to describe the discursive constructions of the body that are employed, and some of their consequences. I do think that law is free to construct multiple bodies and that the choice for the body as privacy interest is necessarily a choice for a body that is quite substantially open at the boundaries and available to others.

Someone who felt the police were searching too many bodies would probably be better off, strategically, in seeking to substitute a sacred or inviolable body, behind firm boundaries that could not be transgressed, rather than trying to nail the custard that is "privacy interest" to the wall. A recent survey in which a small sample of nonlawyers was asked to rank the intrusiveness of fifty different government searches, drawn from leading cases, suggests that "transgressing body boundaries" does make searches exceptionally intrusive: the three such searches on the list were all in the top eleven in intrusiveness, including searches that the courts permit.[19]

By contrast, certain sociopolitical uses of the body do not create constitutional law problems. For example, bodies may be drafted into military service, an extraordinarily invasive social use of the body.[20] This is not even arguably

[18] O'Connor v. Ortega, 480 U.S. 709, 719 (1987) (neither warrants nor probable cause are necessary to support office and desk searches by public employers of their employees' desks and offices; legality of such searches is to be evaluated according to a balancing test).

[19] The three searches on the list that involved transgressing the boundaries of the body were hospital surgery on shoulder (based in *Winston v. Lee*), ranked fortieth (where fiftieth was the *most* intrusive); needle in arm to get blood (based on *Skinner v. Railway Labor Executives' Assn.,* discussed in chap. 12), ranked forty-sixth; and body cavity search at border, discussed in chapter 9, ranked fiftieth. By contrast, body searches limited to the exterior surface of the body were not ranked as particularly intrusive: watching person in front yard with binoculars was ranked thirty-third; dog sniff of body, twenty-third; pat-down, nineteenth; and viewing car occupants at a roadblock, ninth. Christopher Slobogin and Joseph E. Schumacher, "Reasonable Expectations of Privacy and Autonomy in Fourth Amendment Cases: An Empirical Look at 'Understandings Recognized and Permitted by Society,'" 42 *Duke L. J.* 727, 738–39 (1993).

[20] "That the adult human being cannot ordinarily without his consent be physically 'altered' by the verbal imposition of any new political philosophy makes all the more remarkable, genuinely awesome, the fact that he sometimes agrees to go to war, agrees to permit this radical self-alteration to his body." Elaine Scarry, *The Body in Pain: The Making and Unmaking of the World* 112 (New York: Oxford U. Pr., 1985).

a deprivation of liberty in constitutional law terms, though arguably the most invasive sociopolitical use of the body in our culture.[21] Why? Because of our concepts of individual and society? Because Congress's power to "raise armies" implies the power to draft involuntarily?[22] Because the military draft was known to the framers of the Fifth Amendment, so presents no problem of constitutional legitimacy?[23] Because in a democracy, "[i]f citizens' bodies are appropriated by the state, the citizens themselves are the appropriating agents"?[24] Because citizens gain their identity in appropriation of their bodies by an organic state?[25]

I know of no convincing metatheory that explains which social demands on the body are just and which not, and my own intuitions are rarely firm. It could be otherwise, of course, if we happened to live in a culture with more apparent agreement on the boundaries and sacredness of the body than may be constructed from the legal materials we are surveying. Given, however, the absence of any coherent metatheory of the body in these cases, some sort of balancing test that at least purports to identify all the relevant reasons for action may seem like, sadly, the best that law can do.

I think, however, that the balancing test commonly employed in criminal search (and other) cases is a fraud, for it effaces any individuated element of the body and then balances only law's own artifact. The body, constructed as privacy interest, is an abstract, universal body that citizens share, and *not* the Durkheimian body, mentioned in the introduction, that is the very "individualizing factor."[26] Law might construct Rudolph Lee's body as inviolable, or the sacred temple of his soul, or his property, or as a body that an appropriate authority figure (such as his employer or the state) has put on ocular display, or, as we do, a privacy interest that competes with other interests and constructs a body open to others. Each of these competing constructions fits into a certain legal structure, but each effaces the individual and particular. Each construction is destabilized by the trick I have been employing throughout of referring to the legal subject by name (e.g., Rudolph Lee). The "proper" name constructs the *propre* individual self that denies generalization and homogenization, suggesting that a missing element of these cases is Rudolph Lee's

---

[21] Arver v. U.S., 245 U.S. 366 (1918) (upholding draft law); see also Martin v. Mott, 25 U.S. (12 Wheat.) 19 (1827) (draft into state militia under presidential orders).

[22] Arver, 245 U.S. at 377.

[23] 245 U.S. at 380 (colonial drafts). For a critique of the assumption that national government automatically succeeded to colonial powers on this point, see Akhil Reed Amar, "The Bill of Rights as a Constitution," 100 *Yale L. J.* 1131, 1165–73 (1991).

[24] Paul W. Kahn, *Legitimacy and History: Self-Government in American Constitutional Theory* 52 (New Haven: Yale U. Pr., 1992).

[25] Id. 62–63 for elucidation of this theory.

[26] Emile Durkheim, *The Elementary Forms of the Religious Life* 305 (Joseph Ward Swain trans.) (New York: Free Pr., 1965) [1915].

individual sense of his body, that might or might not be the same narrative as anyone else's.

Indeed, if Peter Brooks's account of body narratives in literature is correct, we can be fairly certain that the body constructed by the judge will be untrue to the judge's experience. The judge will construct a body quite substantially shaped by the judge's erotic desire, individual experience (that is, which competing cultural explanations of individual experience the judge characteristically deploys), love of power, freedom to construct bodies—*all* of which will be hidden from the judge himself or herself. The construction and deployment of a privacy interest works powerfully to estrange the decision maker from his or her own body, own thought process, and to make appear objective what might just as well symbolize the radically subjective, unstable, problematized, that is, the boundaries of the body.

BODY CAVITIES

To illustrate the way balancing privacy interests balances only judicial artifacts, which may be constructed among many contested possibilities, consider a case in which the same Supreme Court, a few years before *Winston v. Lee,* approved an intrusive body search, short of surgery. The case involved the treatment of pretrial detainees, that is, people who have not yet been convicted of anything, at New York City's Metropolitan Correctional Center (popularly known as "The Tombs"):

> Inmates at all Bureau of Prisons facilities, including the MCC, are required to expose their body cavities for visual inspection as a part of a strip search conducted after every contact visit with a person from outside the institution. [Footnote by the Court: If the inmate is male, he must lift his genitals and bend over to spread his buttocks for visual inspection. The vaginal and anal cavities of female inmates are also visually inspected. The inmate is not touched by security personnel at any time during the *visual* search procedure.] Corrections officials testified that visual cavity searches were necessary not only to discover but also to deter the smuggling of weapons, drugs, and other contraband into the institution. The District Court upheld the strip-search procedure but prohibited the body-cavity searches, absent probable cause to believe that the inmate is concealing contraband. Because petitioners proved only one instance in the MCC's short history where contraband was found during a body-cavity search, the Court of Appeals affirmed. In its view, the "gross violation of personal privacy inherent in such a search cannot be outweighed by the government's security interest in maintaining a practice of so little practical utility."
>
> Admittedly, this practice instinctively gives us the most pause. However, assuming for present purposes that inmates, both convicted prisoners and pretrial detainees, retain some Fourth Amendment rights upon commitment to a corrections facility, we nonetheless conclude that these searches do not violate that

Amendment. The Fourth Amendment prohibits only unreasonable searches, and under the circumstances, we do not believe that these searches are unreasonable.

The test of reasonableness under the Fourth Amendment is not capable of precise definition or mechanical application. In each case it requires a balancing of the need for the particular search against the invasion of personal rights that the search entails. Courts must consider the scope of the particular intrusion, the manner in which it is conducted, the justification for initiating it, and the place in which it is conducted. A detention facility is a unique place fraught with serious security dangers. Smuggling of money, drugs, weapons, and other contraband is all too common an occurrence. And inmate attempts to secrete these items into the facility by concealing them in body cavities are documented in this record, and in other cases. That there has been only one instance where an MCC inmate was discovered attempting to smuggle contraband into the institution on his person may be more a testament to the effectiveness of this search technique as a deterrent than to any lack of interest on the part of the inmates to secrete and import such items when the opportunity arises.

We do not underestimate the degree to which these searches may invade the personal privacy of inmates. Nor do we doubt, as the District Court noted, that on occasion a security guard may conduct the search in an abusive fashion. Such abuse cannot be condoned. The searches must be conducted in a reasonable manner. But we deal here with the question whether visual body-cavity inspections as contemplated by the MCC rules can *ever* be conducted on less than probable cause. Balancing the significant and legitimate security interests of the institution against the privacy interests of the inmates, we conclude that they can.[27]

The balancing test that favored the prisoner in *Winston v. Lee* here tips to favor the state. I do not wish to argue that such "body cavity inspections," in jails as we know them, violate the Constitution. (How many assumptions do I have to accept? Must so many people be detained before trial? Must the locations of pretrial detention be the way they are? What would happen if we experimented with developing the kind of security among pretrial detainees that comes from people being induced to trust each other and be open with each other? Could such psychological attitudes be induced and persist after release? Conversely, what price does everyone pay after the release of former inmates brutalized in the fashion of the Tombs? Would the alternative notion of security be more brutalizing, as Foucault might argue?) The *Wolfish* case has been influential in the lower courts, where it tends to stand for the proposition that prisoners lose a significant part of their Fourth Amendment rights. It has recently been cited in support of holdings that prisoners may be tested for HIV infection over their objection, and even though the prison made no at-

---

[27] Bell v. Wolfish, 441 U.S. 520, 558–60 (1979) (emphasis original; two footnotes, record references, and case citations omitted).

tempt to treat or segregate prisoners who test positive.[28] Prisoners may also be required to give blood samples for DNA testing, to be entered into a database for future criminal investigations.[29] As Judge Frank Easterbrook recently (rather deliriously) described the reception of *Bell v. Wolfish* in the lower courts, in the course of his upholding the monitoring of male prisoners' bodies by female guards: "Vigilance over showers, vigilance over cells—vigilance everywhere, which means that guards gaze upon naked inmates."[30]

The discursive construction of the inmates' bodies in *Bell v. Wolfish* actually *creates* searchable bodies-on-display, where alternative constructions open to the Court would not. The searchable body-on-display is unindividuated, fetishized, and desentimentalized.

We have noted before how the legal discourse of privacy constructs the body of an isolated private individual, cut off from other human relations and metaphorically opposed to something called society or the public. This is a functional sort of body to represent privacy or indeed individual selves, but it opens up the possibility, raised by Terry Eagleton in chapter 3, which has threatened much of the legal discourse we have examined: that a society so constituted would lack any basis of solidarity. As reflected in the privacy cases, the problem would be that there would be no "society" that could demand anything from the body, let alone a body cavity search, and no circumstance under which the isolated self should, or conceptually could, yield to any greater interest.

Bell v. Wolfish solves this intellectual problem by discursively deindividuating the embodied legal subjects, the "inmates," as it discursively humanizes the government. In the place of the discursive techniques of "humanization": a "proper" name, feelings, a narrative, a voice—the bodies of the inmates are fetishized collections of body cavities, open for visual display. The inmates are nameless, identitiless, faceless. No anecdotes of particularized searches are admitted. We have observed before the discursive creation of embodied legal subjects, such as Rudolph Lee, George Hawkins, Sondra Tamimi, who do not speak to us and whose feelings about or experiences of their bodies remain unknown. *Bell v. Wolfish* carries this a step further by refusing even to name ("interpellate" is the technical Althusserian term) the bodies lifting their genitals and spreading their buttocks.

Meanwhile, embodiment is metaphorically transferred to the Tombs. "A detention facility is a unique place." Not one of the inmates is a unique person. Only the detention facility has an individual body. But after all, what is "unique" about the Tombs? Isn't it just as accurate to say: "The problems at the Tombs are like those at any metropolitan detention center"?

---

[28] Dunn v. White, 880 F.2d 1188 (10th Cir. 1989), cert. denied 493 U.S. 1059 (1990).

[29] Jones v. Murray, 962 F.2d 302 (4th Cir. 1992).

[30] Johnson v. Phelan, 69 F.3d 144, 146 (7th Cir. 1995).

Sentiment and feelings are likewise effaced from the inmates and transferred to the judge. The weeping judge "admits" in a kind of apophasis, or
affirmation by apparent denial: "Admittedly, this practice instinctively gives
us the most pause." Not much pause, since the Court is able to dispose of it in
four not overly long paragraphs. "Instinctively," because reason brings with it
a change of heart, the mind controls the instincts, resolution restored, the
heart's pause vanquished. "We do not underestimate the degree to which these
searches may invade the personal privacy of inmates." Why "personal"? The
inmates themselves have been rendered mute. Their instincts, pauses, privacy,
names are gone; only the Court appropriates these human instincts.

The Court's fetishizing specularization mimes the efforts of jail officials,
the delegated eyes, of the body politic, discursively created in the opinion. The
Court thus creates its own body as it creates the inmates', both political metaphors. The Court's has eyes and the power that comes with that phallic gaze.
The personified Law may metaphorically bond society in the way that the
fragmented bodies of its citizens cannot.

Chapter 9

THE LEGAL VAGINA

LAW CONSTRUCTS the vagina largely as a hiding place, full of secrets the eye cannot behold from outside, where drugs or other mysterious narratives lurk. The four figurations through which law characteristically constructs the vagina may seem contradictory but actually reinforce each other. First, the vagina is constructed as a thing, a possession, a space that may be searched: the apartment-vagina. Second, remarkably, the vagina, unlike any other body part, is often represented in relation to other people. Third, and related to the relational vagina, is the pornographic construction of the vagina on display, also searchable, open to the gaze. Finally, the vagina, as Freudians would predict, is often constructed as a lack, a gap, empty, an absence. All four discursive figurations share the construction of the vagina as a fetishized body part separate from the body.

The vagina thus discursively constructed turns out to be the least private, most specularized body we shall encounter in this book. Most people find this surprising. I know that I do. When I discuss vaginal searches with people, I encounter with equal frequency the argument that there's "nothing special" about the vagina, that searches of it should be conducted under the same standard as searches of mouths or rectums; and the argument that the vagina, being (in this view) partly constitutive of women's identities as women, should to some extent be a refuge from police searches. I don't believe I've ever heard an argument that the vagina ought to be uniquely searchable. Here, law's discursive construction of the vagina enacts this very argument in a way that political theory cannot. While I confess to some uncertainty as to how the language of the private body discussed in the preceding chapter affects the results of those cases, I am absolutely convinced that law's language of vaginas—as things, spaces, constituted by relations with others, on display, and empty—facilitates vaginal searches, though I express no opinion on whether there ought to be more or fewer such searches.

We may begin to see the distinctiveness of the legal vagina by contrasting *Winston v. Lee,* the case in the last chapter that refused to order surgery to retrieve a bullet, describing that surgery as an "intrusion into the body," with a later case brought by a woman named Shirley Mello Rodriques, in which the court's ordering a medical search of her vagina was not, apparently, an "intrusion into the body":

> Search warrants for appellant's apartment and vagina were issued by an assistant clerk of the Taunton (Massachusetts) District Court to appellee Joseph Fur-

tado, a thirteen year veteran of the Taunton Police Force and one of eight officers on the force authorized to apply for search warrants without first securing prior approval from a superior officer. Appellee David Westcoat is the chief of the Taunton Police Force.

The warrant was issued upon Furtado's three page Affidavit in Support of Application for Search Warrant, which contained various allegations that appellant was actively involved in the distribution of narcotics. Upon securing the warrant, Furtado went to appellant's apartment where a search of the premises was conducted by police and the occupants were subjected to sniff searches by police canine units. Police discovered what appeared to be a block of heroin in the bedroom. Appellant was informed of the warrant to search her vaginal cavity, informed that the warrant directed that the search be conducted by a physician at the Morton Hospital, and was offered the opportunity to remove whatever might be hidden in her vagina voluntarily, thus alleviating the necessity of the search. Appellant declined this suggestion and was escorted to the Morton Hospital by a female police officer.

What exactly occurred at the Morton Hospital is disputed, but this much appears clear: Sometime after 3:00 A.M., appellant and the female officer arrived at the Morton Hospital emergency room, where the female officer presented the vaginal cavity search warrant to appellee Phillip Falkoff, M.D. Falkoff telephoned the hospital's acting president and Admnistrator-on-call for advice and was informed of the hospital's consent policy and its requirement to act and comply when presented with a court order. The hospital did not have any official policy regarding warrants to conduct body cavity searches.

Assisted by a nurse, Dr. Falkoff conducted a visual and manual inspection of appellant's vaginal cavity. Appellant claims she was subjected to threats of physical coercion and was held down on the examining table. Dr. Falkoff denies these allegations. The search revealed an absence of foreign bodies in appellant's vaginal cavity.[1]

Shirley Rodriques sued the officer, physician, town, and hospital for damages under the Civil Rights Act of 1871 but lost when summary judgment was granted to all defendants.

In a moment we will do our own visual inspection of the court's legal analysis, but stopping now just to examine this narrative, it is one of the more tortured statements of fact that I have ever read. First, I have to say that I have been collecting legal constructions of the human body for several years now and didn't think anything could surprise me, but I was completely disarmed by the conjunction of "Search warrants for appellant's apartment and vagina." Are they really parallel? Strictly analyzing the property concepts, they may not be: she may own the vagina, although we learned in chapter 3 that she may not own her spleen, and may only rent the apartment. Are lawyers proud to be part of a profession that can refer unblinkingly to "apartment and vagina"?

---

[1] Rodriques v. Furtado, 950 F.2d 805, 807 (1st Cir. 1991) (two footnotes omitted).

A footnote detailed the factual basis for the search warrant; there was plenty of evidence that Rodriques and her husband were dealing drugs from her apartment, and one confidential informant, and an anonymous tipper who may or may not have been a different person, reported that she hid heroin or opiate painkillers in her vagina. The story really gets weird when the police search the apartment. A search of the apartment revealed "what appeared to be a block of heroin in the bedroom." Was it or wasn't it? What complexities of trial strategy kept the court and us in the dark on this point? "What exactly occurred at the Morton Hospital is disputed." But since the case ends without any trial, but with summary judgment for the defendants, the court must be holding that Shirley Rodriques's civil rights were not violated even if her narrative of the search is correct, and that narrative was that "she was pushed down on the examining table and held there by the nurse, while Dr. Falkoff inserted a probe inside her vagina and conducted a bimanual palpation of appellant's abdomen and vagina."

Before Dr. Falkoff proceeded, hospital administrators informed him of "the hospital's consent policy." We learn no more about this, but as Shirley Rodriques did not consent to the search of her vagina, the policy must be one in which the hospital consented to do searches for the police, not one requiring the owner of the vagina to consent. The act of consenting is metaphorically transferred from the human legal subject to the hospital. (Indeed, the brief statement of facts reeks with other pathetic fallacies besides consenting hospitals. *Pain* can be alleviated, but I don't think "necessity" can be "alleviate[d].")

"The search revealed an absence of foreign bodies," only Rodriques's body, which may or may not be foreign. (The body with drugs ingested is often conceptualized as a foreign assault on a pure American national body, to be discussed in chapter 12). But whether or not Rodriques is "foreign," one would have thought it undeniable that the "body" in question was hers. Yet the search did not "reveal a presence of Rodriques's body," because the discursive construction of that search and that body is designed precisely not to reveal the presence of Rodriques as a human subject. So the search, amazingly, reveals absences, not presences: foreign bodies that might have been, but were not, present. Once again the physical body of Shirley Rodriques is metaphorically transferred to the nonexistent foreign body.

Finally, of course, how like a man to find that the search of a vagina "revealed an absence," for what is the vagina, say the Freudians, but an absence, a lack? What does the boy's eye see but the lack of the penis, the anxiety over castration, the missing, the lost, the unattainable and thus, to some extent, imaginary?[2] I do not think that the odd phrase "search revealed an absence" is

[2] Sigmund Freud, "The Sexual Life of Human Beings," in *Introductory Lectures on Psychoanalysis* 317–18 (James Strachey ed. and trans.) (New York: Norton, 1977) [1916–17]. See also Peter Brooks, "The Body in the Field of Vision," in *Body Work: Objects of Desire in Modern*

careless or coincidental here, although I realize that in context it means an absence of drugs, not an absence of anything. Still, this is not the ordinary way in English of saying that there were no drugs in Shirley Rodriques's vagina; the court reifies absence into a thing that can be revealed, and I find this vocabulary indicative of the court's epistemophilia (in Peter Brooks's sense) and phallocentrism (in Lacan's), though others may disagree.

In analyzing the legality of this vaginal search, the court reviewed the cases seen in the last chapter: *Schmerber v. California,* the blood test of the drunk driver; *Winston v. Lee,* the refusal to order surgery; and *Bell v. Wolfish,* the body cavity searches of inmates. The court noted that it had strongly disapproved of body cavity searches not supported by probable cause: "Body cavity searches are 'demeaning, dehumanizing, undignified, humiliating, terrifying, unpleasant, embarrassing, repulsive, signifying degradation and submission'" representing "the greatest personal indignity."[3] However, it had not ruled on body cavity searches conducted pursuant to a search warrant. The court thought this analysis required "balancing the need for the particular search against the invasion of personal rights the search imposes."[4]

> The invasion here was extreme, constituting a drastic and total intrusion of the personal privacy and security values shielded by the fourth amendment from unreasonable searches. Searches of this nature instinctively give us cause for concern as they implicate and threaten the highest degree of dignity that we are entrusted to protect.
>
> On the other side of the balance, the need for the search was also great. Society's interest in the prevention and punishment of drug trafficking weighs in favor of intrusive searches in certain instances. In the present case, other, less intrusive means of investigation and prosecution may have been available. However, given the circumstances as a whole, the existence of other means of investigation and prosecution in this case does not render the vaginal search unreasonable. The need for this particular search may have been necessary to enable the police to discover whether appellant was trafficking in drugs which she kept hidden in her vagina, as specifically alleged in the affidavit for the warrant.[5]

That's all the analysis there was. I didn't omit any footnotes, because there weren't any. I make no argument that the case is incorrectly decided, although a recent survey of a very small sample found body cavity searches to be the

---

Narrative 88–122 (Cambridge: Harv. U. Pr., 1993). Of course, in Freudian theory the vagina is supposed to be something totally different for women, the natural mature location of sexual fulfillment, to which they gradually become attached after renouncing the clitoris/phallus.

[3] Rodriques, 950 F.2d at 810, quoting from Blackburn v. Snow, 771 F.2d 556, 564 (1st Cir. 1985).

[4] Id. 811, quoting Bell v. Wolfish, 441 U.S. at 559.

[5] Id. 811.

single most intrusive search of the fifty mentioned.[6] I have no method at hand for determining the boundaries of state intrusion into the body. I hope, however, it is plain that the legal body of Shirley Rodriques is, somehow, less firm, more porous, more absent, than the body of Rudolph Lee. Like the body of Rudolph Lee, the body of Shirley Rodriques is a judicial artifact that is discursively constructed, then weighed. His is constructed as subject to "intrusion"; the state wrongfully proposed to "take control." Her body, by contrast, is constructed without reference to boundaries at all, a significant omission in a legal discourse often obsessed (see chap. 12) with the boundaries of the body. In her case (like that of the inmates of the Tombs), the court "instinctively" had cause for concern, but reason was able to vanquish instinct just as mind vanquishes body, and the search was permitted. About their bodies as they experience them, of course, we have no knowledge at all.

I have complained before about a body fetishizing that focuses on body parts in isolation, the sort of discourse of the body that led Monique Wittig to deny that she "had" a vagina.[7] One thing that such fetishization could do, however, if anyone wanted it to, would be to draw a boundary, outside the universalizing "balance" that makes all body parts commensurable with all legal interests. One could imagine a flat rule denying law enforcement personnel access to the insides of the vagina (or under the skin, as *Winston v. Lee* did *not* hold), with exceptions perhaps only for "extraordinary circumstances" or something of the sort. I'm not sure that I personally would favor this sort of flat fetishizing rule, although law may well maintain such a rule for penises, as we shall see in the next chapter. However, it is easy to summon up the hypthetical discourse that would construct such fetishized zones of privacy.

Law does not construct the unsearchable vagina partly because of woman's "to-be-looked-at-ness," but equally because a great deal of heroin really is smuggled into the country inside of vaginas or other body cavities. A recent case awarding damages to a traveler found to have been searched illegally— there was truly no basis for suspecting her of anything, except that she was Nigerian—nevertheless noted how common body cavity concealment has become as a method of drug smuggling, largely superseding clothing, suitcases, and swallowing. In the year before the search held illegal, five people had been apprehended at the same airport smuggling drugs in body cavities. The court did note, however, that three-quarters of the passengers whose body cavities were searched, at the hospital performing such searches for Logan Airport in Boston, had concealed nothing in them; that nationwide many more cavity examinations turn out negative than positive; and that the customs ser-

---

[6] Christopher Slobogin and Joseph E. Schumacher, "Reasonable Expectations of Privacy and Autonomy in Fourth Amendment Cases: An Empirical Look at 'Understandings Recognized and Permitted by Society,'" 42 *Duke L. J.* 727, 738–39 (1993).

[7] Discussed in chap. 7.

vice has displayed no interest in statistical comparisons of negative and positive searches or in refining its profile.[8]

So law does not construct an unsearchable vagina. Having failed to do so, law cannot construct any other vagina except the "private" vagina whose "privacy interests" go into the customary "balance." Shirley Rodriques's body is thus totally up for grabs, losing in the balance to "society's interest in the prevention and punishment of drug trafficking" and a search of which "the need . . . *may have been* necessary," as the court desperately, and pleonastically, puts it. This requires some attention then to the legal vagina, that judicial artifact so light that it can be outweighed by such a far-from-weighty nonnecessity.

Perhaps the most interesting aspect of the legal vagina is the extent to which it is constituted by its relations with other people. This truly sets it apart from other legal bodies that represent individuals isolated from each other, such as the rectums of detainees in the Tombs, which can also be searched, but which are not characteristically constituted in relation to others. The construction, I believe, reflects a traditional view of women as less individualized, more the function of all the vectors of their relationships, than are men.

Because the Milwaukee police had a tip that Robert Salinas had heroin with him as he returned with his family in his car from a trip to Texas, their arrest warrant for him was valid, and so were their body cavity searches of his wife Carolyn and four of their children, all under ten. When law constructs a legal vagina, but only when it constructs the vagina, it abandons its usual insistence on the isolated, individuated body abstracted from any human relations and standing in for the individual self. Vaginas, being after all absences or lacks, are constituted by their relations with others (typically male), so that an arrest warrant for her husband will do to permit searching Carolyn and the children. A valid arrest warrant for Robert lets the court "presume" that there was "probable cause" that drugs were hidden on Carolyn or the children; no individual tips or suspicion as to *them* were required.

In Carolyn Salinas's case, the legal figures mimetically representing the search of her body are as pornographically vivid as her vagina is lacking. "One by one, Carolyn's items of clothing were removed, and her arms, fingers, armpits, and back were searched for needlemarks. Then Carolyn was told to bend over. She then felt pokings in the rectal area and then the vaginal area."[9] The court not only *describes* a striptease, it *mimetically represents* the striptease, as the court assumes the subject position of the Milwaukee police, removing Carolyn's items of clothing "one by one." Like the search of Shirley Rodriques, the search of Carolyn Salinas turned up nothing.

This construction of the vagina as constituted relationally makes it fairly

---

[8] Adedeji v. United States, 782 F.Supp. 688, 694–95 and n. 19 (D.Mass. 1992).
[9] Salinas v. Breier, 695 F.2d 1073, 1075 (7th Cir. 1982).

easy for law's eye to get inside a woman's shorts. The absolute minimum that I have run across that sustained a peak in the underpants, though in this case not a specularization of the vagina, involved a high-school student named Angela Williams, subjected to a strip search because *one fellow student* told the principal that Angela and a girl named Michelle had a clear glass vial containing a white powder, and the school officials, guided by *Michelle's* father, had independent reason to suspect *Michelle* (but not Angela) of drug use. After a search of Angela's lockers, books, and purse produced no evidence of drugs, the principal asked Easley, a female assistant principal

> to take Williams into her office and search her person, in the presence of a female secretary. Inside Easley's office, Williams was asked to empty her pockets which she promptly did. Easley then asked the girl to remove her T-shirt. Although she hesitated and appeared nervous, Williams complied after Easley repeated the request. Williams was then required to lower her blue jeans to her knees. In her deposition, Williams testified that Easley pulled on the elastic of her undergarments to see if anything would fall out, but Easley disputes this contention. . . . Finally, Williams was told to remove her shoes and socks. Easley found no evidence of drugs as a result of this search.[10]

Williams's civil rights suit against the school officials was also thrown out without trial with summary judgment granted to the officials, who were found (again, even assuming Williams's version), not unreasonable.

Paternalism is also invoked in support of searching the vagina, so that the specularization of the vagina is really what she wants, or ought to want. This is also a trope not found in body search cases involving men and seems limited to women. One recent case of airport arrivals involved considerably more evidence supporting individual suspicion of the women required to undergo X rays and pelvic and rectal examinations. Moreover, in their case, unlike Shirley Rodriques's, Angela Williams's, or Carolyn Salinas's, they were actually carrying heroin in their vaginas. Still, the court did not content itself with establishing the individual probable cause so often lacking in these cases. "A medical professional at the hospital in fact informed the two women that they were subjecting themselves to a grave risk by carrying the drugs inside them. Thus, had the procedure not been performed, the health of the women would have remained in jeopardy until all of the packets were expelled. We view these considerations as more substantial than dignitary injury occasioned by the concededly embarrassing procedure." A footnote explained: "Our review of the cases dealing with alimentary canal smuggling suggests that very poor and vulnerable people are used to transport drugs in this fashion."[11] A vagina is a dangerous place, especially for a woman. The vagina needs phallic guid-

---

[10] Williams v. Ellington, 936 F.2d 881, 883 (6th Cir. 1991).

[11] United States v. Oyekan, 786 F.2d 832, 839–40 and n. 14 (8th Cir. 1986).

ance, for the phallus knows better than she does how to protect her health. I am unaware of any other cases involving searches in which the court has attempted to establish, paternalistically, that such searches were genuinely in the interest of those searched, and I therefore do not think it accidental that this odd argument is encountered in a case dealing with African women.

In recent years feminist philosophers have urged women to reclaim their bodies. Woman's very body means what it means as constructed through language, and that language is phallic, male; the body it constructs will always be lost, unattainable, lacking, imaginary.[12] To this general suppression of women's bodies associated with male language, we may now add law's distinctive contribution: a female body fetishized as a vagina that stands in for the body; specularized by law's gaze; empty except as constituted by its relations with men; dangerous to women except as tamed by male authority. Whatever new language of the body emerges from feminist jurisprudence could hardly be worse than this.

---

[12] Luce Irigaray, "Così Fan Tutti," in *This Sex Which Is Not One* 86–105 (Catherine Porter trans.) (Ithaca: Cornell U. Pr., 1985) [1975].

Chapter 10

THE LEGAL PENIS

The Penis's Narrative: Constitutional Restrictions on Penile Plethysmography

A few months after the United States Court of Appeals for the First Circuit in Boston constructed the searchable vagina of Shirley Rodriques, it had occasion to construct the unsearchable penis of Norman Harrington.[1] Norman Harrington's penis, like Shirley Rodriques's vagina, had a tale to tell, a narrative to decode, secrets to disclose—none of which the state may know, at least in the way the state had hoped to learn them.

Norman Harrington is a police officer in the City of Old Town, Maine. Four children, siblings, accused Harrington, among others, of sexually abusing them. Two years earlier, the children had accused their parents and some of their parents' friends and relatives of sexual abuse, as a result of which the children were placed in foster care and nine adults, including the children's parents, were eventually convicted of sex crimes. The children began to accuse others and, within a few months after accusing Harrington, had accused over 170 individuals of sexual abuse, including other police officers and a United States senator. "Apparently having serious doubts as to the credibility of the children's allegations against those on the expanding list of persons accused, the Bangor Police and the District Attorney's Office sought no further criminal charges. Harrington was never indicted."[2]

Harrington meanwhile had, as a result of the charges of sexual abuse, temporarily lost custody of his own son and been suspended with pay from his duties as a police officer. When the district attorney decided that the sexual-abuse investigation "wasn't going anywhere," Harrington requested reinstatement. The city manager, who had requested that Harrington resign, eventually compromised by agreeing to reinstate Harrington if he undertook a "psychological examination." Harrington initially agreed but refused to participate on learning that what was contemplated was a penile plethysmograph.

A penile plethysmograph consists of a pressure-sensitive ring or tube, made of rubber and filled with mercury, that is placed around the penis. The ring is connected to a plethysmograph, a computerized monitor, that measures changes in the circumference of the penis. The device measures sexual

---

[1] Harrington v. Almy, 977 F.2d 37 (1st Cir. 1992). Andrea Culler made research contributions to this chapter.

[2] 977 F.2d at 39.

arousal. It was created in 1908 to calculate the effect of drugs on animal research subjects and later became used in studying impotence. Beginning in the 1970s, however, its manufacturer began marketing it for use in programs for the diagnosis of sexual offenders. Subjects are shown sexually explicit slides and are sometimes asked to describe verbally what they see. The plethysmograph measures the differential arousal to different stimuli. There is a fair amount of criticism of the penile plethysmograph on the grounds that there is no really good evidence correlating laboratory responses to sexual crime, particularly among adolescent boys who have erections in response to a wide variety of stimuli. Nor have laboratory responses ever been standardized. The principal manufacturer of the devices has recently decided to stop making them.[3]

Because of Harrington's refusal to take the penile plethysmograph, he was fired as a police officer, and, independently, the district attorney announced that he would refuse to prosecute the cases of any person arrested by Harrington, should Harrington return to work. By the time of the trial, an arbitrator had reinstated Harrington to his police job. However, the district attorney's order had the effect of forcing Harrington to a desk job. He sued, claiming the requirement that he submit to a penile plethysmograph violated his constitutional rights to privacy and to substantive due process. The court of appeals, reversing the district court, agreed with the latter contention. Although the plethysmograph was never administered, it was a potential constitutional violation for the city to condition Harrington's reinstatement on his taking it.[4] At a subsequent trial, a jury awarded Harrington $950,000 compensatory damages and $10,000 punitive damages for the violation of his civil rights, and the case was settled when the city paid Harrington more than $900,000.[5]

My juxtaposing this case with Shirley Rodriques's is obviously unfair. There are many distinctions that might lead the rational mind to favor a search of her vagina and oppose the probe of his penis. Rodriques's vagina was searched as part of a criminal investigation with probable cause; Harrington was only nominally a criminal suspect, and the plethysmograph was proposed on the question of whether he should get his job back (although presumably had the test "disclosed" that he was perversely sexually attracted to children,

---

[3] James G. Barker and Robert J. Howell, "The Plethysmograph: A Review of Recent Literature," 20 *Bull. Am. Acad. Psychiatry & L.* 13 (1992); "Skinnered Alive," 4 *Lingua Franca* 8, 10 (March–April 1994).

[4] Harrington, 977 F.2d 37 (1st Cir. 1992). The refusal of the district attorney to prosecute Harrington's cases was absolutely immune from judicial review under cases such as Imbler v. Pachtman, 424 U.S. 409 (1976).

[5] Police Officer and City Settle Sex-Arousal-Test Case, 8 BNA Individual Emp. Rts. (December 21, 1993) at 1; Cop Who Refused Sex-Arousal Test Gets $960,000, 8 BNA Individual Emp. Rts. (July 6, 1993) at 1.

the criminal investigation of Harrington might well have been revived). The confidential informant in her case was presumably more reliable than the child informants in his. Perhaps for this reason, a search warrant had been issued for the search of Rodriques's vagina but not for Harrington's penis. The search of her vagina involved no issues of reliability. It did not involve technology and either would have found drugs or not. By contrast, the proposed search of his penis was for its semiotic ability to signify psychological urges, of dubious reliability. I do not have firm intuitions on which search was the more "intrusive," either physically or psychologically, but perhaps some readers do. The only real factor in her favor in this comparison is that Shirley Rodriques's vagina was actually searched, while Norman Harrington's penis never was.

In any case, the two cases well demonstrate at least the manipulability of the searchable legal body. However distinguishable the situations, if law had something like a standard on body searches, one might expect to see it employed in both cases. Instead, Harrington's case does not cite Rodriques's, and the discursive construction of his body bears little resemblance to hers. It almost goes without saying that his penis is not-to-be-looked-at; that it is not constructed as an absence (even an absence-of-suspicion); that it is not constructed solely in relation to other persons; that it is not, in short, a vagina. I think that the case also demonstrates some singular aspects of the penis as a narrator of tales, specifically the way in which the erection of a penis falls outside a man's conscious control and therefore threatens a carefully constructed master legal narrative in which bodily self-control graphically represents the self-government contemplated by a democratic legal society. But before developing this point, I want first to explore a few technical legal aspects of Harrington's case, again mainly to establish that these did not drive the discursive construction of his mute penis.

A somewhat technical curiosity of the case is that the penile plethysmograph was held not to violate Harrington's right to privacy. The court invoked an unusually narrow notion of privacy, treating the privacy claim as a claim "to be free from the gathering of highly personal information regarding his psychological fitness." This is certainly a highly restricted notion of privacy and does not address such recognized constitutional rights of privacy as the right to abort or contracept without state interference. Limited to a right to control information, Harrington's right to privacy yielded to the city's interest in psychological information, had that been gathered by less intrusive means.[6] The court's approach to privacy, as to the penis, recalls Peter Brooks's exploration of the constitutional concept of privacy: that the human body is a "space to which we assign final secrets"; that this dynamic mixes with erotic desire in an "epistemophilic drive" to know these secrets; and that the constitutional

[6] 977 F.2d at 43.

concept of private information is formed largely as a representation of the body and sexuality.[7]

The penile plethysmograph did, however, in the court's view, raise issues of substantive due process. That is, conditioning employment on the examination deprived Harrington of liberty protected by the Fourteenth Amendment, either liberty from unnecessarily intrusive police methods or an unwarranted search.

Both of these alternative approaches to substantive due process analysis have focused on state action undertaking unwanted manipulations of an individual's body. While *Rochin* [v. California, 342 U.S. 165 (1952)] found a due process violation when evidence was extracted from the body of a criminal defendant against his will by means of a stomach pump, the courts have not established a per se bar to unwanted intrusions upon or manipulations of a citizen's body by agents of the state. Thus, the Supreme Court has upheld against a substantive due process challenge the use of a hypodermic needle to extract blood from an unconscious accident victim in order to test for alcohol. *Breithaupt v. Abram,* 352 U.S. 432 (1957). This holding was reaffirmed in *Schmerber v. California,* 384 U.S. 757 (1966). Critical to the *Breithaupt* court's determination was the understanding that "the test as administered here would not be considered offensive by even the most delicate" and involved a procedure which "has become routine in our everyday life" (352 U.S. at 436).

More recently the Court [in Winston v. Lee, discussed in chapter 8] revisited the limitations on state intrusions into an individual's body in the context of a Fourth Amendment challenge to a surgical procedure under a general anesthetic designed to remove a bullet lodged in the chest of an armed robbery suspect.

The evolving case law governing unwanted body intrusions or manipulations has weighed several relevant considerations. Once it is established that, as here, the state is entitled to the information the bodily intrusion is designed to obtain, the means used will be measured by its reasonableness in light of the need to obtain the evidence in this way. To the degree the procedure would not be considered offensive even by the most delicate and is routine, it will be less likely to involve a constitutional violation. By contrast, nonroutine manipulative intrusions on bodily integrity will be subject to heightened scrutiny to determine, inter alia, whether there are less intrusive alternatives available.

A reasonable finder of fact could conclude that requiring the plethysmograph involves a substantive due process violation. The procedure, from all that appears, is hardly routine. One does not have to cultivate particularly delicate sensibilities to believe degrading the process of having a strain gauge strapped to an individual's genitals while sexually explicit pictures are displayed in an effort to determine his sexual-arousal patterns. The procedure involves bodily manipulation of the most intimate sort. There has been no showing regarding the proce-

[7] Peter Brooks, *Body Work: Objects of Desire in Modern Narrative* 49–52 (Cambridge: Harv. U. Pr.) (1993).

dure's reliability, and, in light of other psychological evaluative tools available, there has been no demonstration that other less intrusive means of obtaining the relevant information are not sufficient.[8]

We have seen courts tongue-tied over the analysis of body searches before, but it bears repeating that, if there is any justification for the court's discursive construction of the penis, it surely does not lie in the service of this complete nonanalysis. For whatever psychological reason courts hold the body at a distance, avoid making it physically present, it cannot be shown that this language of distance helps courts avoid passion, abstracts from the distracting particular, helps treat like cases alike. For the court's analysis of the problem is full of passion and, moreover, results in nothing that could, even in theory, generate a consistent and principled result. (Consistency and principle do not loom as large in my own jurisprudence as they might in some others. I am trying to dispose of potential self-justifications for this way of talking, were courts ever to be put on the spot as to why they talk this way).

Consider what the court does *not* derive from its brief consideration of the two Supreme Court cases, that is, the case permitting blood sampling for alcohol testing and the case denying general surgery to remove the bullet in Rudolph Lee's chest. It does not derive any legal standard other than "reasonable" and not "offensive," "degrading" and not "routine," which is no legal standard at all. (It could conceivably be a legal standard if there were fairly firm social understandings about body boundaries and body intrusions; however, it is just these understandings that do not exist and are normally constructed by law as it justifies its own power.) The court simply fails (as the Supreme Court has failed before it) to offer any explanation why blood extraction is different from surgery, and were this court to extend its analysis to its own uncited vaginal-search case, the rule would become even more elusive. Again, this is commonplace and tedious, but I think one must always consider the possibility that discourse has some internal legal function.

Here the only possible legal function would be to preserve maximum possible freedom of action for this and future courts addressing the constitutionality of intrusive bodily searches. A sentence like "To the degree the procedure would not be considered offensive even by the most delicate and is routine, it will be less likely to involve a constitutional violation" is a comical parody of a legal standard. We already knew that something that wouldn't offend "the most delicate" wouldn't be offensive to anyone else. So why does the court invoke this spectral "most delicate" individual, who performs no role in its analysis? Who is this "most delicate" individual? A proper lady? A delicate male, like that great nineteenth-century literary invention, the homosexual? How does the court figure this absurd creation, the "most delicate"

---

[8] 977 F.2d at 43–44.

person, empowered to authorize brutal police practices merely by whispering gently "I am not offended"?

The second part of this sentence, suggesting that routine police practices can't violate the Constitution, isn't acceptable in that form. The Court is thinking about extracting blood. The notion must be that if police practices mime some larger social practice that lots of middle-class people accept, the police practices can't violate the Constitution, can't violate the body of the Constitution unless it violates the body of a proper middle-class person. But of course a police search for evidence isn't a voluntary blood donation to transfuse into a patient, and consent to one doesn't imply consent to the other, not even in the case of one individual. If the class of people consenting to the social intrusion isn't the same as the class consenting to the police practice, the argument breaks down entirely. For all I know, there might be a subculture of people who employ the rings from penile plethysmograph machines for sexual enjoyment, but even if this practice became routine in the "general" (heterosexual) population, what would it have to do with personnel practices of police departments? Adult people routinely engage in sexual intercourse, and do not always regard this as coercive or intrusive, but that doesn't mean it could be part of the employment examination for police officers.

So the court's nonstandard really just preserves its own freedom to react subjectively to each body intrusion as it comes along. To this end of maximizing its own power and discretion, the court refrains from even the most commonplace imaging of the body of Norman Harrington (or Rudolph Lee, or Schmerber), lest the very image of the body constrain law's power to appropriate it. So absent is any imaging of the body that Harrington's penis itself disappears from display. In the quoted passage, the court substitutes the euphemism "genitals," which is a good deal less precise, substituting the vaguer general term for the more precise and accurate "penis."[9]

Standing in for the missing penis are a now-familiar string of epithets. The adjectives describing Harrington's forbidden penile plethysmograph ("degrading," "intimate," "intrusive") do not much differ from the similar parade used to describe Shirley Rodriques's permissible vaginal search ("demeaning, dehumanizing, undignified, humiliating, terrifying, unpleasant, embarrassing, repulsive, signifying degradation and submission"). The rhetoric in each case displaces representation of the body of the searched with a set of emotional adjectives: the adjectives belong in the narrative *not* because they represent anything particular to Norman Harrington or Shirley Rodriques, but because they represent, in universalized form, the emotions of the judge.

---

[9] Interestingly, the word *penis* itself was originally a euphemism. "Cicero observes that the Latin *penis* 'tail' had been a euphemism for *mentula:* 'At hodie *penis* est in obscenis.' But nowadays *penis* is among the obscenities." Keith Allan and Kate Burridge, *Euphemism and Dysphemism: Language Used as Shield and Weapon* 22 (New York: Oxford U. Pr.) (1991), quoting Cicero, *Epistulae ad Familiares,* IX, xxii.

The search is relevant insofar as it makes the viewer sympathetically examine his or her *own* sensibilities, excites his or her sympathies. Adam Smith: "Though our brother is on the rack . . . our *senses* will never inform of us of what he suffers. . . . By the *imagination* we place ourselves in his situation, we conceive ourselves enduring all the same torments, *we enter as it were into his body,* and become in some measure the same person with him."[10] The court short-circuits that process; it jumps right to its own sensibilities without employing the literary visualization that might feed the imagination. (We will have much more to say about sympathy with the suffering body in the next chapter on criminal punishment and will return to a reinvigorated, discursive, representation of the body in the conclusion).

I do not think it is necessary to belabor the sexual difference here. Much has been written, particularly in the Freudian and Lacanian traditions, about the symbolic significance of the penis, the taboos around its unveiling from the tale of Noah to the present, the comparative ease with which male judges might identify with the subject of a penile plethysmograph.

On the other hand, it is not the case that the state is prohibited from ever administering penile plethysmographs. Convicted sexual offenders, out on parole and undergoing psychiatric treatment to modify their behavior, have been required to undergo penile plethysmography to monitor their progress.[11]

While I think it true that cases like *Harrington v. Almy* construct a penis that is a privileged symbol of male authority, privileged precisely from disclosing its narratives, I would like to explore an interesting, and perhaps less obvious, symbolic meaning of the penis that links many of the disparate discursive legal bodies that we have already identified. Central to any of law's constructions of the body is, as we have seen, the idea we have been calling Cartesian, of the body as a thing other than the person. It is also true that the thing-body is subject to the mental and physical control of that person, indeed, constructed, as we have seen and will see further, precisely to represent a self-governing individual. Even if it is in some sense "demeaning" or "humiliating" for the doctor to search Shirley Rodriques's vagina, the search was only for the drugs that she was thought (erroneously) to have placed there. The degrading search of her body is necessary only because of the potential agency of Shirley Rodriques (the person) in breaking the law.

The search was thus to bring a narrative to life, and not just drugs. The narrative uncovered in a search is a kind of classic novel, with a protagonist who freely made choices that shaped her life, and in conclusion receives whatever desert is appropriate. In a Fourth Amendment case, the searchee is the

---

[10] Adam Smith, *The Theory of Moral Sentiments* 9 (D. D. Raphael and A. L. Mackie eds.) (Oxford: Clarendon, 1976) (final emphasis supplied, others original).

[11] Walrath v. United States, 830 F.Supp. 444 (N.D. Ill. 1993); State v. Emery, 593 A.2d 77 (Vt. 1991).

protagonist of this novel. Law searches Shirley Rodriques's vagina to reveal drugs, but more importantly to reveal this normalizing narrative of Shirley Rodriques's choices and actions.

Thus, when the state intrudes into a body, this need not be represented as control or domination of that body. In a way, searches paradoxically vindicate the freedom of the hypothesized real individual, the person inside the body, to use that body. Law's searches do this by performing this novelistic narrative of the freedom of this self-using-a-body to make moral choices and face novelistic consequences. Indeed, in this novel, the individual protagonist's freedom *causes* the intrusion. Where that freedom is misused, and sin is chosen, the intrusion, represented by the body search, is the very denouement already willed by the free choices of the searched subject. As Chief Justice Rehnquist wrote in a different case, upholding the warrantless detention of a suspected "balloon smuggler" of drugs until the drugs were defecated: "Respondent's detention was long, uncomfortable, indeed, humiliating; but both its length and its discomfort resulted solely from the method by which she chose to smuggle illicit drugs into this country."[12]

This narrative of the body as the sum total of a lifetime of moral choices by a choosing subject is directly threatened by the penis, that body part that men consistently experience as *not* under their control. The penile plethysmograph exploits for diagnostic or social-control purposes the unamenability of the penis to mental control. For that reason, it coexists uneasily with the larger background legal narrative in which minds control bodies, and it may be inscribed into that narrative only if, somewhat inaccurately, the plethysmograph may be figured as part of the normal novelistic narrative of mental control of the body.

BODIES THAT OUR MINDS DO NOT CONTROL: THE PENIS AS AGENT

> What we touch is always
> an Other: I may fondle
> my leg, not Me.[13]

Once the legal body is constructed as a thing distinct from the person, a potential political struggle opens up over who is to be the master of the two. Law mostly averts this struggle by uncompromisingly supposing that it is the person, specifically the person's mind, that controls the body. As St. Augustine says, "The mind commands the body and is instantly obeyed. The mind commands itself and meets resistance."[14] This is a rather inert and submissive

---

[12] U.S. v. Montoya de Hernandez, 473 U.S. 531, 544 (1985).

[13] W. H. Auden, *Collected Poems* 854 (Edward Mendelson ed.) (New York: Vintage, 1991).

[14] Saint Augustine, *Confessions*, chap. ix, par. 21 (Henry Chadwick trans.) (Oxford: Ox. U. Pr., 1991) (p. 147).

legal body that fits well with the machine body and property body and might be thought to be in tension with more sacred conceptions in which the body is particularly significant, inviolable, definitive of the person, or even, in the conception that law does *not* adopt, the person "himself" or "herself."

It follows that for purposes of criminal law, the body has no independent status or legal agency and certainly can't commit crimes all by itself. Of course, it is not hard to imagine a criminal law discourse that would constitute the body of the criminal as a threat requiring control beyond its simple isolation and confinement. In normal criminal law discourse, however, as we shall consider more carefully in the next chapter, law seizes hold of the body (isolation, discipline, injection of psychotropic medication) as a way of reaching the "person" within. In this Cartesian discourse, the body of the criminal may be constituted a threat only when, as is usual with law, it can be separated from the person who is that criminal, and, as is rare, attributed independent agency.

One such unusual case is an English criminal law case, *Regina v. Charlson*.[15] The defendant hit his ten-year-old son over the head and threw him out of the window. He was permitted a defense of involuntariness on the theory that his behavior was caused by a brain tumor. The case is a difficult one for theories of criminal responsibility and is generally described by English commentators as anomalous if not incorrect, and not followed in later decisions.[16]

Meir Dan-Cohen has recently revived this case as part of his general philosophic treatment of responsibility. While the general thrust of his argument is to expand concepts of legal responsibility beyond the limits of traditional free will, the *Charlson* case for Dan-Cohen represents an appropriate legal category of actions in which the human subject is *not* responsible because its body *is*. Dan-Cohen argues that the most compelling reading of the case "requires us to view the tumor as an external and intrusive agency rather than a part of Charlson himself. Charlson is not subject-responsible for his tumor—it is simply not part of him."[17]

Dan-Cohen contrasts Charlson with a hypothetical rapist who raises a defense of involuntariness, claiming that he cannot control his sex drive any more than Charlson could control his brain tumor. The rapist, argues Dan-Cohen, will be unsuccessful. "[T]he contrast between the brain tumor's relationship to the self and that of the sexual glands" is a "sharp one," though "not absolute." "Although it takes some effort, we can imagine a self for whom the

---

15 1 W.L.R. 317 (1955).

16 Glanville Williams, *Criminal Law: The General Part* §157 n. 22 (at 489) (London: Stevens, 2d ed., 1961). Williams discusses a later case, Regina v. Kemp, [1957] 1 QB 399, a verdict of insanity for conduct attributable to arteriosclerosis, as a repudiation of the acquittal in *Charlson*. Criticism similar to Williams's is expressed in Owen Dixon, "A Legacy of Hadfield, M'Naghten, and Maclean," 31 *Aus.* L. J. 255, 257–60 (1957).

17 Meir Dan-Cohen, "Responsibility and the Boundaries of the Self," 105 *Harv. L. Rev.* 959, 991 (1992).

sexual drive is an intrusive external force no different in kind from the per-
nicious emanations of a brain tumor. The effort needed to imagine such a self,
however, is evidence that our culture (by which I mean at least contemporary
Western culture) does not encourage the enactment of such a self. Hence the
relative ease with which [the rapist] would be held responsible: 'I am not
responsible for my sexual drive' is simply not a viable argument in our culture. One of the ways in which this culture helps constitute a self that inexora-
bly integrates the sexual drive but not a brain tumor is by ascribing responsibility for the former while withholding responsibility for the latter."[18]

I certainly agree generally with Dan-Cohen's attention to the discursive
process by which the self is constituted in legal culture and have been arguing
throughout that the body is a subject of a similar process of discursive construction. The general product of these discursive processes is the same: the
"nice body with a self at home in it," the humanistic, individuated body that
we experience, not as our own discursive construction, but as the site of an
individuated person in the world. Such a body is not the same as the person,
belongs to the person, but normally lies within the control of that person. I
wonder though whether Dan-Cohen hasn't got his Charlson/rapist hypothetical exactly backward.

Charlson seems to me to represent the legal category that never was: the
body that controls the mind. *Charlson* does indeed attempt to stake out such a
category, but it is a discredited case without much influence. I have tried as
hard as I can to find cases that might expand this category, in the interest of
accurate description of the legal system, but have been unable to do so. For
example, as I mentioned in chapter 2, someone who commits an assault with
hands does not normally assault with a deadly weapon, and in any case this
way of putting the point shows that the mind is thought to control the hands,
not the other way around.[19] Hysteria, for another example, that discredited
medical diagnosis in which the body represents and performs a mental state,
has never functioned as a legal category, however fashionable it was once and
is again as a literary and artistic category; legal flesh is constructed so as not to
escape the legal word.[20]

It is the opposite theme, rather, that runs through *all* of the cases we have
studied to date. The property body, machine body, private body, narrated

[18] Id. 992.

[19] People v. Dozie, 224 Cal.App.2d 474 (1964) (naked hands or fists not dangerous or deadly
weapons); People v. Bias, 131 Ill.App.3d 98 (1985) (fingernail not a deadly weapon); Commonwealth v. Davis, 10 Mass.App.Ct. 190 (1980) (teeth not dangerous weapon); People v. Vollmer,
299 N.Y. 347 (1947) (bare fists not dangerous weapon). See "Parts of the Human Body as Dangerous Weapons," 8 ALR4th 1268.

[20] Sander Gilman et al., *Hysteria beyond Freud* (Berkeley: U. Cal. Pr., 1993); Allon White,
"Prosthetic Gods in Atrocious Places: Gilles Deleuze/Francis Bacon," in *Carnival, Hysteria, and
Writing: Collected Essays and Autobiography* 160 (Oxford: Clarendon, 1993).

body, body on display, sentimentalized body in pain, all are constructed as distinct from the person, yet fundamentally under that individual's control. Even when that individual, with few bargaining resources, has made such putatively foolish and self-harming choices as to agree to work his machine body longer than ten hours a day, law posits his ultimate control of that body, or there would be no point in legal limits on maximum hours to "restore" the fair bargains of a lost state of nature. The legal narratives thus reinforce a sort of Cartesian dualism and establish the hierarchical domination of body by mind.

What is more interesting than the unusual *Charlson* is this normal *refusal* of law to develop a jurisprudence of "body responsibility" or "bodies that threaten minds" or "bodies controlling minds." Law's refusal to construct this category is *not* because the contrasting construction of "self-control" is more accurate biologically. The plain truth is that we do not much control our bodies. As Lewis Thomas writes:

> If I were informed tomorrow that I was in direct communication with my liver, and could now take over, I would become deeply depressed. I'd sooner be told, forty thousand feet over Denver, that the 747 in which I had a coach seat was now mine to operate as I pleased; at least I would have the hope of bailing out, if I could find a parachute and discover quickly how to open a door. Nothing would save me and my liver, if I were in charge. For I am, to face the facts squarely, considerably less intelligent than my liver. I am, moreover, constitutionally unable to make hepatic decisions, and I prefer not to be obliged to, ever. I would not be able to think of the first thing to do.[21]

Our minds don't normally control our heartbeat, or blood circulation, or whether we blush, and it requires careful instruction in meditation or biofeedback for the mind to gain any control at all of them. Of course these uncontrolled bodily movements don't usually harm other people, and thus law doesn't much care whether the "body" or the "person" is responsible for them. Still, it is ideology, not biology, that drives the master legal narrative in which bodies are variously constructed but invariably under the control of constructions called minds. Sex, once again, is more complicated. Popular vulgar expressions often attribute agency to the body ("thinks with his dick"), but law never does, again with the exception of the unusual *Charlson* case.

But as the last comment shows, while law may present a uniform narrative on this point of mental, not bodily, agency, culture does not. The body part that is often portrayed in male cultural narrative as controlling the mind is precisely the penis. It is not a dirty joke, but Montaigne, who writes: "Every man knows from his own experience that he has a part of his body which often stirs, erects, and lies down again without his leave. Now such passive move-

---

[21] Lewis Thomas, *The Lives of a Cell* 78 (New York: Bantam, 1974).

ments which only touch our outside cannot be called ours."[22] What Dan-Cohen says was true of Charlson's tumor—that he is not responsible for it, it is not part of him—is just what Montaigne said about the penis that others might (inaccurately, he says) consider "his."

If law were to construct bodies with agency, bodies that acted without minds, without "our leave," bodies that had their own civil and criminal responsibility, I am confident that the penis would become that body part par excellence to which independent agency would be attributed. While I agree with Dan-Cohen that law does not generally construct a body with agency and so holds this narrative at bay, I am not quite so confident as he that the penis-agent is entirely absent from the law of rape.

It is true that a rapist is not acquitted simply by attributing agency to a discursive construction called a "sexual drive." As the work of feminist legal scholars has shown us, however, I do not agree that rapists in contemporary American legal culture are convicted with "relative ease," or that the argument "I am not responsible for my sexual drive" has no resonance as a legal defense. The argument certainly seems implicated in all the successful rape defenses of the general form: "I am not responsible for my sexual drive *because she was.*" I will not review the feminist critique of American rape law here. Dan-Cohen is correct that acquittals do not ordinarily construct a criminally responsible sex drive (or body or penis) distinct from the legal subject, so let us return to that possible construction, in the hopes that, should we clarify the structure of such a possible construction, we might well find it operating in rape law under another name.

The *Charlson* case returns us again to the issue of control over the body as a metaphor for human autonomy and self-control. "I am the master of my fate, I am the captain of my soul" works well for those who consider themselves master of their souls and bodies. The gradual process of civilizing the body, of controlling appetites and emissions, is a bodily experience that, as reconstructed in discourse, serves as a handy metaphor for the political process of individuation, self-government, and legal responsibility. Political freedom, as we saw in chapter 3, is often represented to us metaphorically as our freedom to control our own bodies: "My freedom to swing my arm ends at your nose," and so forth. Like any embodied representation of freedom, this is a construction; one could just as well describe this freedom of bodily movement as an alienated mystification of our subjection to others, or deny that we actually have such bodily freedom.

Law facilitates the standard construction of the free-yet-controlled body, doing so in the larger service of political liberalism. Law's standard discourse in which the *person* controls the *body* is part of a larger story in which people

---

[22] Michel de Montaigne, "On Practice," in *The Essays of Michel de Montaigne* 422 (M. A. Screech trans.) (London: Allen Lane/Penguin, 1991).

experience their freedom to move their bodies as freedom. We do not dwell on the nemesis story, in which bodies move as the very display of social control and discipline. A striking feature of this suppressed nemesis narrative might be that, as we noted above, not so long ago African-Americans and women of all backgrounds were not legally free to move their bodies however they liked. The system that Adrienne Rich calls "compulsory heterosexuality" is also a fairly significant restriction on the freedom of bodily movement, yet states are said to be able to outlaw other sexual expression.[23] Moreover, the freedom that law gives even free heterosexual males to control their bodies may easily be exaggerated. Anyone who spends a few minutes in a law school or courtroom can be trained to notice the subtle surveillance and discipline that encourages certain body postures, deportments, and expressions.

I argued above that the history of constituting the body as property, to facilitate domination, made the strategy of constituting the body as a locus of self-control radically unstable, since the property body may be owned or rented by others and enacts power and self-control only insofar as it is authorized to ignore other property bodies. *Charlson* lets us see that a discourse of bodily self-control is even less stable than we thought before. Even the English male father may not, in the eyes of the law, control his body; his body may control him. It is not very difficult in "our culture" to unearth a language of bodies controlling us, particularly when "we" are males and what the body "controls" is "our" male sexuality.

Which is it? Both, obviously. Just as the body is both public and private, is both controlled by the one inside it and by others, is both owned and alienated, is both individual and social, so is the body both controlled and controlling, and we surely can find elements of both in our individual experiences. This set of body metaphors, like all body metaphors, is self-contradictory, and can never tell us what we ask of them. It is patriarchy, not metaphor, that constitutes the body as *controlled* when men control women and constitutes the male body as *controlling* the "self" when excusing or justifying male violence, particularly sexual. The metaphor doesn't determine its own usage, though it may disguise the politics of the choice. The function of the porous, self-contradictory legal language is to provide a vocabulary to construct any sort of body required by male power. Still, again with the exception of *Charlson* and an equally discredited line of rape cases, the discursive construction of the body controlled by the mind, in an embodied metaphor of self-government, is normally the more powerful.

It is this construction of self-government that the penile plethysmograph threatens. It is "degrading" and "intrusive," not only for the reasons mentioned by the court, with which I certainly agree, but also because it purports to reveal sexual desires that men may not even disclose to themselves, about

[23] Bowers v. Hardwick, 478 U.S. 186 (1986).

which they may be ignorant or may lie. And there is the penis, potentially telling the plethysmograph a kind of truth of which the man is unaware or wishes to keep secret. Better restrict the plethysmograph, as law does, to the paroled sex offender who has "consented" to its use, in whose case the plethysmograph may function in the service of his gaining self-knowledge and self-control. As applied to the paroled sexual offender, the penile plethysmograph thus reinforces rather than threatens the construction of the body as the narrative of all the subject's past moral choices. The plethysmograph becomes the denouement willed by the protagonist, just as the drug smuggler wills her vaginal search.

Law determines whether or not to permit a penile plethysmograph then, not because of how intrusive it is, or because of the presence or absence of other means of obtaining the information it reveals. Rather, whether or not a penile plethysmograph will be used depends on whether or not it can be inscribed into the master narrative of the individual's control of his body and his life. Thus the terrifying fact, for it is a fact, of our lack of control of our bodies, can be soothingly reinscribed into a larger novelistic narrative of the individual's progressive mastery of the self.

Chapter 11

TRANQUILIZING THE PRISONER

There is no law that is not inscribed on bodies. Every law has a hold on
the body. . . . Every power, including the power of law, is written first of
all on the backs of its subjects.[1]

IN MICHEL FOUCAULT's familiar periodization, criminal punishment sharply
altered its relation to the body in the nineteenth century. Criminal punishment
in the eighteenth century created a "spectacle of suffering" in which the body,
sometimes tortured, sometimes branded or hung, was on display as an object
lesson. Increasingly in the nineteenth century criminal punishment became
hidden, no longer spectacularized, rather, the sober imposition of discipline on
prisoners.[2]

Foucault, momentarily forgetting his own methodological prescripts, called
this disappearance of public executions "a slackening of the hold on the body"
and modern penal practice as "non-corporal," but I think it much more accurate (and perhaps more Foucauldian) to see modern criminal punishment as
profoundly holding the body, profoundly corporal.[3] Foucault recognized of
course that penitentiaries, work requirements, and the like do affect the body.
(Body intrusion and subjection is even more graphic under such modern penal
practices as the administration of psychotropic drugs.) Foucault nevertheless
considered these practices noncorporal in the sense that they work on the body
"only to reach something other than the body itself," for example a deprivation of right or property.

I find the phrase "the body itself" to be rather un-Foucauldian. I have been
arguing that legal cases reveal that, while there are indeed material bodies,
people have access to them only as mediated by a fantastic parade of constructed images, often constructed quite self-consciously to represent another
person. In this sense, all punishments necessarily touch both a material and a
discursive body. And, since the body is always a symbol, a problem of interpretation, all touchings of the body are necessarily symbolic, and thus all
punishments necessarily touch the body in order to reach something other than

[1] Michel de Certeau, *The Practice of Everyday Life* 139–40 (Steven Rendall trans.) (Berkeley
and Los Angeles: U. Cal. Pr., 1984).

[2] Michel Foucault, *Discipline and Punish: The Birth of the Prison* 3–22 (Alan Sheridan trans.)
(New York: Pantheon, 1977). For England, see V. A. C. Gatrell, *The Hanging Tree: Execution and
the English People, 1770–1868* (Oxford: Ox. U. Pr., 1994).

[3] The Foucault quotations are from *Discipline and Punish* 10 and 16 respectively.

the body. The brutal tortures that Foucault described were conducted, as he emphasized, in order to deter others. And since, as we saw in the last chapter, modern legal bodies are always constructed as distinct from legal "minds" or "persons," any legal use of the body always reaches "something else," namely that mind or person.

What changes in the nineteenth century is precisely the discursive body that is touched. Criminal punishment reinforces the larger social movement by which the body becomes the mimetic representation of the individual person, the "nice body with a self at home in it."

This contrasts with the earlier symbolism, in which the body was more likely to represent society. In some eighteenth-century penal practices, as reinforced by the accompanying assize sermons, the body mimetically represented the social order; the body's dismemberment, a visual representation of the amputation of the diseased and polluting member from the body politic.[4] In some nineteenth- and twentieth-century juridical and medical practices, the body mimetically represents rather the hypothesized individual, subject to particular bodily restraints and practices in order to educate, discipline, alter the person within. Some criminal practices now seem barbaric, however, just because there is a new consciousness, or rather construction, that there is an individual person inside that body.

Both sets of practices, however, work on the body. In both, that body symbolizes fundamental political theories. Most importantly, since it continues to be true, as we have seen, that the body importantly symbolizes *both* the social order *and* a constructed realm of the private and autonomous, Foucault's periodization will not work out neatly, and the lines drawn will be continually contested, redrawn, threatened. Contemporary penal practices will discursively construct *both* bodies.

THE SPECTACLE OF CRIMINAL PUNISHMENT FROM TORTURE TO COURT TV

The contrast between a discursive construction of a body that represents society and is therefore completely available for the mimetic representation of cultural messages, and a humanized sentimental body with someone inside it, is neatly captured by Randall McGowen's discussion of the late-eighteenth-century reformer William Eden, commenting on an execution charge delivered in the preceding century by Attorney General Sir Edward Coke, in the Gunpowder Plot Judgment of 1606. Eden quoted Coke at length and so shall we:

> These traitors have exceeded all others their predecessors in mischief; yet his
> majesty in his admirable clemency and moderation will not invent any new tor-
> tures or torments for them, but hath been graciously pleased to afford them as

[4] See generally Randall McGowen, "The Body and Punishment in Eighteenth-Century England," 59 *J. Mod. Hist.* 651 (1987).

well an ordinary course of trial, as an ordinary punishment much inferior to their offense, and surely worthy of observation is the treatment by law provided and appointed for high treason.

For first, the traitor shall be drawn to the place of execution, as not being worthy any more to tread upon the face of the earth whereof he was made; and with his head declining downwards, and as near the ground as may be, being thought unfit to take the benefit of the common air.

He shall next be hanged up by the neck between heaven and earth, as deemed unworthy of both or either, as likewise that the eyes of men may behold, and their hearts condemn him. Then is he to be cut down alive, and to have his parts of generation cut off, and burnt before his face, as being unworthily begotten, and unfit to leave any race after him. His inlayed parts shall be also taken out, and burnt; for it was his heart, which harbored such horrible treason. His head shall be cut off, which imagined the mischief; and lastly, his body shall be quartered, and the quarters set up in some high and eminent place, to the view and detestation of men, and to become a prey for the fowls of the air. And this is the reward due to traitors; for it is the physic of government to let out corrupt blood.[5]

Legal prose this good doesn't come along every day, of course, but many of the specific images were indeed, as Coke claimed, "ordinary" in seventeenth-century criminal law discourse. The final image, in which magistrates administered to the body politic as physicians to the diseased patient, was quite standard (recall John Locke's progress from the latter to the former, discussed in chapter 3, and, a century and a half later, Henry Fielding's political essays, mentioned briefly in chapter 4.). Standard, too, was the indicated therapy: cutting disease out, or off, or letting out blood. This metaphor corresponded to standard therapeutic practice of the day. Michel de Certeau notes that this "therapeutics of extraction (the disorder is caused by an excess, something extra or superfluous—which has to be taken out of the body through bleeding, purging, etc.)" would be replaced in the early nineteenth century by a "therapeutics of addition (the disorder is a lack, a deficit, which has to be compensated for or replaced by drugs, supports, etc.)"[6] (We will be looking momentarily at the contemporary "therapeutics of addition" of psychotropic drugs).

By identifying the therapeutics of extraction, or cutting off, with the eighteenth century, I do not mean to suggest that the only possible body metaphor for society at this time would inevitably have represented society as a body threatened by a diseased member. Richard Sennett, drawing on earlier work by Marie-Christine Pouchelle, has recently drawn our attention to an older,

---

[5] William Eden, First Baron Auckland, *Principles of Penal Law* 133–35 (London: B. White and T. Cadell, 1771) (quoting Edward Coke). The charge may also be found, with slight textual variation, at 2 *Complete Collection of State Trials* 184 (T. B. Howell ed.) (London: Hansard, 1816).

[6] Michel de Certeau, *Practice of Everyday Life* 143.

competing medical tradition that does not, however, seem to have had any influence on law. Parisian physicians of the fourteenth century noted the tendency of one organ of the body to compensate for the weakness of another and attributed this to the "pity" that an organ had "on the one which suffers more," which compassionate reaction they called "syncope."[7] Coke, however, could not imagine a kind of Christian commonwealth in which the other organs responded to a diseased member with pity and charity, and indeed I have not found any legal use of this version of the "body politic."

As a body, the body politic was natural and legitimate; it "arose within a theological narrative in which it existed to compensate for the imperfections that had crept into the human frame as a result of the Fall."[8] Like a body, however, it had to be vigilant against disease, and the magistrates who through misconceived mercy failed to amputate the diseased member from society "were as guilty as those who violated the law by putting the interests and concerns of the individual body ahead of a concern with the social body."[9]

Similarly the ritual of the drawing, the head positioning, the mutilation did not merely inflict pain, but, in the phrase Foucault applies only to later penal practice, seeks "to reach something other than the body itself," uses the body "as an instrument or intermediary," in this case, an instrument of education through theater. "The destruction of the physical body of the condemned transformed the individual into a restorative example capable of reestablishing the health of the social body. . . . It was a cure that operated by being seen, and what was seen was less the suffering of the individual than the theater of justice—not just the mangled body but also the restored body politic."[10]

It was this theater of justice that Edward Coke's execution charge served. It was just this aspect of the charge that William Eden, and the generation of reformers for whom he stands in, missed. "Eden used the passage to display what he characterized as the unthinking barbarity of past punishment. While admitting that the charge was full of a 'great profusion of learning,' he thought that it also revealed 'a total want of common benevolence' and offered 'a sentence full of horrors.' . . . He saw what was done to the body and in his imagination shared its pain. . . . In doing so he turned his eyes from everything that Coke wanted to be seen."[11]

While this sort of torture may have disappeared from modern legal systems, it does not follow that the body of the criminal is not punished, is not specularized, is not used as the vehicle for political education in which the body of

[7] Richard Sennett, *Flesh and Stone: The Body and the City in Western Civilization* 164–68 (New York: Norton, 1994); Marie-Christine Pouchelle, *The Body and Surgery in the Middle Ages* (Rosemary Morris trans.) (New Brunswick, N.J.: Rutgers U. Pr., 1990).

[8] McGowen, "Body and Punishment," 655.

[9] Id. 665.

[10] Id. 665–66.

[11] Id. 676–77.

the criminal is a condensed symbol of the political order. (It doesn't even follow that there is nothing more to be said about judicial torture itself; Elaine Scarry has written an outstanding book largely on that subject).[12] There is nothing eighteenth-century in the appearance of the metaphor in Franz Kafka's short story "In the Penal Colony," in which torturing needles literally inscribe the "sentence" of each prisoner into his body, writing whatever commandment has been disobeyed by that prisoner.[13] Law may be words, but the words are inscribed into the body. In Kafka's modernization of the myth, however, it is only the ideal torturing machine that inscribes the sentence; the actual machine malfunctions and makes only a mess.

Specularization of the body may simply have moved backward in the criminal justice process. If punishment is now more private, less spectacular, the criminal trial itself is an important occasion for mass political education in which the body of the accused will be employed for educational purposes. (Even earlier in the criminal justice process is the spectacularization of the body discussed in chapters 8 through 10 and again in chapter 12, the examination and invasion of the body in the search for evidence of wrongdoing. Law figures these displayed and searchable bodies in particular ways that facilitate their availability. However, vaginal searches and penile plethysmography do not yet take place on national television).

As Katherine Fischer Taylor has recently written, criminal justice trials in nineteenth-century France were as spectacular as the punishments of an earlier era, particularly after the opening in 1868 of the new wing for criminal trials in the Palais de Justice. The presence of the public graphically enacted the central ambiguity of Second Empire political theory (did justice emanate from the king, Louis-Napoléon, or from the sovereign people?) by physically placing both the public and the judge in confrontation with the body of the accused. The public often reacted to evidence or lawyers' arguments, when it was not the overt target of these arguments, and, consistent with the underlying political theory, there was decided ambiguity in nineteenth-century French legal theory over the propriety of these reactions.[14] It is not hard to see the contemporary American analogue in the televising of trials, which symbolically constitute democratic authority out of an assembled audience. A dispersed nation of television viewers is thus electronically constituted a sovereign source of justice, an imagined body politic. Although the viewers of Court TV, unlike the spectators of nineteenth-century trials, have no way of reacting audibly or visibly to the trial techniques, talk radio may serve that purpose.

[12] Elaine Scarry, *The Body in Pain: The Making and Unmaking of the World* (New York: Oxford U. Pr., 1985).

[13] Franz Kafka, "In the Penal Colony," in *The Complete Stories* 140 (Nahum N. Glatzer ed.) (New York: Schocken, 1971) [1919].

[14] Katherine Fischer Taylor, *In the Theater of Criminal Justice: The Palais de Justice in Second Empire Paris* 26 (Princeton: Prin. U. Pr., 1993).

Nor, of course, has the spectacularization of punishment disappeared either. For one thing, public executions lingered long after Foucault drops their story and coexisted with the penitentiary throughout Europe.[15] The last public execution in America took place in 1936.[16] Executions may be less frequent today and may no longer feature the rituals of being drawn in a cart with head hanging, but they are thoroughly covered in print and mass media, which have substituted their own ritualized narrative of the condemned's last day. The repeated discussions of the condemned's last meals, religious observances, and words operate as a kind of repeated performance by which the body of the condemned is employed for mass moral edification. The discussions about televising executions betray precisely contemporary ambivalence about the body being constructed and the competing claims of social education and individual privacy.[17]

More might be said about these repeated and well-documented punishments, and someone who wanted to write a history of the physical body in law, rather than its discursive representation, might well start with the physical deployment of the bodies of the condemned, their treatment, position, specularization. Closer to our own time is the account of the war in the H-Blocks over the control of the bodies of Irish Republican Army members who used their bodies as a means of protest (refusing to dress, smearing cells with excrement, smuggling messages in body orifices) and encountered increased body regulation and control.[18] Still, the body of the condemned is necessarily constructed in discourse as it is subjected to punishment. Indeed, the discursive construction of the punished body follows a common pattern in which the humanistic, sentimentalized body in pain emerges as a site of empathy and identification, yielding in more recent times to an abstracted, distanced body removed from the direct apprehension of the reader. But first, the nineteenth-century transition. As torture gave way to the penitentiary, the public trial, the private execution, law constructed a new body: the sentimentalized body in pain.

CRIMINAL PUNISHMENT IN THE AGE OF THE SENTIMENTAL BODY

Coke's displayed and dismembered body began to pass from the scene, along with judicial torture, dismemberment, and public hangings. Eden's sentimental body held sway for most of the next two centuries and may still, though it

---

[15] Petrus Spierenburg, *The Spectacle of Suffering: Executions and the Evolution of Repression: From a Preindustrial Metropolis to the European Experience* (Cambridge: Cam. U. Pr., 1984).

[16] Martin R. Gardner, "Executions and Indignities—an Eighth Amendment Assessment of Methods of Inflicting Capital Punishment," 39 *Ohio St. L. J.* 96, 118 (1978).

[17] Wendy Lesser, *Pictures at an Execution* (Cambridge: Harv. U. Pr., 1993).

[18] Allen Feldman, *Formations of Violence: The Narrative of the Body and Political Terror in Northern Ireland* 204 (Chicago: U. Chi. Pr., 1991).

competes with later constructions. We have noted the sentimental body before; let us review some of its aspects, with particular reference to criminal punishment.

The sentimental body is not a machine. Indeed, in much popular thought, as well as Carlyle or Rebecca Harding Davis, the sentimental body is opposed to the machine. The sentimental body feels pain, it has feelings and sensibilities.

The sentimental body is *like us* in this amenability to feeling. This is a tricky point for the sentimental body to mediate, for the sentimental body is also the site of differentiation and uniqueness. For example, we have seen how the machine body has fungible hands and organs that all doctors might treat the same way when diseased and all juries might evaluate similarly when damaged. We have also seen how someone opposing this machine construction will surely invoke a kind of sentimental body that is the unique bearer of an individual personality, with individual life experience and sensibility. Insurance schemes, statistical persons, uniform-hours legislation that trumps liberty of individual contract, organs available for medical research, all require uniform machine bodies and might become undone by sentimental bodies that *too* uniquely represent an incommensurable human subject. So sentimental bodies must be somewhat like us, neither exactly like us, nor wholly different.

However sentimental bodies construct difference, the limit of such differentiation—the very essence of constructing a sentimental body—is always that such a body *feels pain* and to that extent may excite what we call *empathy* (in the eighteenth century, *sympathy*), for which the contemporary idiom is often precisely "I feel your pain." The notion that we empathize with the humanity of others because they are in pain seems so natural to us that it is difficult to realize that this body, too, has a history.[19] For William Eden, this is what separated his times from the "barbarism" of the previous century. Empathy with the pain of another is bound up with what Norbert Elias calls "the rising threshold of disgust" that is part of the "civilizing process" and Richard Bushman "the refinement of America."[20]

The sentimental body in pain dominated nineteenth-century law and politics; it is surely impossible to imagine the literature, opera, or ballet of the nineteenth century without it. Elizabeth Clark has written about the process by which abolitionist literature came to focus on the suffering body of the slave in pain, a figure of empathy to the reader. Christians know about suffering bodies, of course, but they did not always figure in abolitionist rhetoric. Rather, the suffering body of the slave has a specific history that largely coincides with the decline in judicial torture, contemporaneous campaigns against

[19] See generally David Marshall, *The Surprising Effects of Sympathy* (Chicago: U. Chi. Pr., 1988).

[20] Norbert Elias, *The History of Manners* (*The Civilizing Process:* vol. 1) (Edmund Jephcott trans.) (New York: Pantheon, 1978) [1939]; Richard L. Bushman, *The Refinement of America: Persons, Houses, Cities* (New York:Knopf, 1992).

naval flogging and corporal punishment, and the growth of a civil and criminal punishment by moral discipline, what Richard Brodhead calls "disciplinary intimacy" or "discipline through love." As Clark argues, and as I help show below, our modern culture of individual constitutional rights is hardly imaginable apart from this culture of moral sympathy.[21]

The concern that punishment not inflict physical pain, the empathy with the victim of pain, also lies behind the curious search in American legal history for painless methods of execution. In an endlessly repeating ritual, electrocution, gas chambers, lethal injections are each introduced with tremendous fanfare as a painless form of death, until each is revealed to promote its own kind of suffering on the way to death.

The rhetoric rarely varies. A century after William Eden persuaded himself that Edward Coke had been barbaric, Governor David B. Hill of New York, in creating the commission that eventually led New York from hanging to electrocution, noted, echoing Eden's very metaphors: "The present mode of executing criminals by hanging has come down to us from the dark ages, and it may well be questioned whether the science of the present day cannot provide a means for taking the life of such as are condemned to die in a less barbarous manner." The commission was charged to research "the most humane and practical method known to modern science of carrying into effect the sentence of death in capital cases."[22] It recommended electrocution, which, as the legislature later imagined it, would "pass through the body."[23]

Each generation constructs its own refinement and sensitivity to pain; its own distance from the "barbarism" of the "dark ages," as figured in its *technological* discovery. None seems to make any advance in understanding of or empathy with the victims of execution, as silent now as ever; the technological advances substitute metaphorically for the bodies of the condemned as the objects of human sensibility; indeed the quest for technology has less to do with pain and more to do with effacing contact between the executioner and the condemned, and graphically representing society's mastery of death. The sentimental body, in other words, substitutes a different spectacle of suffering for Coke's, but is still an object in the eye of a moral subject and exists for that eye as the proof of the viewer's own refinement and sensitivity. The sentimental body on display is not necessarily a good way into human interaction. (We

[21] Richard H. Brodhead, "Sparing the Rod: Discipline and Fiction in Antebellum America," in *Cultures of Letters: Scenes of Reading and Writing in Nineteenth-Century America* 18 (Chicago: U. Chi. Pr., 1993); Elizabeth B. Clark, "The Sacred Rights of the Weak: Pain, Sympathy, and the Culture of Individual Rights in Antebellum America," 82 *J. Am. Hist.* 463 (1995).

[22] In re Kemmler, 136 U.S. 436, 444 (1890), quoting Gov. David B. Hill, Annual Message to the Legislature (Jan. 6, 1885).

[23] 1888 New York Laws chap. 489, at 780, as quoted in Maeve L. O'Connor, "Silencing the Body: The American Quest for Capital Punishment without Pain" 12 (unpublished seminar paper), the source for much of the information in this and the next paragraph.

will return to this point in the Conclusion when we imagine alternative discourses of the body that render other people present to us).

The sentimentalized body is also intact, one might say perfect, the better to serve as a representation of our own empathy and refinement. The humane versions of capital punishment express their humanity in just this: that they leave the body visibly intact, without dismemberment or marks. "The body of the condemned is a text that tells the story of physical punishment with brutal honesty. . . . By taking life without marking the body, reformers retain both literal and figurative control over the story told by the execution. Concealing the violence deprives the body of its ability to speak, and thus opens the door to denial."[24]

The sentimentalized body thus supports some aspects of the contemporary practice of capital punishment: its technologies of assumed "painlessness" and nonmarking of the body; its rituals of humanization (last meals, last words); its public specularization. On the other hand, capital punishment is also a kind of performed limit of the sentimentalized, empathized body, and in crucial moments the law of criminal punishment must construct an alternative body that disappears, lest it serve as a potential site of empathy.

When particular executions are challenged as cruel and unconstitutional, law constructs a body that is neither displayed nor sentimentalized but is, to the extent possible, absent. For example, in 1946 the United States Supreme Court rejected the claim of a Louisiana prisoner named Willie Francis, the survivor of a badly botched execution, that submitting him to a second would constitute cruel and unusual punishment in violation of the Eighth Amendment. Writing for the Court, Justice Reed described the first, failed attempt without even mentioning the human subject: "The executioner threw the switch but, presumably because of some mechanical difficulty, death did not result." Physical aspects of Francis's body were effaced and such aspects of his humanity as human intentions metonymically transferred to the state: punishment, the Court held, was cruel only if cruelly intended, not if the suffering was necessary to what the Court oxymoronically described as the "method employed to extinguish life humanely." It was the dissent, by contrast, that quoted from eyewitness testimony of the first, failed execution:

> I saw the electrocutioner turn on the switch and I saw his lips puff out and swell, his body tensed and stretched. I heard the one in charge yell to the man outside for more juice when he saw that Willie Francis was not dying and the one on the inside yelled back he was giving him all he head. Then Wilie Francis cried out "take it off. Let me breathe." Then they took the hood from his eyes and unstrapped him.[25]

[24] O'Connor, "Silencing the Body," 8.

[25] Louisiana ex rel. Francis v. Resweber, 329 U.S. 459 (1947). The quoted passages are at 460, 464, and 480 respectively.

The Tranquilized Body: Contemporary Specularization and Symbolization of the Body of the Prisoner

Injecting prisoners with psychotropic medication problematizes further Foucault's distinction between an obsolete punishment of public spectacle and a contemporary punishment of private discipline. For where that "private" discipline requires the seizure and invasion of the body, the state may do it. That discipline is administered neither to an eighteenth-century body symbolically representing the social order, nor a nineteenth-century sentimental body, but rather to our distinctive late-twentieth-century artifact, the absent body.

The body in question belonged to Walter Harper, and the result of the case bearing his name is that he may now be involuntarily medicated with psychotropic medication without any judicial hearing.[26] Walter Harper was convicted of robbery and sent to prison, where he was diagnosed as schizophrenic and medicated with antipsychotic drugs, initially with what the Court was pleased to call his "consent." (Since schizophrenics cannot lawfully consent to a retirement plan that is not in their best interests, the construction of their ingesting psychotropic drugs, while incarcerated, as legal "consent" is at least opportunistic.) Harper was paroled on condition that he continue to take his medicine, but he assaulted two nurses, parole was revoked, and he was returned to prison and sent to a Special Offender Center for prisoners with serious mental problems. Harper was now rediagnosed as suffering from a manic-depressive disorder; at various times in his commitment he has been diagnosed as manic-depressive, schizophrenic, or suffering from schizoaffective disorder. Curiously, though, the drug therapies do not vary, suggesting to this reader, though not, as we shall see, the Supreme Court, that the drugs may be more for Harper's keepers' benefit than Harper's.

In any case, about a year after coming to the Special Offender Center, Harper refused to continue taking the psychotropic medications. It is typical of the Supreme Court's opinion that his precise reasons for refusing are not disclosed. The dissent noted that the record of one of his hearings noted: "Inmate Harper stated he would rather die th[a]n take medication" and attributed this to the serious side-effects.[27]

Harper's treating psychiatrist then requested permission to medicate him involuntarily. The hospital's procedures required that this request be heard before a committee consisting of a psychiatrist, psychologist, and the Associate Superintendent of the Center, none of whom might be, at the time of the hearing, involved in the inmate's treatment or diagnosis. Harper was told of this hearing and was present at it. The committee found Harper to be a danger to others as a result of a mental disease or disorder and approved involuntary

---

[26] Washington v. Harper, 494 U.S. 210 (1990).
[27] 494 U.S. at 239 (Stevens, J., dissenting).

medication. The Washington Supreme Court found the hospital's procedures for approving such medication to be constitutionally inadequate, but the United States Supreme Court reversed.

Justice Anthony Kennedy, who some eleven months earlier had inveighed against the menace of drugs in upholding the involuntary urinalysis of customs agents (see the next chapter), now set about administering some psychotropic drugs of his own. The body of Walter Harper was discursively constructed as a "liberty interest," then made to disappear.

In earlier chapters we have seen the discursive construction of the body as a privacy interest, and the structure of this construction, the construction of the body in a plane of competing interests, the simultaneous production of law as a seeing eye that mimes the body, giving life to the body, rather than, as is really the case, deriving its own life from the body, a law that constructs isolated dismembered subjects that could never bond together to form society, then bonds that society itself.

Walter Harper's body is said to be a "liberty" as opposed to "privacy" interest. In this the dissent and majority joined forces. The dissent was intent on establishing a liberty interest of greater "dimensions" than the majority's; for the dissent the liberty was "both physical and intellectual."[28] However, it does not seem to matter, here or elsewhere in the law, whether, once the body has been constituted as an interest, that interest is described as a "privacy," "liberty," or other "interest."[29]

"[R]espondent possesses a significant liberty interest in avoiding the unwanted administration of antipsychotic drugs under the Due Process Clause of the Fourteenth Amendment."[30] I can't prove that our limited set of tropes for the legal body leads to this ugly sentence. Plainly, this is not a sentence written by someone who is attempting to see, grasp, apprehend, identify with the body of Walter Harper. Rather, the body of Walter Harper has been turned into a "liberty interest." As we shall see again in the next chapter in the customs agents' case, Justice Kennedy in particular, while not a great literary stylist at best, has particular difficulty in talking about the body and is prone to bizarre sentences that construct distanced, abstract bodies where equally "natural" constructions would have displayed bodies as specularized, sentimentalized, or otherwise present. I have, incidentally, no explanation for the placement of the last nine words of the quoted sentence. Despite their placement, they plainly modify "interest" and not "drugs." Perhaps Justice Kennedy subconsciously regards the psychotropic drugs themselves as somehow emanating from the Due Process Clause. This might be the case if the Due Process

---

[28] 494 U.S. at 237.

[29] A later case cites *Harper* for the proposition that "the Constitution places limits on a State's right to interfere with . . . bodily integrity." Planned Parenthood of Southeastern Pennsylvania v. Casey, 505 U.S. 833, 849 (1992).

[30] 494 U.S. at 221–22.

Clause were a sort of mimetic representation of a universe of order and discipline, in which judicial hearings, hierarchies of rights, and the orderly, disciplined bodies of prisoners all performatively enact a ritual of order and hierarchy. Drugs that keep prisoners in line might then seem metaphorically to
subsist "under the Due Process Clause." More likely, however, Justice Kennedy just has trouble writing good sentences.

Justice Kennedy thus sets up the familiar clash (not, however, describing it
as a "balance") between Harper's individual liberty interest and a state interest
in drugging him. Both interests may be defined at many different levels of
generality. Harper's, as we have seen, is not defined as his interest in bodily
control, or bodily integrity, or bodily purity, or privacy, or control of his
property, or any of the dozen or more legal discursive constructions of the
body that might have been deployed, but rather simply as a liberty interest
deriving from the state's drug policy itself.

The definition of the state's "interest," while not the primary focus of this
book, is also not without interest. The state may prevail over Harper's "liberty" interest "if the inmate is dangerous to himself or others and the treatment
is in the inmate's medical interest."[31] One might have thought (if one were the
sort of person who believed in individual and state interests that weren't simply mutually constitutive) that the inmate's medical interest, and danger at
least to himself, were individual interests. Here, however, the state is able to
appropriate Walter Harper's diseased body and assert it as an interest over the
objection of the person inside the invaded body. Walter Harper loses his body
to the state and must be content with a "liberty interest," as unsatisfactory a
substitute for the body as anything the Lacanians might find offered as a
substitute for the phallus.

Once the medication of Walter Harper was discursively constructed as
something to be balanced against a liberty interest, as opposed to an invasion
of the body, the game was essentially over. (The Court cites *Winston v. Lee,*
the case discussed in chapter 8 that refused to order surgery on a prisoner, for
the proposition that Harper has such a liberty interest but does not discuss the
case.)[32] The case goes on to discuss the procedural requirements that the state
must satisfy before medicating prisoners, but as the body has long since disappeared from the opinion, we may leave this discussion to others.[33] (To my
mind, the dissent's most effective argument stressed the conflicts of interest
of, and influences on, the purportedly neutral special committees.)[34] The fail-

[31] 494 U.S. at 242.

[32] 494 U.S. at 229.

[33] Good introductions to the legal issues are Susan Stefan, "Leaving Civil Rights to the Experts: From Deference to Abdication under the Professional Judgment Standard," 102 *Yale L. J.*
639 (1992); Jami Floyd (student author), "The Administration of Psychotropic Drugs to Prisoners: State of the Law and Beyond," 78 *Cal. L. Rev.* 1243 (1990).

[34] 494 U.S. at 250–57.

ure of any empathy with the affected human, or even a discursively constructed sentimental body, is total. Walter Harper is simply not present in the
opinion in any embodied way. I can't discuss the Court's rhetoric of the body;
there isn't any. Though the case deals with body boundaries, the body is absent. Even the effects of the medication with which Harper was injected show
up only in the dissent.[35]

Since the law cannot see the body, the law evaluates the other things it likes
to talk about: the "reasonableness" of the state's procedures, the strength of
the state interests, the needs of the public. Law constitutes the body as an
interest so that it can make that body disappear.

EPILOGUE: THE PRIVACY THAT KILLS

The sentimental body in pain discussed in this chapter has an intimate historical relationship with the idea of a civil society, discussed in chapters 4 and 5,
with zones of "private" activity that may be regulated only with difficulty, if at
all. Both the sympathetic body and civil society trace back to Adam Smith and
the Scottish Enlightenment, and they have thus historically always coexisted.
Yet the kind of privacy for civil institutions that is implied in the notion of
civil society places severe limits on the protection society can actually offer
the body in pain.

By the sympathetic body, I mean the body that is the uniquely differentiated
home of a unique human person, the body that is the sole medium through
which that person has a world, relates to others, others who can enter relations
with that person precisely because they feel that body's pain. In the words of
Adam Smith, quoted in chapter 10: "Though our brother is on the rack . . . our
senses will never inform of us of what he suffers. . . . By the *imagination* we
place ourselves in his situation, we conceive ourselves enduring all the same
torments, *we enter as it were into his body,* and become in some measure the
same person with him."[36]

The nineteenth-century history of the whipping of servants and slaves, the
beating of wives and children, the carnage of industrial accidents, reminds us
that Adam Smith's sympathetic body did not become fully established all at
once in the late eighteenth century.[37] Indeed, down to the present day, husbands beat wives; the boss may strike the employee but is even more likely to
maintain and ignore unsafe workplaces, "accidents waiting to happen" where
death or dismemberment lie around the corner.[38] Here, in what we are pleased

[35] 494 U.S. at 240.

[36] Adam Smith, *The Theory of Moral Sentiments* 9 (D. D. Raphael and A. L. Mackie eds.)
(Oxford: Clarendon, 1976) (final emphasis supplied, others original).

[37] See generally Brodhead, "Sparing the Rod"; Reva B. Siegel, "The Rule of Love": Wife
Beating as Prerogative and Privacy, 105 *Yale L. J.* 2117 (1996).

[38] See, e.g., Arthur F. McEvoy, "The Triangle Shirtwaist Factory Fire of 1911: Social Change,

today rosily to call "civil society," rests this decidedly uncivil violence. Walking the streets today, we see bodies, like the defendants in the Gunpowder Plot, that in their bruises, deportment, and disfigurement visually represent where power lies in our own society.

Because we inhabit modern, sentimental bodies in pain, because we, like Adam Smith, feel the pain of our brother on the rack, the physical violence of whipping or wife-beating or industrial accident is uniquely horrifying to us, quite literally the worst thing we can imagine about a bad marriage or a bad job. It is difficult for us to obtain critical perspective on the extent to which the sentimental body in pain, so natural to us, is a discursive creation with an origin and a history, though this book has been devoted to the effort. There are ways of destroying a human spirit without physical violence. Lives can be deprived of hope, of meaning, of love, and if these deprivations strike the reader as amorphous, airy, less real than physical violence, I would suggest that this reaction confirms the very power of the sentimental body over our thoughts.

I repeat that the sentimental body in pain that therefore communes with others is one of our finest cultural creations; it is vastly preferable to the clinically distanced or invisible bodies of Walter Harper or Willie Francis or other subjects of criminal punishment discussed earlier in this chapter. While the sentimental body in pain was created in many artistic and literary forms, law, too, had a distinctive role to play in its creation. For one thing, law's case narratives, as discussed in chapter 5 in connection with the *Rodriguez* case on consortium, bring pain vividly before our eyes and help trigger the "imagination" that Adam Smith described.

More distinctive is the legal concept of the *private,* discussed in chapters 4 and 8–11, conceptualized precisely as a sphere, a prosthetic extension of the body into an imaginary *space,* into which states, laws, interests, constitutions do or do not "intrude" or "penetrate." The very metaphors of our constitutional rights show that rights are extensions of, mimeses of, the modern body, like the chairs and tools described by Elaine Scarry.[39] Law defines a private sphere in civil society by extension from this seemingly irreducible instance of privacy, the imagined, sentimental body.

The paradox thus is that the body is protected in contemporary law only by means guaranteed to subjugate it. Because the body is dignified and sacred, because it is the unique way of having a world of a unique human spirit, law imagines that body at the center of a sphere that law shapes but cannot enter. And, to the extent that law does not enter that space, wives, children, workers will suffer preventable pain and die preventable deaths. As Reva Siegel has

---

Industrial Accidents, and the Evolution of Common-Sense Causality," 20 *L. & Social Inquiry* 621 (1995).

[39] Scarry, *The Body in Pain* 278–328.

shown, an obstacle to every proposed criminal or tort regulation of domestic (or workplace) violence is always the presumptively private and self-regulating family (or workplace) that is the body's prosthetic extension.[40] As Lea VanderVelde has pointed out, since the abolition of slavery, the United States has had no functional law on the limits of workplace discipline: workers are not slaves, and if they don't like their jobs, they are supposed to quit. The very discursive construction of the body that puts its pain and humiliation before our sympathetic eyes guarantees that there will be limits to society's protection of it.

The sphere of privacy that is the body's prosthetic extension is not a natural or material fact but a discursive artifact that we adopt precisely to make other people present to us. The horror of whipping or beating is the harm to the real person inside, and that harm, unlike the discursive body, is never just private, but necessarily social, commensurable, accessible. Law desperately needs new ways of "imagining," becoming one person with, our brothers and sisters, imaginings that do not depend on the visualized body, carrying with it its prosthetic sphere of privacy. Self-consciousness about how we construct those bodies is the first step in this reimagining. The second is to try to commune with others without the mediation of the discursive private body. Imagined communion with others can lead to the successful abolition of cruelty, where the hypostatized body gives us the privacy that kills.

---

[40] DeShaney v. Winnebago County Department of Social Services, 489 U.S. 189 (1989) (civil rights laws do not reach public authorities' placement of child with natural father who beat child, causing brain damage requiring permanent institutionalization); Siegel, "The Rule of Love."

PART THREE

Abjection

Chapter 12

BODY WASTES

WE TURN NOW to a disparate group of cases that have in common the discursive casting out of disfavored bodies constructed as threats to the social order: drugged bodies, diseased bodies, bodies in disfavored racial classifications, odorous bodies. I shall argue that the discursive construction of these bodies responds more to infantile psychological processes of identity formation than to self-conscious reasoning, as a result of which law's discursive constructions are less easy to periodize, have longer histories, and will probably be harder for readers to imagine separating from.

Every body survives by shedding itself regularly of wastes such as urine and feces. Imaginary universes have been built on this simple fact. The elimination of wastes in our culture is a sort of metonym of the private, the shameful, the disgusting. Bodies define their boundaries through the expulsion of wastes. Societies define their boundaries in part through their rituals concerning bodily wastes, "abjecting" the threat as the body abjects waste. In Julia Kristeva's account, part of the personality is formed in the infant's early experiences abjecting waste. Finally, human urine occasioned one of the most curious Supreme Court constructions of the body, one in which the body, constituted as a privacy interest, disappeared.

While the practice of eliminating body wastes is of great medical, anthropological, and psychoanalytic interest, as we shall see momentarily, it is unlikely that the Supreme Court would ever have had to get a grip on the practice but for the fact that human urine may also be constituted as the bearer of narrative. The substances ingested into the body leave chemical traces in its urine. When the substances are drugs such as cocaine or marijuana, the gaze of the state seeks to uncover the veiled narrative of drug use, in the sort of sexual pleasure in seeing (scopophilia) and knowing (epistemophilia) that is the subject of Peter Brooks's recent book.[1]

As a result of tests developed by the military in Vietnam, chemical analysis of a urine sample is a cheap way of obtaining information about substances that have entered the body. I will explain a bit about the enzyme-multiplied-immunoassay technique (EMIT) test, which came before the Supreme Court when the Customs Service required employees, under no individualized suspicion of drug use, nevertheless to submit urine samples for chemical analysis. From the outset, however, I want to guard against easy assumption of the

[1] Peter Brooks, *Body Work: Objects of Desire in Modern Narrative* (Cambridge: Harv. U. Pr.) (1993), discussed at the beginning of chap. 8.

Court's structure of analysis, under which the government as employer has a sort of exogenous interest in the chemicals ingested by employees, and the urine test is but a means to achieve the government's end.

I shall argue instead that the construction of the body as a bearer of narratives in its urine is inseparable from the construction of the body as free of drugs, pure and inviolate. Both are part of a larger ritual of social abjection under which the society deals with threats and anxieties by a ritualized identification of a foreign threat and corresponding social rituals of expulsion and purification. (I should add that the word *ritual* here carries no normative or critical force; it does not mean to suggest that drug testing is "primitive" or that advanced societies could in any way be entirely without ritual. I have written elsewhere, at greater length, about the power of the anthropological concept of ritual in explaining legal behavior.)[2]

In this larger ritual, the body is a synecdoche for society. Drug tests of no other functional value serve to construct a perfect, pure body of inviolable borders as a symbolic enactment of social desire for this lost body. Drug testing combines a sort of Freudian erotic desire for the lost, a Foucauldian regulation of the body, and a Kristevan social abjection of the impure. The Supreme Court's version may best be approached as an attempted evasion of these constructions, in which the true narrative is revealed in the parapraxes and evasions of the Court's particularly tortured prose.

The EMIT test that the Reagan administration began administering to randomly selected federal employees is not particularly accurate. It is particularly easy to trigger, for example; while false negatives are almost unheard of, false positives are quite common. Nor does it yield information of the greatest interest. It does not tell us much about the most serious drugs. The test will be positive for marijuana exposure—either through smoking *or* passive inhalation (for example, when someone else smokes in the car)—as long as thirty-six days after exposure, while cocaine and heroin will show up only for two or three days after ingestion. As a result the test in no way shows whether motor or mental functions are impaired, since it may literally be set off by marijuana smoking weeks before. The test may also be positive for poppy seed bagels, certain herbal teas, and numerous over-the-counter cold medications. These are not false positives, since the substances truly are in the body, but they are not very informative either.

The ostensible virtue of EMIT testing is that it is cheap to administer, requiring no great training in its analysts and little special equipment. (The Customs Service's program upheld in the *Treasury Employees* case did require confirmation of positive specimens through the more accurate and expensive gas chromatography/mass spectrometry [GC/MS] test. The Court did not hold that this was constitutionally required). As I have said, the test performs social

---

[2] Alan Hyde, "A Theory of Labor Legislation," 38 *Buffalo L. Rev.* 383, 450–61 (1990).

functions at the level of ritual that dwarf any value it may possess as a device for obtaining relevant information about employees.

These social functions may be speculative and of course did not figure in the Supreme Court's analysis, but this is not because they were, even under the Court's legal theory, irrelevant to it. The Court, unsurprisingly, adopted the familiar framework in which the bodies of the customs agents were constituted as privacy interests, assigned weights, and then weighed against asserted governmental interests in "intrusion." (The Court might have avoided this "weighing" by adopting either of two rejected rules under which urinalysis would have required either a search warrant or probable cause. However, the Court evaluated both these rejected proposals precisely through the "balance [of] the individual's privacy expectations against the government's interests.")[3]

We have seen this mode of analysis before. Constituting one's body as a privacy interest is a deliberately strange, and estranging, vocabulary, which unlike some other legal constructions of the body seems deliberately selected for its lack of consonance with ordinary everyday speech about the body. As we saw above, the body constituted as privacy interest is normally so constituted so that it may be open and available to the demands of others. Law has other constructions of the body employed to render the body less available to others, such as the inviolable body that need not share bone marrow with a sibling.

So much, but by no means all, of the game was over when the Court characterized the search for urine samples as a question of privacy interests. The Court had still to define that privacy interest. What exactly is my interest in the disposition or availability of my urine?

The Court had a great deal of understandable difficulty with this question and might well have profited from the excursion we shall soon undertake into the social and psychoanalytical meaning of urination. The Court's difficulty was only partly the invariable difficulty with privacy interests: their circularity; their definition in terms of "reasonable expectations of privacy" when that is precisely what is to be decided; the arbitrariness with which the Court can assign weight to the weightless. The privacy interest in one's bodily waste partakes of all these difficulties but adds others, noted by some of the lower courts that had grappled with the problem but ignored by the Supreme Court.

Everyone would agree that in our culture, privacy expectations attach to the *acts* of urination and defecation. Of course this is a cultural construct, and there are other cultures where such expectations are absent, but in our culture nearly everyone expects to be able to perform these functions unobserved. The Customs Service program however did not subject urinating employees to the directly observing gaze, but only to unspecified "monitoring."

[3] National Treasury Employees Union v. Von Raab, 489 U.S. 656, 665 (1989).

The problem concerns privacy expectations in the urine itself. Is the urine part of the body? Do we have privacy expectations in it?

These questions can only be answered with reference to the drug-testing program that was the very subject of the case. After all, most people normally are content to see their urine flushed down the toilet. This is not privacy in the sense of retention, holding, excluding others. It is privacy in the sense that no one else may have access to the urine for whatever narratives it bears. My concern to protect my urine does not arise abstractly; that concern arises only when someone seeks that urine and is thus heavily dependent on the purpose for which the urine is sought. When the court fits the case into the usual grid in which a particular interest in "privacy" is opposed to a general interest in "information," it renders itself incapable of answering the question. The two interests are not in opposition; they are mutually constitutive.

In the event, the Court, speaking through Justice Anthony Kennedy, failed to follow even the illogic of its own position: it did not establish just what is the privacy interest in one's urine. Justice Kennedy did not make any attempt to survey social practices or expectations concerning urination but contented himself (in a companion case) with repeating the following observation made by the lower court in the custom agents' case:

> There are few activities in our society more personal or private than the passing of urine. Most people describe it by euphemisms if they talk about it at all. It is a function traditionally performed without public observation; indeed, its performance in public is generally prohibited by law as well as social custom. While individuals may choose not to urinate in private but instead to use public toilet facilities, they make this choice themselves.[4]

While this passage might suggest that the privacy interest in urine approaches the theoretical maximum, the Court did not hold this, finding instead that the public interests actually diminished the private interests.[5] The difference between a public interest *outweighing* a private interest, and a public interest *diminishing* a private interest, may seem purely semantic, but it does reinforce the sense that all these interests are imaginary constructions assigned arbitrary weights.

More significant is the point that in privacy cases, only the employer's "need to know" does any work in the analysis, that privacy, far from having

---

[4] National Treasury Employees Union v. Von Raab, 816 F.2d 170, 175 (5th Cir. 1987), affirmed in part and remanded in part, 489 U.S. 656 (1989). The Supreme Court quoted this passage in Skinner v. Railway Labor Executives' Assn., 489 U.S. 602, 617 (1989). See also Lovvorn v. City of Chattanooga, 846 F.2d 1539, 1545 (6th Cir. 1988) ("There are few other times where individuals insist as strongly and universally that they be let alone to act in private"), vacated 861 F.2d 1388 (6th Cir. 1988), on rehearing, 915 F.2d 1065 (6th Cir. 1990).

[5] Treasury Employees, 489 U.S. at 672 (1989). The relevant passage is quoted at n.20.

some magic internal integrity, is simply a name for a residual category meaning "Nobody has any need to know this." Jed Rubenfeld has made a similar point about the constitutional concept of privacy, however, so I shall not elaborate on this one here, despite the fact, which we have noted before, that all concepts of privacy function as metaphors for the body.[6] The Court does not decide whether the nameless customs agent has more or less expectation of privacy in the products of his or her body than a public employee had in his desk, searched by his employer, largely because we lack any sort of vocabulary for creating hierarchies of privacy of this kind.[7] Rather, all information is presumptively private, unless another claims to know it, in which case the need to know is evaluated. There is literally nothing however to "weigh" against the employer's claim to know, or we would have to be able to say whether a urine sample weighs more than a desk. Of course, in the physical universe, desks weigh more than urine samples, but in the law either may turn out to weigh more than the other. In this case, since (the Court finds) the Customs Service needs to know what its employees ingest, this diminishes the weight of their legal bodies, and a diminished body, poor thing, can hardly outweigh anything at all.

We are far from the sacred body, sanctified in privacy, that we have seen before; far, even, from a specific interest in "bodily" privacy as distinct from privacy unmodified. It is not necessarily surprising that the public employer may, in the end, search urine as it searches a desk (though it is not obviously correct either). It *is* surprising that the formal legal analysis makes *absolutely no distinction* between the two searches: both purportedly weigh a privacy interest, assigned a weight, against a claim to know, and that privacy interest gets no added heft from being a bodily product.

Justice Kennedy's language supports this analysis, not by invoking other bodies-on-display, but rather by carefully avoiding the embodied nature of the customs agents. Bodily references barely appear in the opinion. Consider his description of the "program":

> After an employee qualifies for a position covered by the Customs testing program, the Service advises him by letter that his final selection is contingent upon successful completion of drug screening. An independent contractor contacts the employee to fix the time and place for collecting the sample. On reporting for the test, the employee must produce photographic identification and remove any outer garments, such as a coat or a jacket, and personal belongings. The employee may produce the sample behind a partition, or in the privacy of the bathroom stall

[6] For an account of "privacy" that stresses not the rights of the individual but the improper conduct of the government, see Jed Rubenfeld, "The Right of Privacy," 102 *Harv. L. Rev.* 737 (1989).

[7] O'Connor v. Ortega, 480 U.S. 709 (1987), discussed briefly in chapter 8.

if he so chooses. To ensure against adulteration of the specimen, or substitution of
a sample from another person, a monitor of the same sex as the employee remains
close at hand to listen for the normal sounds of urination.[8]

At this point in the opinion, the word "urine" has yet to appear. (This is the
first appearance of "urination," and "urinalysis" has appeared twice.) Indeed,
the word "urine" appears only a few times in the opinion, generally modifying
"sample." The preferred locutions are those of the excerpt above: the "testing
program," the "specimen," or "produce the sample." The opinion is not incomprehensible if read by an American who knows all about the practice of
urinalysis and its employment by the Reagan administration, but for one who
didn't already know what the opinion was about, it would indeed be difficult
to understand.

On this view, the "privacy interest" is never established, the body remains
absent, since all the work in the opinion is done by the Court's finding that the
Customs Service needed to know what employees had been ingesting. Why
does the Customs Service need to know this? "[T]he public should not bear
the risk that employees who may suffer from impaired perception and judgment will be promoted to positions where they may need to employ deadly
force."[9] Since the test before him does not measure impairment of perception
or judgment, Justice Kennedy apparently was making a statistical argument:
that there is a correlation between drug use and impaired job performance.
People who sometimes use drugs will statistically be somewhat likelier to be
impaired on the job someday than people who pass urine tests. But the relationship is quite complex and not the sort of thing over which people should
lose their jobs. While I cannot review the literature on coping with drugs here,
it should be obvious that urinalysis is what constitutional lawyers call over-
inclusive and underinclusive. Many people will fail urine tests (because they
smoked marijuana at home on the weekend) but never display any impaired
job performance, while others will pass urine tests (because they haven't shot
heroin for five days) but will be impaired on the job. Moreover, even heavy
use of harder drugs may never result in impaired performance. Any sports fan
can name an athlete whose finest years, in terms precisely of dexterity and
judgment, came during what were subsequently revealed to be years of heavy
cocaine use. No one who has read Gelsey Kirkland's autobiography would
wish on another human being the nightmare of drug use to which she subjected herself during her dancing years.[10] But no one who saw her dance in
those years could believe that even heavy drug use necessarily leads to impaired job performance.

---

[8] Treasury Employees, 489 U.S. at 661.

[9] Treasury Employees, 489 U.S. at 671 (1989).

[10] Gelsey Kirkland, *Dancing on My Grave: An Autobiography* (Garden City, N.Y.: Doubleday, 1986).

So the Court's analysis fails its own premises; it can specify neither the nature or weight of a privacy interest in one's urine, nor the nature or weight of a governmental interest in obtaining information about drug use.

Examination of the opinion in the case reveals, through its parapraxes and silences, its role in constructing an imaginary, pure body as a synecdoche for lost national innocence. After all, as any anthropologist knows, government security forces are not the only people who perform rituals with other people's urine. There are many anthropological accounts of magic effected with another's bodily wastes, what Frazer called the principle of Contact or Contagion, "that things which have been in contact with each other continue to act on each other at a distance after the physical contact has been severed." Believing that the ritual of testing and analyzing a customs agent's urine will bring about a person of "judgment and dexterity" is not so far from the charms or spells over body wastes described by Frazer or a contemporary anthropologist such as Michael Taussig.[11]

Nor is the choice of body wastes accidental. Other tests exist for detecting drug use, and some even test impairment, but the government performs rituals on urine.

To understand why, I would like to introduce Julia Kristeva's concept of abjection, introduced in *Powers of Horror: An Essay on Abjection,*[12] her first book after becoming a psychoanalyst, which will help us understand, not only the psychodynamics of urinalysis, but also a variety of problems in upcoming chapters in which legal bodies are constructed in order to be cast out from society: bodies in disfavored racial categories, or with diseases or odors. For Kristeva, abjection is the universal infantile experience of gaining a sense of the boundaries of the body through the casting out of wastes. Kristeva is a particularly difficult, prolix, obscure writer, whose metastasizing books are not always necessarily consistent with each other. I shall not present a real introduction to Kristeva, particularly as a good one in English has just appeared, but simply an appropriation of her concept of abjection.[13]

In chapter 6 we discussed Jacques Lacan's celebrated account of the mirror stage in which the infant enters a world of erotic desire that is simultaneously symbolic and unattainable; we also promised an important supplementary account. In Kristeva's account, the mother is abjected, not rejected.

Kristeva focuses on the stage before the mirror stage, at a point when the infant is presymbolic. (Kristeva confusingly calls this stage the "semiotic." I have no idea, and have not read a convincing account, of why she selected

---

[11] Sir James George Frazer, *The Golden Bough* 52 (London: Macmillan, 3d ed., 1911), discussed in Michael Taussig, *Mimesis and Alterity: A Particular History of the Senses* 52–56 (New York: Routledge, 1993).

[12] (Leon S. Roudiez trans.) (New York: Columbia U.Pr, 1982).

[13] The most helpful introduction to Kristeva that I have found is Kelly Oliver, *Reading Kristeva: Unraveling the Double-Bind* (Bloomington: Indiana U. Pr., 1993).

such a rich and pregnant term, so full of allusions for the reader, most of which seem to me unhelpful in understanding Kristeva's project). Before the infant speaks, or has any symbolic competence, how does it interact with the world? Often through abjection of waste products: it urinates, defecates, vomits, spits up. For Kristeva, these homely activities take on an intense psychoanalytic importance that helps explain their continuing source of disgust and shame for us, among other things.

Abjection in some ways is the opposite of desire. Desire starts with a lack—someone wants something (the breast, love) to supplement one's lacking self. Abjection, by contrast, begins in the experience of excess or surplus, which must be got rid of. Both, however, are sources of intense pleasure, as everyone knows, though the literary and artistic representations of the pleasure of abjection are rare and the opposite of elevating. Why do we deny this pleasure?

While presymbolic infants do take delight in their urination, defecation, and vomit, as they enter the symbolic universe they learn to regard these activities as disgusting, to be performed in private, without public reference, discussion, or sign. "Learn" sounds much too cognitive. In fact, any adult or child will involuntarily gag, retch, or vomit if he or she must spend much time around urine, feces, vomit, menstrual blood, or corpses. Thousands of times a day we involuntarily swallow our own saliva. But who could drink a glass of his or her own saliva after it has been abjected from the body?[14]

Of course, acts of abjection continue throughout life, even after infants acquire symbolic competence. However, acts of abjection acquire new psychological significance. The body every day defines itself and its boundaries by what it jettisons; it throws out the abject again and again; yet what it jettisons disgusts and threatens it.

Kristeva doubtless exaggerates the disgusting quality of the abject. The adult mind is not entirely incapable of coping with the abjection of wastes. Women friends in particular have argued with me that Kristeva may overstate the disgusting or frightening quality of menstrual blood, which may rather represent the pleasure and security of knowing that one is not pregnant, if one does not want to be. Still, however welcome that menstrual blood may be in particular instances, it's not something anyone uses as a sacrament or keepsake unless one is deliberately trying to be transgressive.

Kristeva follows accounts common to many Freudians of the difficulty in separating from the *object,* such as the mother, understood and defined as *another.* The separation involved in *abjection* is equally difficult, but different in kind. The uncanniness, the threat of the abject is that *it used to be (part of) ourselves.*

---

[14] Burt Neuborne gave me this example. He's sure it's not original with him, but neither of us can locate the source.

The psychological process first undertaken as abjection becomes the pattern for all processes of drawing boundaries and limits. We draw boundaries between ourselves and the abjected and thus define what Kristeva calls our *corps propre,* meaning both our "own bodies" and our "clean bodies."[15] The very existence of limits and thresholds between ourselves and others depends on acts of abjection through which we learn our bodies' boundaries. If we can separate ourselves from the very product of our bodies, we can, as it were, separate from anything and anyone. "It is thus not lack of cleanliness or health that causes abjection but what disturbs identity, system, order."[16] Moreover, abjection is continuous. The struggle for a "clean and proper body" is never won, that body is never attained, and the impossibility of its attainment haunts the subject and shapes and colors that subject's psychological relationship to the wastes it sheds, wastes that simultaneously purify and defile it.

Kristeva's account of abjection illuminates a number of interesting aspects of the legal construction of the body. First, it helps explain the obvious sense of embarrassment and shame lurking behind the Supreme Court's opinion in the *Treasury Employees* case, an embarrassment expressed in the opinion's very silence about the bodily functions involved. Second, it helps explain the bizarre passages of the opinion in which the body, excluded from the analysis of privacy because of the Court's shame and embarrassment, returns as a synecdoche for national identity.

One might have developed the "privacy interest" assertedly being weighed from a kind of anthropological inquiry into the social practices and understandings surrounding urination in our culture. Such a review might cover the practice of concealment and euphemism, the association of "bathroom humor" with the very young, and the like. The lower court in the *Treasury Employees* case had attempted such a brief characterization in the passage quoted above. By treating privacy so laconically, the Court can declare urine private without having to make urination present in any meaningful way. The Court thus demonstrates just how urine is private, if not shameful—in the very act of refusing to probe very deeply into its meaning, the Court mimes privacy.

Though the lower court states that urination is private, and the Supreme Court agrees, neither needs to decide why this is so. The courts act as if they are merely reporting some social consensus or practice, put together elsewhere. This permits them to avoid any sense of responsibility, as if that sort of social practice were "natural" and entirely free of law. We may want—I surely want—a court to be able to found privacy on something other than its empirical observation of (other) people's practices. We want the court to own its

---

[15] Kristeva informed her translator that both meanings were intended. Julia Kristeva, *Powers of Horror* viii.

[16] Id. 4.

privacy interests; for these privacy interests to turn neither on facts observed in others nor the Court's subjective feelings. How can we antifoundationalists have our wish?

Psychoanalytic concepts like Kristeva's help bridge the gap. Her account shows that the psychological aspects of urination aren't decided by each of us for ourselves, aren't arbitrary, but are powerfully shared by people in a way that (for example) machine constructions aren't. If the shame and disgust in abjection plays a role in the whole process of infantile development, it may have a stronger psychological resonance than a metaphor like property learned much later in life. Nevertheless, the private body *is* a construction. Urination is natural, but abjection configures that urination in a particular way, setting up a particular symbolic relation to the products of our body. Such relations do change in history, but slowly, and not just because particular parents decide they want to raise their child differently. So while I do not want to make any scientific claims for psychoanalysis, I find it a very helpfully worked out set of concepts to capture this middle ground of constructions that are biologically based but not biologically inevitable, culturally grounded but resistant to individual change.

Kristeva is helpfully ambiguous on just this point. She is often criticized, particularly by feminists, for the alleged essentialism of her accounts of the female or motherhood.[17] More sympathetic accounts stress her interest in discourses that are especially ambiguous, that undermine their own foundations, and read her accounts of femininity or mother in this light.[18] I choose the latter reading; for me the very interest of Kristeva, one that she shares with Luce Irigaray despite the many differences between them, is a vocabulary that recognizes the constructed quality of bodies, locates that construction significantly in prephallic processes, and simultaneously recognizes that these prephallic constructions are particularly difficult to dislodge.

Why is urination so hard to write about? Not everyone finds it as hard as did Justice Kennedy, to be sure, but to anyone it seems disgusting, childish. Apart from the point that this seems to prove its "private" quality, we now can see the precise repression, in the psychoanalytic sense, going on here. Understanding abjection as the basis of a kind of repression helps explain Justice Kennedy's distanced, abstract vocabulary; the way urine disappears, in order to become "the sample"; the way in which the body, constructed as a privacy

[17] Judith Butler, *Gender Trouble: Feminism and the Subversion of Identity* 79–93 (New York: Routledge, 1990); Gail M. Schwab, "Mother's Body, Father's Tongue: Mediation and the Symbolic Order," in *Engaging with Irigaray: Feminist Philosophy and Modern European Thought* 351–62 (Carolyn Burke, Naomi Schor, and Margaret Whitford eds.) (New York: Colum. U. Pr., 1994); Gayatri Chakravorty Spivak, *Outside in the Teaching Machine* 17 (New York: Routledge, 1993).

[18] Jane Gallop, *The Daughter's Seduction: Feminism and Psychoanalysis* 115–31 (Ithaca: Cornell U. Pr., 1982); Oliver, *Reading Kristeva* 48–68.

interest, disappears from the opinion. No identifiable individuals inhabit the opinion. No customs agent is named. No one person's fear, shame, sense of invasion emerges from the generic privacy claimed.

Yet the one sure thing about repression is the return of the repressed. Kristeva's second major illumination of *Treasury Employees* is the insight into the intimacy, if not identity, of the psychological processes of abjecting waste products and excluding other humans. "[T]here are lives not sustained by *desire,* as desire is always for objects. Such lives are based on *exclusion.*"[19]

> The Customs Service is our Nation's first line of defense against one of the greatest problems affecting the health and welfare of our population. . . .
>
> It is readily apparent that the Government has a compelling interest in ensuring that front-line interdiction personnel are physically fit, and have unimpeachable integrity and judgment. Indeed, the Government's interest here is at least as important as its interest in searching travelers entering the country. We have long held that travelers seeking to enter the country may be stopped and required to submit to a routine search without probable cause, or even founded suspicion, "because of national self-protection reasonably requiring one entering the country to identify himself as entitled to come in, and his belongings as effects which may be lawfully brought in." *Carroll v. United States,* 267 U.S. 132, 154 (1925). See also *United States v. Montoya de Hernandez, supra,* at 538; *United States v. Ramsey, supra,* at 617–619. This national interest in self-protection could be irreparably damaged if those charged with safeguarding it were, because of their own drug use, unsympathetic to their mission of interdicting narcotics. . . .
>
> We think Customs employees who are directly involved in the interdiction of illegal drugs or who are required to carry firearms in the line of duty likewise have a diminished expectation of privacy in respect to the intrusions occasioned by a urine test. Unlike most private citizens or government employees in general, employees involved in drug interdiction reasonably should expect effective inquiry into their fitness and probity. Much the same is true of employees who are required to carry firearms. Because successful performance of their duties depends uniquely on their judgment and dexterity, these employees cannot reasonably expect to keep from the Service personal information that bears directly on their fitness. . . . While reasonable tests designed to elicit this information doubtless infringe some privacy expectations, we do not believe these expectations outweigh the Government's compelling interests in safety and in the *integrity of our borders.*[20]

We have already referred to two features of this extraordinary discussion: the strange misapprehension that the urine test detects fitness, probity, judg-

---

[19] *Powers of Horror* 6.
[20] Treasury Employees, 489 U.S. at 668–72 (last emphasis supplied, others original).

ment, or dexterity; and the idea that supposed public interests do not merely outweigh but instead diminish expectations of privacy.

I want now to note its passion and desire, particularly in passages omitted from the first paragraph quoted. The body language repressed from the description of the invasion of privacy itself, the drug test, described above in the clinical, distanced language ("produce the sample"), returns here. The bodies of customs agents are figuratively under assault, but not from the government that wants their urine. The government's invasive powers are transferred to a threatening Other. "The physical safety of these employees may be threatened"; "[o]fficers have been shot, stabbed, run over, dragged by automobiles, and assaulted with blunt objects." In dissent, Justice Scalia questioned the relevance of these remarks.[21] While their legal function is indeed hard to determine, they perform the rhetorical and dramatic function of displacing the government's invasion of the body with an invasion from elsewhere.

The passionate body language does not stem from any new apprehension of the physical body, but rather from the catachresis in which the body of the customs agent stands in for the body of the nation. The body of the customs agent is constructed as pure, free of drugs, fit, and with firm boundaries, because the nation must similarly be constructed as pure, free of drugs, fit, and with firm boundaries. (One irony is that the metaphorical body politic is purified only by invading the borders of the agents' bodies. A second is that within a few months, Justice Kennedy would write for the Court that no judicial hearing was necessary before Walter Harper was to be dosed involuntarily with psychotropic drugs.) "The Customs Service is our Nation's first *line of defense* against one of the greatest problems affecting the health and welfare of our population."

The first legal argument offered in support of the government's testing program—after this passionate description of endangered bodies—is a strange analogy. "Indeed, the Government's interest here is at least as important as its interest in searching travelers entering the country." This is not necessarily a good analogy. In dissent, Justice Scalia argued that it was not: some incoming travelers do violate immigration laws, while, he felt, no similar proof had been forthcoming that customs agents represented any genuine threat to drug policies.[22] Other arguments might be raised against the analogy. Obviously, if law had a more coherent concept of body privacy, an embodied search might be different from a search of luggage.

These arguments misapprehend the rhetorical force of the analogy to "travelers entering the country"; this common and remarkably long-lived analogy gains its rhetorical power in part from its legal irrelevance. In its 1837 version:

[21] 489 U.S. at 681–83.
[22] 489 U.S. at 681.

We think it as competent and as necessary for a state to provide precautionary measures against the moral pestilence of paupers, vagabonds, and possibly convicts; as it is to guard against the physical pestilence which may arise from unsound and infectious articles imported, or from a ship, the crew of which may be labouring under an infectious disease.[23]

We will soon see the same analogy, similarly irrelevant, dropped casually into a legal analysis. In *Jacobson v. Massachusetts,* discussed in chapter 14, compulsory inoculation against smallpox was upheld against constitutional challenge. The opinion has become a standard script for the construction of a body available to others and excludable from society. We consider only one aspect of the opinion here. The Court immediately follows the key, though general, assertion that

> in every well-ordered society charged with the duty of conserving the safety of its members the rights of the individual in respect of his liberty may at times, under the pressure of great dangers, be subjected to such restraint, to be enforced by reasonable regulations, as the safety of the general public may demand

with the following familiar, seemingly irrelevant, analogy:

> An American citizen, arriving at an American port on a vessel in which, during the voyage, there had been cases of yellow fever or Asiatic cholera, although apparently free from disease himself, may yet, in some circumstances, be held in quarantine against his will on board of such vessel or in a quarantine station, until it be ascertained by inspection, conducted with due diligence, that the danger of the spread of the disease among the community at large has disappeared.[24]

This passage, like its equivalent in *Treasury Employees,* calls up what Susan Sontag, writing about AIDS, calls "the usual script for plague: the disease invariably comes from somewhere else."[25] While pauperism, smallpox, and narcotics only ambiguously, if at all, illustrate danger actually arriving from elsewhere, the metaphor of invasion is as central to our mythology of narcotics as is the rhetoric of purity, specifically understood as racial purity. "From the Opium Wars in the mid–nineteenth century up to the current details of U.S. relations with Turkey, Colombia, Panama, Peru, and the Nicaraguan Contras, the drama of 'foreign substances' and the drama of the new imperialisms and nationalisms have been quite inextricable. The integrity of (new and contested) national borders, the reifications of national will and vitality, were readily organized around these narratives of interjection."[26] As Auden said,

[23] City of New York v. Miln, 36 U.S. 102, 142 (1837).

[24] Jacobson v. Massachusetts, 197 U.S. 11, 29 (1905).

[25] Susan Sontag, *Illness as Metaphor and AIDS and Its Metaphors* 135 (New York: Doubleday, Anchor, 1990).

[26] Eve Kosofsky Sedgwick, *Epistemology of the Closet* 173 (Berkeley: U. Cal. Pr., 1990).

"The ship, then, is only used as a metaphor for society in danger from within or without."[27]

Justice Kennedy's language in *Treasury Employees,* the passionate language in the lengthy passage quoted, similarly constructs a body politic, under external invasive threat, preserving its existence through the "integrity of its borders"; one might be forgiven thinking that the last phrase referred to the integrity of the Customs agents' body borders, but for the fact that their body borders are being invaded in order to preserve the integrity of the borders of what is known in plague rhetoric, from smallpox to AIDS, as "the general public" or "community at large."

"[T]he symbolism of the body's boundaries is used in [a] kind of unfunny wit to express dangers to community boundaries," writes Mary Douglas.[28] "The body is a model which can stand for any bounded system. Its boundaries can represent any boundaries which are threatened or precarious. The body is a complex structure. The functions of its different parts and their relation afford a source of symbols for other complex structures. We cannot possibly interpret rituals concerning excreta, breast milk, saliva and the rest unless we are prepared to see in the body a symbol of society, and to see the powers and dangers credited to social structure reproduced in small on the human body."[29]

The opinion in *Treasury Employees* demonstrates at least this general point. The precise justification for urinary ritual is the threat to the boundaries of the nation. The body of the customs agent is constructed to symbolize the larger society. Firm boundaries are part of a characteristically modern narrative of nationality in which "state sovereignty is fully, flatly, and evenly operative over each square centimetre of a legally demarcated community," as opposed to earlier imaginings of nationalism in which "states were defined by centers, borders were porous and indistinct."[30]

In this world of nations with boundaries, narcotics represent an external threat to "the general public." This way of putting the point is inherently racist; in earlier periods of narcotics regulation the racism was explicit in the regulation, but now need no longer be expressed overtly since it lies implicit in the basic structure of the hypothesized "clean" land of "health," threatened

---

[27] W. H. Auden, *The Enchafèd Flood; or, The Romantic Iconography of the Sea* 8 (New York: Random House, 1950).

[28] Mary Douglas, *Purity and Danger: An Analysis of the Concepts of Pollution and Taboo* 122 (London: Routledge, 1966).

[29] Id. 115.

[30] Benedict Anderson, *Imagined Communities: Reflections on the Origin and Spread of Nationalism* 19 (London: Verso, rev. ed., 1991). Legal implications are powerfully explored in Robert S. Chang, "A Meditation on Borders," in *Immigrants Out! The New Nativism and the Anti-Immigrant Impulse in the United States* (Juan Perea ed.) (New York: New York U. Pr., 1996).

from without.[31] As we have seen, criminal punishment in the eighteenth century, in England at least, was routinely justified in assize sermons by imagining the nation as a body that needed a diseased or infected limb removed.[32] Some have seen the disappearance of this imagery,[33] but, as the *Treasury Employees* case shows, it has merely been updated to remain current with contemporaneous medical thought, which now protects the body from infection not by amputation, but rather by hygiene, purification, and healthy immune systems, typically figured as militaristic lines of defense against invasion.[34]

"Excrement and its equivalents (decay, infection, disease, corpse, etc.) stand for the danger to identity that comes from without: the ego threatened by the non-ego, society by its outside, life by death."[35] Such an account takes no stand on whether the danger is "real" or not. In Mary Douglas's account, it is particularly important that rituals of body purification not be understood as attempts "to cure or prevent personal neuroses." Rather, rituals of purification "enact the form of social relations and in giving these relations visible expression they enable people to know their own society. The rituals work upon the body politic through the symbolic medium of the physical body."[36]

Drug testing through urinalysis is just such a ritual, our society's precise

---

[31] Drug cases from the early decades of this century often figure the addict as the corrupted victim of others, a status never accorded the Chinese or African-American characters in the cases, who instead represent the threat itself. See, e.g., Ex parte Yun Quong, 114 P. 835, 837 (Cal. 1911) ("Statistics show that the vice of using opium is increasing in this country. It must be conceded that its indiscriminate use would have a very debilitating effect upon our race"); Luck v. Sears, 44 P. 693, 694 (Or. 1896) (narcotics use "has no place in the common experience or habits of the people of this country"); State v. Shimoaka, 251 P. 290, 292 (Wash. 1926) (permitting jury to draw inference from fact that defendant had entered a Chinese house: "there is a widespread belief, however unfounded it may be, that the members of the Chinese race of people now remaining in the Pacific Coast states are more addicted to the use of narcotics drugs than are the members of any other race of people there residing"). See generally David F. Musto, *The American Disease: Origins of Narcotics Control* 17 (New Haven: Yale U. Pr., 1973); Douglas Clark Kinder, "Shutting Out Evil: Nativism and Narcotics Control in the United States," in *Drug Control Policy: Essays in Historical and Comparative Perspective* 117, 118 (William O. Walker III ed.) (University Park: Penn. St. U. Pr., 1992); Patricia A. Morgan, "The Legislation of Drug Law: Economic Crisis and Social Control," 8 *J. Drug Issues* 53 (1978); and the unpublished paper by my student Eric Stahl, "The Metaphors of Narcotics Prohibition," the source of the material in this footnote. For the Australian story, substantially similar, see Desmond Manderson, "Health and the Aesthetics of Health—an Historical Case Study," 11 *J. Contemp. Health L. & Policy* 85 (1994).

[32] Randall McGowen, "The Body and Punishment in Eighteenth-Century England," 59 *J. Mod. Hist.* 651, 653–62 (1987).

[33] McGowen, "Body and Punishment," 676–79.

[34] Emily Martin, *Flexible Bodies: Tracking Immunity in American Culture—From the Days of Polio to the Age of AIDS* (Boston: Beacon, 1994).

[35] Kristeva, *Powers of Horror* 71.

[36] Douglas, *Purity and Danger* 128.

equivalent to the purification rituals described by Mary Douglas. As the reference to her work implies, calling it a ritual does not call drug testing neurotic, or uncalled-for, or the threat of drugs necessarily nonexistent. (It doesn't prove the contrary of these propositions either). The federal government tests urine for drugs, not for its exiguous instrumental value, but as part of a national ritual of purification, which states symbolically that this is all one nation, united behind firm borders, united in resolve to combat drugs. By calling drug testing a ritual, I am, once again, not sneering, but trying to use the term as an anthropologist might, to describe social actions that are repeated and integrate the minds and emotions of participants through condensed metaphors.[37]

Who is to say that such rituals of national identification might not indeed play a part, an important part, in any coherent policy against narcotics use? The United States of America is famous for such problems of national identity as the expansion of boundaries, the cultivation of the natural, and the creation of internal tranquility; it is hardly surprising that the body figures prominently in our self-imagination of all these political processes, or that judges make legal decisions that create national identity through the deployment of constructions of the body.[38] But for the arguable invasion of the employees' privacy, no one could object generally to such rituals. They are an inherent part of life in society.

The precise embarrassment of the opinion in *Treasury Employees* may now be identified. The opinion, as we have seen, does not fit the grid into which it is mangled, in which an individual interest in privacy is weighed against a public interest in information. The individual interest does not exist apart from this very invasion and in any event cannot be specified, while the public interest is not one of information. Rather, the entire program is a public ritual of purification in which the very construction of the weak body "privacy" of the customs agents plays a part in the drama of uniting against an external threat and purifying the society by strengthening its borders.

We do not have a very sophisticated constitutional law discourse of this kind of use of the body, as a symbol in a larger communicative message. Our tempered language of weighing interests seems inadequate here. We may sense that some such rituals are a necessary part of social life without any sense that judges could determine how necessary is the ritual, what social function it performs, whether bodies must be used just in the specified way, or some other.

[37] See generally Stanley Jeyraja Tambiah, *Culture, Thought, and Social Action: An Anthropological Perspective* (Cambridge: Harv. U. Pr., 1985); David Kertzer, *Ritual, Politics, and Power* (New Haven: Yale U. Pr., 1988).

[38] Sharon Cameron, *The Corporeal Self: Allegories of the Body in Melville and Hawthorne* 6–7 (Baltimore: Johns Hopkins U. Pr., 1981).

The malleability of construction of the legal body rescues us from this embarrassment. Once again, the discursive construction of the body accomplishes what political theory cannot. By constructing the body of the customs agent as an abstract "privacy interest," we simultaneously avoid any apprehension or description of the physical body; invoke a world of accepted legal analyses in which interests are weighed; while in no way limiting our ability to make and remake the body to achieve important social purposes.

Chapter 13

THE RACIAL BODY

[A]n aversion to their corporeal distinctions from us . . . militates against
a general incorporation of them with us.[1]

RACE, insofar as the word has any distinctive meaning, is a construction of the
body. For any sentence containing the word *race,* in which the word cannot be
completely replaced by *ethnicity* or *group* without loss of meaning, a body is
being constructed, and a claim is being made about physically identifiable
bodies as the bearers or carriers of some other trait.[2] A theory of race is not
merely a theory of differences among people, but a theory that locates, figures,
inscribes those differences, not in the mind, history, experience, or likely reactions of others, but in the body. It is not surprising that race will be performatively enacted in legal discourse, a discourse that constructs and naturalizes
what it claims to find.

Whatever the pitfalls of trying to say something about the racialized body in
a short chapter of a subencyclopedic work, the pitfalls of ignoring this crucial
construction of the body are far worse. I shall be drawing on some of the
outstanding recent legal scholarship that interrogates the concept of race, rendering it visible and analyzing its grammar and deployment. This work frees
me of the burden of a comprehensive discussion of the meaning of race in
American law and permits me to discuss the narrower issue of the way in
which race claims involve body constructions; some of the range of such body

---

[1] St. George Tucker, letter (June 1795) to Jeremy Belknap, quoted in Winthrop D. Jordan,
White over Black: American Attitudes toward the Negro, 1550–1812 (New York: Norton, 1977)
[1968] at 556.

[2] The Supreme Court's current version of some of the Reconstruction era statutes that are
popularly understood as bans on "racial" discrimination (though they do not employ the word
race) substitutes the idea of any "ethnic" discrimination. The law now 42 U.S.C. §1981 provides
that "all persons . . . shall have the same right . . . to make and enforce contracts, to sue, be
parties, give evidence, and to the full and equal benefit of all laws and proceedings for the security
of persons and property as is enjoyed by white citizens." A naturalized Iraqi may sue under this
section alleging discrimination against Arabs. Any group discrimination based on "ancestry or
ethnic characteristics" is covered; "a distinctive physiognomy is not essential." Saint Francis
College v. Al-Khazraji, 481 U.S. 604, 613 (1987). Similarly, 42 U.S.C. §1982 guarantees all
citizens the same property rights "enjoyed by white citizens." Jews, presumptively white, may
nevertheless sue other white people who desecrated their synagogue, under this statute. Shaare
Tefila Congregation v. Cobb, 481 U.S. 615, 617–18 (1987). The racial classification of Jews is a
particularly rich history of shifting social construction, to be discussed further.

constructions in history; their relation to some of the other bodies of law discussed in this book; and some notes on a utopian legal discourse that could construct bodies with races only to empower persons.

My basic point is to criticize the account under which race is a natural fact that inheres in each body from birth. This account is not easy to dislodge. I pointed out in the introduction that it is standard to most ordinary talk of race, even the avowedly antiracist speech of President Clinton urging people to vote for people "who look different." The naturalizing account of race as inherent in the body is enjoying a revival in popular sociology and psychology as a marker of supposedly distinct genetic inheritances.[3]

I shall instead be emphasizing the constructed nature of race in legal discourse. Race is a claim that necessarily involves the construction of a specularized body by a privileged eye. I shall try to show that this construction inevitably performatively enacts a kind of domination of the body by the eye. Race is thus not a thing or a state but a relationship, and the question is always not just what state has been constructed, but who is doing that construction and for what purpose.

Some readers will immediately see, perhaps if they have been reading Hegel or Lacan, or the works on the construction of gender by Judith Butler and Thomas Laqueur that I have cited before,[4] that racial constructions of the body always and necessarily represent constructions, and performances of political domination at that, with only tenuous connection to biology. At the moment, though, I want to write also to readers who reject the Butler-Laqueur approach to gender, who think that there are such things as real biological differences among bodies, of which sex is one, and that saying that such differences are overemphasized, or misunderstood, is not the same thing as saying they exist only as an artifact of language. Perhaps sex is just this kind of fact about bodies. Race, however, and however natural it may seem to us, just plain isn't, and legal discourse, from St. George Tucker (in the introductory quotation to this chapter) to Clinton, plays a large role in naturalizing the racial divisions we construct.

The alternative discursive construction of the raced body that I will develop is one in which race is always already experienced as a construction, as a performance in which a person self-consciously creates her own race, as an act of existential self-affirmance, in some specified relation with others. Race becomes always already unstable, willed, somewhat artificial, like the other body constructions of this book, a way of living through complex political and

---

[3] Charles Murray and Richard Herrnstein, *The Bell Curve* (New York: Free Pr., 1994) is a most unoriginal best-selling revival of this school.

[4] Judith Butler, *Gender Trouble: Feminism and the Subversion of Identity* (New York: Routledge, 1990), and *Bodies That Matter: On the Discursive Limits of "Sex"* (New York: Routledge, 1993); Thomas Laqueur, *Making Sex: Body and Gender from the Greeks to Freud* (Cambridge: Harv. U. Pr., 1990).

social notions, but always experienced as constructed not natural, and always
carrying with it a boundless set of alternative constructions, present even if not
expressed.

RACE CLAIMS AS BODY CLAIMS

The standard version of race as a natural trait inherent in the body may appear
well-entrenched in ordinary thought, but it is not particularly old. Race is
nowhere near as old as the fear of the outsider or stranger, or the claim to
superiority of one's own people.[5] Race is the comparatively late development,
in the history of group identity, of the claim that the Other is different from us
in his or her body.

Kwame Anthony Appiah's recent book *In My Father's House* is probably
the most thoroughgoing and influential critique of racial classifications.[6]
(Some of Appiah's unpublished work since that book may represent a partial
retreat from its formulations; I will consider this below.) Appiah argues that
the racial categories that seem natural to naive speakers today, the nineteenth-
century division of humanity into three supposed races, represent a new formulation that owes little to the divisions employed in earlier centuries. While
ancient cultures practiced cultural identity and superiority, they did not conceptualize race in modern, embodied terms. For what it's worth, the studies of
legal discourse in this volume support this idea of the early nineteenth century
as a crucial period for the rethinking and making of the modern body. The
people who habitually constructed bodies as the representations of others, who
developed phrenology and prosopography and physical descriptions of Shakespeare's characters (discussed in chap. 6), who exported the body to traditional societies, gave us race as an important construction of the modern
body.[7] The concept of race that they gave us, however, is neither consistent
nor coherent, as Appiah shows in his discussion of its use by as sophisticated a
thinker as W. E. B. Du Bois.

Race stands in for neither geography, nor language, nor culture. In the first
place, the racial categories in current use are fluid and directly responsive to
political needs. The tortured history of the various racial categories used in the
American West to classify people either of Asian or Latin American origin is
tribute to the substantial political choice or domination involved in the construction of racial categories: persons of Mexican ancestry have been both

---

[5] Julia Kristeva, *Strangers to Ourselves* (New York: Colum. U. Pr., 1991).

[6] Kwame Anthony Appiah, *In My Father's House: Africa in the Philosophy of Culture* 10–45
(New York: Oxford U. Pr., 1992).

[7] Missionary: "En somme c'est la notion d'esprit que nous avons portée dans votre pensée?"
New Caledonian: "L'esprit? Bah! Vous ne nous avez pas apporté l'esprit. Nous savions déjà
l'existence de l'esprit. Ce que vous nous avez apporté, c'est le corps." Maurice Leenhardt, *Do
Kamo* 212 (Paris: Gallimard, 1947).

white and a separate category; Chinese have at times been Indian.[8] "Mr. Plessy could not ride in that notorious 'Whites Only' rail car in Louisiana because he was not a White, but rather, a Colored man, an 'Octaroon.' He was, however, an 'Octaroon' not in the genuinely scientific sense in which he was 'male' (the possessor of both an X and a Y chromosome), but because one of his great-grandparents possessed some vague amalgam of physical and cultural characteristics that led White Southerners to judge him or her a 'Negro' of 'full' blood."[9] Asian-American arose as a label in the 1960s in response to governmental racial regulation.[10] Frantz Fanon wrote: "In 1939, no West Indian in the West Indies proclaimed himself to be a Negro, claimed to be a Negro." Negroes lived in Africa, and West Indians identified with Europeans.[11] Other examples of such fluid racial categories could be multiplied.

Nor is race a good proxy for cultural or ethnic experience or attitudes; what is the significant experience or attitude that links the median citizen of Abidjan, Port-au-Prince, Texarkana (Arkansas), and Bedford-Stuyvesant, just because all may trace ancestry to Africa, and excludes most of the rest of the world? There can be only two nonexclusive answers to the question of what links these four persons: their own identification, or the identification placed upon them by others. In truth, all humans can trace ancestry to Africa, according to current anthropological theory, so all Americans are African-American.

Most importantly, race is not a helpful guide to genetic inheritance. There is now a very strong scientific consensus that the division of the world's populations into distinct races is simply useless for any scientific project. Of course classifications can be made and repeated by other researchers, just as all the people of the world might be classified by foot size, or eye color, or shirt size.

Race, it turns out, is about as helpful a classification as the three I mentioned. Appiah argues the point particularly strongly as part of his general and influential critique of the concept of race. "[F]or two people who are both 'Caucasoid,' the chances of differing in genetic constitution at one site on a given chromosome have recently been estimated at about 14.3 percent, while for any two people taken at random from the human population the same calculations suggest a figure of about 14.8 percent. . . The truth is that there are no races: there is nothing in the world that can do all we ask race to do for us. . . . [W]here race works—in places where 'gross differences' of morphol-

---

[8] People v. Hall, 4 Cal. 399 (1854). See generally Neil Gotanda, "A Critique of 'Our Constitution Is Color-Blind,'" 44 *Stan. L. Rev.* 1 (1991); Michael Omi and Howard Winant, *Racial Formation in the United States: From the 1960s to the 1980s* 75–80 (New York: Routledge and Kegan Paul, 1986).

[9] Christopher A. Ford, "Administering Identity: The Determination of 'Race' in Race-Conscious Law," 82 *Calif. L. Rev.* 1231, 1274 (1994) (footnote omitted).

[10] Omi and Winant, *Racial Formation* 84.

[11] Frantz Fanon, "West Indians and Africans," in *Toward the African Revolution: Political Essays* 21 (Haakon Chevalier trans.) (New York: Monthly Review Pr., 1967) [1955].

ogy are correlated with 'subtle differences' of temperament, belief, and intention—it works as an attempt at metonym for culture, and it does so only at the price of biologizing what *is* culture, ideology."[12]

Race, in other words, is useful primarily to those who want to divide people in order to naturalize domination, precisely, the domination of a caste that draws a line of "race" to create a purified dominant group and an excluded outside. As Dorothy E. Roberts writes:

> [G]enetic makeup is not critical to the meaning of race in African-American culture. Whites defined enslaved Africans as a biological race. Blacks in America have historically resisted this racial ideology by defining themselves as a political group. "Afro-Americans invented themselves, not as a race, but as a nation."[13]

As Roberts points out, race fails as a proxy for genetic inheritance in a crucial respect that Appiah does not notice: in a system of race, genetic ties that are scientifically indistinguishable will have quite different social meanings depending on the status of the affected races. A white genetic tie will have no social significance in the case of an individual who appears dark, for example.

One function of "race" in this discourse of domination is to overcome competing discursive constructions of bodies, in which bodies represent human solidarity.

A RACED BODY AS AN ABJECTED BODY

There is an obvious intellectual problem in this modern location of difference in the body. The body, as we have seen, is just as easily invoked as the very symbolic expression of human likeness and universality. As the quotations in the introduction from Mary Douglas, Shakespeare, and the theater director Peter Brook suggest, "the human body is common to us all." The statement reveals a kind of puzzle. The body is always there, always to hand, always ready and available as the easiest source of analogies and metaphors to help people visually and cognitively think through their situations. This ubiquity of the body is why "most symbolic behavior must work through the human body."[14]

However, one can indeed experience one's own bodies and others' as sites of differentiation. Indeed, under regimes of sexual differentiation, universal in human culture as we know it, the body is always a site of differentiation, in

---

[12] Appiah, *In My Father's House,* 35–45 (New York: Oxford U. Pr., 1992).

[13] Dorothy E. Roberts, "The Genetic Tie," 62 *U. Chi. L. Rev.* 209, 231–32 and n. 90 (1995). The internal quotation is from Barbara Jeanne Fields, "Slavery, Race, and Ideology in the United States of America," 181 *New Left Review* 95, 115 (1990).

[14] Mary Douglas, *Natural Symbols: Explorations in Cosmology* vii (New York: Pantheon, 1970).

which thick layers of discursively created difference magnify limited ana-
tomic variation.

The ubiquity of the body may seem to make it an ambiguous or poor symbolization of difference. If "the human body is common to us all," how is it
that this natural fact does not make racial exclusion impossible? We have seen
with some precision precisely how the body may be constructed as the very
thing that unites people with each other: erotic attraction; all alike under the
skin (and why not in it?); machine bodies that respond alike to medical therapy or tort damages; sentimental bodies in pain; "Hath not a Jew eyes?" It
would seem that any attempt to construct raced bodies as a way of dividing
people would have to swim upstream against this flood of embodied attraction, similarity, sympathy, and solidarity.

The question of why cultures identify hated Others and create group solidarity around their persecution and exclusion is too broad for our attention
here, and I'm sure I have little to add to its discussion. The question of *how*
they enact this persecution through the discursive construction of the body is,
however, more manageable, and I believe that legal texts provide illuminating
examples of the construction of the abjected body. The modern body, an entity
inevitably symbolic, that stands in for but is not the same as the "person," the
specularized, distanced body that displays, as if it were natural, its social and
discursive construction, plays an important role in the discourse of racism.

The Kristevan account of abjection, the hopeless search for an unattainably
pure body, purified continually by the expulsion of the polluting internal
member, clarifies the mental psychological script available to anyone who, for
whatever exogenous reason, participates in racial or ethnic prejudice.[15] Our
existing stock of explanations as to which societies will call on this mental
script does not seem entirely satisfactory to me. Doubtless it is true that threatened societies become obsessed with defining and defending boundaries, as
Mary Douglas has illustrated. Though a threatened society is a good habitat
for racial anxiety and exclusion, it seems too pat and psychologically reductionist to reduce all racism to social anxiety, and of course it is not hard to
come up with examples of the most complacently self-satisfied societies that
enforce cruel and rigid schemes of racial categorization and exclusion.

Doubtless it is also true, as Julia Kristeva has discussed, that *some* anxiety
over the boundaries of the self is a basic fact of human existence, necessarily
lived in bodies that daily redraw, reenact, reexperience their boundaries
through acts of expelling surplus wastes, wastes that daily threaten our self-
control and self-definition. I agree that this may give every adult anywhere a
kind of "abjection script" that may be drawn on by "normal," psychologically

---

[15] These themes are briefly explored in Iris Marion Young, "The Scaling of Bodies and the
Politics of Identity," in *Justice and the Politics of Difference* 141–48 (Princeton: Prin. U. Pr.,
1990).

althy people. It seems to be true, however, that individuals and cultures do vary in their propensity to live out the abjection script at a social level, so the emphasis on universal infantile bodily experiences will not give us a very good social theory of racial exclusion.

While I thus cannot explain why we observe ethnic differentiation at particular times and places, I believe that I can help illuminate the question of *how* this differentiation expresses itself through the discursive construction of the body as a site of differentiation. Successful regimes of *racial* exclusion *must* discursively construct bodies that symbolize differentiation, not universalism, lest the fact that "the human body is common to us all" prevent differentiation from being figured discursively.

Our desire for the bodies of at least some Others is so powerful that it might be difficult to abject them unless their bodies could be discursively constructed as something other than the imaginary object of desire—something threatening, threatening our boundaries, our self-definition. Of course, one need look no further than Bosnia or Northern Ireland to find quite virulent hatred among groups that do not appear physically different to outsiders or perhaps to themselves.

Interestingly, however, body differences are easy to construct where there is a will to differentiate. Joanne Conaghan has told me of growing up in Northern Ireland in a Catholic family, attending Catholic schools, and knowing no Protestants as a child. Her parents moved in wider circles, but there was still some excitement the first time a Protestant family came to the house. Conaghan as a child was alert for physical differences between these Protestants and the people she knew, and concluded, as soon as they arrived, that Catholics have blue eyes, Protestants brown.

The American experience has involved a far more detailed imagery of body difference in support of domination and exclusion, and law has played no small part in the construction of this imagery of body difference. I will examine two older cases that construct the white race. Since Ian F. Haney López has recently ably dispatched the line of naturalization cases denying whiteness to claimants, I shall examine two cases in which people successfully demonstrated that they were white.[16]

How American Law Helped to Create Racial Bodies

Like others who have explored the legal construction of race, we may take the 1806 decision of the Virginia Supreme Court of Appeals in *Hudgins v. Wrights* as a key text in figuring the body as the location of human differentiation, though, interestingly, positioning this differentiation in nose shape and hair

---

[16] Ian F. Haney López, *White by Law: The Legal Construction of Race* (New York: New York U. Pr., 1996).

texture, not skin color.[17] Three generations of women sued for their freedom on the very brink of being sent out of state, alleging that they were white people with an Indian ancestor and could not therefore be held in slavery.

The law of slavery in 1806 and long before distinguished white from Negro in that only Negroes could be slaves. Indians, by a series of treaties dating back to the seventeenth century, could not be slaves. Explaining this racial distinction, incidentally, illustrates the general problem described above of dating and explaining racial distinctions. Before 1806 or so, it is far from clear that the "race" of Negroes that alone could be held in slavery really represented a biological race in the modern conception. There is no consensus among historians of American slavery whether the earliest African slaves were not more or less like white indentured servants, the racial distinction having been made only later in the seventeenth century and largely for instrumental reasons of labor control, or whether, conversely, deep hatred of the African created a regime of difference from the beginning.[18]

Whatever the origins or function of this racial distinction, it is not easy to maintain in a world in which whites and Negroes, who are really all people despite the obfuscation of this fact by the ideology of race slavery, may have sex and produce offspring. Obviously such interracial sex was endemic, largely enforced by rape and coercion, though perhaps sometimes reflecting mutual attraction. If race were conceptualized as a matter of genetic makeup, few Virginians would be able to produce the necessary proof of their backgrounds due to the combined effects of transatlantic travel and hidden sex. Legal decisions on the burden of proving race were thus not just technical, since whoever bore this burden would probably lose.

Hudgins v. Wrights was probably typical of the kind of proof involved. Oral testimony established some, but not all, of the plaintiffs' ancestors, including one old Indian woman known as Butterwood Nan. Still, there were gaps in the witnesses' record (including, as two justices and the headnote writer pointed out, Butterwood Nan's mother), discrepancies between the witnesses' testimony and the plaintiffs' original allegations, and nothing that could be described as written evidence one way or the other.

The case was originally heard by Chancellor Wythe, who granted the

---

[17] 11 Va. (1 Hen. and Mumf.) 134 (1806). The case is discussed in Ian F. Haney López, "The Social Construction of Race: Some Observations on Illusion, Fabrication, and Choice," 29 *Harv. C.R.-C.L. L. Rev.* 1 (1994); A. Leon Higginbotham Jr., and Barbara K. Kopytoff, "Racial Purity and Interracial Sex in the Law of Colonial and Antebellum Virginia," 77 *Geo. L. J.* 1967, 1983–86 (1989).

[18] A brief, lively, tendentious introduction to the debate is Theodore W. Allen, *The Invention of the White Race* (vol. 1: *Racial Oppression and Social Control*) 1–24 (London: Verso, 1994), emphasizing economic factors of labor control and denigrating psychological explanations. See also Edmund S. Morgan, *American Slavery, American Freedom: The Ordeal of Colonial Virginia* 154 (New York: Norton, 1975).

women their freedom "on the ground that freedom is the birth-right of every human being, which sentiment is strongly inculcated by the first article of our 'political catechism,' the bill of rights—[H]e laid it down as a general position, that whenever one person claims to hold another in slavery, the *onus probandi* lies on the claimant."[19]

The Virginia Supreme Court of Appeals unanimously affirmed the grant of freedom, but on narrower grounds. The burden of proving race did not always rest on the claimed slaveholder. Instead, the burden of proof depended on the physical appearance of the alleged slave. As St. George Tucker put it in his opinion:

> Nature has stampt upon the *African* and his descendants two characteristic marks, besides the difference of complexion, which often remain visible long after the characteristic distinction of colour either disappears or becomes doubtful; a flat nose and woolly head of hair. The latter of these characteristics disappears the last of all: and so strong an ingredient in the *African* constitution is this latter character, that it predominates uniformly where the party is in equal degree descended from parents of different complexions, whether white or *Indian;* giving to the jet black lank hair of the *Indian* a degree of flexure, which never fails to betray that the party distinguished by it, cannot trace his lineage purely from the race of native *Americans.* Its operation is still more powerful where the mixture happens between persons descended equally from *European* and *African* parents. . . . Upon these distinctions as connected with our laws, the burthen of proof depends. . . .
>
> Suppose three persons, a black or mulatto man or woman with a flat nose and woolly head; a copper-coloured person with long jetty black, straight hair; and one with a fair complexion, brown hair, not woolly nor inclining thereto, with a prominent *Roman* nose, were brought together before a Judge upon a writ of *Habeas Corpus,* on the ground of false imprisonment and detention in slavery: that the only evidence which the person detaining them in his custody could produce was an authenticated bill of sale from another person, and that the parties themselves were unable to produce any evidence concerning themselves, whence they came, &c. &c. How must a Judge act in such a case? I answer he must judge from his own view. He must discharge the white person and the *Indian* out of custody, . . . and he must redeliver the black or mulatto person, with the flat nose and woolly hair to the person claiming to hold him or her as a slave. . . . This case shews my interpretation how far the *onus probandi* may be shifted from one party to the other: and is, I trust, a sufficient comment upon the case to shew that I do not concur with the Chancellor in his reasoning on the operation of the first clause of the Bill of Rights. . . .[20]

[19] 11 Va. at 134.

[20] 11 Va. at 139–41 (Tucker, J.). Roane, J., also wrote individually, and three judges concurred in a brief statement. All made clear that they disapproved the chancellor's placing the burden of

Applying this standard, the plaintiffs in *Hudgins v. Wrights* were correctly given their freedom, since "it is not and cannot be denied that the appellees have entirely the *appearance* of white people."[21] (The chancellor had actually found, "perceiving from his own view, that the youngest of the appellees was perfectly white, and that there were gradual shades of difference in colour between the grand-mother, mother, and grand-daughter." Perhaps this remark explains why the Supreme Court minimized the significance of skin color and chose rather to emphasize hair texture.)[22]

Hudgins v. Wrights marks the moment when the legal concept of race changed from genotype to include also phenotype (appearance); when race ceased to be simply a kind of shorthand for genetic background and became rather a kind of embodied spectacle.

This is the moment in American legal history when race became a legal concept distinct from ethnicity or heredity or any other concept into which some might wish to subsume it. Race was a necessary concept with which to divide people into enslavable and not enslavable. A strictly genetic or biological conception of race would not have served the underlying purpose, so law did not adopt it. To divide the slave from the free, race had to combine the visual with the genetic; in fact, the visual had to dominate the genetic. Once again, law constructs a body to serve a political purpose, and, thereafter, no one can experience her body apart from the bodies of law.

RACE AS A BODY PLUS AN EYE

Race in American law is thus unthinkable without a body and an eye. The body displays race, but only as perceived by the eye of the chancellor, the figure of authority who knows, as Justice Tucker knew, "from his own view," how to read bodies for their racial identity. This kind of race does not offer any scope for "choosing" or "identifying with" a race, for it enacts a scheme of power relations as it surveys the body; only the eye of the chancellor, not the voice of the subject, performs the legal act of racialization.

Law veils its own power in a case like *Hudgins* by pretending to find what it in fact makes itself. Law pretends to be able to allocate burdens of proof because of natural facts about the hair and noses of people in the world: as natural as Renee Rogers' hair before she put it into cornrows. The natural is always and everywhere a social construction, however, and unavailable as a source of differentiation that is found, not made. As the next case shows,

---

proof on the person claiming to hold, as a slave, one of African appearance. A decade earlier, before his appointment to the Supreme Court of Appeals, Tucker had written a proposal for the extremely gradual abolition of slavery. Tucker's views are discussed in Jordan, *White over Black* at 555–60.

[21] 11 Va. at 141 (Roane, J.).

[22] 11 Va. at 134.

racial categorization could not survive a multiplicity of authoritative eyes classifying the people of the world. To be a legal category, race cannot exist "just" in a body; there must be an eye that sees it there. Law constructs racial categories by reifying particular things it sees. The lines drawn when law looks at hair texture and nose shape will not quite correspond to those drawn by skin color, and other tests might be imagined that would vary things more. The absurd peak was *Plessy v. Ferguson,* upholding state-imposed segregation, which insisted simultaneously that racial identity was a function of "physical differences," distinctions "[l]egislation is powerless to . . . abolish," while acknowledging that the definition of "colored person" varied from state to state according to the statutes of each.[23] Law can deny its own agency in differentiation, and domination—for every differentiation is a domination—by assuming the role of the passive eye recording natural variation.

On this account, there is never anything "natural" about race, because the very concept implies a signifying, authoritative eye, which constructs the racial classification of the specularized Other. This corresponds to one possible but not inevitable reading of W. E. B. Du Bois's famous observation:

> [T]he Negro is . . . born with a veil, and gifted with second-sight in this American world,—a world which yields him no true self-consciousness, but only lets him see himself through the revelation of the other world. It is a peculiar sensation, this double-consciousness, this sense of always looking at one's self through the eyes of others, of measuring one's soul by the tape of a world that looks on in amused contempt and pity.[24]

In Adam Lively's paraphrase, "double-consciousness" is here "the existential struggle between the self as a thing in the eyes of others and the self in the limitless, invisible depth of its authenticity."[25]

This "existential" reading of Du Bois raises the question whether race might be an emancipatory concept, if the defining eye were the very eye of the scrutinized body? Is race a system of domination simply because it constructs a body differentiated from other bodies and thus enables or even compels domination? Or does the domination of racial classification inhere in the kind of body it constructs? Does any construction of the body, particularly any legal construction, enact just the same kind of domination—of one forced to see himself or herself through the eye of one with more power and resources? Or do racial divisions have a certain reality, and the domination lie merely in the attribution of power to one but not another race?

[23] Walter Benn Michaels, *Our America: Nativism, Modernism, and Pluralism* 114 (Durham, N.C.: Duke U. Pr., 1995).

[24] W. E. B. Du Bois, *The Souls of Black Folk,* chap. 1, in *Writings* 364 (New York: Library of America, 1986) [1903].

[25] Adam Lively, "The Talented Tenth: The Ambiguous Lives and Works of Jean Toomer and Nella Larsen in a Jim Crow Society," *Times Literary Supplement,* Dec. 30, 1994, at 5.

Du Bois, as we saw above, suggested the last: he could not, as Anthony Appiah has shown, free himself entirely of a somewhat essentialist concept of race. The quoted passage continues:

> One ever feels his two-ness,—an American, a Negro; two souls, two thoughts, two unreconciled strivings; two warring ideals in one dark body, whose dogged strength alone keeps it from being torn asunder.[26]

Adam Lively again: "This immediately obscures what has gone before. . . . Historical act has become timeless essence."[27] Recent critical race scholarship has, however, begun to explore the constructed nature of race and the question of agency in its construction.

AN ALTERNATIVE CONCEPTION: RACE AS EXISTENTIAL SELF-AFFIRMATION

Race has just this constructed, affiliative quality in the works of some of the most interesting fiction writers who identify as African-American. Race is literally constructed in the life and work of Nella Larsen, born into a "colored" family that became "white," and Jean Toomer, born into a "white" family that passed for "colored."[28] Race is existential in a different way when Langston Hughes and Zora Neale Hurston create the very racial identity with which each identifies.[29]

Just this conception of race has been explored recently in the work of scholars who (among other existential identifications) identify with the Critical Race movement. Influenced by Anthony Appiah's social-constructivist notion of race, they often part company from Appiah in favoring, not the avoiding of any talk of race, but the self-conscious selection of racial terms as acts of identification or affiliation.[30]

For example, Cheryl I. Harris does not end her brilliant dissection of "Whiteness as Property" with a call for the abolition or socialization of all property claims in race. Law also errs when it "refuse[s] to recognize group identity when asserted by racially oppressed groups as a basis for affirming or

---

[26] Du Bois, *Souls of Black Folk* 364–65.

[27] Lively, "The Talented Tenth."

[28] Thadious M. Davis, *Nella Larsen, Novelist of the Harlem Renaissance: A Woman's Life Unveiled* (Baton Rouge: La. St. U. Pr., 1994); Charles R. Larson, *Invisible Darkness: Jean Toomer and Nella Larsen* (Iowa City: Ia. U. Pr., 1993). On the more normal "passing" into whiteness like Nella Larsen's family's, see the extraordinarily powerful accounts in Cheryl I. Harris, "Whiteness as Property," 106 *Harv. L. Rev.* 1707, 1710–13 (1993); Patricia J. Williams, "On Being the Object of Property," in *The Alchemy of Race and Rights* 216, 223 (Cambridge: Harv. U. Pr., 1991); Judy Scales-Trent, *Notes of a White Black Woman: Race, Color, Community* (University Park: Penn. St. U. Pr., 1995).

[29] Michaels, *Our America* 85–94.

[30] See David A. Hollinger, *Postethnic America: Beyond Multiculturalism* 6–8 and passim (New York: Basic Books, 1995) on why "affiliation" is better than "identity": "Affiliation is more performative, while identity suggests something that simply is."

claiming rights"; the deprivileging of whiteness is to come, not in the property claims of mythical Lockean individuals, but in affirmative action. "Black identity is not the functional opposite of whiteness. Even today, whiteness is still intertwined with the degradation of Blacks and is still valued because 'the artifact of "whiteness" . . . sets a floor on how far [whites] can fall.' Acknowledging Black identity does not involve the systematic subordination of whites, nor does it even set up a danger of doing so."[31]

Similarly, Jayne Chong-Soon Lee, in her review of Appiah's book, notes, "When we claim that racial difference precedes the law, however, we obscure the role of the law in constructing these differences." She notes, for example, how in voting rights cases "race" might mean skin color, or experiences of past discrimination. But while she applauds Appiah's denaturalizing of race, she does not adopt his suggestion that we replace *race* with *culture* in our own talk. "Because the meaning of race is constructed by the social contexts in which it is located, there can be no consistent content to race. . . . The constantly shifting topology of race requires us to acknowledge that 'race' can be defined in many different ways, and that all of these ways, even biological and essential conceptions of race, have their place in antiracist struggles."[32] Ian F. Haney López has recently defended such a concept of social race.[33] D. Marvin Jones similarly acknowledges Appiah's influence yet wants also to find "new terms" for "discerning both a sense of race as it appears in our historical consciousness—massive, immovable, and real—and a sense of race as trope."[34]

I obviously find these accounts deeply congenial. This is a particularly good place to reiterate that the aim of this book is not the smoking out and extirpation of incorrect ways of representing the body, but the encouraging of a

[31] Harris, "Whiteness as Property," 1761–91; the quoted sentences are at 1761 and 1785, and the internal quotation in the second sentence is from Andrew Hacker, *Two Nations: Black and White, Separate, Hostile, Unequal* 217 (New York: Scribner's, 1992).

[32] Jayne Chong-Soon Lee, "Navigating the Topology of Race," 46 *Stan. L. Rev.* 747, 750, 779 (1994).

[33] Haney López, "Social Construction of Race." This is a good overview of the literature and a well-argued brief for a continuing concept of race that includes large elements of social fabrication and some scope for individual choice. For most of Haney López's examples of "race," I would normally say "ethnic" or "community" affiliation. (David Hollinger suggests "ethno-racial bloc." *Postethnic America* 9). Haney López rejects (at 19–24) this terminology, largely because he believes that it commits the user to a view that African-Americans or Asian-Americans will "follow the same trajectory of incorporation into American society" of European-American immigrant groups. This just seems like a non sequitur to me. However, as a philosophic pragmatist I can't reject remarks like Haney López's out of hand. The meaning of the term *ethnic community,* like that of the term *race,* for me is just the consequences of using it, and if using the term has the bad consequences that Haney López claims, we ought to find another. I doubt that *race* is it, however.

[34] D. Marvin Jones, "Darkness Made Visible: Law, Metaphor, and the Racial Self," 82 *Geo. L. J.* 437, 508 (1993).

multiplicity of body constructions in the service of human coexistence, under-standing, and empowerment. My goal precisely is to proliferate *so many* dis-cursive representations of the body that none might ever be understood as natural, all instead understood as strategic interventions, self-conscious meta-phors. The property body has, historically, sometimes been a legal performa-tive (the slave is property) but has also, as we saw, been a claim for human freedom and autonomy, though a claim with a particular grammar. Affirming that my body is my property may support my right to sell my organs, or (were I a woman) my right to an abortion. Affirming that my body is a machine may be autism or may be a critique against the dehumanization of industrial factories.

Similarly, there is a liberation involved in the affirmance that a particular body is of a particular race. It might be a politically conservative project to extirpate all talk of race or claims of racial identity, but it is no part of my project at all, which is rather the multiplication of constructions of the body.[35] For example, there exists a movement with politically conservative spin to abolish the section of the census form in which individuals designate their race from a list of categories. From my perspective, this is the most benign of all invocations of race since it is necessarily an act of self-affirmation. (One might question the highly restricted "ethno-racial pentagon—distinctive to the contemporary United States," as David Hollinger calls it, in which every American is *one* of the following: white, African American, Hispanic, Asian American, or Native American. Like Hollinger, I think official discourse should let Alex Haley and Ishmael Reed "be both African American and Irish American without having to choose one to the exclusion of the other.")[36]

Anthony Appiah, in a Tanner lecture given after the publication of his book, explored the idea of a "racial identity," made clear that he did not advocate the replacement of racial claims with cultural claims, but also argued that "there is a danger in making racial identities too central to our conceptions of our-selves." Race is not totally a matter of individual choice; most people can't "pass," and most Americans are unproblematically ascribed races by the eye of others. Racial identities grow in dialogue with a larger culture; they are never generated entirely within themselves. Finally, racial identities may pro-vide the basis for a kind of existential assertion of identity but can never exhaust that process.

> [I]f one is to be black in a society that is racist then one has constantly to deal with assaults on one's dignity. In this context, insisting on the right to live a dignified life will not be enough. It will not even be enough to require that one be

---

[35] Critiques of attempts to eliminate racial claims from law include, in addition to the works cited earlier in this chapter, Patricia Williams, "The Obliging Shell," 87 *Mich. L. Rev.* 2128, 2141–43 (1989).

[36] Hollinger, *Postethnic America* 21–24.

treated with equal dignity despite being black; for that will require a concession that being black counts naturally or to some degree against one's dignity. And so one will end up asking to be respected *as a black*.

I hope I seem sympathetic to this story. I *am* sympathetic. I see how the story goes. It may even be historically, strategically necessary for the story to go this way. But I think we need to go on to the next necessary step, which is to ask whether the identities constructed in this way are ones we can all be happy with in the longer run.[37]

One implication of Appiah's concept of racial identity that he does not point out is the disappearance of the body. Despite his efforts, he has once again subsumed race into culture; his racial identities do not differ from cultural identities. I have been arguing that racial identities are precisely ascribed *bodies*.

However, my embodied version of race, like Appiah's disembodied version, may serve as the basis of identity claims expressed through the body, since, as I have been arguing throughout, bodies are *made* and do not serve well as symbols of the immutable. Is it possible that racial bodies might ever be experienced in this (or Appiah's) "postmodern" way, as the representations of contingency, like the bodies of bodybuilders or body piercers or adoptees of particular hairstyles?

I would like to take up Appiah's challenge by returning to the legal history of embodied racial-identity claims. The Jewish body is an interesting test case of Appiah's views. I raise this suggestion with considerable trepidation; I know how sensitive many African-Americans are to comparison with Jews. I discuss the Jewish body for two precise reasons, neither having anything to do with whether Jews are a model minority or not. First, I am Jewish, so this gives me a body to discuss that is less problematically "mine," once we admit the metaphor of possession at all. Second, and more important, the Jewish body is an interesting test case of a construction that has lost a great deal of meaning in a very short time. In a short historical time, Jewish identity has evolved from a constructed body, that is, a racial identity in my terms, though a racial identity neither comfortably "white" or "nonwhite," to a more existential identity. It suggests that Appiah is correct that a road to human liberation may lead through racial, that is body, identity, to a consciousness precisely of the contingency of the body, and that such an evolution is historically feasible.

WHOSE EYE DEFINES THE RACIAL BODY?: BLACK BODIES, JEWISH BODIES

The eye of the chancellor may be seen to be an indispensable part of the construction of the racial body, if we examine an early-twentieth-century ex-

---

[37] K. Anthony Appiah and Amy Gutmann, *Color Conscious: The Political Morality of Race* 98–99 (Princeton: Princeton U. Pr., 1996).

ample of the construction of racial difference, in the service of Jim Crow segregation of railroads.

In July 1910, Rella Ritchel, age twenty, was forcibly ejected by a conductor from the white car of a train and made to ride in the colored car. The conductor testified that he had taken up Ritchel's ticket, but then received a complaint from another passenger that there was a "colored lady back there," and on looking at Ritchel more carefully, believed that she was a colored person. Ritchel did not dispute the conductor's belief, although she did claim to have offered to show him papers, which he rejected, that would have established her racial identity. (The conductor denied that she had offered him papers).

Rella Ritchel however was "Jewess" from Kiev, "Russia" (today, Ukraine). She had emigrated to Iowa at the age of nine and in 1910 taught English in the public schools of Kokomo, Indiana, and worked in the summer as a traveling representative for the Central Lyceum Bureau of Indianapolis, visiting schools and colleges to book speakers from the Bureau. Witnesses corroborated her rough handling by the conductor and her collapse in nerves and health after the incident. Witnesses also testified "that she was a young lady of refinement and education, and always associated with the white race." (The relevance of this statement was that the conductor had testified, in support of his belief that Ritchel was colored, that a passenger had reported to him that Ritchel had been standing talking to a colored man when the train pulled into the station. Ritchel claimed this was the porter.) Her witnesses also testified that "while she was a person of dark complexion and dark hair and eyes, her features were characteristic of the Jewish race, and bore no resemblance to those of a person of the colored race."

The jury awarded Ritchel $3,750, and the Kentucky Court of Appeals affirmed this judgment.[38] While the conductor no doubt genuinely believed Ritchel to be colored, racial bodies cannot be racialized by just anyone. The eye of the chancellor, not the train conductor, gets to do the racial sorting. Race is an attribute of the body's visual display, but only the eye of the law may authoritatively interpret that display and thus bestow racial identity. Once again, law constructs what it purports to find. There can be no raced bodies without the authoritative eye to bestow, not ascribe, race. (In the contemporary legal order, as Christopher A. Ford has recently shown with care and skill, the authoritative eye is likely to be an "aresponsible" bureaucrat in a federal agency.)[39]

A comprehensive history of race in American law would want to ask many questions of this fascinating case, not least the source of the "nervous shock" Ritchel suffered, and what must have been the ambivalence with which four "colored persons" who had been riding in the colored coach testified to

[38] Louisville and N.R. Co. v. Ritchel, 147 S.W. 411 (Ky. 1912).
[39] Ford, "Administering Identity."

Ritchel's rough treatment. In this study of the construction of the body in legal
discourse, I want only to raise, over the body of Rella Ritchel, the question
Sander Gilman asks in his book *The Jew's Body:* "are Jews white? and what
does 'white' mean in this context?"[40] How did Rella Ritchel get to be a white
woman?

Jews, by self-description, originated in the Near East; spent generations as
immigrants to North Africa; then returned to the Near East, later to be dispersed throughout the Mediterranean and thence, in Ritchel's family's case, to
the Black Sea.[41] Yet Jews are not characteristically classified either as Asian-
or African-Americans. Why?

As Gilman shows, the answer to this is not obvious. "The general consensus
of the ethnological literature of the late nineteenth century was that Jews were
'black' or, at least, 'swarthy.' This view had a long history in European science." Of course, anti-Semitism in one form or another has probably existed
as long as Jews have. Only in the eighteenth century, however, with the general discovery of the modern, specularized body, did religious intolerance
become racial intolerance. By the time of the development of scientific racism
in the nineteenth century, most people who thought seriously about racial
matters saw Jews as dark-skinned, full-lipped, big-nosed. In a scene that
sounds as if it came from a Mel Brooks comedy, Adam Gurowski, a Polish
noble, was amazed on visiting the United States in the 1850s to see Jews
everywhere he turned. He had to be told that he was seeing "light-colored
mulatto[s]."[42]

WORLD WITHOUT RACE; OR, WHATEVER HAPPENED TO THE JEWISH FOOT?

I raise the history of the Jewish body in this context to show not only the
constructed, nonbiological character of racial classification, but more importantly, in order to end this brief discussion on a hopeful note. For, as Gilman
shows, the normal way of thinking about the Jewish body, at least in the
German-speaking world around the turn of the twentieth century, was as a
distinct racial type, set apart from Germans by observable criteria. The hopeful note is how much of the discursive construction of the Jewish body at the
turn of the twentieth century has absolutely no meaning for us today.

Gilman's chapter on "The Jewish Foot" illustrates the point. In German-
speaking countries in the early twentieth century, everyone who thought seri-

[40] Sander Gilman, *The Jew's Body* 170 (New York: Routledge, 1991).

[41] "On the shores of the Black Sea, there were born a pair of Siamese twins called 'civilization' and 'barbarism.' This is where Greek colonists met the Scythians . . . in this particular
encounter began the idea of 'Europe' with all its arrogance, all its implications of superiority, all
its assumptions of priority and antiquity, all its pretensions to a natural right to dominate." Neal
Ascherson, *Black Sea* 49 (New York: Hill and Wang, 1995).

[42] Gilman, *The Jew's Body* 171–74.

ously about the problem was convinced that Jews had weak, flat feet that rendered them incapable of military service. This belief has origins in medieval legend. Anti-Semitic propaganda of the 1920s attempted to prove statistically that Jews had avoided military service in the world war because of their feet. Jewish physicians defended Jews but did not challenge the basic premise that Jews had weak feet. Jews debated whether the "problem" should be solved by different athletic training for Jewish children, such as gymnastics; or by surgery, or ending the misuse of the foot in urban society; or whether Jews didn't limp because of psychological or neurological reasons, as a sort of hysteria.[43]

Perhaps some readers recall echoes of this debate, but I am happy to report that Gilman's discussion was news to me. I had been completely unaware that there had ever been a racial construction called "the Jewish foot." The problem and its solutions all seemed equally unreal to me, and to the students with whom I have read this book.

Now the funny thing is that, for all we know, the statistical studies were right. Perhaps Jews in the first third of the century really did suffer disproportionately from limps, flat feet, and the like. *Perhaps they still do.* It is ideology or collective mentality, not biology, that led German and Austrian Jews and Gentiles to "see" the Jewish foot, while today, at least for me and I suspect for most others, the phrase "Jewish foot" simply has no meaning.

Today it seems impossible that Americans could live in a world without race. Even people who believe that members of all races should be treated alike are normally as confident as Judge St. George Tucker that they can distinguish visually among Africans, whites, Indians, that these observable differences have a social meaning.

The lesson of the story of the Jewish foot is that observable biological differences do not compel either that we "see" difference or not. Is it possible to imagine a future America that discursively constructed skin color and hair texture as "normal" human variations, just as America now discursively constructs foot shape or belt size? In such an America, "African hair" would sound as funny as "Jewish foot," again, not because there was "no such thing" in a statistical sense, but because the statistical variations would have lost any social meaning. People would market combs for thick hair just as they market gymnastics equipment today, without regard to which identifiable social groups needed it more, even if some groups did (in a statistical sense). People could and would assert pride in their ancestors, their families, their cultural traditions. But their bodies would just not be the sorts of things in which people could express pride. It would be like expressing pride in the order of vowels in one's family name.

Under the alternative conception of the body that we have been developing,

---

[43] Gilman, *The Jew's Body* 38–59.

there are no bodies, there are only persons and discursive artifacts. The body is never beyond or under discourse but holds its discursive creation in front of it wherever it walks, so that it would never be possible to imagine the body as natural. A statement about races, or about "looking different than" someone, could only be heard as a performative that creates a particular discursive body, never as a description. Moreover, because everyone would know that "the body" was a discursive artifact, employed to make metaphorically present another person, an invocation of a particular discursive body would automatically invoke all the alternative conceptions, like the joke about the injunction "Don't think about an elephant." In this way of thinking, we could never hate the body of another, because we would always understand the body as a discursive construction. Thus, we could never bring any body to consciousness except as an experience of our own creative agency, an examination of our own self-consciousness. Nor could we love the body of another. Love of the body would not merely be, but also be experienced as, a kind of self-love, a Don Quixote mistaking his own fantasy for reality. We would be condemned to love persons, not bodies.

Chapter 14

DISEASED BODIES: ANTIBODIES AND ANTI-BODIES

THE CANONICAL CONSTRUCTION of a diseased body in American law concerns a body subject to compulsory inoculation against smallpox. There is, by contrast, no canonical legal text constructing the body with AIDS—indeed, the United States Supreme Court has yet to utter the acronym in any opinion—so we will not be examining the enormous literature, associated with cultural studies, on the construction of AIDS in popular culture and medical language.[1]

The total eradication of smallpox is one of the few genuine achievements of this benighted century. Smallpox, "in terms of the sheer numbers of people killed, blinded, crippled, pitted and scarred . . . for at least two thousand years of oral and written history . . . was most probably the worst pestilence ever to afflict humankind."[2] No cure is known for it to this day. Nevertheless, through universal vaccination, the disease is now entirely gone from the face of the earth, except for small quantities of the virus kept frozen in the United States and Russia, to be either destroyed or used for medical research on viruses.[3] I must say that I have always found extremely comforting the image of the last remnants of the virus frozen and imprisoned.

Law schools do not normally study the eradication of smallpox. It illustrates none of the modalities of human interaction that normally interest lawyers. The market did not provide a vaccine. Somehow smallpox was eradicated without anybody making much money out of it. There was probably not a single donation to a law school of money made by eradicating smallpox. Lawyers did not have to create novel organizational forms to reduce agency costs. Public funds, public agencies, and inspired public servants, few of them lawyers, managed to achieve one of the rare unqualified advances in daily life. Why study the campaign against smallpox? Why teach lawyers about cooperation through public regulation where there is little money to be made?

---

[1] Recent English criminal cases are interestingly analyzed in Carl F. Stychin, "Unmanly Diversions: The Construction of the Homosexual Body (Politic) in English Law," 32 *Osgoode Hall L. J.* 503 (1994).

[2] Allan Chase, *Magic Shots: A Human and Scientific Account of the Long and Continuing Struggle to Eradicate Infectious Diseases by Vaccination* 51 (New York: Wm. Morrow, 1982).

[3] Charles Diebert, "Smallpox Is Dead. Long Live Smallpox," *New York Times Magazine,* August 21, 1994, at 30.

THE MISSING BODY OF HENNING JACOBSON

American vaccination campaigns did, however, produce some litigation on whether the government could compel people to be vaccinated, the Supreme Court eventually holding that it could. That case, *Jacobson v. Massachusetts,*[4] is to this day an absolutely standard citation for the proposition that individuals' right to control their own bodies is not absolute and may be subject to public demands; it is cited for that purpose in many decisions on abortion, including *Roe v. Wade*.[5] For all the theoretical importance of the case as a justification for public transgression of the boundary of the body, its language has rarely been studied.

I began with my emotional identification with the eradication of smallpox to make it as clear as possible that I do not regard *Jacobson* as incorrectly decided. As I have mentioned, it is impossible to imagine organized society without some social use of the body, and, like the Supreme Court, I sometimes start my own reasoning process about legitimate and illegitimate "invasions" of the body from this core case of compulsory inoculation.

The Supreme Court upheld the criminal conviction of Henning Jacobson for violating a Cambridge, Massachusetts, law requiring vaccination against smallpox. The vaccine with which Cambridge, in February 1902, required all persons to be injected was not novel; it was more or less what Edward Jenner had developed a century earlier and many Western European countries had required for almost that long. In the winter of 1901–2 a smallpox epidemic in New York City resulted in 3,480 reported cases and 720 deaths, and this boosted local vaccination campaigns.

The report of the case is totally uninformative about Henning Jacobson, and why he refused to be inoculated, partly because the trial court would not let him prove, as he had offered, that he and his son had each suffered long disease in reaction to vaccination. An active antivaccination movement has existed whenever vaccination occurs; at the time of the *Jacobson* case, an Anti-Vaccination League of America was well supported by John Pitcairn, a Scottish-born oil, railroad, and plate glass magnate in Pennsylvania who in 1911 was appointed to head that state's Vaccination Commission. The movement included doctors who pursued alternative therapies, those who feared the consequences of the virus, some who felt sanitation was more important than vaccination, and all-purpose reformers such as George Bernard Shaw, but whether or not it included Henning Jacobson I have been unable to learn.[6] It is also said that resistance to vaccination at the turn of the century was partic-

---

[4] Jacobson v. Massachusetts, 197 U.S. 11 (1905).

[5] 410 U.S. 113, 154 (1973).

[6] Chase, *Magic Shots* 61–75; Joel N. Shurkin, *The Invisible Fire: The Story of Mankind's Victory over the Ancient Scourge of Smallpox* 214 (New York: G. P. Putnam's, 1979); Charles M. Higgins, *Horrors of Vaccination Exposed and Illustrated: Petition to the President to Abolish Compulsory Vaccination in the Army and Navy* (Brooklyn: published by the author, 1921).

ularly strong among recent immigrants from northern Europe, even from countries such as Germany that had required compulsory vaccination for years, but the report of the case does not disclose whether Jacobson was an immigrant.[7] The disappearance of Henning Jacobson from the case bearing his name is, as we shall see, significant; it is part of the discursive construction of his body, which enacts and performs inoculation by making the body disappear.

An Anachronistically Modern Discursive Construction: Jacobson's Body as Privacy Interest

The interest of the *Jacobson* case lies in the discursive process through which the unvaccinated body of Henning Jacobson is constituted a threat to society.

The modern reader assumes that she can reconstruct that discourse. It would be the unusual modern American lawyer who would reason in any way except to posit a liberty or privacy interest in Jacobson to control his own body, which is balanced against a compelling state interest in eradicating disease and protecting the healthy from it, the latter state interest outweighing Jacobson's liberty interest.[8]

What is so interesting about *Jacobson* is that it does not employ that discourse at all. This is not because it was unthinkable, given the date of the case. It is true that constitutional opinions of the *Jacobson* era did not ordinarily "balance."[9] However, they did define categorical "rights" and "liberties." Indeed, Jacobson argued precisely for his liberty to resist vaccination and urged the Court to establish such a liberty.[10] This assertion of a liberty, "an inherent right of every freeman to care for his own body and health in such way as to him seems best,"[11] garnered only a dissent without opinion from two of the Court's stalwart defenders of "substantive due process."[12]

The Court could have affirmed Jacobson's conviction by, as the modern mind would have it, assuming his liberty interest *arguendo* but finding it outweighed by state interest. In fact, the Court did not yield on the question of Jacobson's liberty. "But the liberty secured by the Constitution of the United

---

[7] Donald R. Hopkins, *Princes and Peasants: Smallpox in History* 282 (Chicago: U. Chi. Pr., 1983).

[8] See, e.g., Justice John Paul Stevens, "The Bill of Rights: A Century of Progress," 59 *U. Chi. L. Rev.* 13, 31 n. 62 (1992) (describing *Jacobson* as a balancing test).

[9] T. Alexander Aleinikoff, "Constitutional Law in the Age of Balancing," 96 *Yale L. J.* 943, 948–52 (1987) (balancing appears in 1930s).

[10] 197 U.S. at 14, 26.

[11] 197 U.S. at 26.

[12] Justices Brewer and Peckham, both of whom had been part of the five-to-four majority in *Lochner v. New York*, dissented without opinion. 197 U.S. at 39. (*Lochner* is discussed in chapter 2.) Justices Brewer and Peckham are explored as progenitors of the modern rights revolution in Owen M. Fiss, *Troubled Beginnings of the Modern State, 1888–1910* passim and 32–37 (New York: Macmillan, 1993).

States to every person within its jurisdiction does not import an absolute right in each person to be, at all times and in all circumstances, wholly freed from restraint."[13]

Later on in the opinion, the Court spoke as if there might be some sort of residual right or liberty being balanced. "[T]he rights of the individual in respect of his liberty may at times, under the pressure of great dangers, be subjected to such restraint, to be enforced by reasonable regulations, as the safety of the general public may demand."[14] However, the Court nowhere specified any such right that might apply in Jacobson's case: not a general right to bodily control, or a specific right to medical decision-making, or a right to resist intrusion. At the least, then, *Jacobson* does not clearly adopt the modern framework of separating the "liberty" from the "public interest," and then balancing them. It does not clearly distinguish between invoking public needs in order to define or even eliminate a right, and "balancing" the two.

This may appear to be just a quibble about labels until one reads the rest of the opinion in *Jacobson*. The truly embarrassing thing about the case to modern eyes is that Jacobson had not been permitted at his criminal trial to introduce medical evidence of "alleged injurious or dangerous effects of vaccination."[15] The vaccines used at Jacobson's time would indeed have had side effects and were often contaminated with the bacilli that caused tetanus, although shortly after the date of the case Koch's discovery that glycerin would inhibit bacterial growth was put into practice.[16] Moreover, as mentioned above, Jacobson apparently offered to show that he and his son had been ill in the past after vaccination but was not permitted to introduce evidence to this effect. The Court found no constitutional problem in nevertheless affirming his conviction under these circumstances. This seems more consistent with the view that the Court recognized no "liberty" or right of bodily control at all, for, if the Court really set up a balancing test, how could that balance be conducted in the absence of evidence of the likely impact of vaccination on Jacobson?

Nine Bodies in *Jacobson v. Massachusetts*

So the interest of the *Jacobson* case is not its result, but in the script it provides for constituting the legal body as a threat without rights, indeed, without even a body.[17]

[13] 197 U.S. at 26.
[14] 197 U.S. at 29.
[15] 197 U.S. at 23.
[16] Chase, *Magic Shots* 75.
[17] The analysis that follows draws in part on ideas in Daryl Lee, "The Court's Three Bodies: The Human Body, the Constitutional Corpus, and the Body Politic in *Jacobson v. Massachusetts*" (seminar paper).

The word "body" (or "bodies") appears nine times in the opinion. Not one of these appearances refers to the body of Henning Jacobson. Rather, "body" refers to the text of the Constitution, agencies of government, or an abstract and universal entity subject to disease. Body in *Jacobson* then is a metaphor, used to establish a political hierarchy of meaning and reference among these three images.

The first appearance in the opinion of the word body is in the opening paragraph, which denies the validity of any argument based on the Preamble of the Constitution, which "has never been regarded as the source of any substantive power conferred on the Government of the United States or on any of its Departments. Such powers embrace only those expressly granted in the *body* [1] of the Constitution."[18] The Constitution has a body. Indeed, the Constitution has more than the *word* body. It has a discursive body-as-system, constituent parts integrated systematically, an image often employed to describe the natural world, the political order, or the human body.[19] The Constitution might as well have a text, or main part, or articles, or a structure or other architectural or engineering analogy, or machinery, engine and gears, or mime some example of human solidarity like a team, marriage, family. Why—under what political theory and to what political purpose—does the Constitution have a body? To emphasize the dependence of each part on another? To show that there is no life outside it? To contrast specifically with the absent body of Henning Jacobson, as if to state that the life of his legal body derives from the primordial body of the Constitution, not Jacobson's self?

The second (also fourth, fifth, and eighth) body belongs to the government: "the State may invest local *bodies* [2] called into existence for purposes of local administration with authority in some appropriate way to safeguard the public health and the public safety."[20] This is the most frequent use of the word body in the opinion. It recurs when "The authority to determine for all

[18] 197 U.S. at 22.

[19] On the pervasiveness of the body as a metaphor for the natural or social order, see Leonard Barkan, *Nature's Work of Art: The Human Body as Image of the World* (New Haven: Yale U. Pr., 1975); David Hale, *The Body Politic: A Political Metaphor in Renaissance English Literature* (The Hague: Mouton, 1971); Elaine Scarry, *The Body in Pain: The Making and Unmaking of the World* (New York: Oxford U. Pr., 1985) (all manufactured objects, concepts, and texts as extensions of the body); Susan Sontag, *Illness as Metaphor and AIDS and Its Metaphors* 72–94 (New York: Anchor, 1990) (body as metaphor for political order, e.g. at 94: "the perennial description of society as a kind of body, a well-disciplined body ruled by a 'head.' This has been the dominant metaphor for the polity since Plato and Aristotle, perhaps because of its usefulness in justifying repression. Even more than comparing society to a family, comparing it to a body makes an authoritarian ordering of society seem inevitable, immutable"); Peter Stallybrass and Allon White, *The Politics and Poetics of Transgression* 3–5 (1986) (Ithaca: Cornell U. Pr.) (study of "high/low" oppositions in four "symbolic domains": "psychic forms, the human body, geographical space and the social order": "Divisions and discriminations in one domain are continually structured, legitimated and dissolved by reference to the vertical symbolic hierarchy which operates in the other three domains").

[20] 197 U.S. at 25.

what ought to be done in such an emergency must have been lodged somewhere or in some *body* [4]; and surely it was appropriate for the legislature to
refer that question, in the first instance, to a Board of Health, composed of
persons residing the in the locality affected and appointed, presumably, because of their fitness to determine such questions. To invest such a *body* [5]
with authority over such matters was not an unusual nor an unreasonable or
arbitrary requirement. *Upon the principle of self-defense, of paramount necessity, a community has the right to protect itself against an epidemic of disease
which threatens the safety of its members.*"[21]

This is a remarkable and complex passage. The public authority has a body
because it is personified; it acquires at the same time a right of self-defense
that might otherwise have attached only to a legal subject. By mimetic dis-
placement, the right of self-defense migrates from the body of an individual to
the public body, invested with authority. The individual legal subject is now
discursively a "member," that is, a body part, of the larger, organic body. Of
course, the larger body, the Cambridge Board of Health, is a discursive and
not a natural body, a point emphasized earlier in the opinion, in the paragraph
from which I quoted at the start of the preceding paragraph ("the State may
invest local bodies . . ."). For that paragraph argues that the State may do this
investing under its "police power—a power which the State did not surrender
when becoming a *member* of the Union under the Constitution."[22] What the
"police power" authorizes is precisely "the authority of a State to enact *quarantine* laws and 'health laws of every description'; indeed all laws that relate
to matters completely *within its territory*" and not affecting the people of other
states.[23] That is, the state is itself a member, a body, and a body with space
and boundaries, occupying physical space in the world as it exercises agency
in the world. Its police power, we learn through a body metaphor employed in
the next sentence, "must be held to embrace" public health and safety.

We know, then, that bodies are discursive, not natural, because under different discursive constructions the same entity may be embodied, or may be a
member of a larger discursive body. The individual legal subject may be embodied or a member. The Cambridge Board of Health may be a body or a
member, and so may the Commonwealth of Massachusetts, and the
Constitution.

In saying all this, the Supreme Court enacts and performs its own embodying authority: it does not merely report facts about the world, but actively

---

[21] 197 U.S. at 27 (emphasis supplied). The same figure reappears when "body" is used for the
eighth and final time: "the police power of a State, whether exercised by the legislature, or by a
local *body* acting under its authority . . ." 197 U.S. at 33–34. Here the Cambridge Board of Health
not only has a body, it is a sort of bottom sexual partner that acts *under* the *authority* of the
Commonwealth of Massachusetts.

[22] 197 U.S. at 25 (emphasis supplied).

[23] 197 U.S. at 29 (emphasis supplied).

makes and remakes bodies and members, so in each case demonstrates, establishes, signifies its own powers as it points to the relevant body. The language is not merely descriptive of the constitutional scheme but performative; it structures the reality it purports to describe and locates the judge and the Supreme Court itself in a long chain of performative speech that ritually reenacts its own power to embody or disembody.[24] So the body metaphor naturalizes hierarchy in two related ways: it imagines the state as a body of systematized, hierarchical parts; and it simultaneously performs the Supreme Court's function in constructing, by interpellation, the hierarchy of members of the national body politic.

The third, sixth, seventh, and ninth appearances of "body" refer to a human body, as opposed to a constitution or governmental agency. The body, however, is not Henning Jacobson's:

> The defendant insists that his liberty is invaded when the State subjects him to fine or imprisonment for neglecting or refusing to submit to vaccination; that a compulsory vaccination law is unreasonable, arbitrary, and oppressive, and, therefore, hostile to the inherent right of every freeman to care for his own *body* [3] and health in such way as to him seems best. . . . It is not, therefore, true that the power of the public to guard itself against imminent danger depends in every case involving the control of one's *body* [6] upon his willingness to submit to reasonable regulations established by the constituted authorities, under the sanction of the State, for the purpose of protecting the public collectively against such danger. . . . [Defendant's rejected offers of proof] in the main seem to have had no purpose except to state the general theory of those of the medical profession who attach little or no value to vaccination as a means of preventing the spread of smallpox or who think that vaccination causes other diseases of the *body* [7]. . . . It is easy, for instance, to suppose the case of an adult who is embraced by the mere words of the act, but yet to subject whom to vaccination in a particular condition of his health or *body* [9], would be cruel and inhuman in the last degree.[25]

These are human bodies. But they are not the body of Henning Jacobson, with whatever fears, allergies, bad reactions, and so forth were "in" that body. (The ninth body is expressly *not* the body of Henning Jacobson.) They are, rather, abstract human bodies, abstract bearers of rights belonging to all "free-

---

[24] Cf. Judith Butler, *Bodies That Matter: On the Discursive Limits of "Sex"* 107 (New York: Routledge, 1993) (judge "installed in the midst of a signifying chain, receiving and reciting the law and, in the reciting, echoing forth the authority of the law. When the law functions as ordinance or sanction, it operates as an imperative that brings into being that which it legally enjoins and protects. The performative speaking of the law, an 'utterance' that is most often within legal discourse inscribed in a book of laws, works only by reworking a set of already operative conventions. And these conventions are grounded in no other legitimizing authority than the echo-chain of their own reinvocation").

[25] 197 U.S. at 26, 29, 30, 38–39.

men," a group of human bodies that is larger than Jacobson alone, though not coextensive with humanity, some of whom (not "freemen") might have property bodies that bear different, or no, rights. Jacobson's particular body, however, is never discursively constructed in the opinion, and his rights may be invoked, like other liberal rights, only inasmuch as he is divested of his particularity and rearticulated as a member of an abstracted collective.

The Court discursively *creates, enacts, performs* these "human" bodies every bit as effectively as it enacts and performs the body of the Constitution or the bodies of local government. In fact, the abstract human bodies *mime* the governmental bodies more than they reflect Jacobson's: they are abstract, general, and public.

IS BODY TO SPIRIT AS THE LETTER OF THE LAW IS TO SPIRIT?

These "human" bodies may mimetically represent the legal text itself. Consider the last excerpt quoted, the Court's ninth and final "body."[26] That a person can be "embraced" by an act, no less by its "mere words," jumps out at even the casual reader. Even though the case is imagining how the act's words may not fit the empirical reference, that it suggests the teasing embrace of the act is mildly funny: the Court is implying that the temptation posed by the seductive embrace of language should be spurned because "cruel and inhuman."

Giving the "words" of a statute a body that "embraces" is not a casual metaphor. The statute has a body because, like a human, its body stands opposed to spirit or intent or mind. I argued in the Introduction that *any* invocation of "body" necessarily implicates at least this opposition. Moreover, the Court claims to be able to transcend "mere words" in order to touch intention. In stating this conclusion, the Court cuddles a phrase from an earlier decision: "It will always, therefore, be presumed that the legislature intended exceptions to its language which would avoid results of [unjust, oppressive, or absurd] character. *The reason of the law in such cases should prevail over its letter.*"[27]

Does the Court deliver on this promise? How successfully does this very legal text practice the privileging of reason over letter? This is most relevant to the discursive construction of the body, for the very distinction, spirit of the statute/letter of the statute, must itself be fashioned after the Hellenistic–Judeo-Christian spirit/body. So the Court's construction and depriviling of the letter of the law, and that letter's false embrace, is clearly a kind of construction and depriviling of the desired body, too. The Court purports to privilege spirit over letter, in just the same way it privileges mind over body.

---

[26] The next three paragraphs are taken with minor modification from Lee, "The Court's Three Bodies."

[27] 197 U.S. at 39, quoting United States v. Kirby, U.S. (7 Wall.) 482 (1868).

But the case had already raised the issue of intention, words, and the spirit, immediately following the first appearance of the word "body," cited above. Immediately after rejecting Jacobson's argument from the Preamble to the Constitution, the Court likewise rejected an argument that the Massachusetts vaccination statute

> is opposed to the spirit of the Constitution. Undoubtedly, as observed by Chief Justice Marshall, speaking for the court in Sturges v. Crowninshield, 4 Wheat. 122, 202, "the spirit of an instrument, especially of a constitution, is to be respected not less than its letter, yet the spirit is to be collected chiefly from its words." We have no need in this case to go beyond the plain, obvious meaning of the words in those provisions of the Constitution which, it is contended, must control our decision.

An apparent contradiction: in the concluding remarks, intention exceeds language, reason goes beyond letter; whereas what we read at the beginning says something entirely different.

The Court *construes* legal texts that are sometimes bodies subordinate to spirit and sometimes bodies that control, if not indeed constitute, spirit. The whole matter must be carefully watched, for the texts may falsely embrace a man, even when the seductive embrace is cruel and false. Similarly, the Court *constructs* bodies with the same teasing, ambiguous relationship to spirit, bodies that may tease us, seduce us, falsely alluring, desirable, but, ultimately to be tamed, if body yields to reason. The Court promises us that it can put reason where body was, not yield to the poisoned embrace. Yet it disappoints us in this very promise, for in the very same text it lets the words of the text hold us in their embrace, casting reason and spirit away.

The Abjected Diseased Body

Having appropriated the word *body* to represent the Constitution, government, abstract right; having represented its own authoritative power to make bodies as a "member" of the hierarchy of the "body politic"; having performatively represented its own ambiguous, weak response to the seductions of legal words, the Court, in perhaps the most enduring contribution of the *Jacobson* case, discursively constructs (without the word *body*) the diseased body of Henning Jacobson as a polluting threat to the pure public body politic. A few pages after identifying the police power with "quarantine,"[28] the Court delivers the following passage, which we have noted in chapter 12:

> There is, of course, a sphere within which the individual may assert the supremacy of his own will and rightfully dispute the authority of any human government, especially of any free government existing under a written constitution, to inter-

[28] 197 U.S. at 29.

fere with that will. But it is equally true that in every well-ordered society charged
with the duty of conserving the safety of its members the rights of the individual
in respect of his liberty may at times, under the pressure of great dangers, be
subjected to such restraint, to be enforced by reasonable regulations, as the safety
of the general public may demand. An American citizen, arriving at an American
port on a vessel in which, during the voyage, there had been cases of yellow fever
or Asiatic cholera, although apparently free from disease himself, may yet, in
some circumstances, be held in quarantine against his will on board of such vessel
or in a quarantine station, until it be ascertained by inspection, conducted by due
diligence, that the danger of the spread of the disease among the community at
large has disappeared.[29]

Earlier in the same paragraph, states' public health powers (and their limits)
were illustrated with reference to an earlier case involving

> the right of a State to pass sanitary laws, laws for the protection of life, liberty,
> health or property within its limits, laws to prevent persons and animals suffering
> under contagious or infectious diseases, or convicts, from coming within its
> borders.[30]

I would suggest that the endurance of *Jacobson* as a reference point for the
public use of the body stems, not from its inherent logic or consistency, or the
beauty of its prose, but from the strong visceral reaction that the government is
right and Jacobson wrong, and also, as we see here, from the skill with which
it calls up that same deeply implanted infantile script of abjection that Julia
Kristeva has identified. The body politic, the "general public" so familiar to us
from contemporary discussions of AIDS, purifies itself by identifying, spec-
ularizing, and abjecting the foreign, polluting Other.

The script loses none of its power even when we realize how little any of it
has to do with Henning Jacobson's case. For one thing, there was not actually
any prospect that Jacobson would be inoculated involuntarily. The opinion is
written as if justifying his actual vaccination. Jacobson's actual sentence in the
Massachusetts courts, however, was to pay five dollars or stand committed
until the fine was paid. So if Henning Jacobson's unvaccinated body was a
threat to the Commonwealth before the decision that bears his name, he remained so afterward.

Another inaccuracy in the abjection script, as applied to Jacobson, was the
coding of smallpox as the foreign pollutant, kin to "yellow fever or Asiatic
cholera," permitting the American body politic to be constructed as clean,
pure, behind firm borders. Once again, the Supreme Court invokes what Susan
Sontag, writing about AIDS, calls "the usual script for plague: the disease

---

[29] 197 U.S. at 29.
[30] 197 U.S. at 28, citing Railroad Co. v. Husen, 95 U.S. 465, 471–73 (1877).

invariably comes from somewhere else."[31] The reality of smallpox is that its history coincides precisely with Western culture (ancient mideastern and Mediterranean). If anyone can tell a pollution-from-without myth about smallpox, it would be the first nations of North America, who really were devastated by the smallpox spread as early as 1507 by European arrivals, the most famous incident being Sir Jeffrey Amherst's distribution of smallpox-contaminated blankets to the Iroquois.[32]

The "yellow fever or Asiatic cholera" reference in Jacobson's case is more than adventitiously racist; it calls up the infantile abjection scenario. The myth tells the story of a primordially pure culture that isolates and expels invading pollution. But there was no prospect in real life that Jacobson would be quarantined or deported; the only real options were whether he would pay five dollars or be committed, presumably to prison.

So, like the drug-testing cases over eighty years later (discussed in chap. 12), the measures upheld in *Jacobson* are less an efficacious public health measure than a national ritual psychodrama in which cultural activity is mobilized through ritual enactments of solidarity. As with drug testing, I do not offer this observation in the belief that it argues against the ritualistic aspects of inoculation, for I firmly believe that cultures need rituals to create group action of any kind.

Law does not, however, have a very developed jurisprudential or political theory on when and how the body may be drafted into such national rituals of solidarity, to put it mildly. This is partly, of course, because law does not recognize that ritual psychodrama is what it does. However, there is also no political theory of ritual because there would be no cultural agreement on the answer to the question of the use of the body, were it confronted directly. The very national solidarity that is the point of the ritual would thus be fragmented from the beginning were its nature to be experienced by its participants.

[31] Susan Sontag, *AIDS and Its Metaphors* 135.

[32] Hopkins, *Princes and Peasants* 270–74 on the impact of smallpox on American Indians.

Chapter 15

OFFENSIVE BODIES

He whose odor is unpleasant shall be punished and ostracized.
—Egyptian pyramid inscription[1]

LAW FACILITATES the construction and abjection of hated Others whenever it permits classification and exclusion around issues of sameness or propriety. Abjection is not just about hatred of immigrants or particular races. It is, as we have seen, part of the psychological process of the formation of the self and is particularly associated with the purification of the body and maintenance of body boundaries. Social concern with hygiene is inseparable from division of the population into high and low, and control of the lower orders. Such abjection is well illustrated by a recent case upholding the power of a public library to exclude a homeless patron who smelled bad.

Richard Kreimer is a homeless man who lives in various outdoor public spaces in Morristown, New Jersey, and at one time spent a great deal of time in the public library. The library expelled him more than once because his offensive odor "prevented the Library patrons from using certain areas of the Library and prohibited Library employees from performing their jobs." The library also asserted that Kreimer, in addition to smelling bad, stared at and followed patrons and talked loudly to himself and others. Inasmuch as Kreimer's attack on library rules was "facial," the courts made no factual findings on the library's allegations.[2] Lawyers close to the case have told me that, in their opinion, Kreimer's alleged odor was the fundamental reason for his exclusion from the Library.

The court held that Richard Kreimer had a right under the First Amendment to receive information,[3] and that the public library was a "limited public forum," "intentionally opened . . . to the public *for expressive activity,* namely 'the communication of the written word.' "[4] The library's rule provided that "patrons whose bodily hygiene is offensive so as to constitute a nuisance to other persons shall be required to leave the building."[5] The court noted that this rule "would require the expulsion of a patron who might otherwise be

---

[1] Louis Speleers, *Traduction, index et vocabulaire des textes des pyramids égyptiennes* 89 (Brussels, 1934), as quoted in Annick Le Guérer, *Scent: The Metaphors and Essential Powers of Smell* 30 (New York: Turtle Bay Books, 1992).

[2] Kreimer v. Bureau of Police for the Town of Morristown, 958 F.2d 1242 (3d Cir. 1992).

[3] Id. 1250–55.

[4] Id. 1259 (emphasis original).

[5] Id. 1264.

peacefully engaged in permissible First Amendment activities within the purposes for which the Library was opened."[6]

Nevertheless, held the Court, the library's rule was "narrowly tailored" (as Mr. Kreimer surely was not) "to serve a significant government interest." That interest is ensuring, in the library's words, that "all patrons [may] use its facilities to the maximum extent possible during its regularly scheduled hours." Since, according to the library, "Kreimer's odor was often so offensive that it prevented the Library patrons from using certain areas of the Library and prohibited Library employees from performing their jobs,"[7] a regulation excluding Kreimer would protect library attendance by everyone else.

The main reason the court permitted the library to exclude Kreimer was then that his odors allegedly prevented others from using the library. (The rule also "promotes the Library's interest in maintaining its facilities in a sanitary and attractive condition.") If this should be true, it may say more about library patrons than it does about Kreimer. We do not have a history of American odors to match Alain Corbin's or Georges Vigarello's of France.[8] Moreover, we do not know with much precision how Kreimer smelled, as a legal matter, because no findings of fact were made and, as a discursive matter, because our language of odors is nowhere near as precise as our language for sight and sound. Odors cannot be named in any European language; the closest we can come is to say something smells like something else.[9] Indeed, it has been suggested that the physical location of the sense of smell, in the most primitive, reptilian part of the brain, makes it inaccessible to the language centers of the brain that develop much later.[10]

However, if Kreimer's were simply the odors normally attendant on one who does not bathe—they may well have been worse—it is likely that there have been patrons with similar odors ever since there have been public libraries. Offense at the unbathed other is a comparatively late development in American social history; it is intimately linked with social stratification.

Bathing was in fact widely believed until the 1850s to constitute a hazard to health. As Vigarello summarizes the legal bans on bathing in plague-infested areas of sixteenth- and seventeenth-century Western Europe:

> The skin was seen as porous, and countless openings seemed to threaten, since the surfaces were weak and the frontiers uncertain. Behind the simple refusal of proximity lay a very specific image of the body: heat and water created openings,

---

[6] Id. 1264.

[7] Id. 1247. Recall that no factual findings to this effect were ever made.

[8] Alain Corbin, *The Foul and the Fragrant: Odor and the French Social Imagination* (Cambridge: Harv. U. Pr.) (1986); Georges Vigarello, *Concepts of Cleanliness: Changing Attitudes in France since the Middle Ages* (Cambridge: Camb. U. Pr.) (1988).

[9] Constance Classen, David Howes, and Anthony Synnott, *Aroma: The Cultural History of Smell* 3 (London: Routledge, 1994).

[10] Robert Rivlin and Karen Gravelle, *Deciphering the Senses: The Expanding World of Human Perception* 88–89 (New York: Simon and Schuster, 1984).

the plague had only to slip through. . . . Baths and steam-baths were dangerous because they opened up the body to the atmosphere.[11]

It thus followed that dirty bodies would be healthier than clean ones.[12]

These attitudes disappeared very slowly. Throughout nineteenth-century America, baths were an occasional indulgence for the upper classes. They were not part of anyone's daily life; they were not accessible to the lower classes; and they were still associated with health hazards. Law played a role, in constructing this normative unbathed body, that was even more direct than *Kreimer*'s contemporary construction of the normatively bathed body. Law in Boston as late as 1845 prohibited bathing during the winter except on medical advice, and Philadelphia nearly adopted a similar ban the decade before.[13] Law did not need to construct the denial of access of the poor to bathing, beyond law's general regime of private property and conceptualizing of bathing as a private privilege.

The rise of bathing in nineteenth-century America has been documented by Richard L. Bushman and Claudia L. Bushman, and attributed to a combination of a general "civilizing process"; changing medical thought as to the skin and perspiration, now emphasizing the unhealthy quality of perspiration and the need to remove it from the body; and, though of lesser importance, religious tracts and preaching on cleanliness. These intellectual influences were largely in place at the turn of the nineteenth century but took over half a century to alter much behavior. "[P]robably not until 1850 did regular personal washing become routine in large numbers of middle-class households." Baths in which the entire body was immersed were even rarer. "The proposal to install a bathroom in the White House in 1851 raised a furor over the unnecessary expense. By 1860 there were 3,910 baths reported in Boston in a population of 177,840; probably most were portable tubs and not plumbed. Albany, New York, reported just 19." As late as 1906, only one dwelling in five in Pittsburgh had a bathtub.[14]

Interestingly, the medical learning on respiration through the skin and the necessity of cleaned, open pores was linked, at least in France, to thermodynamics and the analogy of the body to a steam engine, running on combustion.[15] So the machine body became a cleaned body just when the machine analogy changed from clockwork to steam engines (discussed in chap. 2). The discovery of microbes by the end of the century gave further impetus to the

---

[11] Vigarello, Concepts of Cleanliness 9.

[12] Corbin, *Foul and Fragrant* 37; Vigarello, *Concepts of Cleanliness* 7–17.

[13] Harold Donaldson Eberlein, "When Society First Took a Bath," in *Sickness and Health in America: Readings in the History of Medicine and Public Health* 340 (Judith Walzer Leavitt and Ronald L. Numbers eds.) (Madison: U. Wis. Pr., 1978).

[14] Richard L. Bushman and Claudia L. Bushman, "The Early History of Cleanliness in America," 74 *J. Am. Hist.* 1213, 1225–26, 31 (1988).

[15] Vigarello, *Concepts of Cleanliness* 170–72.

growing popularity of cleanliness, although as late as 1900 families that never bathed can be identified.[16]

The history of cleanliness alerts us to another aspect of *Kreimer:* the mobilization of norms of cleanliness and good odor in a larger policing project of ethnic and economic elites against poor and minority populations.[17] The discovery of offensive odor is always necessarily at least in part a Kristevan abjection script in which purity is maintained through the expulsion of the polluting member.

The body may indeed be common to us all, as we have noted repeatedly, but an almost universal aspect of human behavior is the insistence that one's own social group is inodorate, while others smell. This attitude is not confined to the uneducated. It finds its way into classics of modern social analysis, such as Georg Simmel's *Soziologie,* which includes the following jarring paragraph in its self-consciously scientific approach to modern society:

> Die Rezeption der Neger in die höhere Gesellschaft Nordamerikas scheint schon wegen der Körperatmosphäre des Negers ausgeschlossen, und die vielfache dunkle Aversion von Juden und Germanen gegen einander hat man auf dieselbe Ursache geschoben.[18]

George Orwell thought he had penetrated "the real secret of class distinctions in the West . . . summed up in four frightful words . . . *The lower classes smell.*"[19] Today we are more inclined to say of Simmel and Orwell what anthropologists say generally: "Rather than a cause of ethnic antipathy, . . . olfactory aversions are generally an expression of it."[20] Since smell can be perceived at a distance, it has been speculated that smell may be particularly salient in the observation of people with whom one is not intimate, does not converse or embrace.[21]

Every step in the history of public health measures for the encouragement of personal hygiene, the spread of bathing and eradication of filth, is always and necessarily a form of political hegemony. Distinct odors are attributed to hated ethnic groups, foreigners, the poor, homosexuals.[22] Richard Bushman

---

[16] See Corbin, *Foul and Fragrant* 217–18; Vigarello, *Concepts of Cleanliness* 175.

[17] Corbin, *Foul and Fragrant* 142–75 (increased emphasis during nineteenth century on control of odors of lower classes).

[18] [The exclusion of the Negro from high society in North America appears to be due to his body odor, and the complex and deep mutual aversion of Jews and Germans has been attributed to the same cause.] Georg Simmel, *Soziologie: Untersuchungen über die Formen der Vergellschaftung* 657 ("Exkurs über die Soziologie der Sinne") (Leipzig: Duncker und Humblot, 1908).

[19] George Orwell, *The Road to Wigan Pier* 159 (New York: Harcourt Brace, 1958) [1937].

[20] Classen et al., *Aroma* 165.

[21] Constance Classen, *Worlds of Sense: Exploring the Senses in History and across Cultures* 79–105 (London: Routledge, 1993).

[22] Corbin, *Foul and Fragrant* 142–51; Peter Stallybrass and Allon White, *The Politics and*

and Claudia Bushman document the frequency with which popular literature of the nineteenth century use cleanliness to divide people into two worlds, a high world of refinement and a detested lower world.[23] In the optimistic version of this myth, the freed slave, the immigrant could well ascend into the higher world, should he or she simply be induced to bathe regularly; Simmel's is the pessimistic account in which odor, like race itself, inheres in the body, not in our construction of it.

Kreimer's case represents a post–nineteenth century, individualized version of the myth, in which Kreimer's odors are in some sense peculiar to him as an individual. Sensitivity to each individual's odor and a belief that everyone might become inoffensive graphically represent an individuation of the person; in earlier periods bodily odors, if noticed at all, could only represent the forces of nature or a less differentiated mass of people. An insistence on individuals' controlling their own odors helps reiterate and embody the abstract, liberal political program of self-government.

To describe the library's conduct as Kristevan abjection is not to say that it should stop forthwith. We cannot live without abjection. This detour into Kristevan abjection then does not demonstrate that the *Kreimer* case was wrongly decided. No doubt if so many people thought that Richard Kreimer smelled bad, he did, and if this sensitivity to odor is historically contingent, then so be it—what other sort of sense of odor could we have except that of our own era? If there is to be such a category as people whose odors are so offensive as to prevent others from working, I can think of no alternative source for the definition than the good sense of library staff. Given language's weak range of descriptions of odors, objective rules do not seem feasible. I wasn't in the library with Kreimer, and perhaps removing him really was like the expulsion of waste that lets us live.

Perhaps. Yet I do not think a court that was self-conscious about this complex of abjection problems, in which bodies are figured as polluting, from drugs and immigration to racial segregation, could have written an opinion as unself-conscious as the opinion in *Kreimer,* with its narrow tailoring and weighing of interests.

The benefit of this discussion of abjection might be a greater judicial self-consciousness about what it is doing in a case like *Kreimer*. I would like law to develop a pause here, a sudden stopping of the hand at the recognition that law has constructed and abjected an Other, the kind of recognition that comes when the prototype is firm in our minds and we recognize it everywhere. Perhaps we are too quick to identify our security with firm boundaries and internal purification and fail to see how the security we prize comes only from

---

Poetics of Transgression 125–48 (Ithaca: Cornell U. Pr., 1986) (association of poor, savage, Irish with dirt or filth).

[23] Bushman and Bushman, "Early History," 1227–31.

the way we enter into communication with people around us, particularly people who might as easily be constructed as Other and abjected.

For an alternative treatment of the odorous body, consider John Donne's 1622 Lenten sermon on the text "Jesus Wept," as described by Elaine Scarry. Donne "imagines that Jesus could have looked at the four-day rotting corpse of Lazarus and said, 'There is no such matter, he doth not stink,' but says instead, He is rotting, there is a stench, but yet he is my friend ('but though he do, my friend shall not lack my help'). This, finally, is Donne's most characteristic reflex, to bring forward the human hand at moments of both desire and repulsion; to say, but yet he is my friend."[24]

[24] Elaine Scarry, "Donne: 'But Yet the Body Is His Booke,'" in *Literature and the Body: Essays on Populations and Persons* 97 (Elaine Scarry ed.) (Baltimore: Johns Hopkins U. Pr, 1988). The Donne quotes are from 4 *The Sermons of John Donne* 334 (George R. Potter and Evelyn M. Simpson eds.) (Berkeley: U. Cal. Pr., 1962).

A BODY FANTASIA

THE BODY is the way we represent to ourselves that there are other people, with lives, in the world. The body metaphorically represents those qualities of other people to which we believe we have access, which we can see, hear, sense, or smell. From the thousands of mental, moral, biological, psychological, and spiritual processes that make up another person, the set that at any given time constitutes the set of representable processes is called the body.

Biology places fewer constraints on this process than is commonly supposed. Biology gives us arrays of bodily organs of different shapes and sizes and colors. Discourse gives us male and female as categories to which everyone belongs; discourse further tells us whether the female organs are misshaped male organs or something entirely different.[1] Biology gives us a body that feels pain. A discourse that denied that all bodies, or some people's bodies, felt pain, would be simply a lie, that torturers might tell themselves or others. Still, there is enormous variation in the sensation of pain, and the discourse of pain does not simply report people's internal states. The child knows that "pain" is what it feels because adults teach it that is the word, and those adults do not feel what the child feels, but see the customary behavioral correlates of "pain" and teach the child the presumptively correct word.[2] This inherently social process largely shapes the meaning of pain and what will come to seem "experience."

It follows, then, that over time there is a range of discursive bodies. In our postmodern era, with its overpowering sense of historicism and its access to wide ranges of competing discourses, particular speakers or speaking communities may have access to multiple competing discursive representations of the body. This is true of law.

In general, law's discourse of the body constructs the body as a thing, separate from the person, but the bearer of that person, and a bearer of that person as constructed as a legal subject in civil society.

The legal subject is an individual, and so is that subject's body. Each body is an individuated entity with distinct boundaries, an outside and an inside. Defining those boundaries is an individuated judgment that calls for no con-

---

[1] Judith Butler, *Bodies That Matter: On the Discursive Limits of "Sex"* (New York: Routledge, 1993); Thomas Laqueur, *Making Sex: Body and Gender from the Greeks to Freud* (Cambridge: Harv. U. Pr., 1990).

[2] Ludwig Wittgenstein, *Philosophical Investigations,* §244 (G. E. M. Anscombe ed. and trans.) (New York: Macmillan, 3d ed., 1958).

sideration of other legal subjects. The one exception, which fits poorly with this overall scheme, is the displayable, searchable legal vagina, often constructed as a kind of absence that derives its identity from its relations with other people.

The legal subject has a sort of free will, a mental autonomy. It commands its body, and the body obeys. This is why law rarely constructs a body with independent agency, which acts without mental or moral direction or may even control the mind of the person within it. Biologically speaking, many body functions involve no mental intercession. But it is discourse, not biology, that constructs a body as a tool subject to mental direction.

The legal subject is distinct from the body, not identical to it. This facilitates market transactions and public regulation that would be more difficult if law could not separate the body from the person. Since the person survives alteration of the body, people may sell blood, employers may demand haircuts, workers may sell labor power. Bodies may be displayed in advertising as fetishized objects without anyone experiencing this as a sale of the body or the person. Similarly, police may search body cavities that might be harder to search if this were experienced as invasions of the person.

The legal subject has a relationship to its body, but, as that relationship is not the relationship of identity, further legal analogies are necessary to provide an image of that relationship. It is sometimes said that the subject owns his or her body, but that turns out not to be universally true or accurate.

The legal subject's body is presumptively private. The body is often a kind of master symbol for the private that is of no social interest or concern, information about which need not be disclosed, a body that may not be used. The fundamental liberal division of the world into public and private is characteristically played out on the surface of the body, in which the body serves as a master metaphor for the existence of this realm of the private.

The legal subject must, however, tolerate or consent to some fairly massive social uses of the body, which law facilitates by constructing that body so as to permit such social use. Body cavities and orifices may be searched if warrants are obtained or simply on reasonable suspicion of travelers crossing the border. Men may be drafted into military service. Vaccinations may be compulsory. Pregnant women may be required to carry particular pregnancies to term, for example if they are in their final trimester. Public or even private commercial displays of particular body parts or their representations may be suppressed. Since the body cannot exist in the world without being displayed somehow, the suppression of some forms of body display necessarily legislates others as compulsory. Prisoners may be confined, marked, disciplined, or medicated. Users of public libraries may be required to bathe.

While all these represent permissible social uses or invasions of the body, law facilitates these by constructing various discursive bodies, sometimes defined as interests in liberty or property, sometimes as things or property, sometimes through euphemistic language that makes the body disappear. In the last case, basic attributes or functions of the human body are nearly always metaphorically transferred to such artificial bodies as bodies of government, the state, society, or law.

The legal subject has a tricky relationship to difference. Legal subjects must each be constructed as individuals, not fungible or interchangeable; they are not machines. On the other hand, legal subjects must be enough like each other so that they may communicate with each other, be understood by others so as to permit enforceable contracts or civil government, be able to evaluate each others' pain for purposes of civil damages, be able to adjudicate others so as to permit law. If individuals were so entirely unique that no one could really understand or judge another, and all our purported efforts to do so were just solipsistic delusion, then law would truly be a fraud, something imposed on others but unable to obtain consent, consent being just a convenient fiction. The legal body preserves this tricky relationship to difference by being able to present itself alternatively as the site of human sameness and of human differentiation. Law chooses to treat the internal workings of the body largely as the site of human sameness. We are alike under the skin, the saying goes; hath not a Jew organs? This is a construction, to be sure, for people's internal organs display as much variation as their external appearance, varying in size, shape, color, health: it would not be difficult to construct an elaborate discourse of internal bodily individuation, as was true in medical discourse in the eighteenth and early nineteenth century. Law chooses to construct these aspects of the body as the same. This permits compensation for injury, for example.

At the same time, legal bodies are constructed as different in their sex, race, and disability, and these constructions are experienced as statements of facts inherent in the body, not constructions by the speaker. This may stem from an infantile mental script under which bodies experience both pleasure and shame in the abjection of polluting members, which script is often called on in instances of social abjection. In such cases the body is called on to symbolize the social ritual of shame, purification, or boundary maintenance.

When law's discourse might create an unbearable conflict in our imaging of the body, law normally employs euphemisms to make the body disappear. People in our society believe many contradictory things about bodies and often employ these legalistic euphemisms to reduce cognitive dissonance. People believe both that healthy bodies are pure and free of drugs *and* that obstreperous prisoners and mental patients should be tranquilized against their will; that people have a right to do what they please with their bodies *and* that some social demands on the body are appropriate; and so forth. Law is rich in constructions of the body that emphasize its thingness, its distance from us, that treat the body as object, property, machine. Law is not condemned to these particular constructions but often employs them to mediate difficult moral contradiction.

Law's construction of the body is not transparently a construction. It is often naturalized, so that speakers experience themselves as reporting facts about the race, sex, disability, suffering, value, boundaries, and social meaning of the body as if these features inhered in physical bodies instead of being constructed discursively.

One purpose of this book has been to disable all legal arguments that rest on the construction of the body as a single reification, all legal arguments that purport to derive determinate consequences from the body's being "property" or "mine" or "private" or "different." I have done this in two ways. First, I have tried to induce self-consciousness of law's body language, so that people will stop and realize they are saying something funny when they employ one of these stereotyped constructions. Second, anyone with the price of this book can now deploy the precise counterconstruction: if someone argues the body is "property" or "different," anyone can now show that it is "available" and "like us."

Most importantly, every aspect of the legal body on the above list might be changed. Often competing discursive constructions of the body have a contemporary subterranean existence, or were once popular but have passed from the scene, or have a vivid life in literature that has not yet influenced law. Law might, in other words, do any of the following things:

> Construct bodies as the nexus of all the relationships of their lives, meaningless and insignificant except as the sum of those relationships
>
> Construct bodies as moral agents that act without or even against the will of legal subjects
>
> Equate legal subjects with their bodies, so that sale of blood or labor power could only be experienced as a sale of the person
>
> Construct bodies as always presumptively available to social use
>
> Construct bodies that were truly inviolable, in the sense that legal process would be powerless to compel their harmless use even by others, or a state, that would die without them
>
> Construct bodies that differentiated each subject from another in ways that were entirely incommensurable, so that no body damage could even be evaluated
>
> Construct bodies that could never represent any social relationship but sameness, so that differences among people, to the limited extent they were even observed, would be attributed entirely to their mental or moral processes, and not to bodies that were incapable of requiring such difference, at most capable of providing a certain normal variation that became difference only as self-consciously constructed as such

> Always and everywhere treat "body" as a legal construction like "due care" or "good faith," a legal term of art used to facilitate our making present other people, but always understood as a conscious creation employed for that (or some other) purpose, not a natural thing existing independent of our constructions. On this view we might write or say whatever we pleased about the body but would always be aware that we were reaching for figurative language and never be deluded into thinking we were describing reality
>
> Make a very self-conscious effort never to employ our body metaphors of distance or absence, never to forget that legal subjects have bodies, strive for a law and politics of embodied subjects and always employ the most vivid literary imaging of bodies lest we forget that law is about people and people interact in the world through the media of their bodies.

The final question we should consider together is: which, if any, of the things on that list should law do?

I don't think this is the most important question in the book, and I certainly don't think anyone who disagrees with my tentative answer to it is thereby free to ignore the preceding chapters of this book. I have tried to be as comprehensive, fair, and probing as I could be in the descriptive sections, and I believe I have produced a comprehensive catalog of the discursive constructions of the body found in contemporary American law, with some sense of when each is employed and what constellation of political assumptions characteristically is evoked by each body construction. The deepest challenge of the book would be to someone who denied the freedom of body construction or the malleability of our constructions, who insisted that the legal body was quite powerfully shaped by unchangeable biological necessity and that change was therefore impossible. But I think I have shown quite clearly that legal speakers draw on a range of discursive constructions that change over time and that may be used most instrumentally to change outcomes.

Moreover, I think this is a serious blow on behalf of legal creativity. The body so often stands in as a symbol for the foundational, the unchanging, the limits of law. If I really have shown that that very body is to a large extent a legal artifact that could as well have been otherwise, that is a powerful blow for the freedom of the interpreter.

It also follows from the entire corpus of this book that the question of how to construct the body cannot be answered by the body itself. I do not think there is a correct, natural, real way of making the body present in legal analysis: for example a politically left-wing body with gender, without race, its suffering manifest, its economic alienation suspect. Such a body may be discursively constructed of course, but it is a discursive creation and no more real or natural than the machine body. The case for constructing such a suffering body is political, not biological. This doesn't mean that there are no lies about the body; I have already identified as a plain lie the claim that some other never feels pain, invariably put forward in bad faith as an act of subjugation. But there are many fewer lies than one might suppose, and many partial and possible truths to be refracted in legal discourse.

Despite all this, readers may expect some prescription here on some alternative way of constructing the body in law, and as it happens I have one to present, although it in no way follows from the previous fifteen chapters of this book. Oral presentation of this work has convinced me that most people, and even most lawyers, are embarrassed and shamed by language like "search warrant for the apartment and vagina" or "[R]espondent possesses a significant liberty interest in avoiding the unwanted administration of antipsychotic drugs under the Due Process Clause of the Fourteenth Amendment." Such phrasings do not respond to our highest ethical aspirations or our sense of ourselves. They seem like the cumbersome euphemisms of people who cannot talk about the body, like sexless, joyless lawyers in their evasiveness.

What might legal analysis look like if law developed greater self-consciousness about its discursive construction of the body and attempted to develop a discourse of bodily presence not absence, pleasure not pain, wholeness not fetishism, relations not isolation, connection not display, fusion not difference, incorporation not abjection, play not control?

The archaic term *fantasia* describes this proposed alternative discourse of the body. As used by the classical literary theorist known to us as Longinus (and later by Vico), *fantasia* means "image-production." The term "is used generally for anything which in any way suggests a thought productive of speech; but the word has also come into fashion for the situation in which enthusiasm and emotion make the speaker *see* what he is saying and bring it *visually* before his audience."[3] I like the idea of a body fantasia because, to a modern reader, this simultaneously conveys, along with its classical meaning of visualization, the romantic idea of something made, created, fanciful. The body we construct is our construction. It is not offered in the spirit of science or realism or necessity.

In body fantasia, the most important goal in any sort of legal analysis is communion with another person. All rules, formulas, figures, metaphors, and visualizations are experienced as instrumental to the larger goal of communication and understanding. Fantasia is preferred to today's distanced, mechanical legal body, not because it is truer (except perhaps to our ethical aspirations), but just because it better heightens our awareness of the presence of other people. Fantasia is a way of stopping ourselves from denying the significance of others, from excluding them.

In body fantasia, bodies are visualizations, not legal entities, and have no rights as such. But because the body is the site of pleasure, sexuality, and

---

[3] "Longinus," *On Sublimity,* in *Classical Literary Criticism* 159 (D. A. Russell and M. Winterbottom eds.) (Oxford: Ox. U.Pr.) (1989).

fusion with others, it becomes easier to imagine different legal persons, and those persons may have different legal interests or rights, if those terms are still to be employed.

For example, *Bowers v. Hardwick,* the case permitting states to criminalize sodomy, is wrongly decided if the body is fantasized, but not because there is a right to bodily autonomy or control or integrity. Bodies are visualizations and have no rights as such. It is people who have rights. But since we cannot know other people except through the medium of their bodies, and since living with other people is the goal of the entire legal system, people must be imagined as living in fantasized bodies that are the sites of pleasure and love. (People who like rights talk can get there more easily with a "right to love" than a "right to the body." But establishing this right to love would be a subject for another book.) Rights talk is inadequate though, for reasons we have seen repeatedly: bodies and indeed other people can be made to disappear in rights talk, their human attributes wrested from them and metaphorically assigned to an imaginary, invasive, authoritarian state. There may be times—there surely are—when individuals must yield to a greater good, but thinking about these problems is not facilitated when our visualizations deny the humanity of the affected. In body fantasia, people may lose law cases, but they never disappear. The ethical imperative at all time is to use language to the extent possible to assist our visualization of, and hence communion with, another.

Rules of law emerge from body fantasia as the output of hypothesized dialogue with affected individuals who might ultimately come to agree where justice lies. This sounds impossibly naive since some identifiable humans will never agree to anything not in their immediate interest, and some norms simply must be imposed on people. Under body fantasia, such norms are seen as regrettable necessities, not the normal attributes of holding power as a judge. An unconsentable rule is justified only by first undergoing fantasia, empathizing as closely as possible with affected individuals, through listening to them of course, but, where this is not possible, through fantastical visualizations of bodily presence. Whether and how Shirley Rodriques's vagina is searched (and the court to my mind should have said much more about the "how" instead of assuming that the only interesting question is "whether") would be determined in a hypothetical dialogue in which the judge must imagine himself or herself trying to convince a real person, in the flesh, of the location of justice, and employs body fantasia to assist this imaginary dialogue. By contrast, law's lengthy catalog of metaphors of distance or absence would be seen as obstacles to fantasia and thus obstacles to human communion. The body as castle, as impregnable fortress, as locked strongbox is such an evasion, as the body that is the thief hiding relevant evidence, the sneak, the transgressor.

In body fantasia the concrete is preferred to the abstract, the visualized to the hidden, the common name for a body part or function to the euphemism.

We need less Anthony Kennedy (the euphemistic author of the Supreme Court's opinions in *Harper* and *Treasury Employees,* discussed in chapters 11 and 12) and more Jeanette Winterson:

> Articulacy of fingers, the language of the deaf and dumb, signing on the body body longing. Who taught you to write in blood on my back? Who taught you to use your hands as branding irons? You have scored your name into my shoulders, referenced me with your mark. The pads of your fingers have become printing blocks, you tap a message on to my skin, tap meaning into my body. Your morse code interferes with my heart beat. I had a steady heart before I met you, I relied upon it, it had seen active service and grown strong. Now you alter its pace with your own rhythm, you play upon me, drumming me taught.
>
> Written on the body is a secret code only visible in certain lights; the accumulations of a lifetime gather there.[4]

A recent book on euphemism concludes that it is employed by speakers who fear losing face (body metaphor!) without it.[5] Euphemisms are in our culture no longer taboo to people, who do not really fear divine retribution, but are instead rationally adopted, by people who anticipate loss of status if the disfavored noneuphemistic term is employed. Body fantasia employs this analysis, of euphemism as a marker of status. Under body fantasia, higher status would no longer attach to Justice Anthony Kennedy's ability to avoid visualizing the humanity of other people.[6] High-status judging would, instead, involve exquisite facility in the rendering present of affected individual people.

Body fantasia bears some resemblance to what the eighteenth-century moralists called sympathy, but not more than other forms of adjudication that in principle are less self-conscious about the problems. For example, any visualization is of course a sort of power play by the adjudicator and not really an adequate substitute for a human relation with the beaten prisoner, the pregnant unmarried woman, the motel clerk on display. But then making people disappear is a worse power play. If fantasia and empathy were an announced goal of the legal system, judges could be praised or criticized for their achievements in fantasia.

4 Jeanette Winterson, *Written on the Body* 89 (New York: Vintage, 1994).

5 Keith Allan and Kate Burridge, *Euphemism and Dysphemism: Language Used as Shield and Weapon* 11 (New York: Oxford U. Pr.) (1991).

6 The simple eloquence of Justice Kennedy's recent opinion for the Court in Romer v. Evans, 116 S.Ct. 1620, 1629 (1996), striking down Colorado's constitutional prohibition on legislation protecting gay and lesbian people, is a welcome improvement. "We must conclude that Amendment 2 classifies homosexuals not to further a proper legislative end but to make them unequal to everyone else. This Colorado cannot do. A state cannot so deem a class of persons a stranger to its laws."

Of course people's sympathies are constrained by their own life experiences and backgrounds, but this only gets better when people work on the problem, not when judges performatively enact their own lack of sympathy through a discourse of absence. There is even a sense in which sentimentality toward others (specifically, criminals) is, as D. W. Winnicott once told a group of magistrates, a "repressed or unconscious hate" and "sooner or later the hate turns up."[7] But then hatred toward others is also a hate, and indifference to them, or turning them into machines, property, interests, commodities, displays, liberty or privacy is also a kind of unconscious hate.

Body fantasia employs the current social centrality of the body in the service of living with others. It does not idolatrously take the body for the person. It permits the body to fade from our minds, should we find other and better ways of forcing ourselves to take account of others. Acknowledgment of the person is primary, the body merely the way a sensory person represents another person to him or herself.

But this is impossibly utopian. We don't know what law or any of civil society would look like if we changed the way we constructed the body, and perhaps we would all be happier with more modest changes, more sensitivity to our language of the body, the slight hesitation that draws us back from inflicting hurt, the willingness to acknowledge our unity with others, the body at the corner of our eye, trying to catch us, always just beyond our visualization, the lost communion that we seek, recollected, reconstructed, remembered in our representations, our art, our invigorated, embodied legal texts.

[7] D. W. Winnicott, *Deprivation and Delinquency* 114 (London: Tavistock, 1984).

TABLE OF CASES

About the Author

ALAN HYDE is Professor and Sidney Reitman Scholar at the Rutgers University School of Law (Newark).